"This is a 'must-read' book for all practitioners who interact with families affected by autism. Many of the authors whom Dr. Edelson has brought together in this impressive volume have dedicated much of their adult lives to the treatment of people with autism, and they know just how devastating and difficult to treat self-injurious behavior can be. While it is important to study the causes of ASD, it is equally important to identify and treat co-occurring conditions that jeopardize the longevity and quality of life of affected individuals. This is an important step in bringing awareness to the larger community about self-injurious behavior as a critical issue in ASD."

—*David G. Amaral, Ph.D., Research Director, The MIND Institute*

"Self-injurious behaviors, a not-uncommon family of conditions in autism, vary in severity and are sometimes very damaging to the body. Typically, they are difficult to treat. *Understanding and Treating Self-Injurious Behavior in Autism*, edited by Dr. Stephen M. Edelson and Jane Botsford Johnson, is an important effort to advance knowledge regarding these poorly understood and challenging behaviors that receive inadequate scholarly attention. In this volume, Edelson and Johnson insightfully bring together experts from diverse clinical and research backgrounds who discuss general medical, neurological, genetic, and pharmacological issues that can contribute to causation of self-injurious behaviors, as well as different therapeutic approaches that may be useful in specific clinical contexts. This work communicates current knowledge regarding self-injurious behaviors and advances our understanding in this important area of medicine. *Understanding and Treating Self-Injurious Behavior in Autism* is highly recommended for clinicians who care for persons with such behaviors and for researchers interested in learning diverse perspectives on the field."

—*Marvin Natowicz, M.D., Ph.D., Clinical Geneticist, Clinical Pathologist, Pathology & Laboratory Medicine Institute, Cleveland Clinic Cleveland, OH*

"The root of self-injurious behavior can be different for each person on the autism spectrum. An individualized approach, considering all options and combinations of treatments, provides the best chance for a healthy and happy life. This book is long overdue."

—Laurie Mawlam, Executive Director, Autism Canada

"This immensely valuable book guides us through multiple potential target etiologies of self-injurious behavior for effective treatment. Thoughtfully assembled and edited, it represents a much-needed practical and integrative handbook of use to every practitioner who works with individuals with autism spectrum and related disorders. I whole-heartedly recommend it!"

—Robert L. Hendren, D.O., Professor of Psychiatry,
University of California, San Francisco

Understanding and Treating
Self-Injurious Behavior in Autism

of related interest

Infantile Autism
The Syndrome and Its Implications for a Neural Theory
of Behavior by Bernard Rimland, Ph.D.
50th Anniversary Updated Edition
Edited by Stephen M. Edelson
ISBN 978 1 84905 789 9
eISBN 978 1 78450 057 3

Families of Adults with Autism
Stories and Advice for the Next Generation
Edited by Jane Johnson and Anne Van Rensselaer
ISBN 978 1 84310 885 6
eISBN 978 1 84642 766 4

Siblings
The Autism Spectrum Through Our Eyes
Edited by Jane Johnson and Anne Van Rensselaer
ISBN 978 1 84905 829 2
eISBN 978 0 85700 281 5

UNDERSTANDING AND TREATING SELF-INJURIOUS BEHAVIOR IN AUTISM

A MULTI-DISCIPLINARY PERSPECTIVE

EDITED BY STEPHEN M. EDELSON AND JANE BOTSFORD JOHNSON

FOREWORD BY TEMPLE GRANDIN

Jessica Kingsley *Publishers*
London and Philadelphia

Figures 13.1–13.4 are reproduced by kind permission of Helen Marcos and the Groden Centre.
Figure 13.6 reproduced from Groden 2011 by kind permission of Mary Pendergast.
Figures 13.7 and 13.8: the Picture Communication Symbols © 1981–2010 by Mayer-Johnson LLC. All Rights Reserved Worldwide. Used with permission.
Boardmaker™ is a trademark of Mayer-Johnson LLC.
Appendix C is reproduced by kind permission of Jamie Bleiweiss.

First published in 2016
by Jessica Kingsley Publishers
73 Collier Street
London N1 9BE, UK
and
400 Market Street, Suite 400
Philadelphia, PA 19106, USA

www.jkp.com

Library of Congress Cataloging in Publication Data
Names: Edelson, Stephen M., editor. | Johnson, Jane, 1966- editor. | Van
    Rensselaer, Anne, editor.
Title: Understanding and treating self-injurious behavior in autism : a
    multi-disciplinary perspective / edited by Stephen M. Edelson with Jane
    Johnson and Anne Van Rensselaer.
Description: London ; Philadelphia : Jessica Kingsley Publishers, 2016. |
    Includes bibliographical references and index.
Identifiers: LCCN 2015043474 | ISBN 9781849057417 (alk. paper)
Subjects: LCSH: Autistic children--Treatment. | Self-mutilation--Treatment.
Classification: LCC RJ506.A9 U53 2016 | DDC 618.92/85882--dc23 LC record available at http://
lccn.loc.gov/2015043474

British Library Cataloguing in Publication Data
A CIP catalogue record for this book is available from the British Library.

ISBN 978 1 84905 741 7
eISBN 978 1 78450 189 1

Printed and bound in Great Britain

MIX
Paper from
responsible sources
FSC
www.fsc.org   FSC® C013056

This book is dedicated to Dr. Edward Carr, who was a true pioneer in understanding and treating self-injury as well as other challenging behaviors. Dr. Carr was a dedicated researcher, and his contributions to the field of autism and other developmental disorders have helped tens of thousands of individuals in the past and present, and will help hundreds of thousands in the future. We are fortunate that many of his colleagues and students have contributed to this book.

ACKNOWLEDGMENTS

The contributors to this book have agreed to donate their royalties to support research in understanding and treating self-injurious behavior. The Autism Research Institute will match the royalties and distribute this book to treatment centers worldwide.

CONTENTS

Foreword   9
Temple Grandin, author of Thinking in Pictures *and* The Autistic Brain

Introduction   11
Stephen M. Edelson, Ph.D., Autism Research Institute, San Diego, California

1. Targeted Medical Therapies and Self-Injury   18
    Mary Coleman, M.D., Foundation for Autism Research, Sarasota, Florida

2. Self-Injurious and Aggressive Behaviors in Autism: Looking Below
    the Surface   27
    Margaret L. Bauman, M.D., Boston University School of Medicine,
    Boston, Massachusetts

3. Self-Injurious Behavior, Aggression, and Epilepsy in Autism
    Spectrum Disorder   38
    Manuel F. Casanova, M.D., and Emily L. Casanova, Ph.D., University of South
    Carolina, Greenville, South Carolina

4. A Neuropsychiatric Model for Evaluating and Treating Self-Injurious
    Behavior in Autism   55
    Paul Millard Hardy, M.D., Autism Research Institute, San Diego, California

5. Examining the Impact of Medication Side Effects on Problem Behavior   68
    Jamie D. Bleiweiss, Ph.D., Hunter College, New York

6. Self-Injurious Behaviors in Children with Autism Spectrum Disorder:
    Impact of Allergic Diseases   91
    Harumi Jyonouchi, M.D., Saint Peter's University Hospital,
    New Brunswick, New Jersey

7. Medical and Nutritional Approaches to Treating Self-Injurious Behavior
    and Aggression in Autism Spectrum Disorder: Fifteen Case Studies   109
    John Green III, M.D., Evergreen Center, Portland, Oregon, and
    Nancy O'Hara, M.D., Center for Integrative Health, Wilton, Connecticut

8. Dietary and Nutrition Intervention to Address Self-Injurious Behavior in Autism: Thoughts from Five Years of Clinical Care   128
   Kelly M. Barnhill, MBA, CN, CCN, The Johnson Center for Child Health and Development, Austin, Texas

9. Sensory Processing Disorder and Self-Injurious Behaviors   138
   Lucy Jane Miller, Ph.D., OTR/L, and Karen Misher, MFA, Sensory Processing Disorder Foundation, Greenwood Village, Colorado

10. Assessment and Intervention for Self-Injurious Behavior Using Positive Behavior Support   151
    Lauren J. Moskowitz, Ph.D., St. John's University, New York, Caitlin E. Walsh, Ph.D., University of Colorado School of Medicine, Denver, Colorado, and V. Mark Durand, Ph.D., University of South Florida, St. Petersburg, Florida

11. Using Functional Communication Training to Treat Self-Injurious Behavior   186
    V. Mark Durand, Ph.D., University of South Florida, St. Petersburg, Florida, and Lauren J. Moskowitz, Ph.D., St. John's University, New York

12. Assessment and Intervention for Self-Injurious Behavior Related to Anxiety   198
    Lauren J. Moskowitz, Ph.D., and Alexis B. Ritter, M.S., St. John's University, New York

13. A Stress-Reduction Approach to Addressing Self-Injurious Behavior in Individuals with Autism   231
    June Groden, Ph.D., Leslie Weidenman, and Cooper R. Woodward, The Groden Center, Providence, Rhode Island

    APPENDIX A: BIOLOGICAL CONTRIBUTORS TO SELF-INJURIOUS BEHAVIOR   276

    APPENDIX B: TARGETED QUESTIONNAIRE TO IDENTIFY CHAPTERS OF INTEREST   277

    APPENDIX C: THE STRUCTURED INTERVIEW FOR ASSESSMENT OF MEDICATION SIDE EFFECTS (SIAMSE)   280

    APPENDIX D: COMPREHENSIVE LIST OF BEHAVIORAL INDICATORS OF ANXIETY   289

    SUBJECT INDEX   291

    AUTHOR INDEX   297

Foreword

Temple Grandin

Autism represents a broad spectrum, with those affected ranging from brilliant math geniuses to individuals with much more severe problems. Numerous books are available for people on the high end of the spectrum, but there is a huge lack of materials for those individuals with bigger challenges. Self-injurious behavior (SIB) is one of the most serious problems for some on the autism spectrum.

The first step in stopping SIB is to rule out any hidden painful medical problems that a non-verbal person is not able to tell you about. Many parents have told me that acid reflux (heartburn) is one of the most common medical problems associated with their child's meltdown, tantrums, or hitting. When the pain is relieved, behavior improves. Other painful conditions might be earaches, toothaches, constipation, yeast infections, or urinary tract infections. This book has many chapters on medical problems associated with challenging behavior.

Many on the spectrum have problems with sensory over-sensitivity. Loud noises or bright lights may cause pain. When I was a child, the school bell was like a dentist's drill hitting a nerve. Self-injurious behavior may be more likely to occur in crowded, noisy places. In my own books, Thinking in Pictures and The Autistic Brain, I have included self-reports of sensory over-sensitivity problems from many people on the spectrum. The best insights can be gained from verbal individuals who are able to tell you how they experience sensory stimuli that cause pain.

There are two excellent chapters on positive behavior supports and functional communication. These two chapters give lots of practical information on how to use positive behavior methods to stop SIB. Frustration with not being able to communicate caused me to have many tantrums when I was a child. I did not start speaking until age four, and I can remember the frustration of not being able to tell people what I needed.

In some cases, medication will be needed to help stop SIB. In my own case, a low dose of antidepressants greatly reduced anxiety and panic attacks. Careful, conservative use of medication combined with positive behavioral intervention can sometimes work wonders. The two interventions combined may work better than either one of them alone. A third intervention might be to allow the individual to wear noise-cancelling headphones in noisy places, but if headphones are used, they need to be off for half of each day to prevent the ears from becoming more sound sensitive.

Combinations of medical, dietary, sensory, and behavior programs work best. It is a big mistake to depend on a single intervention. Single-minded use of a single method can lead to big trouble. When drugs alone are used, the person may turn into a zombie who is so sedated that he sleeps all the time. When medication is never used, there is a danger of resorting to severe aversives and punishments that are cruel. Severe aversive treatments, such as electric shocks, must never be used, because they are torture.

This book combines medical, biomedical, and behavioral approaches together. It is essential reading for parents, teachers, therapists, and doctors who are working with persons who have self-injurious behavior.

Temple Grandin, author of *Thinking in Pictures* and *The Autistic Brain*

Introduction

Stephen M. Edelson, Ph.D., Autism Research Institute, San Diego, California

Self-injurious behavior (SIB) is one of the most devastating and challenging-to-treat behaviors of people with an autism spectrum disorder or a related developmental disability. The types of behavior vary greatly, but they all can lead to tissue damage, ranging from mild (e.g., redness, bruising) to moderate (e.g., bleeding) to severe (e.g., fractures). The most common forms of self-injury include banging and hitting the head; biting the arm, hand, and wrist; and excessive scratching or pinching of the skin. Less common forms include pressing and poking of the eyes, hair pulling (trichotillomania), and scratching or "digging" of the rectal area.

Researchers in the medical and behavioral fields have investigated the underlying reasons and treatments to reduce or eliminate these behaviors. In many cases, treatment is moderately successful. Growing consensus and documentation indicate numerous physical and social reasons for these behaviors: anxiety, pain, seizures, and attention seeking, to name a few. This book provides the reader with various approaches to assist in understanding and treating SIB. The chapter contributors are knowledgeable researchers and experienced health care practitioners.

In general, practitioners rely on treatment strategies that are consistent with their training; a physician is likely to prescribe medications, a psychologist is more likely to administer a behavior-modification program, an occupational therapist will probably apply a sensory-intervention technique, and so forth. Given the multitude of possible contributing factors, practitioners may not be aware of the most appropriate intervention(s) to treat a specific type of behavior in a particular person.

A Comprehensive Approach to Self-Injurious Behavior

By approaching SIB in a multifaceted, multidisciplinary manner, many of these behaviors can be understood and treated successfully. This book provides a discussion of the various approaches and suggests the most appropriate interventions to reduce or eliminate these behaviors. These approaches can be classified in two main categories. Using a "targeted" approach, a specific contributor is known or suspected and the treatment strategy is aimed directly at the underlying cause. (For example, low calcium levels [hypocalcinuria] may contribute to eye pressing, and the behavior may be eliminated by prescribing calcium supplements. Head banging and ear hitting may be associated with otitis media [i.e., middle ear infection], so the individual should be checked for an ear infection.)

On the other hand, there are cases in which it is quite difficult to determine the underlying reason for SIB; a more general intervention, termed a "non-targeted" approach, may be administered to reduce or possibly eliminate the behavior. For example, anxiety is quite common in those who engage in self-injury, and the underlying reason for the anxiety may never be determined. Steps to reduce anxiety may include a behavioral relaxation program, a deep pressure sensory-related intervention, or perhaps an anxiolytic medication.

In this book, both kinds of approaches are discussed in relation to different treatment models, including physical health (i.e., medical, biomedical, immunological, neurological, nutritional, sensory) and behavior (e.g., positive behavior support, functional communication, relaxation). These interventions have been reported to be effective based on clinical research and/or clinical experience.

The location of the tissue damage may provide clues to help determine the underlying contributor(s) to the behavior, such as rectal digging due to inflammation immediately inside or around the anus, and head hitting due to severe pain from a migraine or ear infection. We have provided a list of biological contributors to self-injurious behavior in Appendix A.

We do not want to give the impression that it is a simple process to uncover the underlying contributor(s) to SIB. In many cases, much effort is needed to properly assess the behavior, and there is an element of trial and error. In fact, given the multitude of potential contributors, an efficient strategy would be to rank order the possible reasons, from most likely to least likely, and then administer one intervention at a time until the behavior is reduced. Unfortunately, there are no guarantees.

Several of the contributors in this book discuss pain or discomfort as primary contributors to SIB. It is good to remember that pain or discomfort may stem from the environment, such as ear hitting as a result of sensory-experienced pain soon after hearing a loud sound, as well as from physical pain.

There are also instances in which there may not be an obvious relationship between pain and challenging behaviors. Dr. Timothy Buie has conducted upper endoscopies on individuals who displayed posturing and stereotypic body movements, and found evidence of gastroesophageal reflux disease. Consequently, these behaviors were eliminated by administering medications to treat reflux. In addition, pressing one's abdomen against a hard surface, such as a table's edge, may provide relief for gastrointestinal-related pain, such as flatulence, which medication may also relieve.

To address undetermined cases in which a "non-targeted" approach is indicated, there are several interventions discussed in this book that are, for example, designed to reduce anxiety in individuals whose cause for anxiety is unclear.

A brief summary of the chapters is presented below to guide the reader. A questionnaire, located in Appendix B, may be useful to help select which chapters to read. We strongly recommend that health care practitioners familiarize themselves with all the various contributors and interventions for self-injury. It would be impossible to discuss every underlying cause for this set of behaviors since the possibilities are endless. Over time, we expect that research and clinical experience will reveal additional underlying contributors and more effective treatments.

Chapter 1 discusses self-injury associated with specific autism-related disorders including phenylketonuria (PKU), Lesch-Nyhan syndrome, Smith-Lemli-Opitz syndrome, tuberous sclerosis, pyridoxine-dependent seizures, cerebral folate deficiency, and biotinidase deficiency. The author also describes how hypocalcinuria may be an underlying contributor to ocular (eye) poking that can be treated successfully with calcium.

Chapter 2 describes self-injury in relation to numerous underlying medical conditions, many of which are associated with discomfort or pain. This includes gastrointestinal pain, hormonal imbalance (i.e., menstrual cycle), seizures, otitis media (middle ear infection), dental pain, headaches, and sleep disorders.

Chapter 3 describes self-injurious and aggressive behaviors within the context of epilepsy, including seizures in the temporal and frontal lobes. The authors also write about intermittent explosive disorder, tuberous sclerosis, limbic encephalitis, and herpes simplex encephalitis.

Chapter 4 provides a psychopharmacological perspective and discusses many aspects of SIBs, including comorbidities. In addition, it stresses the need for physicians to obtain a solid understanding of the patient's biochemistry prior to prescribing a medication to control these behaviors.

Chapter 5 describes the author's research documenting how drugs that are commonly prescribed to treat self-injurious and other challenging behaviors may also be associated with adverse effects, such as fatigue, increased appetite, and gastrointestinal pain and discomfort.

Chapter 6 explains how immune-mediated issues may sometimes play a role in self-injury. In other words, asthma, allergic rhinosinusitis, and atopic dermatitis may lead to chronic inflammation of the mucosa or skin. As a result, this can cause pain and discomfort, which may, in turn, lead to SIB. The author also explains the epidemiological-supported associations between neuropsychiatric conditions such as anxiety and allergic/immune conditions, including asthma and allergic rhinitis.

Chapter 7 provides several interesting clinical case reports involving self-injury and aggression. This includes pain associated with gastrointestinal dysfunction as well as other forms of pain (e.g., constipation, foreign objects lodged in the nasal cavity), allergies, upper-respiratory infection, and monilial vaginitis (vaginal yeast infection).

Chapter 8 discusses how dietary interventions may reduce self-injury. This includes the removal of "offending" foods in the person's diet as well as providing nutritional support.

Chapter 9 approaches SIB using a sensory processing framework and discusses many sensory-related hypotheses. It also discusses the relationship between SIB and non-injurious repetitive behaviors.

Chapter 10 explains positive behavior support to assist parents, teachers, and practitioners in understanding the underlying causes of challenging behaviors and how to select the best treatment strategy.

Chapter 11 describes how SIB may be inadvertently reinforced by others. Functional communication training involves determining the "function" for the behavior and then teaches the individual how to communicate more appropriately.

Chapter 12 discusses the role of anxiety in relation to self-injury, and illustrates ways to prevent, replace, and respond to these anxiety-related behaviors.

Chapter 13 explains how stress is often associated with SIB and how established stress-reduction techniques can be implemented successfully. These interventions include relaxation techniques, picture rehearsal, cognitive restructuring, and other positive psychological techniques.

Additional Comments on Self-Injury

Definition of Self-Injury

Although there are several ways to define what constitutes self-injury, the focus of this book is on behaviors exhibited by those with developmental disabilities who engage in behaviors that will likely lead to tissue damage, such as redness, bruising, open wounds, and fractures. These behaviors may be chronic and repetitive, such as constant skin picking or slow rhythmic head banging. For other individuals, these behaviors may be associated with sudden outbursts, such as head banging or wrist biting as part of a severe tantrum. Other types of behaviors leading to harm, such as cutting and suicide, are infrequent in this population and are not addressed in this book.

Diagnosis and Prevalence

A large-scale survey of adults with intellectual disabilities documented a prevalence rate of 14% for some form of self-injury ($n = 10,000$; Griffin *et al.*, 1986). More recently, surveys have shown that these behaviors are more common in those with autism, with estimates as high as 50% in young children ($n = 222$; Baghdadli *et al.*, 2003). In addition, adults with autism are more likely to engage in self-injury than those with intellectual disabilities ($n = 57$; Rojahn *et al.*, 2010).

An unpublished survey involving individuals on the autism spectrum found that those who are classified with Kanner's syndrome or "classic" autism are more likely to engage in self-injury than those who have other subtypes of autism. The Autism Research Institute has distributed the Diagnostic Checklist E-2, which consists of questions regarding developmental histories and behavioral symptoms, since the mid 1960s. Dr. Bernard Rimland, who created the checklist, developed a rather conservative scoring method to diagnose Kanner's syndrome. Basically, a behavior consistent with Kanner's original description of autism in 1943 was scored a "+1," and a behavior inconsistent was scored a "−1." According to calculations performed by Rimland, a total score of +20 or higher would be categorized as Kanner's syndrome. Based on 39,880 cases, only 3.7% of cases exhibited symptoms and behaviors consistent with Kanner's description of autism. Of these cases, 79.6% engaged in some form of self-injury, as opposed to 43.6% who did not belong to this subgroup.

Severe Forms of Self-Injury

In some instances SIBs may lead to permanent damage to one's body. Hair pulling can lead to bald spots, and excessive scratching of the skin can lead to scarring. In some cases, severe head banging has led to a protruded forehead, and frequent ear hitting can lead to deformed ears, often termed "cauliflower ears." There are also reports of individuals who have poked their eyes, causing permanent blindness. Other clinical reports have included biting off fingers and even part of one's tongue.

Use of Aversives and Drug Therapy

The importance of determining the underlying contributors to self-injury is illustrated by Dr. Edward Carr, who often spoke about an incident that troubled him over the years. Carr and his colleagues administered an electric shock to reduce severe head banging in an adult who lived in a state residential facility. The aversive had only a moderate impact on reducing his head banging. Later, it was uncovered that this individual suffered from migraine headaches, and he reacted to this internal pain by banging his head rather severely. According to Carr, the electric shock simply "added to his misery."

Much research in the 1960s and 1970s was focused on using aversives to control self-injury as well as other challenging behaviors. It is important to mention that the chapter authors in this book feel strongly that aversives are inappropriate and should never be given to anyone, no matter the situation. Although the individual may be able to inhibit a behavior in order to stop punishment by a therapist, there are numerous humane and effective ways to treat challenging behaviors, many of which are discussed in this book.

Another treatment approach that is no longer supported by many physicians is the prescription of rather strong drugs to decrease the individual's level of energy, often leading to a semiconscious or drugged state. Although the challenging behavior may be reduced or eliminated, in many cases the person's cognitive abilities and expressions of emotion are also diminished. Chapter 5 provides a discussion of research on how drug treatment can actually worsen the individual's condition and lead to an increase in challenging behaviors. Admittedly, there are a few extreme cases where these types of drugs may be necessary, but every attempt should be made to treat the individual in a health-oriented manner.

Collecting Data on the Behavior

Functional analysis is a data-driven assessment approach to help understand the cause of a behavior. The assessment involves detailed and careful observations, including documentation of the antecedents and consequences of the behavior, along with the physical and social context. Given that many forms of behavior may have an underlying biological cause, we recommend that the functional analyses also include a physical examination, and the type of examination will likely depend on the location of the tissue damage.

It is advantageous to eliminate self-injury when the individual is relatively young, especially when the severity is moderate to severe. The behaviors can become much more damaging and possibly more difficult to treat in teenage and adult years.

It is important to mention that even when administering an appropriate treatment, the behavior may not be completely eliminated, or it may take a relatively long time to do so. Health care practitioners and parents should start with an initial goal of simply decreasing the behavior's frequency, duration, and/or severity.

Once a decision is made to administer a specific intervention, data on the behavior should be collected prior to (baseline), during, and after the intervention. This documentation should include frequency, duration, and severity along with antecedents and consequences. An opinion on treatment effectiveness based solely on memory is neither professional nor fair to the individual receiving the treatment.

We often hear reports that a challenging behavior, such as self-injury, reoccurs at a later time. One common reason for this reappearance is termed "program decay." Basically, if a challenging behavior is successfully treated, the therapeutic strategy may be reduced or even discarded. As a result, the behavior may return. For example, self-injury may reappear if the individual begins to feel anxious again. The anxiety could be due to the same stimulus as before, or something new. Health care providers should be vigilant and monitor the behavior on a regular basis in order to prevent a possible reappearance or escalation.

It is also important to comment on "program delay." In this case, an intervention is delayed until a later time or the "right time." For example, a treatment strategy may be postponed because of an upcoming holiday, a staff member's vacation, and so forth. There are almost always good excuses. Such delays in treatment will lead to continued challenges for the care providers, and more importantly, continued suffering by the individual.

As mentioned earlier, the treatments mentioned in this book are based on clinical research and/or clinical experience. The distinctions between these two forms of expertise are acknowledged throughout the book. We chose to include both empirically and non-empirically based approaches, because self-injury is such a devastating behavior. One should not give up on an individual or simply administer the same ineffective treatment repeatedly just because there is a lack of scientific evidence for the benefits of other therapies. It should also be noted that when there is little or no research on the efficacy of a treatment, this does not necessarily mean that the treatment is invalid. In many cases, the treatment has not yet been evaluated scientifically. This is particularly true in fields where government and private foundations do not target certain treatment domains for funding, such as the areas of nutrition and sensory issues.

Given the above information, we also want to stress that health care practitioners should not waste valuable time implementing an intervention that has already been found ineffective.

This book is not intended to be an extensive scientific review of the research literature on SIB. For those who are searching for a review on various aspects of self-injury, we recommend a recent review by Minshawi and colleagues (2014). Other excellent research-oriented books include one by Schroeder, Oster-Granite, and Thompson (2002), and one by Simeon and Hollander (2001).

Many of the interventions discussed in this book have also been successfully administered to treat other challenging behaviors such as aggression, destructiveness, and severe tantrums. Throughout the book, the contributors may mention how their approach may be applied to understanding and treating these other behaviors.

References

Baghdadli, A., Pascal, C., Grisi, S., and Aussillous, C. (2003). Risk factors for self-injurious behaviours among 222 young children with autistic disorders. *Journal of Intellectual Disability Research, 47*(8), 622–627.

Griffin, J.C., Williams, D.E., Stark, M.T., Altmeyer, B.K., and Mason, M. (1986). Self-injurious behavior: A state-wide prevalence survey of the extent and circumstances. *Applied Research in Mental Retardation, 7,* 105–116.

Minshawi, N.F., Hurwitz, S., Morriss, D., and McDougle, C.J. (2014). Multidisciplinary assessment and treatment of self-injurious behavior in autism disorder and intellectual disability: Integration of psychological and biological theory and approach. *Journal of Autism and Developmental Disorders, 45*(6), 1541–1568.

Rojahn, J., Wilkins, J., Matson, J.L., and Boisjoli, J. (2010). A comparison of adults with intellectual disabilities with and without ASD on parallel measures of challenging behaviour: The Behavior Problems Inventory-01 (BPI-01) and Autism Spectrum Disorders-Behavior Problems for Intellectually Disabled Adults (ASD-BPA). *Journal of Applied Research in Intellectual Disabilities, 23*(2), 179–185.

Schroeder, S.R., Oster-Granite, M.L., and Thompson, T. (2002). *Self-Injurious Behavior: Gene-Brain-Behavior Relationships*. Washington, DC: American Psychological Association.

Simeon, D., and Hollander, E. (2001). *Self-Injurious Behaviors: Assessment and Treatment*. Washington, DC: American Psychiatric Association.

CHAPTER 1

Targeted Medical Therapies and Self-Injury

Mary Coleman, M.D., Foundation for Autism Research, Sarasota, Florida

Introduction

The ideal way to treat the complications of a disease, such as self-injury, is to anticipate the possibilities of these complications long before they occur by preventing or ameliorating the disease process itself. Autism is not a disease, any more than intellectual impairment (mental retardation) is a disease. They are both large syndromes caused by a huge number of separate and rare diseases (Betancur and Coleman, 2013), each disease with its own individual mechanism of action. Both autism and intellectual impairment are the symptomatic expression of impaired final common pathways in the central nervous system, pathways that were altered well before birth in almost all cases and whose inadequate function begins to show up as the infant's brain grows, connecting and pruning essential developmental pathways.

Sometimes the same patient may have both of these sets of neural pathways impaired; in fact, many patients with self-mutilation are low functioning, making it even more imperative that we find their precise diagnosis in order to identify the exact failed mechanism of action of their disease entity in order to successfully treat them.

Unfortunately, in the majority of individuals who present with the signs and symptoms of autism, the detection and medical treatment of the underlying disease and its symptoms, including self-injury, is not yet possible. However, for some diseases and some groups of patients, a targeted medical therapy that is based on an understanding of the mechanism of action causing the disease in the first place has been devised. Such specific therapies can prevent, reverse, or ameliorate the symptoms of self-injurious and other behaviors. Also, a biochemical abnormality has been found in individuals with autism that, when corrected, can stop a specific form of self-injury. These medical entities should be ruled out before other, more general approaches to self-injury are initiated.

Targeted Medical Therapies of Specific Diseases

Phenylketonuria

We start with phenylketonuria (PKU), both because it was historically the first underlying disease identified in patients who were called "autistic," and also because it has a special lesson to teach us today.

In 1960, Dr. C.E. Benda took a group of psychiatrists to a ward of pediatric patients, letting them examine the children. The psychiatrists diagnosed the children as autistic or with childhood schizophrenia (Benda, 1960). He then revealed to the psychiatrists that the children all had PKU, a metabolic disease. This was one of the early examples establishing that autism was a syndrome of more than one disease, instead of a disease itself.

PKU was first diagnosed in 1934, but its treatment of a very low-phenylalanine diet was not developed until 1953. However, the diet therapy only worked if started within weeks of birth. This led to the institution of neonatal screening, which made PKU an almost vanished disease in most countries by the twenty-first century. Unfortunately for patients missed by the screening, and thus not diagnosed in time for dietary therapy, some have prominent autistic symptoms (Fombonne, 1999; van Karnebeek *et al.*, 2002).

The special lesson PKU has to teach us today involves an elderly man with PKU who had never received dietary treatment for it. At an advanced age, he was placed for the first time on a phenylalanine-restricted diet (Williams, 1998). He had been suffering what was described as "severe self-injury." Monitoring of plasma phenylalanine levels and his behavioral state at identical intervals indicated that the severe self-injury was only reversible when plasma phenylalanine concentrations were titrated to near-normal ranges. In other words, in spite of his age, when his underlying disease was treated medically by an adequate protocol, it was possible to reverse at least the self-injury.

Biotinidase Deficiency

Biotinidase deficiency, a rare syndrome, is, like PKU, now part of neonatal screening programs. The treatment is administration of biotin. Again, like PKU, if the therapy is not started almost immediately after birth, it is not so effective in preventing the clinical presentation of the syndrome. A boy with partial biotinidase deficiency with stereotyped and other autistic behaviors did not improve on biotin therapy, yet his younger brother who was identified by a neonatal screening program and placed on early therapy never developed the autistic behaviors or any other symptoms (Zaffanello *et al.*, 2003).

In a study of 187 Greek patients with autism spectrum disorder (ASD), 3% had minor-to-significant improvement in autistic features following supplementation with biotin (Spilioti *et al.*, 2013). This result has not been duplicated elsewhere. On the American continents, biotinidase deficiency is more commonly seen in Hispanic patients (Borsatto *et al.*, 2014) and is starting to be identified with greater frequency in California neonatal screening programs.

Smith-Lemli-Opitz Syndrome

Smith-Lemli-Opitz syndrome (SLOS) is a congenital anomaly syndrome with an extremely broad clinical phenotype. The syndrome occurs in 1:20,000 newborns with an estimated gene frequency in the United States Caucasian population of 1–2% (Boctor and Wilkerson, 2014). Various series have found that between 50 and 86% of the children with SLOS have autistic features (Coleman and Gillberg, 2012).

For those who survive the neonatal period, both physical and behavioral/ cognitive problems persist. Physical anomalies often include microcephaly, a small upturned nose, ptosis, micrognathia, cleft palate, and hypospadias. Limb anomalies are common, and 80–95% of these patients have a distinctive syndactyly of the second and third toes (Ryan *et al.*, 1998), making it easier for clinicians to suspect their underlying disease on the initial examination.

The behavioral phenotype is first seen in infancy with irritability, lack of interest in feeding, and preferring not to be held. As they grow, self-injurious behavior (SIB) may begin, including self-biting, head banging, and trichotillomania as well as irritability, hyperactivity, and sleep disturbances. Many children meet the full diagnostic criteria for autism (Coleman and Gillberg, 2012).

Smith-Lemli-Opitz syndrome is caused by a mutation in the gene *DHCR7* encoding 7-dehydrocholesterol $\Delta 7$ reductase, the enzyme that catalyzes the last step of cholesterol biosynthesis. More than 130 different mutations of *DHCR7* have been reported in individuals with SLOS. This defect causes low or low-to-normal plasma cholesterol levels and increased 7- and 8-dehydrocholesterol (DHC) levels. The clinical suspicion of SLOS is best confirmed by testing for elevated 7DHC by gas chromatography relative to the cholesterol level.

There are a number of reports of treatment of SLOS by cholesterol supplementation (Elias *et al.*, 1997; Irons *et al.*, 1997; Nwokoro and Mulvihill, 1997; Ryan *et al.*, 1998; Linck *et al.*, 2000; Aneja and Tierney, 2008; Chan *et al.*, 2009; Boctor and Wilkerson, 2014). Sometimes the treatment is combined with statins or other approaches. These reports often, but not always, show improvements in various aspects of SLOS in small groups of patients. Since dietary cholesterol is not believed to cross the blood-brain barrier, it is of interest that a number of these reports of cholesterol supplementation show clear-cut improvements in many different kinds of SIB, including trichotillomania. Although one 2.5-month double-blind study of cholesterol supplementation failed to find a reduction in behavioral abnormalities (Tierney *et al.*, 2010), and although prospective clinical trials with validated outcome measures of medical therapies have not yet been undertaken, the correction of the biochemistry of an autistic individual with SLOS who is self-injurious is well worth a try.

Cerebral Folate Deficiency

Cerebral folate deficiency (CFD) is defined as a neurological syndrome associated with a low cerebrospinal concentration of 5-methyltetrahydrofolate (5-MTHF) in the presence of a normal peripheral folate status. Because there are several known underlying etiologies with different mechanisms of action (Ramaekers, Sequeira, and Quadros, 2013), CFD is itself more than one disease entity—that is, it is a syndrome. The classic symptoms of the syndrome consist of intellectual disability, regression, and, often, seizures. The treatment for the folate deficiency is folinic acid.

In one study (Moretti *et al.*, 2008) in which seven children with the syndrome were studied, five of the seven children met diagnostic criteria for autism. Moretti *et al.* (2005) also had published an earlier case history of a 6-year-old girl with autistic features with CFD. Folinic acid-responsive seizures are a very rare treatable cause of neonatal epilepsy (Al-Baradie and Chaudhary, 2014). Another type of CFD with severe SIB has recently been reported (Leuzzi *et al.*, 2012). A single case of a child with autism who had folate reduced in both plasma and cerebrospinal fluid is in the medical literature; the MRI of this child was suggestive of some kind of demyelination disorder (Engbers *et al.*, 2010). The presence of folate receptor antibodies in one or both parents increases the risk of having a child with autism.

Genotype-phenotype correlations in children with autistic features and metabolic disease are just beginning to be understood. Evidence suggests that autistic features sometimes may be associated with errors in folate metabolism that contribute to the hypomethylation of DNA. In a review of the Autism Genetic Resource Exchange (AGRE) collection, four specific behaviors—including a history of SIB—were more common in individuals with at least one copy of the T allele of the 677C-T polymorphism of the gene *MTHFR*. These behavioral patterns could be explained by the difficulties of converting 5,10-MTHF to 5-MTHF (Goin-Kochel *et al.*, 2009). These patients and others with abnormal folate levels have potentially treatable dysfunctions of folate metabolism.

Pyridoxine-Dependent Epilepsy

Even more rare than the CFD syndrome is pyridoxine-dependent epilepsy. Usually the seizures occur in the neonatal period, but they can start as late as 2 years of age. The seizures are resistant to antiepileptic drugs but can be controlled by lifelong oral pyridoxine. However, autistic features often develop (Rajesh and Girija, 2003; Bennett *et al.*, 2009; Mills *et al.*, 2010). In the case described by Burd *et al.* (2000), self-injury accompanied the autistic disorder.

Lesch-Nyhan Syndrome

Sometimes in a large series of patients labeled as ASD, Lesch-Nyhan syndrome is included, especially if the children have SIB (Spilioti *et al.*, 2013). Various types of self-injury, particularly serious self-biting of lips and fingers, are found in this syndrome.

Lesch-Nyhan syndrome is caused by a nucleotide depletion of purine nucleotides (e.g., ATP, GTP), due to hypoxanthine phosphoribosyltransferase deficiency. A compound, S-adenosylmethione (SAMe), appears to partially alleviate the purine depletion in some patients and result in a reduction of the self-injury. First described by Glick in 2006 as a dramatic reduction of self-injury in a Lesch-Nyhan individual (Glick, 2006), a number of other patients have since been helped by SAMe. Five children from Malaysia, including a girl, had a positive outcome (Chen *et al.*, 2014). In another series of 14 patients, whose authors included W.L. Nyhan, only 4 patients tolerated the drug and reported beneficial effects; the remainder experienced worsened behavior (Dolcetta *et al.*, 2013). SAMe appears to help only certain selected individuals with Lesch-Nyhan syndrome, but it certainly is worth a try in any self-mutilating child.

Tuberous Sclerosis

Between 1 and 3% of children with autistic features have tuberous sclerosis or tuberous sclerosis complex, making it one of the most commonly seen forms of autism by clinicians. Looking at the statistics the other way around, between 20 and 50% of children with tuberous sclerosis have autistic features (Coleman and Gillberg, 2012). This is a genetic disease that causes benign tumors to grow in the brain and other organs. One of two genes underlie this disease entity; children with tuberous sclerosis are found to have mutations either in the gene *TSC1* or the gene *TSC2*. There is increased risk for developing autistic behavior in children with tuberous sclerosis in the presence of the following features: *TSC2* mutations, temporal lobe tumors, history of infantile spasms, early age of seizure onset, and resistance to antiepileptic treatment. Tuberous sclerosis can present with autistic regression. Between 85 and 90% of individuals with tuberous sclerosis have seizures; however, early surgical removal of tubers in the brain can sometimes result in freedom from seizures (Wu *et al.*, 2010).

The frequency of SIB in tuberous sclerosis is about 10%, most often seen in children with the *TSC2* mutation, autistic features, history of infantile spasms, history of seizures, and intellectual disability (Staley *et al.*, 2008).

The U.S. Food and Drug Administration has approved two treatments for tuberous sclerosis complex; these are everolimus and vigabatrin (Gipson *et al.*, 2013). Both drugs have a number of side effects and have not yet been systematically studied in children with tuberous sclerosis with autistic features. But a trial of these medications would be indicated in a child with tuberous sclerosis and SIB.

In the published medical literature there is one child with tuberous sclerosis who became blind from self-inflicted ocular injuries (Noel and Clarke, 1982). Today there are *two* medical options that might have treated him (see below).

Targeted Medical Therapy of a Biochemical Abnormality

In 1974, a large study of 78 children with autism was conducted in Washington, D.C., made possible by the active support of Dr. Bernard Rimland, who solicited families to participate from all over the country. The children were matched with age, sex, and parent-income controls. After all the analyses were completed, the results were published in 1976 (Coleman, 1976).

The study included 24-hour urine samples for calcium, phosphorus, magnesium, creatinine, uric acid, sodium, and potassium. (Twenty-four-hour urine samples are difficult to obtain in any child; in children with autism it is indeed quite difficult, but the highly motivated parents obtained them, and a check by creatinine levels showed almost all were successful.) Two abnormalities were found to be statistically significant in the autistic children compared with the controls in the 24-hour urines. The first one, levels of uric acid, were abnormal in children under 12 years of age but were not significantly different in older children. This finding was later replicated in other patients, and the age cutoff was found to be correct. The meaning of this finding of purine dysfunction in younger children with autism is unknown.

The other finding from the study was a lower level of calcium, with a significant difference between autistic and control urines of $p < 0.01$ (Coleman, 1976, 1994). Accurate 24-hour urines had been obtained for this variable in 72 patients and 67 controls. Sixteen of the 72 children (22%) with autism had hypocalcinuria (levels below two standard deviations for controls). Serum levels of calcium for all children in the study were within normal limits, except for one of the children with hypocalcinuria who had a serum of 8.1 mg% and a urine of 0 mg%.

A second study by Rosenthal (1985), also conducted in the United States, included calcium in serum and 24-hour urines. Of the 37 children with autism tested, all had normal serum levels and 7 (18%) had hypocalcinuria. A third study in France of 21 children with autism (Rosenberger-Debiesse and Coleman, 1986) found normal levels of calcium in both serum and urine.

Later studies of children with autism and hypocalcinuria in the clinic found no evidence of kidney dysfunction, or abnormalities in parathormone, calcitonin, or 1,25 dihydroxyvitamin D3. However, a clinical abnormality was noted in some of the hypocalcinuria patients—ocular damage ranging from simple eye poking to corneal lacerations to vitreous hemorrhage to retinal detachment to actual enucleation of the eye itself in one case. One young boy told the examiner that he was eye poking because his eyes "felt funny."

Most patients in the clinic with hypocalcinuria did not have ocular self-mutilation. However, all the patients with autism and ocular self-injury did have hypocalcinuria when tested, and they did cease their ocular damage when they were placed on liquid supplements of calcium large enough to cancel out their hypocalcinuria, often quite big doses (Coleman, 1994). Each patient had an individual dose based on their own urine level. Since excess calcium is not good for other organs, such as the heart, patients on calcium supplementation need to be monitored by 24-hour urines twice a year as they grow. Recently it has been reported that six children with autism had calcium levels significantly elevated in their temporocortical gray matter on autopsy (Palmieri *et al.*, 2010), a finding that might help explain why the kidney was conserving calcium—trying to prevent hypocalcemia—in some individuals with self-destructive behavior. Also, genetically there is a list of nine proteins encoded by calcium-related genes found to be involved in autism; mutations in those genes all result in abnormal calcium homeostasis in the patients (Napolioni *et al.*, 2011). Although the mechanisms and locations in the cell involved in each gene mutation are different, they each result in amplifying Ca^{2+} signaling. This need for extra calcium in the brain might help explain why the kidney, whose job it is to regulate calcium levels in the blood, was conserving calcium in one out of five of the patients with autism—trying to prevent hypocalcemia, which could harm other organs in these individuals. One possible example might be to try to prevent the osteoporosis that can develop as early as adolescence in some individuals with autism. Another way to elevate calcium in a child with autism is to add vitamin D; there is a single case in the literature of a 32-month-old boy whose head banging against objects almost stopped with vitamin D supplementation (Jia *et al.*, 2014).

These studies with ocular self-mutilation indicate that an irritating, abnormal neurological sensation in the eye underlies this kind of SIB in some individuals. It is possible that this principle applies to some of the other forms of SIB and could guide us in our various approaches to alleviating the misery of SIB suffered by so many children with autism.

Conclusion

In children and adults with autistic features and SIB, it is important to do a diagnostic check for disease entities that have the possibility of medical treatment. In those individuals with ocular self-mutilation, it also is important to obtain calcium levels in 24-hour urines.

References

Al-Baradie, R.S., and Chaudhary, M.W. (2014). Diagnosis and management of cerebral folate deficiency: A form of folinic-acid responsive seizures. *Neurosciences (Riyadh), 19,* 312–316.

Aneja, A., and Tierney, E. (2008). Autism: The role of cholesterol supplementation in treatment. *International Review of Psychiatry, 20,* 165–170.

Benda, C.E. (1960). Childhood schizophrenia, autism and Heller's disease. *Proceedings of the First International Metabolic Conference, Portland, Maine.* New York, NY: Grune and Stratton.

Bennett, C.L., Chen, Y., Hahn, S., Glass, I.A., and Gospe, S.M. Jr. (2009). Prevalence of ALDH7A1 mutations in 18 North American pyridoxine-dependent seizure (PDS) patients. *Epilepsia, 50*(5), 1167–1175.

Betancur, C., and Coleman, M. (2013). Etiological Heterogeneity in Autism Spectrum Disorders: Role of Rare Variants. In J.D. Buxbaum and P.R. Hof (Eds.), *The Neuroscience of Autism Spectrum Disorders.* Oxford: Elsevier.

Boctor, F.N., and Wilkerson, M.L. (2014). Fresh frozen plasma as a source of cholesterol for newborns with Smith-Lemli-Opitz syndrome associated with defective cholesterol synthesis. *Annals of Clinical Laboratory Science, 44*(3), 332–333.

Borsatto, T., Sperb-Ludwig, F., Pinto, L.L., De Luca, G.R., *et al.* (2014). Biotinidase deficiency: Clinical and genetic studies of 38 Brazilian patients. *BMC Medical Genetics, 15*(1), 96.

Burd, L., Stenehjem, A., Franceschini, L.A., and Kerbeshian, J. (2000). A 15-year follow-up of a boy with pyridoxine (vitamin B6)-dependent seizures with autism, breath holding, and severe mental retardation. *Journal of Child Neurology, 15*(11), 763–765.

Chan, Y.M., Merkens, L.S., Conner, W.E., Roullet, J.B., *et al.* (2009). Effects of dietary cholesterol and simvastatin on cholesterol synthesis in Smith-Lemli-Opitz syndrome. *Pediatric Research, 65,* 681–685.

Chen, B.C., Balasubramaniam, S., McGown, I.N., O'Neill, J.P., *et al.* (2014). Treatment of Lesch-Nyhan disease with S-adenosylmethionine: Experience with five young Malaysians, including a girl. *Brain Development, 36,* 593–600.

Coleman, M. (1976). *The Autistic Syndromes.* Amsterdam: North-Holland Publishing Co.

Coleman, M. (1994). Clinical presentation of patients with autism and hypocalcinuria. *Developmental Brain Dysfunction, 7,* 63–70.

Coleman, M., and Gillberg, C. (2012). *The Autisms* (4th ed.). Oxford: Oxford University Press.

Dolcetta, D., Parmigiani, P., Salmaso, L., Bernardelle, R., *et al.* (2013). Quantitative evaluation of the clinical effects of S-adenosylmethionine on mood and behavior in Lesch-Nyhan patients. *Nucleosides Nucleotides Nucleic Acids, 32,* 174–188.

Elias, E.R., Irons, M.B., Hurley, A.S., Tint, G.S., and Salen, G. (1997). Clinical effects of cholesterol supplementation in six patients with the Smith-Lemli-Opitz syndrome. *Journal of Medical Genetics, 68,* 305–310.

Engbers, H.M., Nievelstein, R.A., Gooskens, R.H., Kroes, H.Y., *et al.* (2010). The clinical utility of MRI in patients with neurodevelopmental disorders of unknown origin. *European Journal of Neurology, 17*(6), 815–822.

Fombonne, E. (1999). The epidemiology of autism: A review. *Psychological Medicine, 29,* 769–786.

Gipson, T.T., Gerner, G., Wilson, M.A., Blue, M.E., and Johnston, M.V. (2013). Potential for treatment of severe autism in tuberous sclerosis complex. *World Journal of Clinical Pediatrics, 2,* 16–25.

Glick, N. (2006). Dramatic reduction in self-injury in Lesch-Nyhan disease following S-adenosylmethionine. *Journal of Inherited Metabolic Diseases, 29,* 687.

Goin-Kochel, R.P., Porter, A.E., Peters, S.U., Shinawi, M., Sahoo, T., and Beaudet, A.L. (2009). The MTHFR 677C→T polymorphism and behaviors in children with autism: Exploratory genotype-phenotype correlations. *Autism Research, 2,* 98–108.

Irons, M., Elias, E.R., Abuelo, D., Bull, M.J., *et al.* (1997). Treatment of Smith-Lemli-Opitz syndrome: Results of a multicenter trial. *American Journal of Medical Genetics, 68,* 311–314.

Jia, F., Wang, B., Shan, L., Xu, Z., Staal, W.G., and Du, L. (2014). Core symptoms of autism improved after vitamin D supplementation. *Pediatrics, 135*(1), 2014–2121.

Leuzzi, V., Mastrangelo, M., Celato, A., Carducci, C., and Carducci, C. (2012). A new form of cerebral folate deficiency with severe self-injurious behaviour. *Acta Paediatrica, 101*(11), e482–e483.

Linck, L.M., Lin, D.S., Flavell, D., Connor, W.E., and Steiner, R.D. (2000). Cholesterol supplementation with egg yolk increases plasma cholesterol and decreases plasma 7-dehydrocholesterol in Smith-Lemli-Opitz syndrome. *American Journal of Medical Genetics, 93,* 360–365.

Mills, P.B., Footitt, E.J., Mills, K.A., Tuschl, K., *et al.* (2010). Genotypic and phenotypic spectrum of pyridoxine-dependent epilepsy (ALDH7A1 deficiency). *Brain, 133*(Pt. 7), 2148–2159.

Moretti, P., Peters, S.U., Del Gaudio, D., Sahoo, T., *et al.* (2008). Brief report: Autistic symptoms, developmental regression, mental retardation, epilepsy, and dyskinesias in CNS folate deficiency. *Journal of Autism and Developmental Disorder, 38,* 1170–1177.

Moretti, P., Sahoo, T., Hyland, K., Bottiglieri, T., *et al.* (2005). Cerebral folate deficiency with developmental delay, autism, and response to folinic acid. *Neurology, 64,* 1088–1090.

Napolioni, V., Persico, A.M., Porcelli, V., and Palmieri, L. (2011). The mitochondrial aspartate/glutamate carrier AGC1 and calcium homeostasis: Physiological links and abnormalities in autism. *Molecular Neurobiology, 44,* 83–92.

Noel, L.P., and Clarke, W.N. (1982). Self-inflicted ocular injuries in children. *American Journal of Ophthalmology, 94,* 630–633.

Nwokoro, N.A., and Mulvihill, J.J. (1997). Cholesterol and bile replacement therapy in children and adults with Smith-Lemli-Opitz (SLO/RSH) syndrome. *American Journal of Medical Genetics, 68,* 315–321.

Palmieri, L., Papaleo, V., Porcelli, V., Scarcia, P., *et al.* (2010). Altered calcium homeostasis in autism-spectrum disorders: Evidence from biochemical and genetic studies of the mitochondrial aspartate/glutamate carrier AGC1. *Molecular Psychiatry, 15,* 38–52.

Rajesh, R., and Girija, A.S. (2003). Pyridoxine-dependent seizures: A review. *Indian Pediatrics, 20,* 633–638.

Ramaekers, V., Sequeira, J.M., and Quadros, E.V. (2013). Clinical recognition and aspects of the cerebral folate deficiency syndromes. *Clinical Chemical Laboratory Medicine, 51,* 497–511.

Rosenberger-Debiesse, J., and Coleman, M. (1986). Brief report: Preliminary evidence for multiple etiologies in autism. *Journal of Autism and Developmental Disorders, 16,* 385–392.

Rosenthal, D. (1985). *Metabolic disorders in autism: A behavioral evaluation of treatment.* Unpublished doctoral dissertation, Ferkauf Graduate School of Psychology, Yeshiva University, Bronx, New York.

Ryan, A.K., Bartlett, K., Clayton, P., Eaton, S., *et al.* (1998). Smith-Lemli-Opitz syndrome: A variable clinical and biochemical phenotype. *Journal of Medical Genetics, 35,* 558–565.

Spilioti, M., Evangeliou, A.E., Tramma, D., Theodoridou, Z., *et al.* (2013). Evidence for treatable inborn errors of metabolism in a cohort of 187 Greek patients with autism spectrum disorder (ASD). *Front Human Neurosciences, 7,* 858.

Staley, B.A., Montenegro, M.A., Major, P., Muzykewicz, D.A., *et al.* (2008). Self-injurious behavior and tuberous sclerosis complex: Frequency and possible associations in a population of 257 patients. *Epilepsy Behavior, 13,* 650–653.

Tierney, E., Conley, S.K., Goodwin, H., and Porter, F.D. (2010). Analysis of short-term behavioral effects of dietary cholesterol supplementation in Smith-Lemli-Opitz syndrome. *American Journal of Medical Genetics, 152A,* 91–95.

van Karnebeek, C.D., van Gelderen, I., Nijhof, G.J., Abeling, N.G., *et al.* (2002). An aetiological study of 25 mentally retarded adults with autism. *Journal of Medical Genetics, 39,* 205–213.

Williams, K. (1998). Benefits of normalizing plasma phenylalanine: Impact on behavior and health. A case report. *Journal of Inherited Metabolic Disease, 21,* 785–790.

Wu, J.Y., Salamon, N., Kirsch, H.E., Mantle, M.M., *et al.* (2010). Noninvasive testing, early surgery, and seizure freedom in tuberous sclerosis complex. *Neurology, 74,* 392–398.

Zaffanello, M., Zamboni, G., Fontana, E., Zoccante, L., and Tato, L. (2003). A case of partial biotinidase deficiency associated with autism. *Child Neuropsychology, 9,* 184–188.

CHAPTER 2

Self-Injurious and Aggressive Behaviors in Autism

Looking Below the Surface

Margaret L. Bauman, M.D., Boston University School of Medicine, Boston, Massachusetts

Introduction

Autism is a behaviorally defined disorder first described by Leo Kanner in 1943 (Kanner, 1943). In his original description, Kanner characterized those affected as having features of "autistic aloneness" and an "obsessive insistence on the preservation of sameness." Over time, additional clinical features were noted, including disordered language and communication, impaired social interaction, isolated areas of interest, repetitive stereotypic behaviors, and a preference for routine. Although initially believed to be caused by psychodynamic factors, it is now recognized that autism is a neurodevelopmental disorder that is believed to begin before birth. With the publication of the fifth edition of the *Diagnostic and Statistical Manual of Mental Disorders* (DSM-5) in 2013 (American Psychiatric Association, 2013), an effort commenced to define more rigorously the clinical features, to include the persistent impairment of reciprocal social communication and social interaction, and restricted repetitive patterns of behavior. Furthermore, the diagnosis now also requires a determination of the presence or absence of cognitive disability, medical or genetic conditions, and/or language impairment. It is now understood that autism is heterogeneous in its etiology, neurobiology, and clinical presentation. As a result, the term autism spectrum disorder (ASD) has come into common usage, a term that recognizes severity and symptomatic variability.

Although disruptive behaviors have not been included within the core diagnostic features of the disorder, episodes of self-injurious behavior (SIB) and aggression have been estimated to occur in approximately 50% of ASD individuals (Bodfish *et al.*, 2000; Baghdadli *et al.*, 2003). Common forms include self-biting, skin picking or pinching, head banging, eye pressing, pulling at the hair, nails, teeth, or fingers, eating non-edible items, and knee-to-head hitting (Rojahn, Schroeder, and Hoch, 2008). It has been reported that individuals who engage in SIB are also more likely to engage in aggressive behavior as well as disruptive and destructive behaviors (Murphy, Healy, and Leader, 2009). Lack of verbal communication, deficits in receptive and expressive language, significant social-skills deficits (Emerson *et al.*, 2001), and sleep disturbances (Symons, Davis, and Thompson, 2000) have been associated with an increased risk of SIB (Murphy *et al.*, 2005). However, the association with comorbid psychiatric conditions has generally been the primary focus as it relates to interventions and therapies, the most prevalent comorbid diagnosis being anxiety disorders.

While it has been acknowledged by some that SIB, aggression, and other disruptive behaviors may serve as a form of social communication, there has been relatively little consideration as to what this mode of "communication" might mean over and above behaviors related to frustration, changes in routine, and anxiety. There has been relatively little consideration with regard to the role of these behaviors in communicating possible pain and discomfort related to a variety of medical conditions, which, when present, may then be overlooked. This chapter addresses some of these medical disorders and the importance of diagnosing and treating them in order to achieve improved behavioral and developmental outcomes.

Gastrointestinal Disorders

Although it is now recognized that gastrointestinal (GI) disorders commonly occur in individuals with ASD, the true prevalence of these disorders remains unknown, with estimations ranging from 9 to 70% or higher (Buie *et al.*, 2010). The evaluation of abdominal pain and discomfort in individuals with impaired communication and processing of sensory information can be challenging. While many ASD patients present with symptoms easily recognized by most gastroenterologists, a substantial number of these patients do not provide these clues. In a consensus paper published in 2010 (Buie *et al.*, 2010), a number of GI disorders reported in individuals with ASD were highlighted, including gastroesophageal reflux, colitis, esophagitis, gastritis, celiac disease, inflammatory bowel disease, and Crohn's disease, as well as chronic constipation, diarrhea, and vomiting. In addition, the consensus group identified a variety of atypical and disruptive behaviors observed in association with GI disorders, including facial grimacing and neck stretching, chewing on non-edibles such as shirt sleeves, putting pressure on the abdomen, constant eating and drinking, unusual gulping, and chest tapping, as well as aggression, motor stereotypies, SIBs, and disturbed sleep patterns (T. Buie, unpublished).

It is not known whether or not GI disorders are more common among those with ASD when compared with neurotypical individuals. Furthermore, it is not known whether GI disorders observed in association with ASD should be treated in the same way as those seen in typically developing persons. Whether or not

GI dysfunction in ASD represents an associated phenomenon unrelated to the ASD disorder itself or whether it might reflect a subset or part of a subset of ASD individuals remains to be determined. In 2009, Campbell and colleagues reported on the observation that an increased risk of ASD associated with GI dysfunction was associated with a disruption of MET gene signaling (Campbell *et al.*, 2009). MET is a pleotropic gene that is known to be important for brain development as well as GI motility and repair. This study suggests that ASD associated with GI disturbances, at least in some cases, may represent a subgroup of individuals on the autism spectrum.

Hormonal Dysfunction

Many parents report that the onset of adolescence in their autistic child is associated with the appearance of, or the increase in, disruptive behaviors, including aggression and self-injury. These changes in behavior have generally been attributed to the hormonal changes occurring during the teenage years. However, there have been no formal studies to examine this hypothesis among individuals with ASD. It is known that sex hormones are modulators of brain plasticity across the lifespan and can thus impact both brain and behavior. Some have speculated that disruptive behavior during adolescence could reflect a number of hormonal changes including those related to precocious puberty, accelerated or reduced physical growth, and, in girls, possible menstrual pain and discomfort.

The relationship between the menstrual cycle and the presence of problem behaviors in adolescent girls, believed to be related to pain and discomfort, has been reported by Carr and colleagues (2003). Those authors raise the possibility that fluctuations in progesterone and estrogen levels during adolescence may be important variables. Studies in non-human primates using positron emission tomography have suggested that fluctuations in ovarian hormones across the menstrual cycle influence activity in brain areas involved in the processing and regulation of emotion (Rilling *et al.*, 2008). In a more recent study, Arelin *et al.* (2015) have shown that the menstrual cycle impacts intrinsic functional connectivity, most especially in regions of the brain associated with contextual memory regulation, the hippocampus, and in progesterone-modulated changes in the sensorimotor cortex. Furthermore, it has been reported that differences in pain perception are modulated by endogenous hormonal fluctuations including areas within the sensorimotor cortex (Riley *et al.*, 1999; Veldhuijzen *et al.*, 2013). Additional studies in women experiencing severe menstrual pain have shown gray matter changes in regions associated with pain modulation, pain transmission, and affective experience generation associated with the primary and secondary sensorimotor cortex—regions involved in sensory discrimination and interoception (Tu *et al.*, 2010, 2013). Burke and colleagues (2010) reported on a study in adolescent girls with autism, Down syndrome, and cerebral palsy assessed retrospectively regarding gynecological complaints. Those with autism were significantly more likely to present with disruptive behaviors than girls in the other two groups. Successful management included the use of non-steroidal anti-inflammatory medications, oral contraceptives, and education. Thus, there appears to be a growing body of evidence supporting the role of hormonal dysregulation during adolescence that may underlie some of the disruptive behaviors observed in some ASD teenage girls, and the suggestion that many of these behaviors may be related to the perception of pain and discomfort. The role of hormonal dysfunction in ASD, particularly during adolescence, requires further research including replication of available data. In addition, similar studies in teenage ASD boys is lacking and merits investigation.

Seizure Disorders

In October 2013, the journal *Neurology* published the proceedings of a forum sponsored by the National Institutes of Neurological Disorders and Stroke (NINDS), in which the relationship between autism, epilepsy, and intellectual disability (ID) was reviewed and discussed (Tuchman, Hirtz, and Mamounas, 2013). It was noted that the risk of epilepsy in ASD combined with ID was 21%, as compared with a frequency of 8% in ASD alone. Furthermore, seizures beginning after the age of 12 years in the ASD population were more likely to continue into adulthood than seizures occurring in other epileptic populations.

Peak risk periods for seizures are said to occur during early childhood and later in adolescence (Volkmar and Nelson, 1990). Although complex partial seizures are most frequently reported, many types of seizures can occur in ASD, including major motor, myoclonic, petit mal, and febrile seizures. Further data suggest that the majority of seizures associated with ASD occur after 12 years of age, with 30% occurring by age 20 years (Rossi *et al.*, 1995).

Although seizure disorders can occur in neurotypical individuals as well as those with ASD, relatively few have been reported to be associated with pain and discomfort. When present, however, seizure pain has been classified into three epileptic categories: (1) cephalic attacks, (2) paroxysmal abdominal pain, and (3) painful somatosensory seizures (PSS). Of the three seizure types, PSS are associated with acute intense pain such as a burning sensation, pricking ache, throbbing pain, or a muscle-tearing sensation, usually lateralized contra- or ipsilateral to the epileptic focus. Pain, accompanied by facial grimacing or screaming, can be a common expression of PSS. Recent data suggest that PSS occur in approximately 0.6% of refractory partial epilepsies and 1.5% of patients with somatosensory seizures (Montavont *et al.*, 2015). Recent research suggests that the secondary somatosensory cortex (SII) and the posterior insula are able to trigger the experience of pain during a seizure. Furthermore, it has been found that these regions are the only regions in the human brain where stimulation triggers acute pain and where focal lesions entail selective pain deficits and give rise to neuropathic pain (Garcia-

Larrea, 2012). Given this scenario, it is possible that paroxysmal lateralized pain can be misdiagnosed as psychogenic or behavioral in origin or as radicular pain, and this symptomatic presentation can be the only manifestation of epileptic seizures arising from the opercular-insular cortex. It is important to consider the epileptic origin of these symptoms and to initiate appropriate evaluations, management, and anticonvulsant medications if and as indicated.

Otitis Media

Ear infections are a fairly common illness during childhood and can be associated with pain and discomfort. There is no evidence that children with developmental disabilities, including ASD, are less susceptible to these infections than typically developing children. A number of investigators have suggested a causal link between otitis media and disruptive behaviors, including self-injury (Bailey and Pyles, 1989; Gardner and Sovner, 1994). In those with developmental disabilities, including ASD, children often lack the communication skills to indicate their discomfort, or to accurately localize their pain, possibly due to impaired processing of sensory information. Thus, disruptive behavior may be their only means of conveying physical discomfort.

Although not the only problem behavior that may be associated with otitis media, head banging has been reported in normal infants and toddlers in association with upper respiratory illnesses as well as middle-ear infections (de Lissovoy, 1962, 1963). In 1989, Gunsett et al. published a case report documenting the association between head-banging behavior and a middle-ear infection in an adult (Gunsett et al., 1989). Thus, given the evidence to date, accompanied by the fairly common occurrence of middle-ear infections during childhood, adolescence, and adulthood, ASD individuals of any age with disruptive behaviors, including self-injury and aggression, should be evaluated for possible otitis media and treated accordingly.

Dental Pain

Orofacial pain can be difficult to diagnose in individuals with developmental disabilities, atypical social interaction, and impaired communication, and, in ASD, may be associated with or result in aggravation of core symptoms including self-injury and aggression (Zeidan-Chulia et al., 2011). Orofacial pain may be felt in the region of the mouth, face, nose, ear, eyes, head, and neck. Prevalence rates in the general population have been estimated to range from 17.5 to 26% and can become chronic in a subset of these cases (Sarlani, Balciunas, and Grace, 2005). Etiological factors include temporomandibular joint disorders, gingivitis, impacted wisdom teeth, malocclusion of the jaw, dental abscesses, and, most commonly, dental caries. Studies have provided evidence of higher rates of caries in ASD, as compared with non-autistic subjects and those with schizophrenia (Vishnu-Rekha, Arangannal, and Shahed, 2012; Delli *et al.*, 2013). Evaluation of orofacial pain can be challenging in patients with developmental disabilities, and it is often labeled as "psychogenic" when the etiology remains obscure. In many cases, orofacial pain remains undiagnosed or is labeled "idiopathic."

The invasive nature of oral health care in patients with ASD can trigger disruptive behaviors including self-injury, head banging, aggression, or temper tantrums (Friedlander *et al.*, 2003). Further complicating oral care is the fact that many ASD individuals exhibit damaging habits such as picking at their gums, lip biting, chewing on non-edible items, and bruxism. In addition, many ASD patients exhibit a high sensitivity to sensory stimuli (including sound, touch, and lights), further complicating their daily oral hygiene and dental care.

Despite increasing awareness among the medical and dental community, orofacial pain can easily elude diagnosis and remain a "silent disease," masked by the fact that many ASD patients cannot express their pain and discomfort nor localize their symptoms (Zeidan-Chulia *et al.*, 2011). It is therefore important that family members and health care professionals consider orofacial pain as a possible cause for new or ongoing disruptive behaviors, including aggression and self-injury, in the ASD population.

Headaches

It is estimated that approximately 10% of school-age children and 15–27% of adolescents experience headaches (DeBlasio, 2014). Headaches can be brought on by a variety of causes including inadequate hydration, diet/hunger, sleep deprivation, stress, vision problems, and a positive family history. However, the prevalence of headaches in the ASD population has received relatively little attention. In a study of 18 ASD patients, 61% reported symptoms consistent with migraine headaches, with and without aura. Age at presentation was 5–16 years. All patients were verbal and had comorbid mental health and behavioral conditions (Victorio, 2014).

Among the ASD population, a relationship between sensory hyperactivity and migraine headaches has been proposed (Casanova, 2008; Gargus, 2009). Migraine headaches are a relatively common condition in the neurotypical population, with symptoms characterized by unilateral throbbing headache, increased pain sensitivity, photophobia, and increased reactivity to sensory input (Sullivan *et al.*, 2014). A general hyperexcitability or imbalance of cortical inhibitory/excitatory activity has been hypothesized, possibly reflecting a dysfunction of subcortical sensory modulation systems (Goadsby, 2007). Similar patterns of neural and behavioral processes have been reported in ASD (Casanova, 2008; Gargus, 2009). ASD and migraine headaches have both been associated with anxiety and sensory reactive differences. In a pilot study of 81 ASD children (ages 7–17 years) who were evaluated for anxiety, sensory processing disorder, and sensory over-responsiveness, children with ASD and migraines showed significantly more generalized anxiety symptoms and more sensory over-reactivity than those without migraines; the study utilized a number of parent-reported scales (Sullivan *et al.*, 2014). Although this study was limited by a small sample size and lack of direct examination of each child, the data suggest a significant link between migraines in ASD and sensory hyperactivity, and support previous studies connecting sensory hyperactivity and anxiety (Green and Ben-Sasson, 2010). Thus, given the presence of a triad of sensory hyper-reactivity, migraine headaches, and anxiety in an individual with ASD, it should not be surprising that disruptive behaviors may be a presenting or associated clinical symptom which, when present—especially in non-verbal patients—merits an in-depth medical assessment.

Sleep Disorders

Sleep problems are highly prevalent in ASD children and rank as one of the most common concurrent medical conditions associated with this disorder. Prevalence rates vary widely, ranging from 40 to 86% (Richdale, 1999; Richdale and Schreck, 2009; Humphreys *et al.*, 2014), leading to a growing interest in the causes and consequences of these dysfunctions, and possible remediation. It is known that disordered sleep affects daytime health and can result in neurocognitive dysfunction and behavioral disruptions. Although sleep disruptions are common in ASD, it is not clear why disordered sleep patterns are so prevalent in this population. Proposed hypotheses include (1) factors in the home or environment that are not conducive to good sleep, (2) potential intrinsic biological or genetic abnormalities that alter brain structure and/or chemistry, or (3) psychological or behavioral disorders associated with the core features of ASD (Richdale and Schreck, 2009). However, recent reports (Tudor *et al.*, 2014; Moore, 2015) suggest that pain-related distress may also be a factor in some cases, with pain predicting three specific sleep problems: sleep duration, parasomnias, and sleep-disordered breathing.

In typically developing children, sleep disruptions may lead to daytime sleepiness as well as hyperactivity, inattention, disruptive behaviors, and aggression (Owens *et al.*, 1998). Similar patterns have been reported in ASD children (Fadini *et al.*, 2015), with additional correlations with impulsivity, anxiety, and depression. Furthermore, it has been noted that there is a direct relationship between a reduction in the hours of nighttime sleep and the severity of behavioral stereotypies, impaired social interaction, communication, and family stress (Richdale, 1999; Miano and Ferri, 2010; Minkel *et al.*, 2012).

Given the prevalence of sleep disorders in ASD and their behavioral consequences, it has been recommended that all children on the spectrum be screened for potential sleep disturbances (Johnson, Giannotti, and Cortesi, 2009). A number of questionnaires are available that can be used for this purpose. Depending upon the responses to these questionnaires, further studies may be needed to clarify the nature and cause of the presenting behaviors, including the use of polysomnography and actigraphy, and possible referral to specialty providers, including a sleep specialist, gastroenterologist, otolaryngologist, neurologist, and dentist. Evidence suggests that the identification and treatment of an underlying cause of a sleep disorder can have a positive effect on behavioral outcomes (Fadini *et al.*, 2015).

Other Medical Conditions

Suffice it to say that any medical disorder that can present in neurotypical persons can also impact the ASD child, adolescent, and adult. Disorders highlighted in this chapter tend to be among some of the more common conditions requiring medical attention. However, other causes of discomfort can be related to injury and fractures, foreign bodies in orifices, sinus infections, skin lesions such as eczema, allergies associated with itchiness, bladder and kidney infections, muscle spasms, angina, neuropathic pain, neoplasms, and some cases of respiratory distress, to name a few. It is important that a thorough physical and neurological evaluation be conducted on any ASD individual who presents with significant or new-onset episodes of disruptive behaviors, and that appropriate medical assessments be conducted to rule out possible causes of pain and discomfort.

Discussion

Since its original description, most of the research related to ASD has been focused on studies of the brain and associated psychiatric and neurological symptoms. However, over the past 5–10 years, there has been a growing appreciation that organ systems outside of the brain can be, and often are, involved in many cases. Additionally, there has been increased and convincing evidence that pain and discomfort, often secondary to any number of medical conditions, can result in disruptive, self-injurious, repetitive, and/or aggressive behaviors. The relationship between physical discomfort and problem behaviors has been reported by Carr and Owen-DeSchryver (2007) in minimally verbal, developmentally disabled individuals. Since it has been estimated that approximately 50% of the ASD population are non-verbal or hypo-verbal, coupled with the fact that many show deficits in processing and localizing sensory information, it seems highly probable that many of the challenging behaviors exhibited by these individuals may, at least in some cases, represent a means of conveying their physical discomfort.

Although there is an increased awareness of the role of medical comorbidities and the impact of these conditions on some of the behavioral patterns seen in individuals with ASD, much research remains to be done relative to the prevalence of intercurrent illnesses in ASD, their mode of presentation, and how they can best be identified and effectively treated. To date, many of these conditions have been either ignored or have been difficult to identify, in large part due to challenges involved in obtaining a meaningful medical history and conducting a detailed physical examination in an often non-verbal patient whose behavior may interfere with an adequate assessment. Further complicating diagnosis has been the common lore, based on a number of case studies, that individuals with ASD experience an insensitivity to pain, highlighting how impaired sensory perception may mask and therefore delay the ability of health care providers to make an accurate diagnosis and provide treatment. However, a recent review of the literature indicates that this view needs to be challenged (Alley, 2013). Current evidence suggests that more research needs to be directed toward the appreciation that pain expression in ASD individuals differs from that of neurotypical peers, and that recognition of these differences has important implications for accurate diagnosis and treatment.

Conclusion

It is becoming increasingly evident that ASD, in many cases, involves more than the brain in its presentation and underlying neurobiology, and that children, adolescents, and adults impacted by this disorder can and often do experience comorbid medical conditions that can be challenging to diagnose. The nature and prevalence of many of these health care conditions remain poorly defined. However, there is a growing awareness that many medical disorders can have an impact on behavior, often resulting in disruptive outbursts, self-injury, and aggression toward others. Prior to assuming that such symptoms are "just part of the autism" or are "behavioral," it is critically important to ensure that possible painful and uncomfortable medical conditions have been carefully considered and thoroughly investigated before psychotropic medications and behavioral strategies are considered as primary treatment options. More research is needed relative to how ASD individuals interpret and express pain and discomfort, as well as the prevalence and expression of medical conditions involving any number of organ systems, and how these conditions might present themselves in non-verbal and sensory-challenged persons. Given what is now known with regard to pain and behavior in association with ASD, it is imperative that both primary care providers as well as specialists remain aware of the complexity of health care issues in the ASD population, and that interdisciplinary clinical approaches to medical and behavioral disorders may be required for best outcomes.

References

Alley, C.S. (2013). Pain sensitivity and observer perception of pain in individuals with autism spectrum disorder. *The Scientific World Journal, 2013,* doi:10.1155/2013/916178

American Psychiatric Association (2013). *Diagnostic and Statistical Manual of Mental Disorders* (5th ed.). Washington, DC: American Psychiatric Publishing.

Arelin, K., Mueller, K., Barth, C., Rekkas, P., *et al.* (2015). Progesterone mediates brain functional connectivity changes during the menstrual cycle: A pilot resting state MRI study. *Frontiers in Neuroscience, 9*(44), 1–15.

Baghdadli, A., Pascal, C., Grisi, S., and Aussilloux, C. (2003). Risk factors for self-injurious behaviors among 222 young children with autistic disorders. *Journal of Intellectual Disability Research, 47*(Pt. 8), 622–627.

Bailey, J.S., and Pyles, D.A.M. (1989). Behavioral Diagnostics. In I. Cipani (Ed.), *The Treatment of Severe Behavior Disorders*. Washington, DC: Monograph of the American Association of Mental Retardation.

Bodfish, J.W., Symons, F.J., Parker, D.E., and Lewis, M.H. (2000). Varieties of repetitive behavior in autism: Comparisons to mental retardation. *Journal of Autism and Developmental Disorders, 30*(3), 237–243.

Buie, T., Campbell, D.B., Fuchs, G.J. III, Furuta, G.T., *et al.* (2010). Evaluation, diagnosis, and treatment of gastrointestinal disorders in individuals with ASDs: A consensus report. *Pediatrics, 125*(Suppl. 1), S1–S18.

Burke, L.M., Kalpakjian, C.Z., Smith, Y.R., and Quint, E.H. (2010). Gynecological issues of adolescents with Down syndrome, autism and cerebral palsy. *Journal of Pediatric and Adolescent Gynecology, 23*(1), 11–15.

Campbell, D.B., Buie, T.M., Winter, H., Bauman, M., *et al.* (2009). Distinct genetic risk based on association of MET in families with co-occurring autism and gastrointestinal conditions. *Pediatrics, 123*(3), 1018–1024.

Carr, E.G., and Owen-DeSchryver, J.S. (2007). Physical illness, pain, and problem behavior in minimally verbal people with developmental disabilities. *Journal of Autism and Developmental Disorders, 37*, 413–424.

Carr, E.G., Smith, C.E., Giacin, T.A., Whelan, B.M., and Pancari, J. (2003). Menstrual discomfort as a biological setting event for severe problem behavior: Assessment and intervention. *American Journal of Mental Retardation, 108*(2), 117–133.

Casanova, M.F. (2008). The minicolumnopathy of autism: A link between migraine and gastrointestinal symptoms. *Medical Hypotheses, 70*(1), 73–80.

DeBlasio, N. (2014). Six reasons for headaches in school-age children and how parents can help relieve pain. *Science Daily*, 28 July.

de Lissovoy, V. (1962). Head banging in early childhood. *Child Development, 33*, 43–56.

de Lissovoy, V. (1963). Head banging in early childhood: A suggested cause. *The Journal of Genetic Psychology, 102*, 109–114.

Delli, K., Reichart, P.A., Bornstein, M.M., and Livas, C. (2013). Management of children with autism spectrum disorder in the dental setting: Concerns, behavioral approaches and recommendations. *Medicina Oral, Patologia Oral y Cirugia Bucal, 18*(6), 862–868.

Emerson, E., Kiernan, C., Alborz, A., Reeves, D., *et al.* (2001). The prevalence of challenging behaviors: A total population study. *Research in Developmental Disabilities, 22*, 77–93.

Fadini, C.C., Lamonica, D.A., Fett-Conte, A.C., Osorio, E., *et al.* (2015). Influence of sleep disorders on behavior of individuals with autism spectrum disorder. *Frontiers in Human Neuroscience, 9*(347), 1–15.

Friedlander, A.H., Yagiela, J.A., Paterno, V.I., and Mahler, M.E. (2003). The pathophysiology, medical management and dental implications of autism. *Journal of the California Dental Association, 31*(9), 681–682, 684, 686–691.

Garcia-Larrea, L. (2012). The posterior insular-opercular region and the search of a primary cortex for pain (review). *Neurophysiologie Clinique, 42*(5), 299–313.

Gardner, W.I., and Sovner, R. (1994). *Self-Injurious Behaviors*. Willow Street, PA: Vida Publishing.

Gargus, J.J. (2009). Genetic calcium signaling abnormalities in the central nervous system: Seizures, migraine and autism. *Annals of the New York Academy of Sciences, 1151*, 133–156.

Goadsby, P.J. (2007). Recent advances in understanding migraine mechanisms, molecules and therapeutics. *Trends in Molecular Medicine, 13*(1), 39–44.

Green, S.A., and Ben-Sasson, A. (2010). Anxiety disorders and sensory over-responsivity in children with autism spectrum disorder: Is there a causal relationship? *Journal of Autism and Developmental Disorders, 40*(12), 1495–1504.

Gunsett, R.P., Mulick, J.A., Fernald, W.B., and Martin, J.L. (1989). Indications for medical screening prior to behavioral programming for severely and profoundly mentally retarded clients. *Journal of Autism and Developmental Disorders, 19*(1), 167–172.

Humphreys, J.S., Gringras, P., Blair, P.S., Scott, N., *et al.* (2014). Sleep patterns in children with autism spectrum disorders: A prospective cohort study. *Archives of Disease in Childhood, 99*(2), 114–118.

Johnson, K.P., Giannotti, F., and Cortesi, F. (2009). Sleep patterns in autism spectrum disorders. *Child and Adolescent Psychiatric Clinics of North America, 18*(4), 917–928.

Kanner, L. (1943). Autistic disturbances of affective contact. *Nervous Child, 2*, 217–250.

Miano, S., and Ferri, R. (2010). Epidemiology and management of insomnia in children with autism spectrum disorders. *Paediatric Drugs, 12*(2), 75–84.

Minkel, J.D., Banks, S., Htaik, O., Moreta, M.C., *et al.* (2012). Sleep deprivation and stressors: Evidence for elevated negative affect in response to mild stressors when sleep deprived. *Emotion, 12*(5), 1015–1020.

Montavont, A., Mauguiere, F., Mazzola, L., Garcia-Larrea, L., *et al.* (2015). On the origin of painful somatosensory seizures. *Neurology, 84*(6), 594–601.

Moore, D.J. (2015). Acute pain in experience in individuals with autism spectrum disorders: A review. *Autism, 19*(4), 387–399.

Murphy, G.H., Beadle-Brown, J., Wing, L., Gould, J., Shah, A., and Holmes, N. (2005). Chronicity of challenging behaviours in people with severe intellectual disabilities and/or autism: A total population sample. *Journal of Autism and Developmental Disorders, 35*(4), 405–418.

Murphy, O., Healy, O., and Leader, G. (2009). Risk factors for challenging behaviors among 157 children with autism spectrum disorder in Ireland. *Research in Autism Spectrum Disorders, 3*(2), 474–482.

Owens, J., Opipari, L., Nobile, C., and Spirito, A. (1998). Sleep and daytime behavior in children with obstructive apnea and behavioral sleep disorders. *Pediatrics, 102*(5), 1178–1184.

Richdale, A.L. (1999). Sleep problems in autism: Prevalence, cause and intervention. *Developmental Medicine and Child Neurology, 41*(1), 60–66.

Richdale, A.L., and Schreck, K.A. (2009). Sleep problems in autism spectrum disorders: Prevalence, nature and possible biopsychosocial aetiologies. *Sleep Medicine Reviews, 13*(6), 403–411.

Riley, J.L. III, Robinson, M.E., Wise, E.A., and Price, D.D. (1999). A meta-analytic review of pain perception across the menstrual cycle. *Pain, 81*(3), 225–235.

Rilling, J.K., Lacreuse, A., Barks, S.K., Elfenbein, H.A., *et al.* (2008). Effect of menstrual cycle on resting brain metabolism in female rhesus monkeys. *Neuroreport, 19*(5), 537–541.

Rojahn, J., Schroeder, S.R., and Hoch, T.A. (2008). *Self-Injurious Behavior in Intellectual Disabilities.* New York, NY: Elsevier.

Rossi, P.G., Parmeggiani, A., Bach, V., Santucci, M., and Visconti, P. (1995). EEG features and epilepsy in patients with autism. *Brain and Development, 17*(3), 169–174.

Sarlani, E., Balciunas, B.A., and Grace, E.G. (2005). Orofacial pain. Part I: Assessment and management of musculoskeletal and neuropathic causes. *AACN Clinical Issues, 16*(3), 333–346.

Sullivan, J.C., Miller, L.J., Nielsen, D.M., and Schoen, S.A. (2014). The presence of migraines and its association with sensory hyperreactivity and anxiety symptomatology in children with autism spectrum disorder. *Autism, 18*(6), 743–747.

Symons, F.J., Davis, M.L., and Thompson, T. (2000). Self-injurious behavior and sleep disturbance in adults with developmental disabilities. *Research in Developmental Disabilities, 21*, 115–123.

Tu, C.H., Niddam, D.M., Chao, H.T., Chen, L.F., *et al.* (2010). Brain morphological changes associated with cyclic menstrual pain. *Pain, 150*(3), 462–468.

Tu, C.H., Niddam, D.M., Yeh, T.C., Lirng, J.F., *et al.* (2013). Menstrual pain is associated with rapid structural alterations in the brain. *Pain, 154*(9), 1718–1724.

Tuchman, R., Hirtz, D., and Mamounas, L.A. (2013). NINDS epilepsy and autism spectrum disorders workshop report. *Neurology, 81*(18), 1630–1636.

Tudor, M.E., Walsh, C.E., Mulder, E.C., and Lerner, M.D. (2014). Pain as a predictor of sleep problems in youth with autism spectrum disorders. *Autism, 19*(3), 292–300.

Veldhuijzen, D.S., Keaser, M.L., Traub, D.S., Zhuo, J., Gullapalli, R.P., and Greenspan, J.D. (2013). The role of circulating sex hormones in menstrual cycle-dependent modulation of pain-related brain activation. *Pain, 154*(4), 548–559.

Victorio, M. (2014). Headaches in patients with autism spectrum disorder. *The Journal of Headache and Pain, 15*(Suppl. 1), B37.

Vishnu-Rekha, C., Arangannal, P., and Shahed, H. (2012). Oral health status of children with autistic disorder in Chennai. *European Archives of Paediatric Dentistry, 13*(3), 126–131.

Volkmar, F.R., and Nelson, D.S. (1990). Seizure disorders in autism. *Journal of the American Academy of Child and Adolescent Psychiatry, 29*(1), 127–129.

Zeidan-Chulia, F., Gursoy, U.K., Kononen, E., and Gottfried, C. (2011). A dental look at the autistic patient through orofacial pain. *Acta Odontologica Scandinavica, 69*(4), 193–200.

CHAPTER 3

Self-Injurious Behavior, Aggression, and Epilepsy in Autism Spectrum Disorder

Manuel F. Casanova, M.D., and Emily L. Casanova, Ph.D.,
University of South Carolina, Greenville, South Carolina

Introduction

The term "challenging behaviors" was introduced in the United States sometime in the 1980s in order to describe problematic behaviors observed in certain patients with mental retardation (Xeniditis, Russell, and Murphy, 2001). Challenging behaviors are often defined as "culturally abnormal behaviors of such intensity, frequency, or duration that the physical safety of the person or others is placed in serious jeopardy" (Emerson *et al.*, 2001, p.3). These behaviors may prevent an individual from participating in certain aspects of community life, thus leading to social deprivation. In effect, by interfering with his or her social development and preventing the child from receiving proper education, these behaviors are challenging for the child.

Challenging behaviors include self-injurious behaviors (SIBs), inappropriate sexualized behaviors (e.g., public masturbation, groping), tantrums, physical or verbal aggression, and stereotyped behaviors (e.g., repetitive rocking). These behaviors are sometimes interrelated; as an example, stereotypies may by themselves constitute an SIB or serve as a precursor to the same (Sarkhel, Praharaj, and Akhtar, 2011). On other occasions SIBs may be conceptualized as a variant of another mental condition (e.g., obsessive-compulsive disorder) or as a psychiatric comorbidity (e.g., alcohol abuse/dependence, body dysmorphic disorder) (Wilhelm *et al.*, 1999).

Other labels for challenging behaviors include oppositional, out-of-control, high-needs, maladaptive, aberrant, and antisocial behaviors. Some people do not like the appellation of "challenging," as it invokes a threatening connotation that necessitates battling or engaging the same in a fight. Indeed, when the child grows older, bigger, and stronger, such behaviors may reach crisis situations posing physical challenges to caregivers. However, although some behaviors and physical characteristics of individuals can be viewed as potentially harmful and in need of restraint, some experts have suggested adopting the alternate term: "behavior of concern" (Chan *et al.*, 2012).

Challenging behaviors are now known to be prevalent in many psychiatric disorders, especially those with intellectual disabilities (ID) (Felce, Kerr, and Hastings, 2009) and autism spectrum disorder (ASD) in particular (Kanne and Mazurek, 2011). In ASD a study using a cohort from the Simons Simplex Collection found that, among 1380 children ages 4–17 years, 56% of them engaged in aggressive behaviors towards their caregivers, while a smaller number (32%) directed their aggression towards non-caregivers (Kanne and Mazurek, 2011). The results indicate a very high prevalence of aggressive behaviors in ASD as compared with people having ID but who are not autistic. There is even a higher discrepancy when comparing the results to neurotypicals, for whom the prevalence of aggression ranges from 7 to 11% (Emerson *et al.*, 2001; Holden and Gitlesen, 2006).

In ASD, those children at highest risk for exhibiting challenging behaviors are most often males of low IQ who experience increased severity of autistic symptoms: more frequent repetitive behaviors, resistance to change, and an increased degree of severe social impairment (Matson and Rivet, 2008). The presence of challenging behaviors requires the investment of considerable resources that may compound the treatment of other ASD symptoms as well as the acquisition of education, life skills training, and social development. Because of their severity and chronicity, challenging behaviors are a heavy burden on parents, professionals, and direct-care staff.

Self-Injurious Behavior

Specific behaviors that have the potential to inflict tissue damage upon oneself are denoted as self-injurious behaviors. They are common in children with neurodevelopmental conditions, and have been described in Cornelia de Lange syndrome (Basile *et al.*, 2007), Lesch-Nyhan disease (Schretien *et al.*, 2005), and Smith-Magenis syndrome (Finucane, Dirrigl, and Simon, 2001). There is no single cause for SIBs. In many cases self-injury is a way of expressing feelings, and is not an attempt by the patient to injure himself or herself, or to commit suicide. They do not have psychodynamic connotations. Treatment options include outpatient therapy, environmental changes, behavior modification, psychotropics, and hospitalization. On occasion, anticonvulsants have been used off-label to treat challenging behaviors in autistic individuals (Hollander *et al.*, 2001). Clear conclusions cannot be drawn from the latter attempts because mixed results have been found both between and within studies (NIHCE, 2012).

Self-injurious behavior is possibly the most devastating symptom observed in a significant number of individuals with ASD. Illustrative clinical examples are derived from the children initially treated by Lovaas who, because of self-abusive behaviors, had been placed in physical restraints (tied to a bed or placed in arm restraints) throughout much of their lives (Lovaas and Simmons, 1969). One of the children in this early study had been tied down for so long that his legs atrophied, and he could no longer walk. Laura Schreibman, in her book *The Science and Fiction of Autism*, relates the horrifying instances of young children blinding themselves because of eye gouging, beating their faces bloody against the faucet of a bathtub, or dying from skull fractures after escaping from restraints to beat their heads against a metal bedframe (Schreibman, 2005).

Self-injurious behaviors are described as deliberate, repetitive, or episodic. In the case of ASD they are also described as stereotyped and stimulus dependent. In some cases the behaviors may be health- or life-threatening or cause physical harm. Life expectancy is severely compromised in individuals who partake in these behaviors. Self-injurious behaviors take the form of head banging, hand biting, hair pulling, excessive self-rubbing, and scratching. In autism the most common SIB is hand biting, often co-occurring with other troublesome behaviors (Murphy, Healy, and Leader, 2009).

Although common in ASD, SIBs are not considered a core feature of the condition. Lifetime prevalence of these behaviors in ASD is about 50%, while cross-sectional studies indicate a point prevalence of approximately 25% (Bodfish *et al.*, 2000). Baghdadli and colleagues (2003) reported that increased severity of ASD correlated with greater levels of SIB. This behavior is chronic and usually persists through adulthood.

Aggressive Behavior

There are two types of aggressive behaviors: predatory and defensive (Vitiello and Stoff, 1997). Predatory aggression is well structured, proactive, goal oriented, and performed in a controlled state of mind. It is usually associated with antisocial personality disorders, thus presenting a major problem to public health and the criminal justice system. Proactive aggression has been associated with later delinquency and disruptive behaviors. In contrast, defensive aggression is both impulsive and reactive. It is usually seen in emotionally charged situations and is associated with signs of fear or anger. The majority of instances involving humans belong to the defensive subset, occurring as a reaction towards a perceived threat, be it real or not (Albert, Walsh, and Jonik, 1993). The scarcity of studies within the medical literature prevents drawing conclusions regarding the role of comorbidities, treatment response, and long-term prognosis (Vitiello and Stoff, 1997).

Aggression is such a problematic behavior that it often takes precedence over the treatment of other core symptoms of autism. Although research on the subject has been ongoing for over two decades, there is a surprising dearth of studies on the subject. Furthermore, flaws in experimental design limit the usefulness of these studies. Most studies of aggression in ASD suffer from a selection bias (they focus on children, with only a handful focusing on adults) that hampers attempts at generalization (Matson and Jang, 2014). Many studies are case reports or have a limited study population. In a recent overview of potential treatments for aggression in ASD, 13 of 27 studies reported on one or two individuals, while only two studies involved over 100 individuals. Thus, although existing data provide some guidance, the available information falls short of a critical mass of evidence from which to draw firm conclusions (Matson and Jang, 2014).

Epilepsy

Epilepsy and intellectual disability are the most commonly cited comorbidities for ASD. Approximately 30% of individuals with ASD have epilepsy (Tuchman, Cuccaro, and Alessandri, 2010) and 15% of patients with epilepsy are diagnosed with autism (Matsuo *et al.*, 2010). Contrary to expectations, many of these autistic individuals are idiopathic; only a minority are syndromic. In this patient population the most common type of epilepsy is complex partial seizure. In almost half of the cases ASD is diagnosed after beginning seizure activity (Matsuo *et al.*, 2010). Multiple studies have shown that there is a bimodal distribution to the onset of seizures: one peaks in early childhood and the other during adolescence, continuing through adulthood (Tuchman *et al.*, 2010).

The heterogeneous nature of aggression and SIBs is the result of multiple causations, which provides difficulties in classification. These behaviors may be due to many factors, including some that are biological, social, environmental, and/or psychological in nature. In the same vein, epilepsy is a complex disorder whose neuropathology and heterogeneous clinical characteristics preclude a singular pathophysiological mechanism. Compounding characterization for both challenging behaviors and epilepsy is the fact that none of them are static in nature, but rather continue to evolve over the lifespan of the individual. At present, we lack a clear understanding of both a critical time window for the emergence of these disorders and predictive markers of their chronicity, frequency, and severity.

Epilepsy is a disorder of nerve activity stemming from an imbalance in the excitatory/inhibitory bias of the brain. A common definition for epilepsy is the occurrence of two or more unprovoked seizures that happen 24 or more hours apart. Because epilepsy alters the normal activity of neurons, it can affect any process coordinated by the brain. During a seizure muscles may jerk or become stiff, and there may be perceived changes as to how things look, smell, or feel. Additional symptoms may be noted between seizures, the so-called interictal period (Latin *ictus*, meaning a blow or a stroke). The strong association between some of these symptoms, especially psychiatric disorders, and epilepsy has led some authors to describe them as comorbidities (Nascimento *et al.*, 2013).

It is noteworthy that, contrary to the complex motor behaviors of ASD, epileptic seizures are characterized by stereotyped and non-directed behaviors. According to most authorities, the more organized, directed, and modifiable a behavior is by the environment, the less likely it is the result of epilepsy (Treinman, 1991). This observation pertains to ictal events. Behavioral manifestations between seizures may be organized and directed, but their intentionality may be questioned.

Temporal and Frontal Lobe Seizures

Approximately 20–30% of patients with epilepsy suffer from a psychiatric disturbance (Vuilleumier and Jallon, 1998). The percentage may be closer to 70% for those with intractable complex partial seizures (i.e., seizures of local origin that impair consciousness while the individual is still able to perform routine tasks and/ or manifest automatisms), wherein 58% of patients will have a history of depressive disorders, 32% suffer from agoraphobia, and 13% have psychosis (Tucker, 1998). When depressive disorders are combined with irritability, pain, phobic fears, and/ or euphoric moods, an "interictal dysphoric disorder" may be present (Gilliam, Kanner, and Sheline, 2005). Interictal mood changes appear to occur without external triggers. Although interictal dysphoric disorders are typical of epilepsy, a similar diagnostic construct can be observed in other central nervous system disorders (Mula *et al.*, 2008).

A specific association between behavioral changes and epilepsy was first reported by Gibbs in a series of patients having a characteristic electroencephalographic (EEG) pattern of temporal lobe seizures accompanied by mental, emotional, motor, and autonomic manifestations (Gibbs, Gibbs, and Fuster, 1949). Older studies suggested that approximately 33% of patients with "psychomotor seizures" of temporal lobe origin manifested interictal behavioral changes (Gibbs, 1951). In psychomotor epilepsy some behavioral manifestations, by themselves uncommon, seem to cluster together into syndromes. Gastaut and colleagues reported on the association of emotional viscosity, hyposexuality, hypoactivity, and aggressiveness in epilepsy patients, and suggested that the same stood in contrast to the stereotyped behaviors observed in the Kluver-Bucy syndrome. The latter syndrome, also known as temporal lobectomy behavior, provides for a combination of symptoms that includes hyperphagia, hypersexuality, hyperorality, visual agnosia, and docility (Gastaut, Morrin, and Lesevre, 1955). This syndrome is usually caused by the bilateral destruction of the amygdaloid body caused by herpes simplex encephalitis (see the section "Herpes Simplex Encephalitis").

Temporal lobe epilepsy also provides for a personality disorder characterized by hypergraphia, hyperreligiosity, atypical sexuality (usually hyposexuality), circumstantiality, and intensified mental life (deepened cognitive and emotional responses) (Waxman and Geschwind, 1975). At present, the disorder is known by the eponym of the Geschwind or Gastaut-Geschwind syndrome. The diagnostic validity of this syndrome has been questioned due to the complex interplay of the symptoms with: (1) psychosocial factors, (2) a selection bias of studies to include primarily treatment-refractory patients, and (3) changes in cognitive function caused by epilepsy. However, the association of behavioral changes to interictal spike activity in temporal lobe structures suggests a pathophysiological basis for this syndrome (Waxman and Geschwind, 1975). It is believed that intermittent spike foci in the temporal lobe may alter the responsiveness of the limbic system, leading to a heightened emotional response to many stimuli as well as to diminished sexual responsiveness (Geschwind, 1983).

Abnormalities of the temporal lobe and its limbic structures can alter emotion and drive-related behaviors. It is not surprising that when brain regions are richly intertwined with the limbic system, it can result in changes in personality and behavior. Both the orbitofrontal cortex and the anterior cingulate gyrus (ACG) are paralimbic areas heavily connected to the temporal lobes. Common symptoms of ACG seizures include emotional outbursts (poor impulse control), aggression, sociopathic behavior, sexual deviancy, irritability, and autonomic abnormalities. The aggressive behavior in both frontal and temporal lobe epilepsy is more commonly seen in men and children. Patients who are more affected (as compared with controls) tend to have seizure onset before 10 years of age, traumatic brain injury, fewer years of formal education, and lower IQ. The location of the ACG within the mesial surface of the brain hemispheres makes electrophysiological abnormalities difficult to detect with scalp electrodes (Unnwongse, Wehner, and Foldvary-Schaefer, 2012). The deep-seated location of the seizure foci means that patients may pass through the rigmarole of the legal system before they are diagnosed with epilepsy.

Another frontal lobe seizure focus that is difficult to recognize and is heavily intertwined with the limbic portions of the temporal lobe is the orbitofrontal cortex. Seizures that originate in this frontal lobe region may manifest motor, oroalimentary, and/or manual automatisms, depending on spread (Kriegel, Roberts, and Jobst, 2012). Manifestations are often bizarre, non-localizing, and may suggest a psychogenic event. These manifestations may include the intrusion of violent and sometimes horrifying visual hallucinations as well as aggression (Fornazzari *et al.*, 1992).

Challenging Behaviors in Epilepsy

Challenging behaviors are common among children with neurodevelopmental disabilities. It is usually accepted that additive comorbidities provide for a higher prevalence of psychopathology (Smith and Matson, 2010a). However, despite their ubiquitousness and clinical importance, few studies have compared the prevalence of challenging behaviors among specific neurodevelopmental disorders. In a study of child services through Early Steps, 76 children were divided into three groups: Down syndrome (*n* = 27), cerebral palsy (*n* = 18), and those with a history of a seizure disorder (*n* = 29) (Hattier *et al.*, 2012). Patients with ASD were excluded from this study. For the purpose of screening the researchers only used the Tantrum/Conduct behavior subscale of the BISCUIT-Part 2. The results showed that children with a history of seizures exhibited a greater score or were more impaired than those with cerebral palsy or Down syndrome. A surprising result of the study was the lack of gender effects.

Behavior problems in epilepsy can start before the first recognized seizure episode (Austin *et al.*, 2001). According to some researchers, both seizures and behavior problems are caused by the same neurological disorder. This appears to be primarily the case for children who experience recurrent seizures (Austin *et al.*, 2002). The role of seizures in the development of these problems has been attributed to different causal factors: (1) poor child and family response to the condition, (2) side effects of antiepileptic medication, (3) neurological dysfunction that causes both the seizures and the behavioral problem, (4) transient cognitive impairment from interictal epileptiform discharges, and (5) the effect of comorbidities (Austin and Dunn, 2002).

Medications and Comorbidities

Many children with epilepsy are cognitively impaired. For some patients, cognitive problems may antedate the onset of epilepsy, but for others epilepsy may pose a risk factor that influences brain growth. When classified according to seizure type and compared with controls, those suffering from generalized epilepsy perform significantly worse in neuropsychological tests of cognitive assessment than those with focal or partial complex seizures. A similar trend is observed for those with secondary generalization, who do worse than those in whom the ictal focus remains localized to one area of the brain (Mandelbaum and Burack, 1997; Prevey *et al.*, 1998).

As previously stated, there are many reasons for the observed cognitive impairment in epilepsy, including brain damage, the effects of the seizures themselves, the location of the ictal focus, psychological problems, and various combinations of the aforementioned factors (Aidenkamp, 1997). Although antiepileptic drugs do impair cognition in some children, these represent the minority of cases. Studies reporting adverse effects of anticonvulsants on behavior have not controlled for the baseline status of the patient (e.g., underlying neurological condition, seizure type). When cognitive and behavioral profiles are followed longitudinally, few side effects are attributable to anticonvulsant medications (Mandelbaum and Burack, 1997). In the minority of cases in which cognitive side effects have been noted, phenobarbital and topiramate have been the likely culprits (Bourgeois, 2004). In other cases, a persistent impairment of reaction time and reaction-time variability may have been due to carbamazepine therapy (Mandelbaum, Burack, and Bhise, 2009). Discontinuation of carbamazepine in some patients receiving the drug as monotherapy has resulted in improved cognitive function (Hessen *et al.*, 2006). Anticonvulsants with behavioral side effects akin to attention deficit hyperactivity disorder (ADHD) include phenobarbital, gabapentin, vigabatrin, and topiramate (Hamoda *et al.*, 2009).

Comorbidities are frequent in childhood epilepsy. Those that have a significant association include attention deficit hyperactivity disorder, autism, developmental disabilities, accidental injury, stroke, migraine, and depression/anxiety (Pellock, 2004). ADHD is present in approximately 20–30% of children with epilepsy (Barkley, 1990). Initial studies have shown that children with both ASD and ADHD can respond as well to stimulants as children with ADHD alone (Santosh *et al.*, 2006). Data from the 2010 National Health Interview Survey (NHIS) indicate that adults with epilepsy have a higher prevalence of cardiovascular, respiratory, and inflammatory conditions as compared with the general population (Centers for Disease Control and Prevention, 2013). In some cases these comorbidities may affect the quality of life for a person with epilepsy more than the seizures do. According to some researchers, the presence of comorbidities strongly associated with epilepsy suggests a shared underlying pathophysiology (Selassie *et al.*, 2014).

Self-Injurious Behavior and Epilepsy

Self-injurious behavior is common in persons exhibiting both intellectual disabilities and epilepsy. In a recent study 158 people with intellectual disability and epilepsy were compared with 195 people with intellectual disability but without epilepsy. The prevalence for SIBs, using the Italian Scale for the Assessment of Self-Injurious Behaviors, was 44 and 46.5%, respectively (no significant between-group differences) (Buono *et al.*, 2012). In that study the presence of epilepsy did not confer a risk factor for SIBs. Curiously, epilepsy may be considered a risk factor for aggression when the intellectual disability takes the form of an ASD (Smith and Matson, 2010b).

In patients with epilepsy the most common areas affected by SIBs are the hands, mouth, and head. These body parts are usually traumatized by self-biting or self-hitting with hands or with objects. These behaviors are often observed in relation to episodes of high emotional arousal, anger, or fear. All of the latter are gross disorders of emotion commonly seen in temporal lobe epilepsy. Episodes of SIB in the context of temporal lobe seizure are usually not recalled by the patient. When challenging behaviors fail to respond to antipsychotic medication but respond to anticonvulsants, physicians would do well to suspect an underlying seizure disorder (Shakya *et al.*, 2010; Deriaz *et al.*, 2011).

Aggression and Epilepsy

The prevalence of aggression in epilepsy varies between 4.8% (Rodin, 1973) and 50% (Gastaut *et al.*, 1955), with multiple reports indicating an in-between prevalence. Many of these studies were hampered by faulty study design, including a selection bias and lack of control for a variety of social and psychological variables. For these reasons the real prevalence of aggressive behavior in epilepsy, especially that of temporolimbic origin, remains controversial (Lishman, 1998). Behavior problems have been reported to occur in approximately 50% of individuals with comorbid ID and epilepsy in state-run residential facilities (Kerr, 2002). Community-based studies, on the other hand, have not found an increased prevalence of aggressive behaviors in patients with epilepsy (Klingman and Goldberg, 1975). However, a recent community-based study in 318 adults with intellectual disabilities found a higher prevalence of epilepsy associated with greater psychopathology and/or caregiver strain. Among this population, 58 of the participants (18%) had epilepsy, of which 26% were seizure-free, but 36% had extremely poor control of their seizures. The study also supported the high occurrence of epilepsy in people with intellectual disability (Matthews *et al.*, 2008).

Ictal aggression is a rare phenomenon and usually takes the form of resistive violence, that is, when at the end of the seizure the patient finds himself or herself confused and restrained, or when witnesses or caregivers try to assist the patient (Marsh and Krauss, 2000). Violence at the beginning of or during the seizure is rare and difficult to sustain because of the lack of consecutive purposeful goal-oriented movements (Treinman, 1986). Indeed, ictal aggression was witnessed in only 13 of 5400 patients examined by video EEG (Delgado-Escueta *et al.*, 2002). Only five of these patients had a history of having harmed another person. Ictal aggression is usually classified as primary or secondary, resistive violence, and postictal psychosis (Treinman, 1991). Ictal aggressive episodes, as opposed to gestures and facial expressions with emotional valence, are rare and usually not remembered by the patient (Tassinari *et al.*, 2005). These aggressive expressions are usually seen in males, are never organized, and do not result in physical assault (Delgado-Escueta *et al.*, 2002; Tassinari *et al.*, 2005).

Interictal aggression, although rare, appears to be a well-recognized problem of temporal lobe epilepsy, referred to as "episodic dyscontrol" or "intermittent explosive disorder" (IED) (see below). These behaviors are different from automatism (e.g., chewing, swallowing, and lip smacking). These movements are unconscious and tend to be of brief duration (seconds to a few minutes). The involved individual is not aware of their actions. His or her eyes may be open but unable to respond to verbal commands. Unless restrained, the subject is not likely to harm herself or himself, or others, during complex automatism. Exceptions to these generalizations are rare but do occur. Shih and colleagues (2009) reported the case of an 18-year-old man with seizures manifesting interictal aggressive behavior. Video-EEG monitoring captured 11 seizures when he was awake and 3 seizures during sleep. Episodes lasted between 15 and 45 seconds, during which time the patient was able to follow simple commands and demonstrated comprehension of spoken language. Despite comprehension, he struck a nonthreatening hand held two feet away from him and appeared to alter his actions in response to external visual and verbal stimuli. Partial amnesia to the events suggested to the authors the possible spread of the seizure to the mesial temporal cortex. Some of these behaviors may be controlled by anticonvulsants. Coffey (2013) reported the resolution of SIBs with phenytoin treatment in a young man with autism and intellectual disability who suffered from frontal lobe seizures.

Postictal psychosis may involve delusional ideation, hallucinations, thought disorder, and manic or depressive mood changes (Savard *et al.*, 1991). Although psychosis may evolve during the period of postictal confusion, it is more commonly seen after a lucid interval (So *et al.*, 1990), beginning hours or days after the end of the confusional stage (Gerard *et al.*, 1998). In males, episodes tend to recur and to have an onset after seizure clusters. Postictal psychosis may last for less than a day to as long as a few weeks, but, as with confusion, postictal psychosis is a self-limiting condition (Yankovsky *et al.*, 2005).

Aggressive behaviors in epilepsy usually occur with lesions of the frontal lobe and limbic structures. In a study of 252 patients with partial epilepsy, those involving the frontal lobes were more likely to involve version and posturing, without an intervening absence phase, than the ones of temporal lobe origin (Manford, Fish, and Shorvon, 1996). General motor agitation as part of the seizure was associated with lesions of the orbitofrontal (8 of 13 cases) and frontopolar cortices (6 of 13 cases). These frontal lobe lesions may act by disinhibiting the limbic system. Bizarre behaviors stemming from complex partial seizures of medial or orbital frontal origin distinguish these patients from those originating elsewhere. Seizures originating in these regions tend to include complex motor automatisms with kicking and thrashing, sexual automatisms (e.g., genital manipulation), unusual facial expressions, and articulate vocalization (Williamson *et al.*, 1985).

A single case report of a patient with frontal lobe epilepsy reported episodes of intense fear followed by kicking, hitting, and screaming (Sumer *et al.*, 2007). A case series of 11 cases selected from 1000 patients that underwent video-EEG/SEEG monitoring for presurgical evaluation showed a possible correlation between biting and frontotemporal seizures in both hemispheres (Tassinari *et al.*, 2005). Biting behavior in these patients occurred in the context of strong emotional arousal with various threatening gestures. The authors of the study considered biting and related aggressive behaviors to be the result of emerging instinctual behaviors that had adaptive significance for defending their peripersonal space.

Decortication, or removal of the cerebral cortex, in animals produces behaviors such as biting, clawing, hissing, and violent alternating limb movements. The term for these behaviors, as introduced by Cannon and Britton (1925), is "sham rage." In humans a similar phenomenon has been noted for patients with "uninhibited hypothalamic discharge" (Wortis, 1942). The impact of cultural variables in behaviors makes it difficult to extrapolate animal data to humans; however, stimulation of the amygdala in humans has produced agitation, anger, and/or rage. Surgical resection of the amygdala has reduced aggressive behaviors in violent individuals (Treinman, 1991) or, in the case of limbic lesions, it may promote the expression of hyperactivity symptoms (Sumer *et al.*, 2007).

Intermittent Explosive Disorder

Repetitive outbursts of impulsive, aggressive behaviors that are grossly out of proportion to the situation give rise to a condition known as intermittent explosive disorder. This condition is presently classified as a category of impulse-control disorders. It was first described by Esquirol as "instinctual monomania" (Tavares, 2008). The diagnosis is made when other mental disorders that might account for an aggressive disorder are ruled out; in this regard it is considered a diagnosis of exclusion. The disorder is often quoted in cases of domestic abuse, road rage, serious assault, and property destruction. The impulsive actions, as contrasted to planned or premeditated aggressive actions, tend to occur in people who have experienced affective changes prior to the outburst. Relief follows the tension and arousal during the aggressive bout, although the patient may feel remorseful and embarrassed by the incident.

Intermittent explosive disorder has an onset during the early teenage years and may pose a risk factor for later development of depression, anxiety, and substance abuse disorders. Most patients are young men who describe the episodes of aggression as "spells" or "attacks." Autistic patients with mental retardation have difficulties with explosivity and aggression (Horrigan and Barnhill, 1997). A study of self-directed and other-directed aggressive behavior in a forensic sample of 50 habitually aggressive men revealed that they were more likely to receive a diagnosis of mental retardation, organic personality disorder, intermittent explosive disorder, or autism (Hillbrand, 1992). Many of these patients proved resistant to various pharmacotherapeutic interventions; however, risperidone, on occasion, provided substantial clinical improvement (Horrigan and Barnhill, 1997). In these cases discontinuation of risperidone therapy was associated with a rapid return of disruptive and aggressive behaviors in most individuals (Research Units on Pediatric Psychopharmacology Autism Network, 2005).

Tuberous Sclerosis

Tuberous sclerosis is a genetic disorder resulting from a mutation of either the *TSC1* gene on chromosome 9q34 or the *TSC2* gene on chromosome 16p13. In this condition intellectual abilities fall under a bimodal distribution, with 30% being described as showing profound disability and 70% falling within the normal distribution (de Vries and Prather, 2007). About 25–50% of people diagnosed with tuberous sclerosis exhibit an autism phenotype; contrariwise, the prevalence of tuberous sclerosis among ASD is 1–4% (Wiznitzer, 2004). The relationship between both disorders has been variously attributed to tuber location, seizures, cognitive impairment, and a disturbance of brain development.

In a sample population of 257 patients with tuberous sclerosis complex (TSC), 10% of patients exhibited SIBs. When compared with neurotypicals, affected individuals had significantly higher rates of EEG interictal spikes in the left frontal lobe and a history of infantile spasms, seizures, and mental retardation (Staley *et al.*, 2008). Other researchers have similarly found a correlation between SIBs and frontal lobe seizures (Gedye, 1989). However, the idea that SIBs may be the result of frontal lobe dysfunction (not a volitional behavioral problem) is controversial (Coulter, 1991). More recently, data from the Challenging Behavior Questionnaire were collected from 37 children (age range 4–15 years) with TSC. Self-injury and aggression were compared against other neurodevelopmental conditions, including ASD. Although rates for SIB and aggression were high in TSC (27 and 50%, respectively), they did not differ from those of other control groups (Eden *et al.*, 2014).

Limbic Encephalitis

Encephalitis is an acute inflammation of the brain. Symptoms include a flu-like syndrome with headaches and fever. Other symptoms include seizures, confusion, drowsiness, fatigue, weakness, and, in some cases, developmental regression with autistic features (Marques *et al.*, 2014; Scott *et al.*, 2014). Most cases are caused by a viral infection. Those cases associated with bacterial infection may in addition involve the meninges and are known as meningoencephalitis. These patients often exhibit severe nuchal rigidity and changes in the state of consciousness. When the inflammation affects primarily the limbic region, it is known as a limbic encephalitis. Contrary to other types of brain inflammation, limbic encephalitis is often caused by an autoimmune reaction sometimes associated with the presence of cancer. Cases of limbic encephalitis associated with antibodies to the voltage-gated potassium channel complex also provide for status epilepticus, epileptic encephalopathy, and autistic regression (Hacohen *et al.*, 2012). These patients, without any underlying carcinoma, do well in response to immunotherapy.

Most patients with limbic encephalitis are young women with diagnosed or undiagnosed tumors of the ovary. The subacute development of progressive, short-term memory loss is the hallmark of the condition. However, memory loss is often hidden under more prominent symptoms that include simple/complex partial seizures, and progressive changes in behavior and affect that include marked aggression. The patient may exhibit delusions, hallucinations, a low tolerance for frustration, and unpredictable outbursts of uncontrolled rage. Patients are usually admitted to a psychiatric ward with a diagnosis of acute psychosis or schizophrenia before the true diagnosis is uncovered.

Herpes Simplex Encephalitis

Many patients with limbic encephalitis are originally diagnosed with herpes encephalitis, as the conditions cannot be distinguished based on clinical presentation. This is a rare but severe viral infection thought to be caused by the retrograde transmission of a reactivated herpes simplex virus-1 (HSV-1) along a nerve axon (most probably the olfactory pathway or trigeminal ganglia) and into the meninges of the anterior and middle cranial fossa. From the meninges the virus infects the adjacent temporal and inferior frontal lobes first, and then spreads to the rest of the brain. Neuropathological examination reveals a greater degree of brain destruction, inflammation, and reactive response than in any other viral encephalitis. The localization helps explain why the patients often display bizarre behaviors, personality changes, anosmia, and gustatory hallucinations.

DeLong, Bean, and Brown (1981) described three children (age range 5–11 years) who developed an acute encephalitic disorder accompanied by autistic features that resolved after clinical recovery. In two of the patients the underlying inciting agent was never identified. One patient had high serum titers for herpes simplex and a computerized tomography scan that revealed extensive lesions of the temporal lobe, primarily the left side. Ghaziuddin and colleagues (1992) reported two cases that developed herpes infection in either the intrauterine or early postnatal period and presented features of autism at around 2 years of age. In contrast to the previous cases, in which imaging suggested a predominant involvement of the temporal lobes, Ghaziuddin, Al-Khouri, and Ghaziuddin (2002) reported the case of an 11-year-old child who developed symptoms of autism following herpes encephalitis involving the frontal lobes. Gillberg (1986) described the case of a 14-year-old girl who developed what was described as a "typical" autistic syndrome as a result of herpes simplex encephalitis. The autistic symptoms persisted long after the acute symptoms of the encephalitis abated. Similarly, a case report of a 14-year-old boy was reported by Greer and colleagues (1989). The boy was normal till the second grade, when he was hospitalized with herpes encephalitis. He later developed significant and persistent social, language, and memory deficits. This and other cases in which autism developed after an infection at an older age indicate that, at least in syndromic cases, autism is not necessarily a neurodevelopmental disorder (Gillberg, 1991).

Conclusion

Challenging behaviors are not peculiar to either epilepsy or ASD. They have been reported in various psychiatric disorders in which the expression of the behavior usually correlates with the extent of the psychopathology. The fact that these behaviors are often observed in epilepsy suggests a multifactorial origin involving both biological and psychosocial factors. The pathophysiological role of the frontal/temporal lobes in challenging behaviors is underlined by the strong association between maladaptive behaviors and seizure foci in these anatomical structures. Given the high prevalence of subclinical paroxysmal EEG discharges in ASD, some maladaptive behaviors may be due to transitory cognitive impairment. When aggressive behaviors are observed during or after complex partial seizures, the same may reflect a confused state on the part of the patient. Under these circumstances attempts at restraining the person may escalate the aggressive behavior. Treatment with anticonvulsants may ameliorate challenging behaviors in a small minority of patients but may have idiosyncratic behavioral side effects in others.

References

Aidenkamp, A.P. (1997). Effect of seizures and epileptiform discharges on cognitive function. *Epilepsia*(Suppl.), S52–S55.

Albert, D.J., Walsh, M.L., and Jonik, R.H. (1993). Aggression in humans: What is its biological foundation? *Neuroscience & Biobehavioral Reviews, 17,* 405–425.

Austin, J.K., and Dunn, D.W. (2002). Progressive behavioral changes in children with epilepsy. *Progress in Brain Research, 135,* 419–427.

Austin, J.K., Dunn, D.W., Caffrey, H.M., Perkins, S.M., Harezlak, J., and Rose, D.F. (2002). Recurrent seizures and behavior problems in children with first recognized seizures: A prospective study. *Epilepsia, 43*(12), 1564–1573.

Austin, J.K., Harezlak, J., Dunn, D.W., Hustler, G.A., Rose, D.F., and Ambrosius, W.T. (2001). Behavior problems in children before first recognized seizures. *Pediatrics, 107*(1), 115–122.

Baghdadli, A., Pascal, C., Grisi, S., and Aussilloux, C. (2003). Risk factors for self-injurious behaviours among 222 young children with autistic disorders. *Journal of Intellectual Disability Research, 47*(8), 622–627.

Barkley, R.A. (1990). *Attention Deficit Hyperactivity Disorder: A Handbook for Diagnosis and Treatment.* New York, NY: Guilford.

Basile, E., Villa, L., Slicorni, A., and Molteni, M. (2007). The behavioural phenotype of Cornelia de Lange syndrome: A study of 56 individuals. *Journal of Intellectual Disability Research, 51,* 671–681.

Bodfish, J.W., Symons, F.J., Parker, D.E., and Lewis, M.H. (2000). Varieties of repetitive behavior in autism: Comparisons to mental retardation. *Journal of Autism and Developmental Disorders, 30*(3), 237–243.

Bourgeois, B.F. (2004). Determining the effects of antiepileptic drugs on cognitive functioning in pediatric patients with epilepsy. *Journal of Child Neurology, 1*(Suppl.), S15–S24.

Buono, S., Scannella, F., Palmigiano, M.B., Elia, M., Kerr, M., and Di Nuovo, S. (2012). Self-injury in people with intellectual disability and epilepsy: A matched controlled study. *Seizure, 21*(3), 160–164.

Cannon, W.B., and Britton, S.B. (1925). Pseudoaffective medulliadrenal secretion. *American Journal of Psychology, 72,* 283.

Centers for Disease Control and Prevention (2013). MMWR. *Morbidity and Mortality Weekly Report, 62*(43), 849–853.

Chan, J., Arnold, S., Webber, L., Riches, V., Parmenter, T., and Stancliffe, R. (2012). Is it time to drop the term "challenging behavior"? *Learning Disability Practice, 15*(5), 36–38.

Coffey, M.J. (2013). Resolution of self-injury with phenytoin in a man with autism and intellectual disability: The role of frontal lobe seizures and catatonia. *Journal of ECT, 29*(1), e12–e13.

Coulter, D.L. (1991). Frontal lobe seizures: No evidence of self-injury. *American Journal of Mental Retardation, 96,* 81–85.

Delgado-Escueta, A.V., Mattson, R.H., King, L., Goldensohn, E.S., *et al.* (2002). The nature of aggression during epileptic seizures. *Epilepsy and Behavior, 3,* 550–556.

DeLong, G.R., Bean, S.C., and Brown, F.R., III (1981). Acquired reversible autistic syndrome in acute encephalopathic illness in children. *Archives of Neurology, 38,* 191–194.

Deriaz, N., Will, J.P., Orihuela-Flores, M., Galli Carminatu, G., and Ratib, O. (2011). Treatment with levetiracetam in a patient with pervasive developmental disorders, severe intellectual disability, self-injurious behavior, and seizures: A case report. *Neurocase, 18*(5), 386–391.

de Vries, P.J., and Prather, P.A. (2007). The tuberous sclerosis complex. *New England Journal of Medicine, 365,* 92–94.

Eden, K.E., De Vries, P.J., Moss, J., Richards, C., and Oliver, C. (2014). Self-injury and aggression in tuberous sclerosis complex: Cross syndrome comparison and associated risk markers. *Journal of Neurodevelopmental Disorders, 6*(1), 10.

Emerson, E., Kiernan, C., Alborz, A., Reeves, D., *et al.* (2001). The prevalence of challenging behaviors: A total population study. *Research in Developmental Disabilities, 22*(1), 77–93.

Felce, D., Kerr, M., and Hastings, R.P. (2009). A general practice-based study of the relationship between indicators of mental illness and challenging behavior among adults with intellectual disabilities. *Journal of Intellectual Disability Research, 53*(3), 243–254.

Finucane, B., Dirrigl, K.H., and Simon, E.W. (2001). Characterization of self-injurious behaviors in children and adults with Smith-Magenis syndrome. *American Journal on Mental Retardation, 196,* 52–58.

Fornazzari, L., Farcnik, K., Smith, I., Heasman, G.A., and Ischise, M.I. (1992). Violent visual hallucinations and aggression in frontal lobe dysfunction: Clinical manifestations of deep orbitofrontal foci. *The Journal of Neuropsychiatry & Clinical Neurosciences, 4*(1), 42–44.

Gastaut, H., Morrin, G., and Lesevre, N. (1955). Etudes du compartment des epileptiques psychomoteur dans l'interval de leurs crises. *Annales Medico-psychologiques, 113,* 1–29.

Gedye, A. (1989). Extreme self-injury attributed to frontal lobe seizures. *American Journal on Mental Retardation, 94,* 20–26.

Gerard, M.E., Spitz, M.C., Towbin, J.A., and Shantz, D. (1998). Subacute postictal aggression. *Neurology, 50,* 384–388.

Geschwind, N. (1983). Interictal behavioral changes in epilepsy. *Epilepsia, 1*(Suppl.), S23–S30.

Ghaziuddin, M., Al-Khouri, I., and Ghaziuddin, N. (2002). Autistic symptoms following herpes encephalitis. *European Child & Adolescent Psychiatry, 11*(3), 142–146.

Ghaziuddin, M., Tsai, L.Y., Eilers, L., and Ghaziuddin N. (1992). Brief report: Autism and herpes simplex encephalitis. *Journal of Autism and Developmental Disorders, 22*(1), 107–113.

Gibbs, E.L., Gibbs, F.A., and Fuster, B. (1949). Psychomotor epilepsy. *Archives of Neurology and Psychiatry, 60,* 331–339.

Gibbs, F.A. (1951). Ictal and non-ictal psychiatric disorders in temporal lobe epilepsy. *The Journal of Nervous and Mental Disease, 113,* 522–528.

Gillberg, I.C. (1986). Brief report: Onset at age 14 of a typical autistic syndrome. A case report of a girl with herpes simplex encephalitis. *Journal of Autism and Developmental Disorders, 16,* 369–375.

Gillberg, I.C. (1991). Autistic syndrome with onset at age 31 years: Herpes encephalitis as a possible model for childhood autism. *Developmental Medicine and Child Neurology, 33*(10), 92–94.

Gilliam, F., Kanner, A.M., and Sheline, Y. (2005). *Depression and Brain Dysfunction.* New York, NY: Taylor and Francis.

Greer, M.K., Lyons-Crews, M., Mauldin, L.B., and Brown, F.R., III (1989). A case study of the cognitive and behavioral deficits of temporal lobe damage in herpes simplex encephalitis. *Journal of Autism and Developmental Disorders, 11,* 317–330.

Hacohen, Y., Wright, S., Siddiqui A., Pandya, N., *et al.* (2012). A clinic-radiological phenotype of voltage-gated potassium channel complex antibody-mediated disorder presenting with seizures and basal ganglia changes. *Developmental Medicine and Child Neurology, 54*(12), 1157–1159.

Hamoda, H.M., Guild, D.J., Gumlak, S., Travers, B.H., and Gonzalez-Heydrich, J. (2009). Association between attention-deficit/hyperactivity disorder and epilepsy in pediatric populations. *Expert Review of Neurotherapeutics, 9*(12), 1747–1754.

Hattier, M.A., Matson, J.L., Belva, B., and Kozlowski, A. (2012). The effects of diagnostic group and gender on challenging behaviors in infants and toddlers with cerebral palsy, Down syndrome or seizures. *Research in Developmental Disabilities, 33*(1), 258–264.

Hessen, E., Lossius, M.I., Reinvang, I., and Gierstad, L. (2006). Influence of major antiepileptic drugs on attention, reaction time, and speed of information processing: Results from a randomized, double-blind, placebo-controlled withdrawal study of seizure-free epilepsy patients receiving monotherapy. *Epilepsia, 47*(12), 2038–2045.

Hillbrand, M. (1992). Self-directed and other-directed aggressive behavior in a forensic sample. *Suicide and Life-Threatening Behavior, 22*(3), 333–340.

Holden, B., and Gitlesen, J.P. (2006). A total population study of challenging behavior in the county of Hedmark, Norway: Prevalence, and risk markers. *Research in Developmental Disabilities, 27*(4), 456–465.

Hollander, E., Dolgoff-Kaspar, R., Cartwright, C., Rawitt, R., and Novotny, S. (2001). An open trial of divalproex sodium in autism spectrum disorders. *Journal of Clinical Psychiatry, 62*(7), 530–534.

Horrigan, J.P., and Barnhill, L.J. (1997). Risperidone and explosive aggressive autism. *Journal of Autism and Developmental Disorders, 27*(3), 313–323.

Kanne, S.M., and Mazurek, M.O. (2011). Aggression in children and adolescents with ASD: Prevalence and risk factors. *Journal of Autism and Developmental Disorders, 41*(7), 926–937.

Kerr, M.P. (2002). Behavioral assessment in mentally retarded and developmentally disabled patients with epilepsy. *Epilepsy and Behavior, 3,* 1–17.

Klingman, D., and Goldberg, D.A. (1975). Temporal lobe epilepsy and aggression. *The Journal of Nervous and Mental Disease, 160,* 324–341.

Kriegel, M.F., Roberts, D.W., and Jobst, B.C. (2012). Orbitofrontal and insular epilepsy. *Journal of Clinical Neurophysiology, 29*(5), 385–391.

Lishman, W.A. (1998). *Organic Psychiatry: The Psychological Consequences of Cerebral Disorder* (3rd ed.). Oxford: Blackwell Science.

Lovaas, O.I., and Simmons, J.Q. (1969). Manipulation of self-destruction in three retarded children. *Journal of Applied Behavior Analysis, 3,* 143–157.

Mandelbaum, D.E., and Burack, G.D. (1997). The effect of seizure type and medication on cognitive and behavioral functioning in children with idiopathic epilepsy. *Developmental Medicine and Child Neurology, 39*(11), 731–736.

Mandelbaum, D.E., Burack, G.D., and Bhise, V.V. (2009). Impact of antiepileptic drugs on cognition, behavior, and motor skills in children with new-onset idiopathic epilepsy. *Epilepsy & Behavior, 16*(2), 341–344.

Manford, M., Fish, D.R., and Shorvon, S.D. (1996). An analysis of clinical seizure patterns and their localizing value in frontal and temporal lobe epilepsies. *Brain, 119*(Pt. 1), 17–40.

Marques, F., Brito, M.J., Conde, M., Pìnto, M., and Moreira, A. (2014). Autism spectrum disorder secondary to enterovirus encephalitis. *Journal of Child Neurology, 29*(5), 708–714.

Marsh, L., and Krauss, G.L. (2000). Aggression and violence in patients with epilepsy. *Epilepsy & Behavior, 1*, 160–168.

Matson, J.L., and Jang, J. (2014). Treating aggression in persons with autism spectrum disorders: A review. *Research in Developmental Disabilities, 35*(12), 3386–3391.

Matson, J.L., and Rivet, T.T. (2008). Characteristics of challenging behaviours in adults with autistic disorder, PDD-NOS, and intellectual disability. *Journal of Intellectual & Developmental Disability, 33*(4), 323–329.

Matsuo, M., Maeda, T., Sasaki, K., Ishii, K., and Hamasaki, Y. (2010). Frequent association of autism spectrum disorder in patients with childhood onset epilepsy. *Brain and Development, 32*, 759–763.

Matthews, T., Wetson, N., Baxter, H., Felce, D., and Kerr, M. (2008). A general practice-based prevalence study of epilepsy among adults with intellectual disabilities and of its association with psychiatric disorder, behaviour disturbance and carer stress. *Journal of Intellectual Disability Research, 52*(Pt. 2), 163–173.

Mula, M., Jauch, R., Cavanna, A., Collimedaglia, L., *et al.* (2008). Clinical and psychopathological definition of the interictal dysphoric disorder of epilepsy. *Epilepsia, 49*(4), 650–656.

Murphy, O., Healy, O., and Leader, G. (2009). Risk factors for challenging behaviors among 157 children with autism spectrum disorder in Ireland. *Research in Autism Spectrum Disorders, 3*(2), 474–482.

Nascimento, P.P., Oliva, C.H., Franco, C.M., Mazetto, L., *et al.* (2013). Interictal dysphoric disorder: A frequent psychiatric comorbidity among patients with epilepsy who were followed in two tertiary centers. *Arquivos de Neuro-Psiquiatria, 71*(11), 852–855.

National Institute for Health and Clinical Excellence (NIHCE) (2012). *Autism: Recognition, referral, diagnosis and management of adults on the autism spectrum*. Available at www.nice.org.uk/guidance/cg142, accessed on 14 November 2015.

Pellock, J.M. (2004). Understanding co-morbidities affecting children with epilepsy. *Neurology, 62*(Suppl. 2), S17–S23.

Prevey, M.L., Delaney, R.C., Crame, J.A., and Mattson, R.H. (1998). Complex partial and secondarily generalized seizure patients: Cognitive functioning prior to treatment with antiepileptic medication. VA Epilepsy Cooperative Study 264 Group. *Epilepsy Research, 30*(1), 1–9.

Research Units on Pediatric Psychopharmacology Autism Network (2005). Risperidone treatment of autistic disorder: Longer-term benefits and blinded discontinuation after 6 months. *American Journal of Psychiatry, 162*(7), 1361–1369.

Rodin, E.A. (1973). Psychomotor epilepsy and aggressive behavior. *Archives of General Psychiatry, 28*, 210–213.

Santosh, P.J., Baird, G., Pityaratstian, N., Tavare, E., and Gringras, P. (2006). Impact of comorbid autism spectrum disorders on stimulant response in children with attention deficit hyperactivity disorder: A retrospective and prospective effectiveness study. *Child: Care, Health and Development, 32*(5), 575–583.

Sarkhel, S., Praharaj, S.K., and Akhtar, S. (2011). Cheek-biting disorder: Another stereotypic movement disorder? *Journal of Anxiety Disorders, 25*(8), 1085–1086.

Savard, G., Andermann, F., Olivier, A., and Remillard, G.M. (1991). Post-ictal psychosis after partial complex seizures: A multiple case study. *Epilepsia, 32*, 225–231.

Schreibman, L. (2005). *The Science and Fiction of Autism*. Cambridge, MA: Harvard University Press.

Schretien, D.J., Ward, J., Meyer, S.M., Yun, J., *et al.* (2005). Behavioral aspects of the Lesch-Nyhan disease and its variants. *Developmental Medicine and Child Neurology, 47*, 673–677.

Scott, O., Riche, L., Forbes, K., Sonnenberg, L., *et al.* (2014). Anti-N-methyl-D-aspartate (NMDA) receptor encephalitis: An unusual cause of autistic regression in a toddler. *Journal of Child Neurology, 29*(5), 691–694.

Selassie, A.W., Wilson, D.A., Martz, G.U., Smith, G.G., Wagner, J.L., and Wannamaker, B.B. (2014). Epilepsy beyond seizure: A population-based study of comorbidities. *Epilepsy Research, 108*(2), 305–315.

Shakya, D.R., Shyangwa, P.M., Panday, A.K., Subedi, S., and Yadav, S. (2010). Self injurious behavior in temporal lobe epilepsy. *Journal of Nepal Medical Association, 49*(179), 239–242.

Shih, J.J., Leslie-Mazwi, T., Falcao, G., and Van Gerpen, J. (2009). Directed aggressive behavior in frontal lobe epilepsy: A video-EEG and ictal spect study. *Neurology, 73*(21), 1804–1806.

Smith, K.R., and Matson, J.L. (2010a). Psychopathology: Differences among adults with intellectually disabled, comorbid autism spectrum disorders and epilepsy. *Research in Developmental Disabilities, 31*(3), 743–749.

Smith, K.R., and Matson, J.L. (2010b). Behavior problems: Differences among intellectually disabled adults with co-morbid autism spectrum disorders and epilepsy. *Research in Developmental Disabilities, 31*(5), 1062–1069.

So, N.K., Savard, G., Andermann, F., Olivier, A., *et al.* (1990). Acute post-ictal psychosis: A stereo EEG study. *Epilepsia, 31*, 188–193.

Staley, B.A., Montenegro, M.A., Major, P., Muzykewicz, D.A., *et al.* (2008). Self-injurious behavior and tuberous sclerosis complex: Frequency and possible associations in a population of 257 patients. *Epilepsy and Behavior, 13*(4), 650–653.

Sumer, M.M., Atik, L., Unal, A., Emre, U., and Atasoy, H.T. (2007). Frontal lobe epilepsy presented as ictal aggression. *Neurological Sciences, 28,* 48–51.

Tassinari, C.A., Tassi, L., Calandra-Buonaura, G., Stanzani-Maserati, M., *et al.* (2005). Biting behavior, aggression, and seizures. *Epilepsia, 46,* 654–663.

Tavares. H. (2008). [Impulsive control disorders: the return of Esquirol instinctive monomania.] *Rev Bras Psiquitr, 30* (Suppl. 1), S1–2. (Portuguese)

Treinman, D.M. (1986). Epilepsy and violence: Medical and legal issues. *Epilepsia, 27*(Suppl. 2), S77–S104.

Treinman, D.M. (1991). Psychobiology of ictal aggression. *Advances in Neurology, 55,* 341–356.

Tuchman, R., Cuccaro, M., and Alessandri, M. (2010). Autism and epilepsy: Historical perspective. *Brain & Development, 32,* 709–718.

Tucker, G.J. (1998). Seizure disorders presenting with psychiatric symptomatology. *Psychiatric Clinics of North America, 21*(3), 625–635.

Unnwongse, K., Wehner, T., and Foldvary-Schaefer, N. (2012). Mesial frontal lobe epilepsy. *Journal of Clinical Neurophysiology, 29*(5), 371–378.

Vitiello, B., and Stoff, D.M. (1997). Subtypes of aggression and their relevance to child psychiatry. *Journal of the American Academy of Child and Adolescent Psychiatry, 36,* 307–315.

Vuilleumier, P., and Jallon, P. (1998). Epilepsy and psychiatric disorders: Epidemiological data. *Revue Neurologique, 154*(4), 305–317.

Waxman, S.G., and Geschwind, N. (1975). The interictal behavior syndrome of temporal lobe epilepsy. *Archives of General Psychiatry, 32*(12), 1580–1586.

Wilhelm, S., Keuthen, N.J., Deckersbach, T., Engelhard, I.M., *et al.* (1999). Self-injurious skin picking: Clinical characteristics and comorbidity. *Journal of Clinical Psychiatry, 60*(7), 454–459.

Williamson, P.D., Spencer, D.D., Spencer, S.S., Novelly, R.A., and Mattson, R.H. (1985). Complex partial seizures of frontal origin. *Annals of Neurology, 18*(4), 497–504.

Wiznitzer, M. (2004). Autism and tuberous sclerosis. *Journal of Child Neurology, 19*(9), 675–679.

Wortis, H. (1942). Sham rage in man. *American Journal of Psychiatry, 98*(5), 638–644.

Xeniditis, K., Russell, A., and Murphy, D. (2001). Management of people with challenging behavior. *Advances in Psychiatric Treatment, 7,* 109–116.

Yankovsky, A.E., Veilleux, M., Dubeau, F., and Andremann, F. (2005). Post-ictal rage and aggression: A video-EEG study. *Epileptic Disorders, 7*(2), 143–147.

CHAPTER 4

A Neuropsychiatric Model for Evaluating and Treating Self-Injurious Behavior in Autism

Paul Millard Hardy, M.D., Autism Research Institute, San Diego, California

Introduction

This chapter provides a comprehensive approach to the clinical evaluation of self-injurious behavior (SIB) in autism spectrum disorder (ASD). It is important to note that while SIB is not part of the DSM-5 diagnostic criteria for ASD, it is a very disturbing behavior that occurs in about 50% of subjects (Baghdadli *et al.*, 2003). Treatments for SIB, beyond the chains of Bedlam, the straitjackets of state hospitals and developmental centers, have slowly evolved during the past 50 years; however, a cohesive neuropsychiatric model of SIB in autism has yet to be developed: pharmacological and other biological therapies should still be considered as being in their infancy. Unlike what has happened in recent years in the treatment of depression, anxiety, and more recently schizophrenia, research on the fine-tuning of psychopharmacology with behavioral therapy, psychotherapy, and other biological therapies is effectively non-existent (Beitman and Klerman, 1991; Goodwin and Jamison, 2007). However, the recent review by Minshawi and colleagues begins to tackle this complex therapeutic issue. This important review provides a comprehensive multidisciplinary assessment of, and treatment plan for, SIB in ASD (Minshawi *et al.*, 2014). Another comprehensive review on the pharmacology of ASD by Ji and Findling (2015) is an excellent up-to-date general discussion, but it does not focus on SIB. This chapter does not attempt to replicate the Minshawi *et al.* and Ji and Findling papers; instead, it:

- focuses on historical and conceptual issues of the etiology of SIB

- expands the discussion of comorbid neurological and psychiatric diagnoses that can provide key opportunities for pharmacological management

- discusses a hypothesis for the function of severe self-mutilation

- presents information on the opportunities emerging from the field of pharmacogenomics

- discusses the emerging role of inflammatory and autoimmune disorders in SIB

- discusses non-pharmacological biological treatments for SIB in autism.

Progress from 1943 to 1985

From the time of Leo Kanner's 1943 landmark paper identifying and defining autism, until well into the 1980s, the medical community conceived of self-injury as a symptom of psychosis (Kanner, 1943). For this and other reasons, persons with autism were regularly diagnosed and treated as schizophrenic. In 1979 the *Journal of Autism and Childhood Schizophrenia* was renamed the *Journal of Autism and Developmental Disabilities* (Schopler, Rutter, and Chess, 1979). In DSM-I (American Psychiatric Association, 1952), the only reference to autism was under the category of "schizophrenic reaction, childhood type… [P]sychotic reactions in children, manifesting primarily in autism, will be classified here." DSM-II (American Psychiatric Association, 1968) changed the diagnostic label slightly to "schizophrenia, childhood type." A somewhat more extensive description was provided: "This category is for cases in which schizophrenic symptoms may be manifest by autistic, atypical and withdrawn behaviors; failure to develop identity separate from the mother's…"

The concept that schizophrenia in childhood was synonymous with autism led to the widespread over-use well into the mid 1980s of antipsychotic medications for SIB in autism, such as haloperidol, thioridazine, and chlorpromazine (essentially pharmacological sledgehammers) (Andrulonis, 1982; Campbell, 1978; Matson and Barrett, 1982; Sprague, 1968).

While the medical community was stuck on a psychosis model, the psychology community began to conceptualize SIB in a variety of novel ways based upon an operant conditioning model, as outlined by multiple authors in this book. From the late 1960s to the present, these methods have been refined to treat SIB, incorporating a variety of behavioral techniques and functional behavioral assessments (see Chapters 10–13).

Watershed: The Publication of DSM-III in 1980

The modern approach to evaluating and using psychopharmacology for SIB in ASD really did not begin until the mid 1980s. The publication of DSM-III (American Psychiatric Association, 1980) heralded this era, helping to create a slow but significant paradigm shift both conceptually and therapeutically that is now incorporated in DSM-5 (American Psychiatric Association, 2013). DSM-III separated infantile autism from childhood schizophrenia; however, there was no conceptualization of autism as being associated with comorbid disorders. Revised definitions of major depression and bipolar disorder, changing concepts of the anxiety disorders in child and adult psychiatry, attention deficit disorder (previously known as minimal brain damage), and intermittent explosive disorder helped to slowly create the conceptual shift as researchers began to identify these newly defined major psychiatric conditions as being comorbid with autism. Simultaneously, important new developments in the pharmacology of epilepsy (such as valproic acid and carbamazepine) and in psychopharmacology (e.g., lithium, the beta-blockers, and the benzodiazepines) gave physicians new options for autism and SIB (Gaultieri and Hawk, 1982). Soon after, there was the discovery that antiepileptic medications had mood stabilization and behavioral effects (Goodwin and Jamison, 2007; Post *et al.*, 1996).

Panic Disorder as a Cause of SIB

In 1978, having just completed The Joseph P. Kennedy Fellowship in Medical Ethics at Harvard Medical School, followed by a fellowship in behavioral neurology and neuropsychiatry at Boston University School of Medicine, my first full-time job was at the Eunice Kennedy Shriver Center in Waltham, Massachusetts, at the behest of Eunice Shriver. This seemed like an opportunity to not only learn something about the issues facing developmentally disabled persons, but also about neuropsychiatric disorders in this population. Dr. Norman Geschwind, a mentor and world-renowned behavioral neurologist at Harvard, used to say, "There is more neurologic and psychiatric disease in the state hospitals of Massachusetts than in the teaching hospitals of Boston" (N. Geschwind, personal communication, 1977). It quickly became apparent that the evaluation and treatment of an essentially non-verbal population would serve to heighten one's diagnostic curiosity, if not acumen.

Walking into a state institution of over 1300 individuals living in large-brick and cinder-block wards of approximately 20 people made one feel as if not much progress had been made since the days of Bedlam. Approximately 850 residents were on psychotropic medications to control behaviors such as self-injury, aggression toward others, and destruction of property. Ninety-five percent of these psychotropic agents were first-generation antipsychotics such as thioridazine and haloperidol. Almost no anxiolytics or antidepressants were prescribed. In 1977, the prevailing belief in medicine was that if you were mentally retarded (as it was then known) you did not have the mental capacity to become depressed or anxious. No mention is made of anxiety or affective disorders in Michael Rutter and Eric Schopler's landmark edited book, *Autism: A Reappraisal of Concepts and Treatment* (1978). Few papers existed in the literature; a 1977 reference noted that tricyclic antidepressants offered little promise and treatment for the developmental-disorders population (Lipman *et al.*, 1978). Even the second edition of the *Handbook of Autism and Pervasive Developmental Disorders* from

1997 makes no reference to anxiety being comorbid with autism. A very brief section discusses affective disorders associated with autism (Cohen and Volkmar, 1997). The third edition of the *Handbook of Autism and Pervasive Developmental Disorders* briefly mentions anxiety and depression in autism, but not mania or the general concept of comorbidity in autism (Volkmar, 2005).

In DSM-III through DSM-IV-R (American Psychiatric Association, 1980, 1994, 2000) there was no mention of the concept of there being comorbid bipolar disorder in persons with developmental disabilities. The notion of comorbid psychiatric disorders was nonexistent. At that time there was little recognition that there was an increased incidence of Tourette disorder (TD) in autism, or that TD was linked to obsessive-compulsive disorder (OCD). The motor and vocal tics and the repetitive behaviors, including a need for routine, were seen as part of autism as whole, not as a manifestation of a separate comorbid disorder that might have more effective treatments apart from the antipsychotic medications (Hollander, 1993; Stein and Niehaus, 2001).

CASE 1: Panic Disorder in Autism

In assuming responsibility for medication management of the most severe behaviorally disturbed individuals in July 1968, the author began to realize that adjusting doses upward to 1000 mg of chlorpromazine per day, 600 mg of thioridazine per day, or 6–8 mg of haloperidol per day did little to improve SIBs. Then, in 1980, the most self-injurious resident in this large institution provided an opportunity to observe, and to learn something new. This young woman in her mid twenties would have paroxysmal bouts of severe self-mutilation: biting chunks of skin and muscle from her biceps bilaterally, as well as her forearms. It was difficult to dress these wounds, as she tried to pull the bandages off with her teeth. In the heat of July and August, flies would land on her open flesh. Her head was often severely contused despite wearing a helmet, as she would frantically bang her head against the cinder-block walls of the ward. (Helmets had to be replaced frequently due to breakage.) She wrung her hands against each other repetitively and bit them to the extent that they were covered with thick calluses the size of walnuts, as well as many fresh excoriations. Thinking about the English idiom "wringing one's hands" during a time of anxiety, fear, and worry forced one to reconsider whether this was purely the psychotic schizophrenic behavior of autism.

During this resident's paroxysmal rages of SIB, it was noted that she developed extreme diaphoresis and tachycardia of 140–160 beats per minute. This was associated with a widened pulse pressure of 160/60 compared with a resting pulse of 80 and blood pressure of 120/70. Only one hormone in the body could produce this response: adrenalin. Working her up for an adrenalin-producing tumor and collecting several 24-hour urines (very difficult in the back wards of a state institution) revealed elevated adrenalin levels, but a further workup for a pheochromocytoma at a Boston teaching hospital was negative. What else could be causing this?

A review of what little history there was in this patient's record revealed that her mother, who lived within 50 miles, never came to visit her. In fact, she rarely left her home except to travel 60 miles to Boston to see a cardiologist for a "heart problem." Having just studied the newly published DSM-III, the suspicion arose that she had panic disorder, and that her mother probably had panic disorder, mitral valve prolapse, and agoraphobia. (Awareness of these disorders was emerging at that time.) Contemporaneously, Donald Kline's pioneering work at Columbia University on the use of tricyclic antidepressants for anxiety and panic appeared in the literature (Klein, Zitrin, and Woerner, 1978). While lowering this patient's high-dose antipsychotic medication and gingerly introducing a tricyclic antidepressant (considered at the time to be an anti-panic medication), the frequency and severity of her self-injury slowly began to decrease.

A Novel Perspective on the Endorphin Hypothesis of SIB

Why did a human being with severe intellectual disability and all the features of autism engage in what was clearly painful mutilation of his arms, as well as the trauma of severe head banging? At that time, only a few years separated the author from a medical internship and the experience of treating the panicky fear of suffocation in patients with congestive heart failure. Since morphine was the first treatment upon arrival in an emergency department, it was hypothesized that perhaps some of the self-injuries in persons with autism or other forms of developmental disability were an attempt to titrate down their panic or severe anxiety. (The release of endorphins in the context of major trauma, allowing victims to tolerate pain associated with the trauma, has been well documented; Okur *et al.*, 2007.) The thought of trying naltrexone to block the endorphin release, in an attempt to extinguish the SIB, seemed to be unethical since it was not addressing the primary cause and would only increase pain and suffering. The use of anti-anxiety medications, specifically anti-panic medications, seemed more humane. Since there was essentially no literature in the 1980s to support their use, it seemed reasonable to cautiously try benzodiazepines and tricyclic antidepressants known to reduce anxiety. When a benzodiazepine and a tricyclic were introduced, reductions in the frequency and intensity of the SIB became apparent. Over time, the calluses from hand biting diminished in size.

Minshawi *et al.* (2014) have quite thoroughly summarized the conflicting literature on the use of opioids in treating SIB in autism. However, the idea that some forms of SIB are an attempt by the person to reduce his or her own panic is not presented; this may explain why so much of the research on the use of opiate blockers (such as naltrexone) in treating SIB has been confusing and unsuccessful (Campbell *et al.*, 1993; Dove *et al.*, 2012; Tsiouris *et al.*, 2003; Willemsen-Swinkels *et al.*, 1995).

Temple Grandin: Self-Report

The possibility that there is a link between panic disorder, the symptoms of panic embedded in autism, and the role of endorphins was further supported by Temple Grandin in her publications during the mid 1980s, especially *Emergence: Labeled Autistic* (Grandin, 1984; Grandin and Scariano, 1986). Grandin describes in detail that as a child she had "nerve attacks," and episodes of "panic" associated with tachycardia that intensified in adolescence. While spending a summer at her aunt's ranch in Arizona, Grandin, using her savant ability to connect with animals, observed how the most twitchy and fearful cattle were calmed by a squeeze chute. This observation led her to try the squeeze chute herself and she experienced the calming effect it had upon her nerves and feelings of panic. The role of deep pressure and massage in releasing endorphins has been documented. Grandin describes how this became her new fixation in *Emergence*.

Grandin returned that fall to high school in New Hampshire, and with the assistance of her science teacher, she designed her now-famous squeeze machine, which she would use to release her own endorphins. This would calm her significantly. Her psychiatrist in Boston thought her squeeze machine was quite strange, although he could offer her no medical alternative. In fact, both her psychiatrist and psychologist recommended that she be prohibited from using it. Subsequently, after reading an article about imipramine in *Psychology Today* (Wender and Klein, 1981), she sought treatment with this tricyclic antidepressant. In describing the benefits she writes: "Gone are the frenzied searches for the basic meaning of life...since I am more relaxed, I get along better with people, and stress-related health problems, such as colitis, are gone." Grandin also describes how, as a child, experiences of pain were often associated with pleasure, supporting the endorphin hypothesis presented in the previous section (Grandin, 1984, p.110).

Panic Disorder and Seizures

Another subset of individuals with autism, SIB, and panic disorder are those who have comorbid complex partial seizures (Blumer, 1984). Over the years, the present author has worked with over a dozen individuals, both within an institutional setting and in an outpatient practice, who present this complex clinical picture. It is noteworthy that these patients generally do not have a positive family history for anxiety disorders, especially panic disorder; the panic is in fact a manifestation of a complex partial seizure.

CASE 2: Self-Injury and Epilepsy

About the same time, another non-verbal patient gave this physician the opportunity to make a connection between autism and epilepsy. This was in a young woman in her mid twenties, institutionalized since childhood, who had a chronic, deep, crater-like lesion on her forehead that was often bloody. For years she would suddenly, and without warning, get up from her bed or a chair and run across the ward to bang her head into a brick wall. One day while walking past her, it was noted that she appeared to be in a trance with rapid eye rolling upward toward the ceiling. Such rolling of the eyes is essentially pathognomonic for the early stages of partial seizure activity. Given that she was in the hospital unit, she received a STAT injection of 10 mg of diazepam from the nearby emergency cart. This stopped the eye rolling immediately and interrupted the impending seizure. In the ensuing years medical literature has emerged on the association of complex partial epilepsy and panic attacks (Thompson, Duncan, and Smith, 2000). Treating this young woman with anti-seizure medications gradually reduced the seizure activity, associated panic attacks, and resulting SIB. Moreover, it allowed for the reduction of her high doses of thioridazine.

These cases illustrate several things:

- Both SIB and panic disorder occur in autism with uncertain frequency and can have multiple causations.
- The relationship between epilepsy and panic disorder can be missed even by board-certified academic neurologists and epileptologists.
- The diagnosis of autism often clouds diagnostic thinking on the part of the finest physicians: "It's just part of autism."
- Partial epilepsy is a *clinical* diagnosis and should not be dismissed even if routine or 24-hour electroencephalographs are normal.

- A detailed history is the most important factor in making this diagnosis, and it is important not to be seduced by tests and technology.

Affective Disorders, OCD, and TD Associated with SIB in Autism

CASE 3: Self-Injury and Depression

In studying how other DSM-III diagnoses might apply to the residents in this 1300-bed institution for the developmentally disabled during the early 1980s, the present author noticed several individuals who often sat on the floor, or in chairs, with their heads buried between their hands, leaning forward between flexed knees. Among this group was another young woman with severe self-injury in the form of head banging and face slapping, institutionalized since childhood, and on 1200 mg per day of chlorpromazine (a very high dose). Her posture would remind one of Vincent Van Gogh's famous series of drawings entitled *Sorrow*. Working with the hypothesis that this woman might be depressed—and more than schizophrenic—treatment with a tricyclic antidepressant was slowly initiated. Within 2–3 weeks it was observed that her affect brightened and her head banging diminished. Subsequently, she tolerated lower antipsychotic medication without any regression, and we were then able to identify many other non-verbal residents who engaged in SIB who also appeared to be clinically depressed (Hardy, Waters, and Cohen, 1984). Treating these non-verbal residents who engaged in SIB and appeared depressed led to reductions in their SIB (Cole *et al.*, 1985).

CASE 4: Self-Injury and Tourette Disorder

Another interesting group of self-injurious individuals were those who engaged in self-restraint. In working with a young man in his early twenties who had blinded himself in one eye from severe head banging, one had to wonder if his repeated loud, vocal outbursts were not just a symptom of his autism but possibly a sign of comorbid TD. What was most notable about this young man was that he always had a length of shredded cloth wrapped around his waist and tightly held in both hands in front of his abdomen. If the cloth was removed he would begin to bang his face. It appeared that this was a repetitive motor tic in the form of head banging, and the self-restraint was a compulsion to inhibit the motor tic. In this circumstance, the SIB did not release endorphins to titrate down the anxiety/panic—it only inflicted pain and discomfort, and thus he sought to restrain himself.

It has been the present author's experience during the past four decades of treating dozens of individuals with the quadrangle of comorbid autism, SIB, TD, and OCD that this cohort is very resistant to pharmacological and behavioral treatment. In the years since, these early observations (i.e., the associations between autism and TD, and autism and OCD) have been increasingly documented in the literature (Hollander, 1993; Jenike, Baer, and Minichiello, 1990).

PANS/PANDAS

After 15 years of controversy between neurologists and psychiatrists, the clinical syndromes of pediatric autoimmune neuropsychiatric disorder associated with streptococcal infections (PANDAS) and pediatric acute neuropsychiatric syndrome (PANS) are increasingly accepted in the community of health care providers. It is extremely important to consider this autoimmune disorder for SIB in persons with ASD (Chang, Koplewicz, and Steingard, 2015; Murphy *et al.*, 2015; Swedo *et al.*, 2015). Antibiotic and immunomodulatory therapies now need to be added to the pharmacological therapies considered in treating SIB. Some children and adults respond to antibiotics alone; others require more complex evaluation and treatment including consultation with infectious disease experts and immunologists (Frankovich *et al.*, 2015).

In working with both children and adults on the autism spectrum for a eneration, it has been a recent realization by the present author that there is a subset of autistic adults with SIB, tics, unusual fears, and obsessions who probably developed PANS/PANDAS in childhood prior to the syndrome being described by Swedo in 1998 or accepted as a valid medical illness by physicians. Swedo and colleagues support this as being a reasonable hypothesis (Swedo *et al.*, 2015). Not surprisingly, this subset of patients with autism have, over the years, been among the most challenging to treat. Now, taking careful histories for the acute onset of behavioral regression following infections in childhood has opened windows of opportunity for treatment, and indeed has yielded some therapeutic success stories.

Taking careful histories for the onset of regression following childhood infectious, viral, and tick-borne illnesses must be included in the evaluations of SIB in ASD. The rise in tick-borne infections, many of which are not diagnosed easily at this time, is creating a new challenge in the diagnosis of all behavioral problems in children, including autism. Unfortunately, there are no guidelines for how to manage chronic PANS/PANDAS in adults.

The Rapidly Evolving Field of Pharmacogenomics

The emerging new technology of pharmacogenomics will revolutionize the way medications will be prescribed in the years ahead. This breakthrough will help guide medication selection, dosing, and monitoring for possible side effects to a significant degree, based upon genes that influence the rapidity with which medications are metabolized through the liver. Moreover, specific genes that influence the sensitivity of receptors in the brain to medications can now be measured, and more will be added over time (D'Empaire, Guico-Pabia, and Preskorn, 2011; Hall-Flavin *et al.*, 2012; Kung and Li, 2010; Winner *et al.*, 2013). Collection of the DNA specimen involves swabbing inside the cheek of the individual rather than the challenge of drawing blood in a fearful autistic person. In a recent case, a young man with high-functioning autism had been diagnosed with panic disorder, posttraumatic stress disorder (PTSD), bipolar disorder, and probable PANS/PANDAS. Treating him pharmacologically was a challenge, especially since it required a combination of five different medications, including an antibiotic, to stabilize him. However, there was discord between his attorney parents regarding medication choices and dosing. Therefore, it was extremely helpful that this young autistic man—who would bite his hands and sometimes threaten suicide—was found, as a result of pharmacogenomic testing, to be a rapid metabolizer of the major tranquilizer (neuroleptic) that had brought significant stability. This finding provided comfort to this prescribing physician as well as the young man's parents, knowing that not only was he on 50% of the maximum dose, but he probably fell into a lower risk category for developing tardive dyskinesia and other side effects from the neuroleptic.

Psychopharmacological genomics will become a significant new tool in managing medications in SIB. Some of the concerns rightfully expressed by Jamie Bleiweiss in Chapter 5 of this book will likely be diminished by this new medical technology. Several commercial laboratories are now available to do this testing. Genesight (Assurex Health) is one that has emerged out of a collaboration between the Mayo Clinic and the University of Cincinnati.[1]

SIB Options Emerging in Neuropsychiatry

New medications are constantly being developed for medical, psychiatric, and neurological conditions, but other biological therapies are emerging to treat

---

1   It has an informative website on this new technology (www.genesight.com).

suicidality (the severest form of SIB), depression, PTSD, and epilepsy. Such biological therapies include rTMS for depression and autism (Casanova *et al.*, 2015; Oberman *et al.*, 2015) and the anesthetic agent ketamine for severe SIB with suicidality (Diaz-Granados *et al.*, 2010; Price *et al.*, 2009), and a re-evaluation of ECT for SIB is being conducted by Wachtel and colleagues (Wachtel *et al.*, 2009; Wachtel, Griffin, and Reti, 2010). It will be important for those treating and conducting research on SIB to assess how these biological therapies may apply to this most challenging conundrum in autism.

The Significant Improvement in DSM-5 for SIB in ASD

The changes in the definition and criteria for ASD in DSM-5 have been very controversial, especially the deletion of Asperger's syndrome; however, there is one significant improvement: the inclusion of a concept of comorbidity (Baker, 2013). DSM-5 notes under a discussion of comorbidity that many individuals with ASD have psychiatric symptoms not part of the criteria of ASD: "About 70% of individuals with autism spectrum disorder may have one comorbid mental disorder, and 40% may have two or more comorbid mental disorders" (American Psychiatric Association, 2013, p.58). The failure to include or exclude these comorbid disorders by relying solely on the ADOS or ADI in ASD research, especially on SIB, has confounded much ASD evidence-based medicine (EBM) to date. Research in autism should move forward in a more efficient and effective manner by carefully using the new DSM-5 specifiers:

- intellectual impairment
- language impairment
- associated known medical or genetic conditions or environmental factors
- associated other neurodevelopmental, mental, or behavioral disorders
- with or without catatonia.

Indeed, in the present author's view, some of the EBM on SIB in ASD is flawed, as subjects have not been properly subcategorized. What has been presented in this chapter would have been very difficult to accomplish in the current era of EBM in ASD. The new DSM-5 should assist the next generation of clinicians, guided by science and clinical experience, to hone their clinical intuitions while continuing to practice the art of medicine.

References

American Psychiatric Association (1952). *Diagnostic and Statistical Manual of Mental Disorders* (1st ed.). Washington, DC: American Psychiatric Association.

American Psychiatric Association (1968). *Diagnostic and Statistical Manual of Mental Disorders* (2nd ed.). Washington, DC: American Psychiatric Association.

American Psychiatric Association (1980). *Diagnostic and Statistical Manual of Mental Disorders* (3rd ed.). Washington, DC: American Psychiatric Association.

American Psychiatric Association (1994). *Diagnostic and Statistical Manual of Mental Disorders* (4th ed.). Washington, DC: American Psychiatric Association.

American Psychiatric Association (2000). *Diagnostic and Statistical Manual of Mental Disorders* (4th ed., text revision). Washington, DC: American Psychiatric Association.

American Psychiatric Association (2013). *Diagnostic and Statistical Manual of Mental Disorders* (5th ed.). Washington, DC: American Psychiatric Association.

Andrulonis, P.A. (1982). The Psychopharmacology of Emotionally Disturbed and Mentally Retarded Children and Adolescents. In J.I. Jakab (Ed.), *Mental Retardation.* Basel: Karger.

Baghdadli, A., Pascal, C., Grisi, S., and Assilloux, C. (2003). Risk factors for self-injurious behaviors among 222 young children with autistic disorders. *Journal of Intellectual Disability Research, 47*(8), 622–627.

Baker, J.P. (2013). History of medicine. Autism at 70: redrawing the boundaries. *The New England Journal of Medicine, 369,* 12.

Beitman, B.D., and Klerman, G.L. (Eds.) (1991). *Integrating Pharmacotherapy and Psychotherapy.* Washington, DC: American Psychiatric Press.

Blumer, D. (Ed.) (1984). *Psychiatric Aspects of Epilepsy.* Washington, DC: American Psychiatric Press.

Campbell, M. (1978). The Use of Drug Treatment in Infantile Autism and Childhood Schizophrenia: A Review. In M.A. Lipton, A. DiMascio, and K.E. Killam (Eds.), *Psychopharmacology: A Generation of Progress.* New York, NY: Raven Press.

Campbell, M., Anderson, L.T., Small, A.M., Adams, P., Gonzalez, N.M., and Ernst, M. (1993). Naltrexone in autistic children: Behavioral symptoms and attentional learning. *Journal of the American Academy of Child and Adolescent Psychiatry, 32*(6), 1283–1291.

Casanova, M.F., Sokhadze, E., Opris, I., Wang, Y., and Li, X. (2015). Autism spectrum disorders: Linking neuropathological findings to treatment with transcranial magnetic stimulation. *Acta Paediatrica, 104,* 346–355.

Chang, K., Koplewicz, H.S., and Steingard, R. (2015). Special issue on pediatric acute-onset neuropsychiatric syndrome. *Journal of Child and Adolescent Psychopharmacology, 25,* 1–2.

Cohen, D.J., and Volkmar, F.R. (Eds.) (1997). *Handbook of Autism and Pervasive Developmental Disorders* (2nd ed.). Toronto: John Wiley & Sons.

Cole, J.O., Hardy, P.M., Marcel, B., and Salomon, M. (1985). Organic States. In A.F. Schatzberg (Ed.), *Common Treatment Problems in Depression.* Washington, DC: American Psychiatric Press.

D'Empaire, I., Guico-Pabia, C.J., and Preskorn, S.H. (2011). Antidepressant treatment and altered CYP2D6 activity: Are pharmacokinetic variations clinically relevant? *Journal of Psychiatric Practice, 17*(5), 330–339.

Diaz-Granados, N., Ibrahim, L., Brutsche, N., Ameli, R., *et al.* (2010). Rapid resolution of suicidal ideation after a single infusion of an NMDA antagonist in patients with treatment-resistant major depressive disorder. *Journal of Clinical Psychiatry, 71*(12), 1605–1611.

Dove, D., Warren, Z., McPheeters, M.L., Taylor, J.L., Sathe, N.A., and Veenstra-VanderWeele, J. (2012). Medications for adolescents and young adults with autism spectrum disorders: A systematic review. *Pediatrics, 130*(4), 717–726.

Frankovich, J., Thienemann, M., Pearlstein, J., Crable, A., Brown, K., and Chang, K. (2015). Multidisciplinary clinic dedicated to treating youth with pediatric acute-onset neuropsychiatric syndrome: Presenting characteristics of the first 47 consecutive patients. *Journal of Child and Adolescent Psychopharmacology, 25*(1), 38–47.

Gaultieri, C.T., and Hawk, B. (1982). Antidepressant and Antimanic Drugs. In S.E. Breuning and A.D. Poling (Eds.), *Drugs and Mental Retardation.* Springfield, IL: Charles C. Thomas.

Goodwin, F.K., and Jamison, K.R. (2007). *Manic-Depressive Illness: Bipolar Disorders and Recurrent Depression* (2nd ed.). New York, NY: Oxford University Press.

Grandin, T. (1984). My experiences as an autistic child. *Journal of Orthomolecular Psychiatry, 13,* 144–174.

Grandin, T., and Scariano, M.M. (1986). *Emergence: Labeled Autistic.* Novato, CA: Arena Press.

Hall-Flavin, D.K., Winner, J.G., Allen, J.D., Jordan, J.J., *et al.* (2012). Using a pharmacogenomic algorithm to guide the treatment of depression. *Translational Psychiatry, 2,* e172. doi:10.1038/tp.2012.99

Hardy, P.M., Waters, J., and Cohen, M.S. (1984). A Biomedical Basis for Self-Injury. In J.C. Griffin, M.T. Stark, and D.E. Williams (Eds.), *Advances in the Treatment of Self-Injurious Behavior.* Richmond, TX: J.C. Griffin.

Hollander, E. (1993). *Obsessive-Compulsive Related Disorders.* Washington, DC: American Psychiatric Press.

Jenike, M.A., Baer, L., and Minichiello, W.E. (1990). *Obsessive-Compulsive Disorders: Theory and Management* (2nd ed.). Chicago, IL: Year Book Medical Publishers.

Ji, N.Y., and Findling, R.L. (2015). An update on pharmacotherapy for autism spectrum disorder in children and adolescents. *Current Opinion in Psychiatry, 28*(2), 91–101.

Kanner, L. (1943). Autistic disturbances of affective contact. *Nervous Child, 2,* 217–250.

Klein, D.F., Zitrin, C.M., and Woerner, M. (1978). Antidepressants, Anxiety, Panic and Phobia. In Lipton, A. DiMascio, M., and Killam, K. (Eds.), *Psychopharmacology: A Generation of Progress.* New York, NY: Raven Press.

Kung, S., and Li, X. (2010). The clinical use of pharmacogenomic testing in treatment-resistant depression. *Primary Psychiatry, 17*(5), 46–51.

Lipman, R.S., DiMascio, A., Reatig, N., and Kirson, T. (1978). Psychotropic Drugs and Mentally Retarded Children. In M. Lipton, A. DiMascio, and K. Killam (Eds.), *Psychopharmacology: A Generation of Progress.* New York, NY: Raven Press.

Matson, J.L., and Barrett, R.P. (Eds.) (1982). *Psychopathology in the Mentally Retarded.* New York, NY: Grune & Stratton.

Minshawi, N.F., Hurwitz, S., Morriss, D., and McDougle, C.J. (2014). Multidisciplinary assessment and treatment of self-injurious behavior in autism spectrum disorder and intellectual disability: Integration of psychological and biological theory and approach. *Journal of Autism Developmental Disorders, 5*(6), 1541–1568.

Murphy, T.K., Patel, P.D., McGuire, J.F., Kennel, A., *et al.* (2015). Characterization of the pediatric acute-onset neuropsychiatric syndrome phenotype. *Journal of Child and Adolescent Psychopharmacology, 25,* 14–25.

Oberman, L.M., Enticott, P.G., Casanova, M.F., Rotenberg, A., Pascual-Leone, A., and McCracken, J.T. (2015). Transcranial magnetic stimulation (TMS) therapy for autism: An international consensus conference held in conjunction with the international meeting for autism research on May 13th and 14th, 2014. *Frontiers in Human Neuroscience, 8,* 1034.

Okur, H., Kucukaydn, M., Ozokutan, B.H., Muhtaroqlu, S., Kazez, A., and Turan, C. (2007). Relationship between release of beta-endorphin, cortisol, and trauma severity in children with blunt torso and extremity trauma. *Journal of Trauma, 62*(2), 320–324.

Post, R.M., Ketter, T.A., Denicoff, D., Pazzaglia, P.J., *et al.* (1996; first published 1990). The place of anticonvulsant therapy in bipolar illness. *Psychopharmacology, 12,* 115–129.

Price, R.B., Nock, M.K., Charney, D.S., and Mathew, S.J. (2009). Effects of intravenous ketamine on explicit and implicit measures of suicidality in treatment-resistant depression. *Biological Psychiatry, 66*(5), 522–526.

Rutter, M., and Schopler, E. (Eds.) (1978). *Autism: A Reappraisal of Concepts and Treatment.* New York, NY: Plenum Press.

Schopler, E., Rutter, M., and Chess, S. (1979). Editorial: Change of journal scope and title. *Journal of Autism and Developmental Disorders, 9*(1), 1–10.

Sprague, R.L. (1968). Overview of Psychopharmacology for the Retarded in the United States. In P. Mittler and J.M. de Jong (Eds.), *Research to Practice in Mental Retardation: Biomedical Aspects* (Vol. III). Baltimore, MD: University Park Press.

Stein, D.J., and Niehaus, D.J.H. (2001). Stereotypic Self-Injurious Behaviors: Neurobiology and psychopharmacology. In D. Simeon and E. Hollander (Eds.), *Self-Injurious Behaviors: Assessment and Treatment.* Washington, DC: American Psychiatric Publishing.

Swedo, S.E., Seidlitz, J., Kovacevic, M., Latimer, M.E., *et al.* (2015). Clinical presentation of pediatric autoimmune neuropsychiatric disorders associated with streptococcal infections in research and community settings. *Journal of Child and Adolescent Psychopharmacology, 25,* 26–30.

Thompson, S.A., Duncan, J.S., and Smith, S.J. (2000). Partial seizures presenting as panic attacks. *British Medical Journal, 321*(7267), 1002–1003.

Tsiouris, J.A., Cohen, I.L., Patti, P.J., and Korosh, W.M. (2003). Treatment of previously undiagnosed psychiatric disorders in persons with developmental disabilities decreased or eliminated self-injurious behavior. *Journal of Clinical Psychiatry, 64*(9), 1081–1090.

Volkmar, F.R., Paul, R., Klin, A., and Cohen, D. (Eds.) (2005). *Handbook of Autism and Pervasive Developmental Disorders* (3rd ed.). Hoboken, NJ: John Wiley & Sons.

Wachtel, L.E., Contrucci-Kuhn, S.A., Griffin, M., Thompson, A., Dhossche, D.M., and Reti, I.M. (2009). ECT for self-injury in an autistic boy. *European Child and Adolescent Psychiatry, 18*(7), 458–463.

Wachtel, L.E., Griffin, M., and Reti, I.M. (2010). Electroconvulsive therapy in a man with autism experiencing severe depression, catatonia, and self-injury. *The Journal of ECT, 26*(1), 70–73.

Wender, P.H., and Klein, D.F. (1981). The promise of biological psychiatry. *Psychology Today, 75*(2), 25–41.

Willemsen-Swinkels, S.H., Buitelaar, J.K., Nijhof, G.J., and van England, H. (1995). Failure of naltrexone hydrochloride to reduce self-injurious and autistic behavior in mentally retarded adults: Double-blind placebo controlled studies. *Archives of General Psychiatry, 52*(9), 766–773.

Winner, J., Allen, J.D., Altar, C.A., and Spahic-Mihajlovic, A. (2013). Psychiatric pharmacogenomics predicts health resource utilization of outpatients with anxiety and depression. *Translational Psychiatry, 3*(3), e242.

CHAPTER 5

Examining the Impact of Medication Side Effects on Problem Behavior

Jamie D. Bleiweiss, Ph.D., Hunter College, New York

Introduction

Severe problem behavior, including self-injury and aggression, significantly impedes quality of life for individuals with autism spectrum disorder (ASD) and their families, and thus represents a priority for intervention. Psychotropic medications are commonly administered to treat such behaviors; however, these agents often produce new difficulties in the form of adverse side effects. Interestingly, many of the same factors identified as commonly occurring side effects of medications (e.g., fatigue, gastrointestinal pain and discomfort, appetite changes, heightened anxiety, and so forth) have been observed in the behavioral literature, where they occur in the absence of medication, and are referred to as "setting events." These setting events, importantly, are often associated with elevated levels of problem behavior. Thus, it is plausible that medication side effects may function as setting events, paradoxically exacerbating the very behavior the medication intends to treat. In other words, the presence of side effects may make aspects of certain home and community routines more challenging and, in turn, producing greater levels of problem behavior.

This chapter explores the notion that medication side effects essentially function as biological setting events, and the paradoxical role these variables may play in producing increased levels of subsequent problem behavior. Additionally, we examine the intervention implications arising from such a conceptualization, and discuss the potential opportunities for fostering greater collaboration across disciplines, to ultimately improve outcomes for individuals with autism and their loved ones.

Prevalence, Importance, and Treatment of Severe Problem Behavior

Autism spectrum disorder is a neurodevelopmental disorder that is characterized by an array of qualitative impairments in socialization and communication, and the presence of restricted, repetitive, and stereotyped patterns of behaviors and interests (American Psychiatric Association, 2000). As a result of these challenges in the core developmental domains, people with autism often display a variety of interfering behaviors such as self-injury, aggression, and tantrums. For caregivers and practitioners, the most distressing and troublesome are self-injurious behaviors (SIBs) that include any type of action resulting in physical injury directed toward the self (Fee and Matson, 1992). These behaviors are often repetitive and can range in severity from mild instances of repetitive head rubbing to intense episodes of banging one's head against hard surfaces, which can be quite dangerous and cause significant damage. Studies examining the prevalence of these behaviors have indicated that 10–89% of the population engages in at least one type of problem behavior, and individuals experiencing more significant impairments have been found to exhibit more frequent and intense behaviors (Cooper *et al.*, 2009; Emerson *et al.*, 2001; Lowe *et al.*, 2007).

Challenging behavior often compromises multiple aspects of family quality of life, and thus represents a main focus for intervention efforts (Davis and Carter, 2008; Lucyshyn, Dunlap, and Albin, 2002). For example, severe problem behavior may prevent the successful inclusion of children into neighborhood schools, and often leads to social isolation and rejection by peers (Koegel, Koegel, and Dunlap, 1996). In addition, these behaviors significantly reduce opportunities for meaningful participation in valued community activities (Lee *et al.*, 2008) and have been shown to be a major barrier to success in the workplace later in life (Bruininks, Hill, and Morreau, 1988). The negative effect of problematic behavior on those living and working with the individual is evidenced by reports of elevated levels of parental distress and caregiver burnout (Davis and Carter, 2008; Hayes and Watson, 2013; Koegel *et al.*, 1992). Given the negative impact that problem behaviors can have on the person displaying them, as well as on his or her caregivers, a great deal of research and clinical work in both the behavioral and pharmacological fields has been dedicated to the development and implementation of effective interventions.

Behavioral Interventions for Challenging Behavior

The behavioral literature is replete with studies investigating the factors that evoke severe problematic behaviors such as self-injury and aggression; a significant amount of research has been devoted to the assessment and subsequent development of effective interventions that remediate such behavior (Carr *et al.*, 1999; Dunlap *et al.*, 1991; Horner *et al.*, 2002). Behavioral researchers and clinicians have focused on the prevailing notion that all behaviors, including those that are problematic, are a function of the consequences that maintain such behavior and the antecedents or contextual variables that trigger it. A substantial literature has amassed demonstrating that the functions of behavior are identified through an analysis of the patterns of events that occur before and after the interfering behavior.

Traditionally, the behavioral approach to managing aggression and self-injury has focused largely on consequence-based assessment and intervention (see descriptions in Chapters 11 and 12).

In recent years, the focus of research in the behavioral field has shifted as investigators have increasingly begun to explore the pivotal role that *contextual variables* play in producing problematic behavior (Luiselli and Cameron, 1998; McGill, 1999; Smith and Iwata, 1997). Problem behavior occurs as a direct response to two types of contextual variables: *discriminative stimuli* (*antecedents*) and *setting events*. A discriminative stimulus is a discrete event that, when present, sets the occasion for, or is associated with, the reliable reinforcement of a behavior (Skinner, 1938). This event immediately precedes the behavior, essentially triggering it to occur. In illustration, if a child displays tantrums and self-injury when presented with an aversive task demand (e.g., being told to do his homework), and this repeatedly results in the parent's withdrawal of the demand, it is likely that in the future he will respond with tantrums and self-injury in the presence of that task demand ("do your homework"). Thus, the task demand becomes a discriminative stimulus for the problem behavior because he learns that this behavior "pays off" by permitting him to escape from performing the undesirable task.

The other contextual factor, the setting event, is a variable that influences the ongoing relationship between the discriminative stimulus and the problem behavior (Bijou and Baer, 1961; Kantor, 1959). In essence, setting events *set the stage* for the behavior; when present, they make the discriminative stimuli (i.e., immediate triggers) more aversive than they normally would be, and thus increase the likelihood that the child will display problem behavior. While these factors may not directly evoke the behavior, they play a critical role in enhancing our understanding of how challenging behaviors, such as self-injury and severe aggression, arise.

The Four-Term Contingency

Figure 5.1 depicts the four-term contingency model that serves as a conceptual framework for understanding problem behavior (Carr and Smith, 1995). This model describes the relationship between setting events, discriminative stimuli (i.e., immediate trigger), responses (problem behavior), and consequences (i.e., function or purpose). This model is described in detail along with case descriptions in Chapter 10.

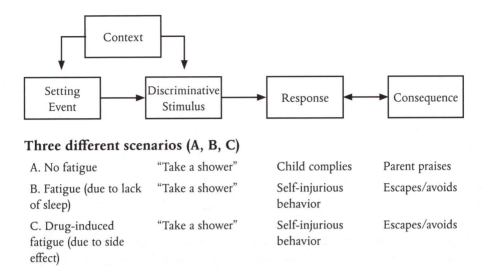

Three different scenarios (A, B, C)

A. No fatigue	"Take a shower"	Child complies	Parent praises
B. Fatigue (due to lack of sleep)	"Take a shower"	Self-injurious behavior	Escapes/avoids
C. Drug-induced fatigue (due to side effect)	"Take a shower"	Self-injurious behavior	Escapes/avoids

Figure 5.1 The Four-Term Contingency: A Conceptual Framework for Understanding Problem Behavior

Three Categories of Setting Events

The important role of context in the four-term contingency model highlights the need for identifying the broad array of contextual variables that can impact problem behavior and help explain why it occurs (i.e., its motivation). A review of the behavioral literature shows that there are three broad categories of setting events commonly associated with problem behavior: social, activities/routines, and biological. Social factors have been found to be correlated with increased levels of problem behavior and can include variables such as the presence or absence of specific people (Touchette, MacDonald, and Langer, 1985), or low levels of attention from others (Taylor *et al.*, 1993). For example, a student with ASD may engage in severe SIB when her favorite teacher is absent from school. The absence of her preferred teacher may make certain tasks or activities more unpleasant than they usually are, and thus increases the likelihood that she will display SIB when a substitute teacher presents her with academic tasks.

Problem behavior has also been found to be associated with contextual factors related to the nature of some activities and certain aspects of ongoing routines, such as having to wait, transitioning from one setting to another, or encountering unexpected changes in routines (Davis, 1987; Doss and Reichle, 1991; McCord, Thomson, and Iwata, 2001). Additionally, activities that are too long, too difficult, or too noisy may serve as setting events (Carr, Newsom, and Binkoff, 1980; O'Reilly, Lacey, and Lancioni, 2000). In other words, the presence of these unpleasant aspects of activities or routines increases the likelihood that the child will engage in challenging behavior in order to escape or avoid it. For instance, an individual with ASD may become extremely distressed when in noisy, crowded settings, and as a result slap the side of their face repeatedly and shriek loudly in order to escape the uncomfortable environment.

An association between physiological states and affective conditions and problem behavior has been well documented in the research literature as well (Bosch *et al.*, 1997; Kennedy and O'Reilly, 2006). This third category, biological setting events, includes factors such as physical pain/discomfort and illness (Carr *et al.*, 2003; Kennedy and Itkonen, 1993), as well as increased fatigue (Kennedy and Meyer, 1996; Wiggs and Stores, 1996). For instance, Carr and colleagues (2003) demonstrated an association between menstrual discomfort (a biological setting event) and increased levels of problem behavior displayed by participants. During instances when participants experienced menstrual pain, they were found to engage in higher rates of problem behavior in response to task demands.

Symons, Davis, and Thompson (2000) investigated a correlation between increased fatigue and daytime problem behavior. They reported that elevated levels of daytime SIB were displayed by individuals who were sleep-deprived (i.e., slept significantly fewer hours as compared with matched controls). The association between physical discomfort and increased problem behavior was further demonstrated by Bosch and colleagues (1997), as they found higher rates of problem behavior displayed by individuals who were experiencing pain caused by gastrointestinal conditions, while O'Reilly (1997) reported higher rates of self-injury correlated with pain caused by otitis media (middle ear infection).

In summary, a number of studies have documented a clear relationship between pain and discomfort affecting different physiological systems, and problematic behavior. These investigations provide compelling evidence that pain and discomfort produced by a range of conditions plausibly function as setting events, thus increasing the likelihood that problem behavior will occur.

Context-Based Assessment and Intervention

Given the increased awareness of how these contextual factors interact with consequences to produce problem behavior, a greater number of studies have begun to focus on the assessment and intervention of context variables (Clarke, Dunlap, and Vaughn, 1999; Vaughn *et al.*, 1997). For instance, Vaughn, Clarke, and Dunlap (1997) demonstrated the efficacy of implementing a context-based intervention to reduce severe problem behavior displayed by an 8-year-old boy during two family routines: using the bathroom in the home and dining in a restaurant. Assessment data indicated that the child displayed problem behavior, including aggression and property destruction, when required to transition to a less-preferred activity (i.e., using the bathroom) and when having to wait during the restaurant routine. Multicomponent interventions implemented in the family routines involved the use of a visual schedule depicting the sequence of steps comprising the activity, and for the restaurant routine, the intervention included increasing the child's participation throughout the activity (e.g., ordering the meal, paying for the food). Following the implementation of the intervention strategies in each context, the child's disruptive behavior was significantly reduced, while his level of engagement and interaction with family members increased.

Carr and Carlson (1993) demonstrated the effectiveness of utilizing context-based assessment and multicomponent intervention to reduce severe problem behavior displayed by three adults with autism in a community setting. Specifically, the individuals exhibited aggression and self-injury during outings to the grocery store, greatly hindering opportunities for them to participate in community activities. Comprehensive intervention plans were designed based on assessment data unique to each participant, and consisted of strategies including: Functional Communication Training (Carr and Durand, 1985), that is, teaching alternative communicative behaviors that are functionally equivalent to the problem behavior (e.g., teaching the individual to request a desired item by saying "I want the cookies," rather than by engaging in self-injury); providing access to preferred items during difficult tasks; and increasing opportunities for making choices during disliked activities. Following implementation of the intervention, all three participants were able to successfully complete the grocery shopping routine without engaging in problem behavior.

In summary, there is mounting evidence revealing the efficacy of assessment-driven, *contextually appropriate* interventions, implemented to reduce disruptive behaviors in a variety of settings, and, importantly, to teach adaptive skills that enhance engagement and enable successful participation in valued routines.

Behaviorally based treatments are not the only type of intervention used to address problematic behavior displayed by individuals with ASD. In the next section, we explore the second major treatment method, namely psychotropic medication.

Pharmacological Intervention

The other main approach to intervention aimed at reducing or eliminating problem behavior is pharmacological. There is a rapidly expanding literature examining the use of different classes of psychotropic medications to treat severe problem behavior displayed by individuals with ASD (Coury *et al.*, 2012; Doyle and McDougle, 2012; RUPP, 2002, 2005; Shea *et al.*, 2004; Siegel and Beaulieu, 2012). Psychotropic medications include any agent that is prescribed to stabilize or improve mood, mental status, or behavior (Julien, 2003). Examples of the various classes of psychotropic drugs commonly used with children and adults diagnosed with ASD include: antipsychotics (e.g., risperidone, aripiprazole), antidepressants (e.g., fluoxetine, paroxetine), anxiolytics (e.g., lorazepam, diazepam), stimulants (e.g., methylphenidate), and mood stabilizers (e.g., carbamazepine, oxcarbamazepine).

Studies have revealed that the use of these medications to treat both children and adults with autism has steadily increased over the past several decades, with the atypical antipsychotic agents representing the class of medication that has evidenced the most significant increase in rate of prescription (Cornell, 2008; Mandell *et al.*, 2008; Matson and Neal, 2009; Schubart, Camacho, and Leslie, 2014). Reported rates of psychotropic medication use among children and adolescents diagnosed with ASD range from 27 to 83% (Coury *et al.*, 2012; Rosenberg *et al.*, 2010; Tureck *et al.*, 2013), with high rates of polypharmacy, that is, the use of more than one type of psychotropic medication concurrently, correlating with more severe behavior and significant challenges (Comer, Olfson, and Mojtabi, 2010). Spencer and colleagues (2015) conducted a large-scale, retrospective study to examine rates of psychotropic medication use and multiclass polypharmacy among children diagnosed with ASD. Over 33,000 children were included in this investigation, and results indicate that 64% had been administered at least one psychotropic drug, 35% had been prescribed two or more medications in different classes, and 15% used three or more medications from different classes concurrently.

Findings from other studies investigating prescribing trends for individuals with ASD suggest that once psychotropic medications are prescribed, there is a high likelihood that the person will remain on those drugs for many years (Esbensen *et al.*, 2009). Additionally, the use of psychotropic medications with children and adolescents diagnosed with ASD has been found to increase with age; thus, as they get older, people with autism are more likely to be treated with one or more psychotropic medications (Aman, Lam, and Van Bourgondien, 2005). Similarly, individuals with more severe forms of autism who have more significant communication and cognitive impairments are also more frequently treated with multiple psychotropic medications used concurrently.

While pharmacological treatments have not been found to be particularly effective in addressing the core characteristics of ASD, there is mounting evidence documenting the benefits of several classes of psychotropic medications in the treatment of comorbid conditions, including serious types of problem behavior (Cornell, 2008; DeLeon *et al.*, 2009; McCracken *et al.*, 2002; Stigler *et al.*, 2009). A number of large-scale, multisite, placebo-controlled studies have been conducted in recent years demonstrating the efficacy of the antipsychotic medications risperidone and aripiprazole in reducing severe problem behavior displayed by children with autism (Marcus *et al.*, 2009; Owen *et al.*, 2009; RUPP, 2002; Shea *et al.*, 2004). Consequently, the U.S. Food and Drug Administration has approved both of these medications for use with children and adolescents for the treatment of aggression, irritability, and agitation associated with ASD (U.S. Food and Drug Administration, 2006, 2009).

As research examining a varied range of psychotropic agents continues to amass, it remains quite common for non-indicated medications to be prescribed in an "off-label," trial-and-error manner to help address problem behavior displayed by those with ASD (Esbensen *et al.*, 2009; Zito *et al.*, 2008). Clearly, additional research investigating the wide gamut of medications that are being administered to this population is needed.

Medication Side Effects

Although psychotropic medications are frequently used as a primary treatment for severe problem behavior, it is important to note that, in addition to their main effects, these drugs are often associated with an array of adverse secondary effects (Cohen *et al.*, 2012; Hess *et al.*, 2010; Jerrell and McIntyre, 2008). Side effects are considered *significant* or problematic due to their frequency and potential severity, particularly with respect to the impact these accompanying symptoms have on the quality of life of the individual being treated. The intensity of a given side effect ranges from mild to severe, and temporally, a side effect may be experienced as an acute event, lasting a relatively short period of time following drug administration and then subsiding, or it may be experienced in a more chronic manner, whereby side effects persist throughout the duration of medication treatment. For instance, increased appetite and subsequent weight gain are common side effects of antipsychotic drugs that tend to be long lasting, with individuals reportedly experiencing greater levels of hunger throughout the day upon starting the drug treatment. This increased appetite that occurs on a daily basis for many individuals taking antipsychotic agents often causes them to eat more food throughout the day, which, in turn, leads to a substantial increase in weight within a relatively short period of time.

Side effects can be transient; that is, the individual experiences more intense symptoms when they first start taking the drug, but the adverse effects become less pronounced and not as bothersome over time as they continue to take the medication. Alternatively, side effects can be more permanent symptoms, such as motor tics or tremors, which tend to persist even after the medication is discontinued (Matson and Hess, 2011).

The pharmacological literature generally describes the side effects of medications as an array of physical symptoms such as sedation, dry mouth, constipation, and dizziness (Jerrell *et al.*, 2008; Martin *et al.*, 2004; Preston, O'Neal, and Talaga, 2009). For example, studies have shown that fatigue, increased appetite/weight gain, and dizziness were the most common side effects experienced by children with ASD who were administered antipsychotic medication to treat aggression and SIB (Cohen *et al.*, 2012; Hellings *et al.*, 2001; Matson and Mahan, 2010; McCracken *et al.*, 2002). Additionally, it has been found that many medications can produce a variety of side effects that are affective in nature, including increased anxiety, elevated irritability and agitation, and changes in mood. For example, stimulant medications, commonly prescribed to treat inattention and hyperactivity, have been found to produce affective side effects such as intense mood swings and increased irritability and crankiness (Doyle and McDougle, 2012). Carlson and Kelly (2003) described what is anecdotally referred to as a "rebound effect" of stimulant medication, in the form of behavioral deterioration once the drug's intended effects wear off. Children experiencing this rebound effect reportedly became more irritable and moody during the late afternoon/early evening hours, coinciding with the time when their medications were wearing off.

The profiles of side effects tend to vary with each class of medication and may even differ for specific agents within the same drug class. Similarly, the presence, absence, and manifestation of medication side effects can vary for each person taking a given drug (Julien, 2003). Importantly, individuals with ASD experience the same array of side effects that accompany psychotropic medications as the general population; however, they may in fact be more susceptible to the negative impact of these drug-induced symptoms (Hess *et al.*, 2010).

The presence of side effects may be difficult to ascertain, given the communication and cognitive skill challenges that are often associated with ASD. Communication difficulties can greatly complicate medication treatment, as individuals may lack the ability to self-report or to communicate their thoughts, emotions, and internal states. For instance, they may be unable to let others know when they are experiencing drug-induced symptoms such as increased fatigue, dizziness, or gastric discomfort. Moreover, individuals with limited ability to communicate that they are experiencing drug side effects may display behaviors that mimic the underlying condition the medication is targeting. Thus, a boy prescribed medication to reduce high rates of self-injurious behavior may experience drug-induced gastric discomfort approximately 30 minutes after they take their medication, yet because he is unable to alert his caregiver that he is in pain, he becomes increasingly agitated and subsequently displays even greater levels of self-injury.

Studies have shown that polypharmacy exacerbates side effects (Mahan *et al.*, 2010; Matson and Neal, 2009); individuals taking more than one psychotropic medication from different drug classes (e.g., antipsychotics and antidepressants) are more likely to experience a greater number of side effects (Hess *et al.*, 2010). Additionally, as the number of medications administered to an individual increases, he or she is more likely to experience more frequent and severe secondary symptoms. Therefore, given the widespread practice of polypharmacy with this population, closer examination of the secondary, unintended effects of drugs is clearly warranted.

Although a wide array of symptoms have been identified as side effects in both the research and in clinical practice, the majority of studies investigating medication side effects have primarily focused on the more severe and permanent adverse events such as tardive dyskinesia, motor tics, and tremors (Jerrell and McIntyre, 2008; Matson and Hess, 2011). There is a need for empirical studies that closely examine other, more commonly experienced side effects such as fatigue, increased appetite, and gastrointestinal pain or discomfort, as many of these *same* symptoms have been noted in the behavioral literature, where they are referred to as *biological setting events*, and, as previously noted, these factors have been found to be associated with greater levels of problem behavior.

Does a Paradox Exist?

Given the parallels that clearly exist between the contextual variables that are described in the behavioral field and the symptoms identified in the pharmacological field as side effects of psychotropic drugs, it is plausible that medication side effects actually function as biological setting events, producing elevated levels of problem behavior. For instance, Bosch and colleagues (1997) reported that individuals experiencing abdominal pain resulting from severe constipation displayed higher rates of self-injury and aggression. Significantly, gastrointestinal disturbances producing pain and discomfort (e.g., abdominal pain, nausea, and constipation) have been documented in the pharmacological literature as commonly occurring side effects of various medications (Julien, 2003). Conceivably, these side effects, as well as numerous others that frequently accompany psychotropic drugs, could operate in the same manner as non-drug-induced pain and discomfort, in that they make specific activities and routines more aversive than they would typically be, thereby increasing the likelihood that problem behavior will be displayed. Therefore, *it may be the case that medication side effects paradoxically exacerbate problem behavior by functioning as setting events in specific contexts.*

The typical cycle of events that tend to occur when medication is used to treat serious problem behavior is presented in Figure 5.2. To illustrate this seemingly paradoxical sequence of events, consider an example of a child who displays high rates of self-injury and is prescribed a psychotropic medication (e.g., risperidone) to treat it. This drug, as with all psychotropic medications, is accompanied by side effects (e.g., increased appetite/weight gain, fatigue), and these symptoms, presumably functioning as biological setting events, make certain home and community routines more difficult for the child to complete, which in turn causes the child to display increased levels of problem behavior in those contexts. As a result, during a follow-up visit with the family to assess the child's response to the medication, the physician may decide to increase the dosage of the drug. This modification to the medication regimen consequently leads back to the start of the paradoxical cycle, as a higher dose of the drug will likely intensify the side effects, further impacting particular activities when the symptoms are present, ultimately resulting in an exacerbation of the problem behavior. Alternatively, the physician may decide to add another medication to the child's regimen instead of altering the dosage of the original drug. This scenario may also set off the cycle of events displayed in Figure 5.2, as this second medication presumably has side effects associated with it, which can compromise the successful completion of certain home and community routines, further contributing to this paradoxical effect of producing elevated levels of problematic behavior.

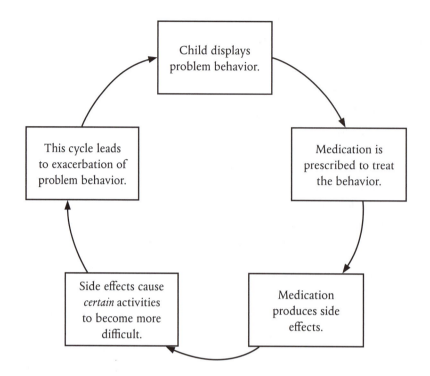

Figure 5.2 The Pharmacological Treatment of
Problem Behavior: A Potential Paradox

CASE 1: Emma

To provide an additional illustration of this proposed paradox, consider the case of Emma, an adolescent girl who displayed significant self-injurious behavior during grooming activities on days when she experienced fatigue. Consider the possibility that due to the severity of the self-injury she exhibited, she is prescribed a psychotropic medication that is accompanied by several side effects, including increased levels of fatigue. This symptom presumably functions in a manner similar to fatigue caused by a lack of sleep (described previously as a biological setting event), and accordingly makes certain tasks, such as taking a shower, more challenging than usual, ultimately resulting in an exacerbation of the self-injurious behavior that the medication treatment is targeting. Therefore, escape from the aversive task, via self-injury (i.e., biting her hands and scratching her face), becomes more reinforcing for Emma; hence, in the future, the combination of drug-induced fatigue and task demands is more likely to set off subsequent self-injurious behavior (see Figure 5.1, line C). *Paradoxically, the drug given to treat the self-injurious behavior sets in motion a process that culminates in even greater levels of problem behavior, in certain contexts.* This outcome argues for a closer examination of how individuals respond to the particular medications they are given, including assessment of potential drug side effects.

Assessing Medication Side Effects

While several assessment measures have been designed to evaluate the side effects of medications, including the Abnormal Involuntary Movement Scale (AIMS) (Guy, 1976), the Monitoring of Side Effects System (MOSES) (Kalachnik, 1986), and the Matson Evaluation of Drug Side Effects (MEDS) (Matson *et al.*, 1998), the majority of these tools tend to focus on the more serious and permanent musculoskeletal effects. There are relatively few measures that assess the broader array of the more common physiological and affective side effects noted in the literature, such as fatigue, appetite changes, and irritability. Moreover, there are few, if any, measures that take into account the *context* in which the side effects occur, that is, the potential impact that these untoward symptoms may have when present in certain activities and routines. Essentially, medication side effects have been "decontextualized" in both the literature and in clinical practice, despite the growing evidence of the significant role that context plays in producing problem behavior (Luiselli and Cameron, 1998; McAtee, Carr, and Schulte, 2004). As a result, potentially valuable information about side effects is most likely not included in the assessment process, thereby hindering the overall efficacy of the interventions targeting severe problem behavior.

A Programmatic Line of Emerging Research Examining the Proposed Paradox

Currently, the most widely used instruments evaluating drug side effects provide a somewhat limited picture of these symptoms. Thus, in an effort to extend previous work in this area and to expand upon the assessment measures that already exist, the Structured Interview for the Assessment of Medication Side Effects (SIAMSE) was created (J.D. Bleiweiss and E.G. Carr, unpublished). This tool was designed to be a comprehensive yet user-friendly measure that assesses the broad array of commonly occurring side effects of psychotropic medications in a *contextualized* manner, to determine whether they negatively impact everyday home and community routines. Derived from existing scales, as well as from input from experts in the fields of psychiatry, pharmacology, and psychology, the SIAMSE is a semistructured interview consisting of a combination of open-ended questions, as well as items rated on a five-point Likert scale. Primarily intended for use with parents or caregivers, this measure provides a finer-grained analysis of medication side effects, such as fatigue or gastrointestinal discomfort, by systematically assessing the context in which these symptoms occur in order to see if they are correlated with increased problem behavior, as would be predicted by a setting-events model. (A copy of the SIAMSE is included in Appendix C.)

Findings from an initial study of the SIAMSE demonstrated the utility of this measure, in that it provides practitioners with a means of collecting a great deal of contextualized information that may reveal a more complete picture about the behaviors that pharmacological treatments target. In turn, this may facilitate the treatment-planning process and lead to more effective practices that produce positive and lasting outcomes. Moreover, results suggest that there is a strong association between the presence of medication side effects and an elevation in the level of problem behavior that was displayed. The SIAMSE was administered to parents who had a child who was taking psychotropic medication to treat severe problem behavior. Parents reported that since starting the medication regimen, their child appeared to be experiencing drug-induced symptoms, such as increased sedation, changes in appetite, or gastrointestinal discomfort. Furthermore, they noted that when these side effects were present, their child had much more difficulty participating in certain home-based routines and/or activities in the community, often resulting in an exacerbation of problem behavior displayed in those contexts.

Interestingly, parents indicated that only *some* routines had become more problematic since starting the medication. In no instances did the parents participating in this study report that all activities had become more challenging for their child to complete. Thus, the medication may indeed have had a positive global effect in reducing the child's overall level of problem behavior; however, in certain contexts, there was evidence of the paradoxical effect (described earlier in this chapter). Essentially, findings from this study suggest that medication side effects may in fact function as biological setting events in particular contexts, contributing to an escalation of problematic behavior.

A Context-Based Approach to Assessment and Intervention of Medication Side Effects

Following the development of the SIAMSE, we took our work a step further and conducted a series of assessment and intervention studies that aimed to experimentally demonstrate the proposed paradox related to medication side effects and problem behavior (J.D. Bleiweiss and E.G. Carr, unpublished). Specifically, the association between drug side effects, compromised performance in common home and community routines, and elevated levels of problem behavior was investigated. A second goal of this research was to evaluate the efficacy of implementing a context-based model of intervention to reduce problem behavior exhibited in select family routines when medication side effects were present and seemingly functioning as setting events. A comprehensive assessment of problematic activities was conducted, and the SIAMSE was administered to participating families, enabling a thorough examination of the potential impact that medication side effects had on those contexts, as well as the mechanisms involved in evoking problem behavior. Uniquely tailored intervention packages, comprising empirically validated behavioral strategies, were designed and implemented to address the problematic home or community-based activities identified by each family. These multicomponent plans, developed in collaboration with each family, consisted of a variety of mitigation strategies and coping techniques.

Mitigation strategies utilized in this study included procedures in which parents were taught ways to modify aspects of the problematic context; they included the use of visual supports, such as activity schedules and timers, as well as choice-making and embedding techniques. The use of visual activity schedules involves visually representing the activities that will occur throughout the day, or depicting the specific sequence of steps involved in a particular task or routine, using pictures or written words. Timers are another effective form of visual support, as they can be used to indicate the amount of time remaining in a disliked or difficult routine, or they can signal an upcoming transition, or the end of a preferred activity. Visual supports have been found to be highly effective in reducing problem behavior displayed by individuals with ASD, as they enhance predictability and make activities and tasks easier to complete (Dettmer *et al.*, 2000; Flannery and Horner, 1994; Lequia, Machalicek, and Rispoli, 2012).

Embedding is a strategy that involves providing an individual with access to preferred items or activities during disliked or difficult tasks, and has been found to be associated with significant decreases in problem behavior displayed by individuals with autism (Blair, Umbreit, and Bos, 1999; Dunlap *et al.*, 1991). Similarly, providing individuals with opportunities to make choices during challenging tasks has been found to effectively reduce problematic behavior exhibited in home and community settings (Bambara *et al.*, 1995; Kern *et al.*, 2001; Shogren *et al.*, 2004). These techniques enhance motivation by increasing interest and promoting active engagement during difficult or unpleasant activities. Additionally, these strategies can be particularly effective in preventing challenging behavior associated with medication side effects that cause physical discomfort, as gaining access to a preferred item can be quite comforting for the child and may serve as a way of shifting their attention away from the unpleasant symptoms they are experiencing.

In the case of mitigation strategies, it is the *adult* (e.g., parent, teacher) who is the driving force responsible for directly implementing strategies and modifying aspects of the environment that may be problematic, in an effort to remediate challenging behavior. However, in the case of coping-skill strategies, it is the *child* who acquires the alternative skills that essentially replace the maladaptive behavior. Thus, coping-skill strategies used in this line of research involved an instructional component, whereby the child was taught to use a variety of adaptive skills to more appropriately get his or her needs met, and included functional communication training (Carr and Durand, 1985; Reichle, Drager, and Davis, 2002) and a variety of relaxation techniques (Cautela and Groden, 1978; Mullins and Christian, 2001; Steen and Zuriff, 1977). These alternative and more adaptive sets of skills impact the problematic context by eventually generating stimuli for appropriate (non-problem) behavior. In illustration, a child who communicates "It's too noisy and crowded!" in response to a loud and crowded setting may influence her parent to alter the problematic context (e.g., lowering the level of noise that she is exposed to, or taking the child to a quieter location, thereby reducing the likelihood that problem behavior will be displayed). Similarly, a child who experiences heightened anxiety or distress in response to an unexpected change in his schedule could be taught to use deep-breathing exercises to help him calm down and more effectively cope with the distress he feels when his schedule is disrupted. Coping strategies have been found to be effective in not only reducing problem behavior but also in engendering a sense of empowerment and increased control over one's environment, which are meaningful outcomes often overlooked in the treatment of individuals with ASD (Wehmeyer, Kelchner, and Richards, 1996).

Following the implementation of the multicomponent intervention packages, all families who participated were able to engage in and more successfully complete highly valued routines that, prior to treatment, had been extremely problematic due to the presence of medication side effects and problem behavior. Across all participants, the percentage of task steps completed in the specified contexts substantially increased following intervention, and the latency for the termination of the activity due to problem behavior was greatly reduced, as families were able to successfully complete their identified routines.

Interestingly, parents reported that the level of intensity of the various drug-induced symptoms experienced by their child did not significantly change over the course of the study. In other words, a majority of the medication side effects that were identified in the initial assessment continued to be present at elevated levels of intensity throughout the baseline and intervention. Importantly, following intervention, the *negative impact* of these symptoms did appear to diminish, as evidenced by reductions in parents' ratings of the level of difficulty that was experienced, as well as by substantial reductions in the ratings of the level of severity of problem behavior displayed by all participants in these contexts. Moreover, evidence of more global reductions in problem behavior and significant improvements in family quality of life was noted for all participants. Families reported a decrease in the number of routines that they considered problematic due to the negative impact of side effects, and significantly, each family noted an increase in the number of activities they were able to successfully participate in upon completion of the study.

CASE 2: Ellie

To illustrate the possible mechanisms by which medication side effects may function as setting events for problem behavior in commonly occurring family routines and, importantly, to demonstrate how behavioral interventions could be utilized to address problem behavior in those contexts, consider the following example of one of the participants involved in the studies. Ellie was an 11-year-old girl diagnosed with autism who had a history of engaging in severe self-injurious behavior that was treated using a combination of psychotropic medications. According to her mother, Ellie experienced a variety of side effects including marked fatigue, heightened irritability, and agitation, as well as a significant increase in her appetite and subsequent weight gain since going on the medication. Her mother noted that when these symptoms were present, they appeared to make certain outings in the community, such as going to the grocery store, much more difficult for Ellie, and consequently led to an exacerbation of self-injurious behavior that she displayed during this valued family activity. Presumably, the medication side effects functioned as setting events for Ellie's problem behavior in this context. In other words, these symptoms, when present, increased the aversiveness of the grocery shopping routine, thereby strengthening any behavior that reliably allowed her to escape the difficult activity. Additionally, given that Ellie's appetite had substantially increased since going on the medication, as evidenced by her increased food consumption throughout the day and the tendency for her to display elevated levels of problem behavior when she was denied access to (or had to wait for) a desired food item, it is likely that the self-injury she displayed during outings to the grocery store may have also functioned as a means of gaining access to desired items (i.e., food). Accordingly, being in the grocery store became exceedingly problematic, as the increased hunger that she experienced enhanced the reinforcing potential of food that was readily accessible at the grocery store, making it much more likely that Ellie would engage in problem behavior in order to gain access to food items she desired.

Although going to the grocery store had previously been an activity that Ellie enjoyed, it had become increasingly more challenging for her to successfully complete since going on the medication regimen; thus, this routine was selected as the priority context and became the primary focus of the intervention. Given the aversiveness of this activity within the context of increased fatigue and hunger, it was logical to implement several mitigation strategies to reduce some of the difficulty Ellie experienced when these side effects were present. A visual schedule (depicting the sequence of steps involved in the activity) was used throughout the grocery store routine to make it easier and more predictable. Embedding was used to address difficulties related to the elevated level of fatigue and the physical discomfort associated with increased hunger that she experienced during the shopping routine. Her parents noted that listening to music was a highly preferred activity for Ellie; thus, she was provided with an MP3 player with headphones that she could use throughout the activity. Additionally, she was able to choose a highly preferred snack item that she could eat while she appropriately participated in the shopping routine. Providing access to desired items of food while shopping presumably reduced some of the aversiveness experienced during the activity and undermined the necessity for escape-motivated problem behavior. A coping strategy was also included in the intervention package, as Ellie was taught a more appropriate method to manage difficulties associated with having to wait in line during the final step in the grocery store routine. Specifically, Ellie was taught to use a deep-breathing exercise to help reduce some of the distress she experienced when side effects were present and she had to wait in the checkout line.

Following the implementation of the multicomponent intervention, Ellie's parents noted considerable improvements in her behavior during the grocery store routine, as evidenced by substantial reductions in the ratings of the level of severity of self-injurious behavior displayed in this context. Moreover, her parents reported that Ellie was able to take part in other home and community activities, and they found that they were able to modify the strategies designed for the grocery store routine and effectively implement them during other activities to reduce the difficulty she experienced when side effects were present.

Implications of a Context-Based Approach to Assessment and Intervention of Side Effects

Findings from this initial line of programmatic research support previous work demonstrating the effectiveness of utilizing a context-based approach to the assessment and intervention of severe problem behavior (Carr and Blakeley-Smith, 2006; Carr *et al.*, 2003; Lucyshyn *et al.*, 2007). Significantly, the use of multicomponent intervention plans composed of both mitigation and coping strategies represents a fundamental shift in the way we approach the treatment of challenging behaviors, as it enables us to adjust our focus from *just managing problem behavior* to *remediating problematic contexts*, which consequently augments the number of efficacious treatment options that are available. Moreover, these preliminary studies serve to highlight the benefits of conducting a comprehensive and "contextualized" analysis of medication side effects in order to determine the potential impact these symptoms may have in relation to the broader context in which they occur. In an effort to help facilitate this process of systematically assessing medication side effects in a contextualized manner, the Structured Interview for the Assessment of Medication Side Effects (SIAMSE) was developed (J.D. Bleiweiss and E.G. Carr, unpublished).

Given the parallels between the side effects of psychotropic medication and biological setting events, broad contextual variables often associated with increased problem behavior, it seems plausible that the untoward drug-induced symptoms function in much the same way as setting events in increasing the aversiveness of certain activities, and paradoxically cause an exacerbation of problem behavior. Thus, it may be beneficial to use a model that conceptualizes medication side effects as biological setting events, as it enhances our understanding of the mechanisms involved in triggering and maintaining the problem behavior and enables us to develop more targeted, context-based interventions that are effective and long lasting.

Such a conceptualization has direct implications for improving our treatment practices and potentially increases the number of treatment options available to treat severe problem behavior. As previously noted, psychotropic medications often do have a beneficial impact on problem behavior; however, the side effects of these drugs may interfere with the positive outcome because they function as setting events for subsequent problem behavior, thereby obscuring or muting some of the intended benefits of the medication. Therefore, it would seem advantageous to use a combination of pharmacological and behavioral approaches, whereby the drugs would address the initially targeted problem behavior and the behavioral interventions would be used to address the side effects. Plausibly, this combination approach could actually enhance the efficacy of the medication in reducing problem behavior, as the primary effect of the drug would no longer be compromised by the presence of the untoward symptoms.

Precedents exist in both the attention deficit hyperactivity disorder (ADHD) and depression literature demonstrating the efficacy of a combination approach to intervention (Conners *et al.*, 2001; Kellner *et al.*, 2000; Klein *et al.*, 2004; Safren *et al.*, 2005). Findings from a number of studies conducted with individuals diagnosed with depression have suggested that the combination of pharmacological and behavioral treatments may be more effective than either treatment alone (Bernstein *et al.*, 2000; Kellner *et al.*, 2000). Similar results have been found in studies investigating interventions for children and adolescents diagnosed with ADHD, highlighting the efficacy of the combination of medication and behavioral interventions (Cuijpers, van Straten, and Andersson, 2009; Safren *et al.*, 2005). Conceivably, the same may be true for problem behavior displayed by individuals with ASD, suggesting that researchers and clinicians in both disciplines may wish to devote their efforts toward greater collaboration and adopt a multimodal approach to treatment of problem behavior associated with autism. Behavioral treatments may improve outcomes on some symptoms, and medication may improve outcomes on others; thus, both approaches would be necessary to maximize meaningful and long-lasting behavior change.

While intervention efforts in the pharmacological and behavioral fields have shared a similar focus in that both areas ultimately seek to reduce problem behavior, differences in training, technical jargon, and publication venues have had the effect of limiting opportunities for collaboration and sharing knowledge across these fields. Rather than continuing to work in isolation, it would seem logical and quite beneficial for professionals from these areas to begin working in tandem, and biological setting events may be aptly suited to serve as a bridge concept to help unite these traditionally disparate fields. Conceptualizing medication side effects as biological setting events accordingly enables us to design efficacious treatments that combine pharmacological methods and behavioral strategies, providing a unique opportunity for genuine collaboration in an effort to improve the lives of individuals with autism and their loved ones.

Conclusion

Given the complex nature of problem behavior frequently displayed by individuals with autism, a great deal of research and clinical effort has been devoted to the development of effective assessment and intervention methods available to address this clinically significant issue. Although a number of psychotropic medications have been used with this population, these drugs are often accompanied by a variety of adverse side effects, which may negatively impact valued family routines, and paradoxically increase problem behavior. Thus, there is a critical need for us to more closely examine commonly occurring side effects in a contextualized manner, in order to bolster our understanding of the mechanisms involved in evoking problem behavior. A model that conceptualizes drug side effects as setting events for problem behavior may help to improve our assessment and intervention practices by enabling us to develop more efficacious treatments that bridge the gap between the behavioral and pharmacological fields and ultimately yield more robust and enduring positive outcomes for individuals with autism and their families.

References

Aman, M.G., Lam, K.S.L., and Van Bourgondien, M.E. (2005). Medication patterns in patients with autism: Temporal, regional, and demographic influences. *Journal of Child and Adolescent Psychopharmacology, 15,* 116–126.

American Psychiatric Association (2000). *Diagnostic and Statistical Manual of Mental Disorders* (4th ed., text revision). Washington, DC: American Psychiatric Association.

Bambara, L.M., Koger, F., Katzer, T., and Davenport, T.A. (1995). Embedding choice in the context of daily routines: An experimental case study. *Journal of the Association for Persons with Severe Handicaps, 20,* 185–195.

Bernstein, G.A., Bordrandt, C.M., Perwien, A.R., Crosby, R.D., *et al.* (2000). Imipramine plus cognitive behavior therapy in the treatment of school refusal. *Journal of the American Academy of Child and Adolescent Psychiatry, 39,* 276–283.

Bijou, S.W., and Baer, D.M. (1961). *Child Development I: A Systematic and Empirical Theory.* Englewood Cliffs, NJ: Prentice-Hall.

Blair, K.C., Umbreit, J., and Bos, C.S. (1999). Using functional assessment and children's preferences to improve the behavior of young children with behavioral disorders. *Behavioral Disorders, 24,* 151–166.

Bosch, J., Van Dyke, D.C., Milligan Smith, S., and Poulton, S. (1997). Role of medical conditions in the exacerbation of self-injurious behavior: An exploratory study. *Mental Retardation, 35,* 124–130.

Bruininks, R.H., Hill, B.K., and Morreau, L.E. (1988). Prevalence and Implications of Maladaptive Behaviors and Dual Diagnosis in Residential and Other Service Programs. In J.A. Stark, F.J. Menolascino, M.H. Albarelli, and V.C. Gray (Eds.), *Mental Retardation and Mental Health: Classification, Diagnosis, Treatment Services.* New York, NY: Springer-Verlag.

Carlson, G.A., and Kelly, K.L. (2003). Stimulant rebound: How common is it and what does it mean? *Journal of Child and Adolescent Psychopharmacology, 13*(2), 137–142.

Carr, E.G., and Blakeley-Smith, A. (2006). Classroom intervention for illness-related problem behavior in children with developmental disabilities. *Behavior Modification, 30,* 1–22.

Carr, E.G., and Carlson, J.L. (1993). Reduction of severe problem behavior in the community using a multicomponent treatment approach. *Journal of Applied Behavior Analysis, 26,* 157–172.

Carr, E.G., and Durand, V.M. (1985). Reducing behavior problems through functional communication training. *Journal of Applied Behavior Analysis, 18,* 111–126.

Carr, E.G., Horner, R.H., Turnbull, A.P., Marquis, J.G., et al. (1999). *Positive Behavior Support for People with Developmental Disabilities: A Research Synthesis.* Washington, DC: American Association on Mental Retardation.

Carr, E.G., Newsom, C.D., and Binkoff, J.A. (1980). Escape as a factor in the aggressive behavior of two retarded children. *Journal of Applied Behavior Analysis, 13,* 101–117.

Carr, E.G., and Smith, C.E. (1995). Biological setting events for self-injury. *Mental Retardation and Developmental Disabilities Research Reviews, 1,* 94–98.

Carr, E.G., Smith, C.E., Giacin, T.A., Whelan, B.M., and Pancari, J. (2003). Menstrual discomfort as a biological setting event for severe problem behavior: Assessment and intervention. *American Journal on Mental Retardation, 108,* 117–133.

Cautela, J.R., and Groden, J. (1978). *Relaxation: A Comprehensive Manual for Adults, Children, and Children with Special Needs.* Champaign, IL: Research Press.

Clarke, S., Dunlap, G., and Vaughn, B. (1999). Family-centered, assessment-based intervention to improve behavior during an early morning routine. *Journal of Positive Behavior Interventions, 1,* 235–241.

Cohen, D., Bonnot, O., Bodeau, N., Consoli, A., and Laurent, C. (2012). Adverse effects of second generation antipsychotics in children and adolescents: A meta-analysis. *Journal of Clinical Psychopharmacology, 32,* 309–316.

Comer, J.S., Olfson, M., and Mojtabi, R. (2010). National trends in child and adolescent psychotropic polypharmacy in office-based practice, 1996–2007. *Journal of the American Academy of Child and Adolescent Psychiatry, 49,* 1001–1010.

Conners, C.K., Epstein, J.N., March, J.S., Angold, A., et al. (2001). Multimodal treatment of ADHD in the MTA: An alternative outcome analysis. *Journal of the American Academy of Child and Adolescent Psychiatry, 40*(2), 159–167.

Cooper, S.A., Smiley, E., Jackson, A., Finlayson, J., et al. (2009). Adults with intellectual disabilities: Prevalence, incidence and remission of aggressive behavior and related factors. *Journal of Intellectual Disability Research, 53,* 217–232.

Cornell, C.U. (2008). Antipsychotic use in children and adolescents: Minimizing adverse effects to maximize outcomes. *Journal of the American Academy of Child and Adolescent Psychiatry, 47,* 9–20.

Coury, D.L., Anagnostou, E., Manning-Courtney, P., Reynolds, A., et al. (2012). Use of psychotropic medication in children and adolescents with autism spectrum disorders. *Pediatrics, 130*(Suppl. 2), S69–S76.

Cuijpers, P., van Straten, A., and Andersson, G. (2009). Psychotherapy versus the combination of psychotherapy and pharmacotherapy in the treatment of depression: A meta-analysis. *Depression and Anxiety, 26*(3), 279–288.

Davis, D.H. (1987). Issues in the Development of a Recreational Program for Autistic Individuals with Severe Cognitive and Behavioral Disorders. In D.J. Cohen and A.M. Donnelan (Eds.), *Handbook of Autism and Pervasive Developmental Disorders.* Silver Spring, MD: V.H. Winston and Sons.

Davis, N.O., and Carter, A.S. (2008). Parenting stress in mothers and fathers of toddlers with autism spectrum disorders: Associations with child characteristics. *Journal of Autism Developmental Disorders, 38,* 1278–1291.

DeLeon, L., Greenlee, B., Barber, J., Sabaawi, M., and Singh, N.N. (2009). Practical guidelines for the use of new generation antipsychotic drugs (except clozapine) in adult individuals with intellectual disabilities. *Research in Developmental Disabilities, 30,* 613–669.

Dettmer, S., Simpson, R.L., Myles, B.S., and Ganz, J.L. (2000). The use of visual supports to facilitate transitions of students with autism. *Focus on Autism and Other Developmental Disabilities, 15,* 1631–1639.

Doss, L.S., and Reichle, J. (1991). Replacing Excess Behavior with an Initial Communicative Repertoire. In J. Reichle, J. York, and J. Sigafoos (Eds.), *Implementing Augmentative and Alternative Communication: Strategies for Learners with Severe Disabilities.* Baltimore, MD: Paul H. Brookes.

Doyle, C.A., and McDougle, C.J. (2012). Pharmacological treatments for the behavioral symptoms associated with autism spectrum disorders across the lifespan. *Dialogues in Clinical Neuroscience, 14,* 263–279.

Dunlap, G., Kern-Dunlap, L., Clarke, S., and Robbins, F.R. (1991). Functional assessment, curricular revision, and severe behavior problems. *Journal of Applied Behavior Analysis, 24,* 387–397.

Emerson, E., Kiernan, C., Alborz, A., Reeves, *et al.* (2001). The prevalence of challenging behaviors: A total population study. *Research in Developmental Disabilities, 22,* 77–93.

Esbensen, A.J., Greenberg, J.S., Seltzer, M.M., and Aman, M.G. (2009). A longitudinal investigation of psychotropic and non-psychotropic medication use among adolescents and adults with autism spectrum disorders. *Journal of Autism and Developmental Disorders, 39,* 1339–1349.

Fee, V.E., and Matson, J.L. (1992). Definition, Classification, and Taxonomy. In J.K. Luiselli, J.L. Matson, and N.N. Singh (Eds.), *Self-Injurious Behavior: Analysis, Assessment, and Treatment.* New York, NY: Springer-Verlag.

Flannery, K.B., and Horner, R.H. (1994). The relationship between predictability and problem behavior for students with severe disabilities. *Journal of Behavioral Education, 4,* 157–176.

Guy, W. (1976). *ECDEU Assessment Manual for Psychopharmacology.* DHEW Publication No. 76-338. Rockville, MD: National Institute of Mental Health.

Hayes, S.A., and Watson, S. (2013). The impact of parenting stress: A meta-analysis of studies comparing the experience of parenting stress in parents of children with and without autism spectrum disorder. *Journal of Autism and Developmental Disorders, 43*(3), 629–642.

Hellings, J.A., Zarcone, J.R., Crandall, K., Wallace, D., and Schroeder, S.R. (2001). Weight gain in a controlled study of risperidone in children, adolescents, and adults with mental retardation and autism. *Journal of Child and Adolescent Psychopharmacology, 11*(3), 229–238.

Hess, J., Matson, J.L., Neal, D., Mahan, S., *et al.* (2010). A comparison of psychotropic drug side effect profiles in adults diagnosed with intellectual disabilities and autism spectrum disorders. *Journal of Mental Health Research in Intellectual Disabilities, 3,* 85–96.

Horner, R.H., Carr, E.G., Strain, P.S., Todd, A.W., and Reed, H.K. (2002). Problem behavior interventions for young children with autism: A research synthesis for the National Academy of Sciences. *Journal of Autism and Developmental Disorders, 32,* 423–446.

Jerrell, J.M., and McIntyre, R.S. (2008). Adverse events in children and adolescents treated with antipsychotic medications. *Human Psychopharmacology, 23,* 283–290.

Julien, R.M. (2003). *A Primer of Drug Action* (10th ed.). New York, NY: Worth Publishers.

Kalachnik, J. (1986). Assessment Sheet for Monitoring of Side-Effects System (MOSES). In A. Poling, K. Gadow, and J. Cleary (Eds.), *Drug Therapy for Behavior Disorders: An Introduction.* New York, NY: Pergamon Press.

Kantor, J.R. (1959). *Interbehavioral Psychology.* Granville, OH: Principia Press.

Kellner, R.B., McCullough, J.P., Klein, D.N., Arnow, B., *et al.* (2000). A comparison of nefazodone, the cognitive behavioral-analysis system of psychotherapy, and their combination for the treatment of chronic depression. *The New England Journal of Medicine, 342,* 1462–1470.

Kennedy, C.H., and Itkonen, T. (1993). Effects of setting events on the problem behavior of students with severe disabilities. *Journal of Applied Behavior Analysis, 26,* 321–327.

Kennedy, C.H., and Meyer, K.A. (1996). Sleep deprivation, allergy symptoms, and negatively reinforced problem behavior. *Journal of Applied Behavior Analysis, 29,* 133–135.

Kennedy, C.H., and O'Reilly, M.F. (2006). Pain, Health Conditions, and Problem Behavior in People with Developmental Disabilities. In T.F. Oberlander and F.J. Symons (Eds.), *Pain in Children and Adults with Developmental Disabilities.* Baltimore, MD: Paul H. Brookes.

Kern, L., Mantegna, M.E., Vorndran, C.M., Bailin, D., and Hilt, A. (2001). Choice of task sequence to reduce problem behaviors. *Journal of Positive Behavior Interventions, 3*(1), 3–10.

Klein, R.G., Abikoff, H., Hechtman, L., and Weiss, G. (2004). Design and rationale of controlled study of long-term methylphenidate and multimodal psychosocial treatment in children with ADHD. *Journal of the American Academy of Child and Adolescent Psychiatry, 43,* 792–801.

Koegel, L.K., Koegel, R.L., and Dunlap, G. (1996). *Positive Behavioral Support: Including People with Difficult Behavior in the Community.* Baltimore, MD: Paul H. Brookes Publishing.

Koegel, R.L., Schreibman, L., Loos, L.M., Dirlich-Wilhelm, H., *et al.* (1992). Consistent stress profiles in mothers of children with autism. *Journal of Autism and Developmental Disabilities, 22,* 205–216.

Lee, L., Harrington, R.A., Louie, B.B., and Newschaffer, C.J. (2008). Children with autism: Quality of life and parental concerns. *Journal of Autism and Developmental Disorders, 38,* 1147–1160.

Lequia, J., Machalicek, W., and Rispoli, M.J. (2012). Effects of activity schedules on challenging behavior exhibited by children with autism spectrum disorders: A systematic review. *Research in Autism Spectrum Disorders, 6,* 480–492.

Lowe, K., Allen, D., Jones, E., Brophy, S., Moore, K., and James, W. (2007). Challenging behaviours: Prevalence and topographies. *Journal of Intellectual Disability Research, 51,* 625–636.

Lucyshyn, J., Albin, R.W., Horner, R.H., Mann, J.C., Mann, J.A., and Wadsworth, G. (2007). Family implementation of positive behavior support for a child with autism: Longitudinal, single-case, experimental, and descriptive replication and extension. *Journal of Positive Behavior Interventions, 9*(3), 131–150.

Lucyshyn, J., Dunlap, G., and Albin, R.W. (Eds.) (2002). *Families and Positive Behavior Support: Addressing Problem Behavior in Family Contexts.* Baltimore, MD: Paul H. Brookes Publishing.

Luiselli, J.K., and Cameron, M.J. (Eds.) (1998). *Antecedent Control: Innovative Approaches to Behavioral Support.* Baltimore, MD: Paul H. Brookes Publishing.

Mahan, S., Holloway, J., Bamburg, J.W., Hess, J.A., Fodstad, F.C., and Matson, J.L. (2010). An examination of psychotropic medication side effects: Does taking a greater number of psychotropic medications from different classes affect presentation of side effects in adults with ID? *Research in Developmental Disabilities, 31,* 1561–1569.

Mandell, D.S., Morales, K.H., Marcus, S.C., Stahmer, A.C., Doshi, J., and Polsky, D.E. (2008). Psychotropic medication use among Medicaid enrolled children with autism spectrum disorders. *Pediatrics, 121*(3), 441–448.

Marcus, R.N., Owen, R., Karmen, L., Manos, G., *et al.* (2009). A placebo-controlled, fixed-dose study of aripiprazole in children and adolescents with irritability associated with autistic disorder. *Journal of the American Academy of Child and Adolescent Psychiatry, 48*(11), 1110–1119.

Martin, A., Schaill, L., Anderson, G.M., Aman, M.G., *et al.* (2004). Weight gain and leptin changes among risperidone-treated youths with autism: 6-month prospective data. *American Journal of Psychiatry, 161,* 1125–1127.

Matson, J.L., and Hess, J.A. (2011). Psychotropic drug efficacy and side effects for persons with autism spectrum disorders. *Research in Autism Spectrum Disorders, 5,* 230–236.

Matson, J.L., and Mahan, S. (2010). Antipsychotic drug side effects for persons with intellectual disability. *Research in Developmental Disabilities, 31,* 1570–1576.

Matson, J.L., Mayville, E.A., Bielecki, J., Barnes, W.H., Bamburg, J.W., and Baglio, C.S. (1998). Reliability of the Matson Evaluation of Drug Side Effects Scale (MEDS). *Research in Developmental Disabilities, 19,* 501–506.

Matson, J.L., and Neal, D. (2009). Psychotropic medication use for challenging behaviors in persons with intellectual disabilities: An overview. *Research in Developmental Disabilities, 30,* 572–586.

McAtee, M., Carr, E.G., and Schulte, C. (2004). A contextual assessment inventory for problem behavior: Initial development. *Journal of Positive Behavioral Interventions, 6,* 148–165.

McCord, B.E., Thomson, R.J., and Iwata, B.A. (2001). Functional analysis and treatment of self-injury associated with transitions. *Journal of Applied Behavior Analysis, 34,* 195–210.

McCracken, J.T., McGough, J., Shah, B., Cronin, P., *et al.* (Research Units on Pediatric Psychopharmacology Autism Network) (2002). Risperidone in children with autism and serious behavioral problems. *The New England Journal of Medicine, 347*(5), 314–321.

McGill, P. (1999). Establishing operations: Implications for the assessment, treatment, and prevention of problem behavior. *Journal of Applied Behavior Analysis, 32,* 393–418.

Mullins, J.L., and Christian, L. (2001). The effects of progressive relaxation training on the disruptive behavior of a boy with autism. *Research in Developmental Disabilities, 22,* 449–462.

O'Reilly, M.F. (1997). Functional analysis of episodic self-injury correlated with recurrent otitis media. *Journal of Applied Behavior Analysis, 30,* 165–167.

O'Reilly, M.F., Lacey, C., and Lancioni, G.E. (2000). Assessment of the influence of background noise on escape-maintained problem behavior and pain behavior in a child with Williams syndrome. *Journal of Applied Behavior Analysis, 33,* 511–514.

Owen, R., Sikich, L., Marcus, R.N., Corey-Lisle, P., *et al.* (2009). Aripiprazole in the treatment of irritability in children and adolescents with autistic disorder. *Pediatrics, 124,* 1533–1540.

Preston, J.D., O'Neal, J.H., and Talaga, M.C. (2009). *Consumer's Guide to Psychiatric Drugs.* New York, NY: Simon and Schuster.

Reichle, J., Drager, K., and Davis, C. (2002). Using requests to obtain desired items and to gain release from nonpreferred activities: Implications for assessment and intervention. *Education and Treatment of Children, 25*(1), 47–66.

Research Units on Pediatric Psychopharmacology Autism Network (RUPP) (2002). Risperidone in children with autism and serious behavioral problems. *New England Journal of Medicine, 347*(5), 314–321.

Research Units on Pediatric Psychopharmacology Autism Network (RUPP) (2005). A randomized, double-blind, placebo-controlled, cross-over trial of methylphenidate in children with hyperactivity associated with pervasive developmental disorders. *Archives of General Psychiatry, 62,* 1266–1274.

Rosenberg, R.E., Mandell, D.S., Farmer, J.E., Law, J.K., Marvin, A.R., and Law, P.A. (2010). Psychotropic medication use among children with autism spectrum disorders enrolled in a national registry, 2007–2008. *Journal of Autism and Developmental Discord, 40*(3), 342–351.

Safren, S.A., Otto, M.W., Sprich, S., Winett, C.J., Wilens, T.E., and Biederman, J. (2005). Cognitive-behavioral therapy for ADHD in medication treated adults with continued symptoms. *Behaviour Research and Therapy, 43,* 831–842.

Schubart, J.R., Camacho, F., and Leslie, D. (2014). Psychotropic medication trends among children and adolescents with autism spectrum disorder in the Medicaid program. *Autism, 18*(6), 631–637.

Shea, S., Turgay, A., Carroll, A., Schulz, M., *et al.* (2004). Risperidone in the treatment of disruptive behavioral symptoms in children with autistics and other pervasive developmental disorders. *Pediatrics, 114*(5), e634–e641.

Shogren, K.A., Faggella-Luby, M.N., Jik Bae, S., and Wehmeyer, M.L. (2004). The effect of choice-making as an intervention for problem behavior: A meta-analysis. *Journal of Positive Behavior Interventions, 6,* 228–237.

Siegel, M., and Beaulieu, A.A. (2012). Psychotropic medications in children with autism spectrum disorders: A systematic review and synthesis for evidence-based practice. *Journal of Autism and Developmental Disorders, 42,* 1592–1605.

Skinner, B.F. (1938). *The Behavior of Organisms.* New York, NY: Appleton-Century-Crofts.

Smith, R.G., and Iwata, B.A. (1997). Antecedent influences on behavior disorders. *Journal of Applied Behavior Analysis, 30,* 343–375.

Spencer, D., Marshall, J., Post, B., Kulakodlu, M., *et al.* (2015). Psychotropic medication use and polypharmacy in children with autism spectrum disorders. *Pediatrics, 132*(5), 833–840.

Steen, P.L., and Zuriff, G.E. (1977). The use of relaxation in the treatment of self-injurious behavior. *Journal of Behavior Therapy and Experimental Psychiatry, 18,* 447–448.

Stigler, K.A., Diener, J.T., Kohn, A.E., Li, L., *et al.* (2009). Aripiprazole in pervasive developmental disorder not otherwise specified and Asperger's disorder: A 14-week, prospective, open-label study. *Journal of Child and Adolescent Psychopharmacology, 19,* 265–274.

Symons, F.J., Davis, M.L., and Thompson, T. (2000). Self-injurious behavior and sleep disturbance in adults with developmental disabilities. *Research in Developmental Disabilities, 21,* 115–123.

Taylor, J.C., Sisson, L.A., McKelvey, J.L., and Trefelner, M.F. (1993). Situation specificity in attention-seeking problem behavior: A case study. *Behavior Modification, 17,* 474–497.

Touchette, P.E., MacDonald, R.F., and Langer, S.N. (1985). A scatter plot for identifying stimulus control of problem behavior. *Journal of Applied Behavior Analysis, 18,* 343–351.

Tureck, K., Matson, J.L., Turygin, N., and Macmillan, K. (2013). Rates of psychotropic medication use in children with ASD compared to presence and severity of problem behaviors. *Research in Autism Spectrum Disorders, 7,* 1377–1382.

U.S. Food and Drug Administration (2006). *FDA approves the first drug to treat irritability associated with autism, Risperdal.* Available at www.accessdata.fda.gov/drugsatfda_docs/nda/2006/020272Orig1s036,s041,020588Orig1s024,s028,s029,21444Orig1s008,s015.pdf, accessed on 2 March 2015.

U.S. Food and Drug Administration (2009). *FDA approves another drug to treat irritability associated with autism, Abilify.* Available at www.accessdata.fda.gov/drugsatfda_docs/nda/2009/021436Orig1s027.pdf, accessed on 2 March 2015.

Vaughn, B.J., Clarke, S., and Dunlap, G. (1997). Assessment-based intervention for severe behavior problems in a natural family context. *Journal of Applied Behavior Analysis, 30,* 713–716.

Vaughn, B.J., Dunlap, G., Fox, L., Clarke, S., and Bucy, M. (1997). Parent–professional partnership in behavioral support: A case study of community-based intervention. *Journal of the Association for Persons with Severe Handicaps, 22,* 186–197.

Wehmeyer, M.L., Kelchner, K., and Richards, S. (1996). Essential characteristics of self-determined behavior of individuals with mental retardation. *American Journal on Mental Retardation, 200,* 632–642.

Wiggs, L., and Stores, G. (1996). Severe sleep disturbance and daytime challenging behavior in children with severe learning disabilities. *Journal of Intellectual Disabilities, 40,* 518–528.

Zito, J.M., Derivan, A.T., Kratochvil, C.J., Safer, D.J., Fegert, J.M., and Greenhill, L.L. (2008). Off-label psychopharmacologic prescribing for children: History supports close clinical monitoring. *Child and Adolescent Psychiatry and Mental Health, 2,* 24. doi:10.1186/1753-2000-2-24

CHAPTER 6

Self-Injurious Behaviors in Children with Autism Spectrum Disorder

Impact of Allergic Diseases

Harumi Jyonouchi, M.D., Saint Peter's University Hospital,
New Brunswick, New Jersey

Introduction

Self-injurious behaviors (SIBs) exhibited by individuals with autism spectrum disorder (ASD) are one of the most detrimental behavioral symptoms and often very difficult to manage. The etiology of SIBs is multifactorial and difficult to assess in children with limited expressive language. Too often, SIBs associated with medical conditions other than ASD are simply attributed to "being autistic." The medical conditions provoking behavioral symptoms are often common childhood diseases that cause pain and discomfort but can be managed easily. Allergic diseases are one such common medical condition. Under-diagnosis and under-treatment of common childhood diseases in ASD children may further aggravate SIBs. Obviously, if SIB is caused by poor health, a child will not respond to behavioral interventions and/or neurotropic medications.

Allergic diseases generally lead to chronic inflammation of respiratory and gastrointestinal (GI) mucosa and skin, but they are also known to cause or aggravate neuropsychiatric symptoms in non-ASD individuals. These symptoms include anxiety, obsessive-compulsive disorder (OCD), and attention deficit hyperactivity disorder (ADHD). For example, excessive picking of skin due to severe pruritus (i.e., itching) can occur in non-ASD individuals suffering from severe eczema, and this may be implicated with OCD behaviors in part.

Immunoglobulin E (IgE)-mediated allergic disorders that include atopic asthma, atopic dermatitis, food allergy, and allergic rhinoconjunctivitis are rising in prevalence in developed countries. One of every four or five individuals are now known to suffer from IgE-mediated allergic diseases, and surprisingly the improvement of environmental hygiene may be partly responsible for the increase

(Daley, 2014). IgE-mediated allergic diseases are expected to be as prevalent in ASD individuals as in the general population, and these allergic diseases are easily treatable in most cases. It is important to address the possible role of allergic diseases in the workup of SIBs in ASD children with limited expressive language, especially if objective symptoms of allergic conditions are present.

It should also be noted that allergic diseases may differ in definition depending on caregivers' medical backgrounds and medical providers' specialties. Non-medical caregivers and medical caregivers who are not trained in the discipline of allergy/immunology (A/I) may apply the word "allergy" to disease conditions not associated with IgE-mediated immune responses. In contrast, subspecialists with A/I training separate IgE-mediated immediate reactions from non-IgE-mediated reactions that may or may not involve immune mechanisms. "Food allergy" (FA) defined by recent FA guidelines include both IgE- and non-IgE-mediated immune reactions to food proteins (Boyce *et al.*, 2010). Asthma, a common childhood respiratory disease, is triggered by multiple environmental factors and not solely attributed to IgE-mediated immune responses. Asthma is often subdivided into atopic asthma and non-atopic asthma on the basis of the presence or absence of IgE-mediated responses to allergens as triggers. However, physicians not trained in the A/I discipline may regard asthma as a single atopic condition.

In this chapter, common childhood conditions that are known to be associated with neuropsychiatric conditions in the general population are discussed. Discussion is limited to the medical conditions associated with the IgE- and non-IgE-mediated immune mechanisms. First, we briefly define IgE-mediated mechanisms and their pathogenesis. In the latter part of the chapter, we discuss the reported high prevalence of "allergic diseases" and the potential contribution of "allergy" to the onset and progress of common neuropsychiatric conditions including depression, bipolar disorders, and schizophrenia. Again, it should be noted, in the literature addressing "allergy" in patients with neuropsychiatric diseases, "allergic diseases" is not strictly defined, as opposed to the literature published in the A/I journals. Lastly, we discuss the potential effects of allergic diseases or other conditions often included in "allergy" in ASD children, although literature addressing the role of "allergy" and behavioral symptoms, including self-injury, is rather scant with regard to ASD individuals.

Neuropsychiatric Symptoms Implicated in IgE- and Non-IgE-Mediated Immune Disorders

Mechanisms of IgE-Mediated Allergy and Non-IgE-Mediated Immune Reactions

The word "allergy" is generally used to describe immediate immune reactions that are mediated by IgE antibodies (Ab). The interactions between allergens and IgE Ab cause the rapid release of mediators from effector cells (mainly mast cells and basophils), resulting in acute symptoms in the skin, airway, and GI tract (Akdis and Akdis, 2009). In contrast, non-IgE-mediated allergic reactions are often cell-mediated or mediated by other isotypes of antibodies, and the onset of symptoms is delayed. In other words, these reactions typically occur several hours after exposure to causative agents. In addition, the reactions tend to be limited to the tissue or organ where the exposure takes place (Jyonouchi, 2008).

ANTIGEN SENSITIZATION

Most allergens causing IgE- and non-IgE-mediated responses are proteins that are absorbed by antigen (Ag) presenting cells (APC); their immunogenic peptides (epitopes) are bound to major histocompatibility (MHC) II molecules and then presented to T-helper (Th) cells (Akdis and Akdis, 2009). Ag presentation to Th cells leads to the differentiation of naive T cells to type 2 Th (Th2) effector cells to produce IgE Ab, depending on properties of the Ag and the genetic predisposition of the host (Akdis and Akdis, 2009; Akdis and Akdis, 2007). Ag presentation to Th cells can also lead to differentiation of other types of Th cells, including Th1 cells, Th17 cells, and regulatory T (Treg) cells.

T-HELPER CELL DIFFERENTIATION

Which types of Th cells develop partly determines subsequent immune responses. Th2 cells activate eosinophilic inflammation that can be triggered by the immediate release of mediators secreted by effector cells (mast cells and basophiles) upon exposure to a minute amount of allergens. Th2 responses are believed to be developed for the clearance of large extracellular organisms such as helminths (parasitic worms). Th1 responses lead to cellular immune responses mediated by monocyte and macrophage lineage cells with major mediators being interferon-gamma (IFN-γ); Th1 responses serve as a major defense against intracellular organisms, augmenting intracellular microbial killing. Antibodies (IgG1, IgG3 in isotype) augmented by Th1 responses are effective for antibody-mediated activation of phagocytic killing. Th17 responses cause neutrophil-mediated inflammation and promote clearance of certain fungi and extracellular organisms.

Differentiation of Th2 cells and the actions of Th2 cytokines are counter-regulated by other Th cell subsets and their mediators (Akdis and Akdis, 2009). For example, IFN-γ, a representative Th1 cytokine, and interleukin (IL)-10, a counter-regulatory cytokine produced by multiple lineage cells including Treg cells, both suppress differentiation of Th2 cells (Akdis and Akdis, 2009; Ochs, Oukka, and Torgerson, 2009; Ozdemir, Akdis, and Akdis, 2009). They also suppress the actions of Th2 cytokines (Akdis and Akdis, 2009; Ochs *et al.*, 2009; Ozdemir *et al.*, 2009). Environmental exposure to Th1-inducing stimulants (endotoxins, livestock, common bacterial and viral infections, and so forth) during the first few years of life has decreased in developed countries with the improvement of general hygiene. This change has been implicated in an increased prevalence of Th2-skewed allergic diseases in developed countries; this concept is referred to as the "hygiene hypothesis" (Chang and Pan, 2008; Tse and Horner, 2008). Improvements in hygiene have also resulted in a lack of immunoregulatory stimuli from exposure to helminths; stimuli provided by helminths induce systemic immunosuppression at the expense of localized, self-limited tissue inflammation (Jackson *et al.*, 2009). This also has been shown to contribute to the increased prevalence of IgE-mediated allergy as well as autoimmune conditions in developed countries (Jackson *et al.*, 2009).

EFFECTOR CELLS

IgE Ab is present in a minute amount in the serum, far less than other Ig isotypes (IgA, IgG, and IgM); it has a very short half-life (2–3 days) but has a high affinity to antigen (Ag). IgE Ab bound to high-affinity IgE receptors (FcεRI), which are expressed on mast cells and basophils, become stable, lasting up to 6 weeks. A cross-linking of IgE Abs on the cell surface of the effector cells can occur with a minute amount of allergen (Jackson *et al.*, 2009). This results in the rapid release of mediators causing immediate allergic responses; these mediators include histamine, leukotrienes, and other enzymes (Metcalfe, Peavy, and Gilfillan, 2009). Chronic exposure to causative allergens then leads to chronic inflammation of the mucosa and/or skin.

In Th1 responses, Th1 cytokines including IFN-γ activate monocyte-macrophage lineage cells for phagocytosis (ingestion of bacteria) and the intracellular killing of phagocytosed microbes, which is executed with the production of toxic reactive oxygen species in the phagosomes. For microbes that are resistant to intracellular killing, granuloma formation is augmented to contain phagocytosed microbes, as typically seen in tuberculosis. In Th17 responses, the main effector cells are neutrophils. Neutrophils exert the intracellular killing of microbes trapped in phagosomes like monocytes and also eliminate pathogens by NETosis, the death pathway mediated by neutrophil extracellular traps (NET). NET was used to describe extracellular strands of DNA that originated from neutrophils and are bound to neutrophil-derived antimicrobial peptides (Nauseef and Borregaard, 2014).

Neuropsychiatric Conditions Observed in IgE- and Non-IgE-Mediated Immune Conditions

In this section, we briefly summarize neuropsychiatric symptoms in IgE- and non-IgE-mediated allergic or immune conditions in the general population. We focus on common childhood diseases.

Allergic Disorders and Neuropsychiatric Conditions

As noted before, in most studies addressing an association between asthma/allergic disorders and neuropsychiatric conditions, asthma and other allergic diseases were defined on the basis of clinical diagnosis, and whether or not the individual had documented IgE-mediated reactivity to allergens was not specifically addressed. In population studies, such diagnoses are often based on parental reports or diagnostic codes used for billing. Population studies tended to combine asthma, allergic rhinitis (AR), eczema, and food allergy into one group. The results of such recent population studies are summarized below, and conclusions appear to be consistent with previous reports (mainly cross-sectional studies) as reviewed previously (Jyonouchi, 2010).

Analysis of data obtained from the National Survey of Children's Health (2007–2008) of 27,566 children (0–5 years of age) revealed that asthma, eczema, hay fever, and food allergy were diagnosed in 6.6, 15.0, 11.6, and 6.1% of children, respectively (Garg and Silverberg, 2014). Garg and Silverberg (2014) report that children with these "allergic" disorders had higher odds of at least one comorbid psychiatric or behavioral disorder (ADHD, depression, anxiety, conduct/oppositional disorder, and learning delay), but not autism/Asperger's disorder. "Allergic diseases" are all based on survey results, not on physician diagnosis.

A nationwide population-based prospective case-control cohort study that included 2294 children with asthma and 9176 controls followed from 2000 till 2010 revealed that children diagnosed with asthma had a higher incidence of developing ADHD, with a moderately elevated risk (hazard ratio: 1.31; 95% confidence interval: 1.07–1.59) (Chen *et al.*, 2013c).

In a longitudinal study of community samples of adolescents ($n = 367$), anxiety is associated with a lifetime history of "allergic" diseases as a group. Slattery and Essex (2011) report that "pure" anxiety was associated with asthma and AR; having both asthma and AR further strengthened the association compared with having either disorder alone.

In a cross-sectional study involving 942 males and 1085 females (all adults), "allergic" disorders were reported to be associated with a 59% increased likelihood of depression (Sanna *et al.*, 2014).

In studies of 144 asthmatic and 144 non-asthmatic control children, Carrera-Bojorges and colleagues (2013) reported an association between asthma and internalizing disorders including panic disorder, social phobia, separation anxiety, and total anxiety.

Supporting the previous results described above, recent studies also addressed whether there were any specific factors contributing to an association between "allergic" diseases and neuropsychiatric symptoms.

Asthma

Depression is reported to be more common in girls (ages 11–14 years) with *non-atopic* (non-IgE-mediated) asthma (Bahreinian *et al.*, 2011). In a study of cross-sectional data on asthma and allergic diseases at the 10-year follow-up of two birth cohorts, Kohlboeck and colleagues (2013) reported a threefold higher likelihood of emotional symptoms in children with non-atopic asthma than non-asthmatic controls, but such an association was not observed in children with atopic asthma.

In another birth-cohort study, more severe and persistent asthma at age 5 years was associated with increased odds of affective, anxiety, somatic, oppositional/defiant, and conduct problems at ages 5–17 years (Goodwin *et al.*, 2013).

It was reported that children with well-controlled asthma ($n = 70$) enrolled in a comprehensive asthma-management program did not reveal an increased risk of anxiety, depression, or poor self-esteem (Letitre *et al.*, 2014). However, Letitre and colleagues (2014) did indicate an association between uncontrolled asthma and neuropsychiatric symptoms.

Higher prevalence of clinically significant depressive and anxiety symptoms was reported in patients with severe, prednisone-dependent asthma ($n = 67$) than in patients with severe non-prednisone-dependent or mild-moderate asthma ($n = 47$ and 73, respectively) (Amelink *et al.*, 2014).

One study reported a 43.5% increased risk of self-reported anxiety in individuals with predominantly mild asthma ($n = 1403$) in a population-based study of a total of 15,675 individuals (Gada *et al.*, 2014); however, in this study, asthma control was not addressed.

The above-described results indicate *the importance of asthma control for neuropsychiatric symptoms*. However, it should also be noted that some studies report the presence of psychiatric conditions as risk factors of inadequate control of asthma as follows: In a longitudinal study of 653 adult asthma patients with 4.3 years of follow-up, Favreau and colleagues (2014) reported that panic disorder and anxiety sensitivity are prospectively associated with poorer asthma control.

Allergic Rhinitis

Many studies have addressed an association between allergic rhinitis (AR) and ADHD as well as other neuropsychiatric conditions. The results of some of these studies in non-ASD AR individuals are as follows:

- In children diagnosed with AR, the prevalence of ADHD was reported to be higher ($p < 0.001$) in a large population-based study ($n = 226,550$) (Shyu *et al.*, 2012). Another study (case-controlled) indicated that the increased prevalence of ADHD in AR children was associated with parenting stress (Lee *et al.*, 2014).

- In another population-based study, ADHD individuals ($n = 4692$) were reported to have increased risk of AR compared with controls ($n = 18,768$) (Tsai *et al.*, 2013); however, in that study, AR diagnosis was not necessarily based on physician diagnosis.

- In one Web-based survey study, Kwon and colleagues (2013) reported that AR was associated with an increased risk of depression and suicidal ideation, which was worsened with sleep deprivation caused by AR.

- In one study, 1673 individuals who were diagnosed with AR at ages 12–15 years between 1996 and 2000 were evaluated for the presence of depressive disorder in 2010, in comparison with case cohorts. Results indicated a positive association between AR in early adolescence and depression in late adolescence and early adulthood (Chen *et al.*, 2013a).

Sinusitis

One study of electronic health records ($n = 446,480$) revealed that patients diagnosed with chronic rhinosinusitis (CRS) had a higher premorbid prevalence of anxiety and headaches (Tan *et al.*, 2013).

In CRS individuals, the scores of anxiety and depression questionnaires are positively associated with CRS symptoms (Nanayakkara *et al.*, 2013), which was partly attributed to poor quality of life.

The above-described results indicate that the presence of AR and sinusitis can be contributing factors to SIBs, such as anxiety and headaches, in ASD children, given the profound neuropsychiatric effects on non-ASD individuals.

Atopic Dermatitis

Many studies report a positive association between neuropsychiatric conditions and atopic dermatitis (AD). The results of some recent studies are as follows:

- Children diagnosed with AD were reported to have a higher prevalence of mental disorders in cross-sectional studies using the 2007 National Survey of Children's Health ($n = 92,642$). The odds ratios for ADHD, depression, anxiety, and conduct disorder were 1.87, 1.81, 1.77, and 1.87, respectively (Yaghmaie, Koudelka, and Simpson, 2013).

- Meta-analysis of non-allergic comorbidities of AD revealed a consistent positive association of AD with ADHD (Deckert, Kopkow, and Schmitt, 2014).

- Analysis of four recent epidemiological studies indicated a positive association between AD and ADHD, revealing a 43% increased risk of ADHD in children with previous or prevalent AD (Schmitt *et al.*, 2013).

- One study indicated that itching intensity in AD was positively associated with depression symptoms, which were assessed by questionnaires (Chrostowska-Plak, Reich, and Szepietowski, 2013).

Although a causal relationship between AD and ADHD is unknown, neuroimmunological mechanisms involving stress responses have been proposed (Buske-Kirschbaum *et al.*, 2013). Such neuroimmune interactions may also be true in other neuropsychiatric conditions with altered stress responses. Interestingly, it was reported that stress and anxiety affect skin-test reactivity in AR individuals, as well as allergic inflammation (Buske-Kirschbaum, Ebrecht, and Hellhammer, 2010; Heffner *et al.*, 2014; Kiecolt-Glaser *et al.*, 2009). Other studies also support the importance of stress and subsequent neuroimmunological mechanisms for allergy flare-up and adult-onset asthma (Patterson *et al.*, 2014; Rod *et al.*, 2012).

Celiac Disease

Celiac disease (CD) is thought to be causally associated with the production of IgA Ab against tissue transglutaminase in genetically susceptible individuals. CD patients are also known to exhibit neuropsychiatric symptoms at high frequency, as reviewed elsewhere (Jackson *et al.*, 2012). Psychiatric complications implicated with CD include anxiety, depression, mood disorders, ADHD, schizophrenia, and possibly ASD (Jackson *et al.*, 2012). Namely, several studies reported an increased risk of ASD in children with a maternal history of CD or family history of CD along with other autoimmune conditions (Atladottir *et al.*, 2009; Valicenti-McDermott *et al.*, 2008).

IgE- and Non-IgE-Mediated Immune Conditions in Neuropsychiatric Disorders

In previous sections, reports of high prevalence of neuropsychiatric symptoms in patients with IgE- and non-IgE-mediated immune conditions were discussed. Such immune conditions are typically regarded as "allergic diseases" in the general population as well as by some medical practitioners not trained in the A/I discipline. If high prevalences of neuropsychiatric symptoms are truly seen in patients with such "allergic diseases," the question arises as to whether allergic conditions are more frequently seen in established neuropsychiatric conditions. If so, it may be questioned whether allergen-induced inflammation is associated with the onset and progress of certain neuropsychiatric conditions, including ASD.

Several studies addressing the possible high frequency of "allergic diseases" in patients with neuropsychiatric conditions have been summarized (Jyonouchi, 2010). More recent studies addressed a possible causal relationship between "allergic diseases" and chronic inflammation and the development of certain neuropsychiatric conditions. The results of such studies are as follows:

- In a population-based study including >5000 individuals, authors Khandaker and colleagues (2014) reported an increased risk of psychotic experience at 13 years of age in children diagnosed with eczema, asthma, or both, at 10 years of age; asthma and eczema diagnoses were based on parental questionnaires and not separated into IgE- or non-IgE-mediated conditions. Diagnoses of eczema and/or asthma were associated with increased serum levels of inflammatory markers (IL-6 and C-reactive protein) (Khandaker *et al.*, 2014). These results may indicate an importance of inflammation for the onset of psychotic conditions in genetically predisposed individuals.

- In another population-based study utilizing the Taiwan National Health Insurance Research Database, Chen and colleagues (2013b) reported a significantly higher prevalence of AR, asthma, AD, and allergic conjunctivitis in patients diagnosed with ADHD and/or tic disorder. Chen and colleagues (2013b) also reported a higher prevalence of OCD and anxiety disorder in these patients.

- Another population-based study also indicated a high prevalence of AR in patients with ADHD (Chou *et al.*, 2013).

- A population-based study conducted in Korea targeting school-age children indicated a higher prevalence of asthma and AR in children diagnosed with ADHD than in non-ADHD children (Kwon *et al.*, 2014).

- In a small pilot study, an association of Tourette syndrome and OCD with "allergic" disease in a pediatric population was reported; allergic diseases include asthma, AR, and eczema (Yuce *et al.*, 2014).

- In another study utilizing two Danish nationwide population-based registries, it was reported that hospital contact with any allergic disorders (AD, urticaria, and AR) increased the risk of schizophrenia (risk ratio 1.59) (Pedersen *et al.*, 2012).

In these population studies, diagnoses of asthma, AR, and eczema are mainly based on the parental report or diagnostic codes used for insurance claims. Therefore, asthma, eczema, and AR likely involve both atopic and non-atopic (non-IgE-mediated) conditions. It is difficult to assess the degree to which IgE-mediated allergic reactions are associated with the apparent high prevalence of asthma, rhinitis, and eczema in patients with the above-described neuropsychiatric conditions. It may be argued that inflammation associated with asthma, eczema, and rhinitis may have aggravated the onset and progress of the disease in the above-described neuropsychiatric conditions irrespective of IgE- or non-IgE-mediated immune mechanisms. In fact, two studies reported inflammation caused either IgE-mediated or non-IgE-mediated mechanisms that are associated with the clinical exacerbation of neuropsychiatric conditions as follows: In bipolar patients, positive pollen-specific IgE was associated with the worsening of depression scores during the allergy season with high pollen count. In other words, this study indicates that pollen-specific IgE-mediated allergic inflammation may have led to worsening depression symptoms (Manalai *et al.*, 2012).

Another study reported that serum levels of IgG antibodies against gut organisms (*Saccharomyces cerevisiae* and *Toxoplasma gondii*) and common food proteins (casein and wheat-derived gluten) are higher in patients diagnosed with schizophrenia, and this association is most evident in IgG antibody levels against *Saccharomyces cerevisiae* (ASCA) (Severance *et al.*, 2012). The authors use IgG antibody levels against these antigens as markers of GI inflammation, but it is unclear how these IgG antibody levels correlate with GI inflammation. ASCA may be the best indicator of inflammation.

Given the above-described results, it may be speculated that neuropsychiatric symptoms associated with both IgE- and non-IgE-mediated "allergic diseases" cause changes in behavioral symptoms in ASD children, with reasons as follows:

- pain and discomfort associated with "allergic diseases"

- aggravation of neuropsychiatric symptoms by inflammation caused by "allergic" diseases

- disease (medical condition)-associated neuropsychiatric conditions that may aggravate behavioral symptoms including SIBs.

Since this book is devoted to SIBs observed in ASD children, how the above-described conditions can lead to SIBs is discussed in the next section. However, it is noteworthy that studies of "self-injurious behaviors" in ASD children in association with underlying medical conditions are very limited, and discussion here may be based on results obtained from non-ASD individuals.

SIBs in Individuals with Limited Expressive Language

It is difficult to assess pain in individuals with limited expressive language. Several studies report that pain and discomfort associated with underlying medical conditions greatly influence behavioral symptoms in such individuals. It has been reported that, in individuals with minimal verbal skills and problem behaviors, aggression, SIBs, and temper tantrums can vary with concurrent medical conditions (Carr and Owen-DeSchryver, 2007).

Negative effects of sleep deprivation due to allergic symptoms are also reported in adolescents (13, 15, and 18 years of age) with mental retardation, aggression, and SIBs (Kennedy and Meyer, 1996).

In 11 children with developmental disabilities, illness-related problem behaviors are reported to be better controlled with a combination approach of behavioral plus medical intervention to address underlying medical problems (Carr and Blakeley-Smith, 2006).

A higher level of problem behavior has also been reported in ASD children in the high-anxiety state in a small case study: anxiety state was evaluated by physiological data (heart rate and respiratory sinus arrhythmia) (Moskowitz *et al.*, 2013). In a previous publication, the present author also presents cases with improvement of behavioral symptoms following optimized treatment for medical conditions (delayed-type food allergy and chronic sinusitis) (Jyonouchi, 2010).

Can SIBs Be Associated with Psychiatric Conditions Associated with "Allergic Diseases"?

In cognitively intact children, SIBs may be best expressed as suicidal ideation and attempts. In such behaviors, is there any role for medical conditions?

In a population-based study with a large number of Taiwanese adolescents ($n = 5027$), anxiety symptoms were often associated with suicidality in adolescents and children (Yen *et al.*, 2014).

In another study in ADHD children 3–18 years of age ($n = 418$), prior to treatment, ADHD symptoms were reported to be associated with an increased risk of suicidality (Balazs *et al.*, 2014).

Suicidal behavior in anxiety disorders among adolescents in a rural population of India has also been reported (Russell *et al.*, 2013).

Multiple population studies indicate a higher risk of ADHD and anxiety symptoms in patients with common childhood conditions discussed in the previous section, including AR and asthma. Given these findings, it may be speculated that anxiety and ADHD symptoms also are closely associated with SIBs in ASD children, apart from pain and discomfort. Since associations between "allergic diseases" and the above-described neuropsychiatric diseases are implicated with chronic inflammation, a question may arise as to how chronic inflammation alters brain functions, leading to SIBs.

Chronic Inflammation Associated with "Allergic Diseases": Is There a Link with SIBs and HPA Dysfunction Associated with "Allergic Diseases"?

SIBs, especially suicidality, have been implicated with altered responses or dysfunction of the hypothalamic–pituitary–adrenal (HPA) axis. Meta-analysis of the literature published from January 1990 to June 2011 revealed a correlation between HPA dysfunction and emotional dysregulation in adolescent suicide (Braquehais *et al.*, 2012). Altered cortisol response to a central serotonin receptor agonist (meta-chlorophenylpiperazine) was also reported in depressed, suicidal adolescent males (Ghaziuddin *et al.*, 2014). Abnormal patterns of HPA-axis activation have been known to occur in patients with schizophrenia and bipolar disorder. One study reports the altered expression of glucocorticoid receptor 1B and 1C (GR-1B and GR-1C) at transcript levels that are partly associated with polymorphisms of GR genes when postmortem brains were examined (Sinclair *et al.*, 2012). Alterations in GR expression in the postmortem brain of teenage suicide victims have also been reported: a study by Pandey and colleagues (2013) reported decreased expression of GR-α at protein and transcript levels in the prefrontal cortex and amygdaloid nuclei.

These results indicate a role of HPA-axis dysfunction in SIBs. If so, chronic inflammation caused by "allergic diseases" may have a role in the alteration of HPA-axis responses. Only scant studies addressed possibly altered stress responses due to allergic inflammation. One study reported blunted HPA-axis responsiveness to stress using a standardized laboratory stressor (Trier Social Stress Test; TSST) in 20 adult patients with seasonal AR as compared with 20 non-AR controls (Buske-Kirschbaum *et al.*, 2010). Furthermore, Buske-Kirschbaum and colleagues (2010) report a negative correlation between symptom severity and cortisol responses to the stressor. Altered HPA-axis responses likely affect allergic inflammation reciprocally. For example, stress and anxiety affect immediate- and late-phase allergic responses in AR individuals by amplifying responses, as evidenced by increased skin-prick test reactivity (Heffner *et al.*, 2014; Kiecolt-Glaser *et al.*, 2009).

These results indicate that HPA dysfunction caused by "allergic" chronic inflammation may have a role in SIBs observed in ASD individuals.

Below are two representative cases with fluctuating behavioral symptoms following various immune insults.

CASE 1: A Case of Marked Exacerbation of Behavioral Symptoms Following Repeated Viral Infection

A 10-year-old Caucasian boy initially presented to our pediatric A/I clinic for evaluation of pediatric acute-onset neuropsychiatric syndrome (PANS). He was diagnosed with high-functioning ASD and had been able to be mainstreamed without an aide. However, a worsening neuropsychiatric syndrome made it difficult for him to attend the mainstream classes. Worsening of his behavioral symptoms was preceded by viral syndrome (Figure 6.1). He underwent home instruction for several months, and his neuropsychiatric symptoms gradually subsided with the use of non-steroidal anti-inflammatory drugs and antibiotics with anti-inflammatory properties. He became able to resume school attendance, but he experienced mild flare-up of his neuropsychiatric symptoms with "flare-up" of his AR during his allergy season. This case illustrates that behavioral symptoms can be aggravated by various medical conditions.

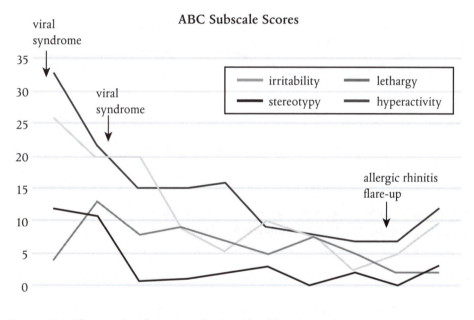

Figure 6.1 Changes in Aberrant Behavior Checklist Scores in Case 1

CASE 2: A Case of Worsening Behavioral Symptoms Secondary to the Under-Treatment of Asthma and Sinusitis

An 11-year-old boy was originally referred to our clinic for evaluation of FA, which was resolved after avoidance of causative food. However, his behavioral symptoms have been noted to flare correlated with asthma "flare-up," which is usually triggered by viral syndrome. Furthermore, when his condition was complicated with sinusitis, which likely caused facial or head pain, head banging started with worsening behavioral symptoms, as shown in Figure 6.2.

It is noteworthy that the worsening of his behavioral symptoms was also associated with onset of vocal and motor tics.

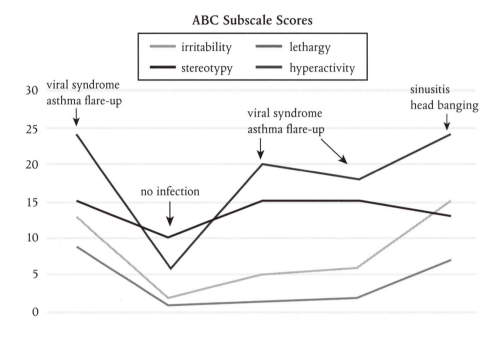

Figure 6.2 Changes in Aberrant Behavior Checklist Scores in Association with His Medical Conditions in Case 2

CASE 3: A Case of Severe Self-Injurious Symptoms Secondary to Severe Allergic Rhinitis

A 12-year-old boy diagnosed with autism was diagnosed with severe seasonal AR (mainly reacting to tree and grass pollens) and has been followed in our A/I clinic. His behavioral symptoms (OCD, anxiety, and irritability) have been worse during spring-summer, and aggression and SIBs, such as head banging, have been observed during this period (Figure 6.3). SIBs completely resolved in this case, when his severe AR symptoms came under control with the use of monoclonal antibodies against IgE.

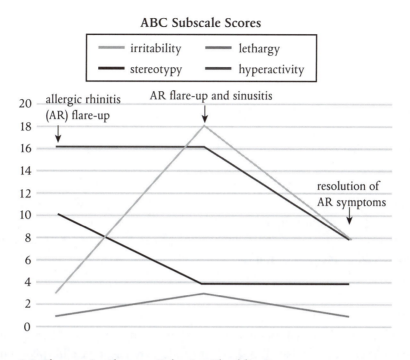

Figure 6.3 Changes in Aberrant Behavior Checklist Scores in Association with His Medical Conditions in Case 3

Diagnostic Approach

Although seldom fatal, allergic diseases mediated by IgE Abs impose significant morbidity in the general population, as evidenced by the mounting medical cost and loss of productivity (missed work or school days) (Bahadori *et al.*, 2009). Allergic diseases are well known to cause discomfort and pain, for example sinus headache with allergic rhinitis, and GI cramping with delayed-type food allergy. In addition, these allergic diseases are also known to cause psychiatric and neurological conditions in neurotypical individuals, as detailed in the first part of this chapter. This is also most likely the case for ASD children as well, as discussed in the latter part of the chapter. This is also what has been observed in our A/I clinic. It must also be emphasized that medical conditions not mediated by allergy or immune responses can also cause similar inflammatory conditions or pain and discomfort. For example, foreign bodies in the ear canal may mimic symptoms of otitis externa (inflammation of the external ear canal), and gastroesophageal reflux disease can cause recurrent respiratory infection and intermittent pain resembling GI cramping. These are relatively common conditions, and skilled clinicians should carefully evaluate ASD subjects with SIBs, keeping their eyes open for common childhood medical conditions.

It has been our experience that, in ASD children, behavioral changes caused by both IgE- and non-IgE-mediated diseases are often attributed merely to being "autistic," and these diseases are under-diagnosed and under-treated prior to evaluation in our clinic. The physicians involved in the care of ASD children need to be aware of the importance of diagnosing common IgE- and non-IgE-mediated immune conditions in ASD children. Therefore, when SIBs and other behavioral challenges are addressed in ASD children, caring physicians should pay attention to possibly underlying medical conditions that may aggravate such behaviors through multiple mechanisms. Such possibilities should be considered especially when such patients are not responsive to behavioral or pharmacological approaches, and also when other objective symptoms are noted. A high index of suspicion is very important for diagnosing and treating ASD individuals with limited expressive language, realizing that "self-injurious behaviors" can be indicators of underlying, possibly treatable, medical conditions.

Acknowledgments

A part of this study was supported by funding from the Jonty Foundation, St. Paul, Minnesota; the Autism Research Institute, San Diego, California; and the Governor's Council for Medical Research and Treatment for Autism, Princeton, New Jersey.

References

Akdis, C.A., and Akdis, M. (2009). Mechanisms and treatment of allergic disease in the big picture of regulatory T cells. *Journal of Allergy and Clinical Immunology, 123,* 735–746.

Akdis, M., and Akdis, C.A. (2007). Mechanisms of allergen-specific immunotherapy. *Journal of Allergy and Clinical Immunology, 119,* 780–791.

Amelink, M., Hashimoto, S., Spinhoven, P., Pasma, H.R., *et al.* (2014). Anxiety, depression and personality traits in severe, prednisone-dependent asthma. *Respiratory Medicine, 108,* 438–444.

Atladottir, H.O., Pedersen, M.G., Thorsen, P., Mortensen, P.B., *et al.* (2009). Association of family history of autoimmune diseases and autism spectrum disorders. *Pediatrics, 124,* 687–694.

Bahadori, K., Doyle-Waters, M.M., Marra, C., Lynd, L., *et al.* (2009). Economic burden of asthma: A systematic review. *BMC Pulmonary Medicine, 9,* 24.

Bahreinian, S., Ball, G.D., Colman, I., Becker, A.B., and Kozyrskyj, A.L. (2011). Depression is more common in girls with nonatopic asthma. *Chest, 140,* 1138–1145.

Balazs, J., Miklosi, M., Kereszteny, A., Dallos, G., and Gadoros, J. (2014). Attention-deficit hyperactivity disorder and suicidality in a treatment naive sample of children and adolescents. *Journal of Affective Disorders, 152–154,* 282–287.

Boyce, J.A., Assa'ad, A., Burks, A.W., Jones, S.M., *et al.* (2010). Guidelines for the diagnosis and management of food allergy in the United States: Summary of the NIAID-sponsored expert panel report. *The Journal of Allergy and Clinical Immunology, 126,* 1105–1118.

Braquehais, M.D., Picouto, M.D., Casas, M., and Sher, L. (2012). Hypothalamic–pituitary–adrenal axis dysfunction as a neurobiological correlate of emotion dysregulation in adolescent suicide. *World Journal of Pediatrics, 8,* 197–206.

Buske-Kirschbaum, A., Ebrecht, M., and Hellhammer, D.H. (2010). Blunted HPA axis responsiveness to stress in atopic patients is associated with the acuity and severeness of allergic inflammation. *Brain, Behavior, and Immunity, 24,* 1347–1353.

Buske-Kirschbaum, A., Schmitt, J., Plessow, F., Romanos, M., Weidinger, S., and Roessner, V. (2013). Psychoendocrine and psychoneuroimmunological mechanisms in the comorbidity of atopic eczema and attention deficit/hyperactivity disorder. *Psychoneuroendocrinology, 38,* 12–23.

Carr, E.G., and Blakeley-Smith, A. (2006). Classroom intervention for illness-related problem behavior in children with developmental disabilities. *Behavior Modification, 30,* 901–924.

Carr, E.G., and Owen-DeSchryver, J.S. (2007). Physical illness, pain, and problem behavior in minimally verbal people with developmental disabilities. *Journal of Autism and Developmental Disorders, 37,* 413–424.

Carrera-Bojorges, X.B., Perez-Romero, L.F., Trujillo-Garcia, J.U., Jimenez-Sandoval, J.O., and Machorro-Munoz, O.S. (2013). [Internalization disorders in children with asthma]. *Revista Alergia Mexico, 60,* 63–68.

Chang, T.W., and Pan, A.Y. (2008). Cumulative environmental changes, skewed antigen exposure, and the increase of allergy. *Advances in Immunology, 98,* 39–83.

Chen, M.H., Su, T.P., Chen, Y.S., Hsu, J.W., *et al.* (2013a). Allergic rhinitis in adolescence increases the risk of depression in later life: A nationwide population-based prospective cohort study. *Journal of Affective Disorders, 145,* 49–53.

Chen, M.H., Su, T.P., Chen, Y.S., Hsu, J.W., *et al.* (2013b). Attention deficit hyperactivity disorder, tic disorder, and allergy: Is there a link? A nationwide population-based study. *Journal of Child Psychology and Psychiatry, and Allied Disciplines, 54,* 545–551.

Chen, M.H., Su, T.P., Chen, Y.S., Hsu, J.W., *et al.* (2013c). Asthma and attention-deficit/hyperactivity disorder: A nationwide population-based prospective cohort study. *Journal of Child Psychology and Psychiatry, and Allied Disciplines, 54,* 1208–1214.

Chou, P.H., Lin, C.C., Lin, C.H., Loh, el-W., Chan, C.H., and Lan, T.H. (2013). Prevalence of allergic rhinitis in patients with attention-deficit/hyperactivity disorder: A population-based study. *European Child & Adolescent Psychiatry, 22,* 301–307.

Chrostowska-Plak, D., Reich, A., and Szepietowski, J.C. (2013). Relationship between itch and psychological status of patients with atopic dermatitis. *Journal of the European Academy of Dermatology and Venereology, 27,* e239–e242.

Daley, D. (2014). The evolution of the hygiene hypothesis: The role of early-life exposures to viruses and microbes and their relationship to asthma and allergic diseases. *Current Opinion in Allergy and Clinical Immunology, 14,* 390–396.

Deckert, S., Kopkow, C., and Schmitt, J. (2014). Nonallergic comorbidities of atopic eczema: An overview of systematic reviews. *Allergy, 69,* 37–45.

Favreau, H., Bacon, S.L., Labrecque, M., and Lavoie, K.L. (2014). Prospective impact of panic disorder and panic-anxiety on asthma control, health service use, and quality of life in adult patients with asthma over a 4-year follow-up. *Psychosomatic Medicine, 76,* 147–155.

Gada, E., Khan, D.A., DeFina, L.F., and Brown, E.S. (2014). The relationship between asthma and self-reported anxiety in a predominantly healthy adult population. *Annals of Allergy, Asthma & Immunology, 112,* 329–332.

Garg, N., and Silverberg, J.I. (2014). Association between childhood allergic disease, psychological comorbidity, and injury requiring medical attention. *Annals of Allergy, Asthma & Immunology, 112,* 525–532.

Ghaziuddin, N., King, C.A., Welch, K., and Ghaziuddin, M. (2014). Depressed suicidal adolescent males have an altered cortisol response to a pharmacological challenge. *Asian Journal of Psychiatry, 7,* 28–33.

Goodwin, R.D., Robinson, M., Sly, P.D., McKeague, I.W., *et al.* (2013). Severity and persistence of asthma and mental health: A birth cohort study. *Psychological Medicine, 43,* 1313–1322.

Heffner, K.L., Kiecolt-Glaser, J.K., Glaser, R., Malarkey, W.B., and Marshall, G.D. (2014). Stress and anxiety effects on positive skin test responses in young adults with allergic rhinitis. *Annals of Allergy, Asthma & Immunology, 113,* 13–18.

Jackson, J.A., Friberg, I.M., Little, S., and Bradley, J.E. (2009). Review series on helminths, immune modulation and the hygiene hypothesis. Immunity against helminths and immunological phenomena in modern human populations: Coevolutionary legacies? *Immunology, 126,* 18–27.

Jackson, J.R., Eaton, W.W., Cascella, N.G., Fasano, A., and Kelly, D.L. (2012). Neurologic and psychiatric manifestations of celiac disease and gluten sensitivity. *The Psychiatric Quarterly, 83,* 91–102.

Jyonouchi, H. (2008). Non-IgE mediated food allergy. *Inflammation & Allergy Drug Targets, 7,* 173–180.

Jyonouchi, H. (2010). Autism spectrum disorders and allergy: Observation from a pediatric allergy/immunology clinic. *Expert Review of Clinical Immunology, 6,* 397–411.

Kennedy, C.H., and Meyer, K.A. (1996). Sleep deprivation, allergy symptoms, and negatively reinforced problem behavior. *Journal of Applied Behavior Analysis, 29,* 133–135.

Khandaker, G.M., Zammit, S., Lewis, G., and Jones, P.B. (2014). A population-based study of atopic disorders and inflammatory markers in childhood before psychotic experiences in adolescence. *Schizophrenia Research, 152,* 139–145.

Kiecolt-Glaser, J.K., Heffner, K.L., Glaser, R., Malarkey, W.B., *et al.* (2009). How stress and anxiety can alter immediate and late phase skin test responses in allergic rhinitis. *Psychoneuroendocrinology, 34,* 670–680.

Kohlboeck, G., Koletzko, S., Bauer, C.P., von Berg, A., *et al.* (2013). Association of atopic and non-atopic asthma with emotional symptoms in school children. *Pediatric Allergy and Immunology, 24,* 230–236.

Kwon, H.J., Lee, M., Ha, M., Yoo, S.J., *et al.* (2014). The associations between ADHD and asthma in Korean children. *BMC Psychiatry, 14,* 70.

Kwon, J.A., Lee, M., Yoo, K.B., and Park, E.C. (2013). Does the duration and time of sleep increase the risk of allergic rhinitis? Results of the 6-year nationwide Korea youth risk behavior Web-based survey? *PloS One, 8,* e72507.

Lee, Y.S., Kim, S.H., You, J.H., Baek, H.T., *et al.* (2014). Attention deficit hyperactivity disorder like behavioral problems and parenting stress in pediatric allergic rhinitis. *Psychiatry Investigation, 11,* 266–271.

Letitre, S.L., de Groot, E.P., Draaisma, E., and Brand, P.L. (2014). Anxiety, depression and self-esteem in children with well-controlled asthma: Case-control study. *Archives of Disease in Childhood, 99,* 744–748.

Manalai, P., Hamilton, R.G., Langenberg, P., Kosisky, S.E., *et al.* (2012). Pollen-specific immunoglobulin E positivity is associated with worsening of depression scores in bipolar disorder patients during high pollen season. *Bipolar Disorders, 14,* 90–98.

Metcalfe, D.D., Peavy, R.D., and Gilfillan, A.M. (2009). Mechanisms of mast cell signaling in anaphylaxis. *Journal of Allergy and Clinical Immunology, 124,* 639–646.

Moskowitz, L.J., Mulder, E., Walsh, C.E., McLaughlin, D.M., *et al.* (2013). A multimethod assessment of anxiety and problem behavior in children with autism spectrum disorders and intellectual disability. *American Journal on Intellectual and Developmental Disabilities, 118,* 419–434.

Nanayakkara, J.P., Igwe, C., Roberts, D., and Hopkins, C. (2013). The impact of mental health on chronic rhinosinusitis symptom scores. *European Archives of Oto-Rhino-Laryngology, 270,* 1361–1364.

Nauseef, W.M., and Borregaard, N. (2014). Neutrophils at work. *Nature Immunology, 15,* 602–611.

Ochs, H.D., Oukka, M., and Torgerson, T.R. (2009). TH17 cells and regulatory T cells in primary immunodeficiency diseases. *Journal of Allergy and Clinical Immunology, 123,* 977–983.

Ozdemir, C., Akdis, M., and Akdis, C.A. (2009). T regulatory cells and their counterparts: Masters of immune regulation. *Clinical & Experimental Allergy, 39,* 626–639.

Pandey, G.N., Rizavi, H.S., Ren, X., Dwivedi, Y., and Palkovits, M. (2013). Region-specific alterations in glucocorticoid receptor expression in the postmortem brain of teenage suicide victims. *Psychoneuroendocrinology, 38,* 2628–2639.

Patterson, A.M., Yildiz, V.O., Klatt, M.D., and Malarkey, W.B. (2014). Perceived stress predicts allergy flares. *Annals of Allergy, Asthma & Immunology, 112,* 317–321.

Pedersen, M.S., Benros, M.E., Agerbo, E., Borglum, A.D., and Mortensen, P.B. (2012). Schizophrenia in patients with atopic disorders with particular emphasis on asthma: A Danish population-based study. *Schizophrenia Research, 138,* 58–62.

Rod, N.H., Kristensen, T.S., Lange, P., Prescott, E., and Diderichsen, F. (2012). Perceived stress and risk of adult-onset asthma and other atopic disorders: A longitudinal cohort study. *Allergy, 67,* 1408–1414.

Russell, P.S., Nair, M.K., Chandra, A., Subramaniam, V.S., *et al.* (2013). ADad 9: Suicidal behavior in anxiety disorders among adolescents in a rural community population in India. *Indian Journal of Pediatrics, 80*(Suppl. 2), S175–S180.

Sanna, L., Stuart, A.L., Pasco, J.A., Jacka, F.N., *et al.* (2014). Atopic disorders and depression: Findings from a large, population-based study. *Journal of Affective Disorders, 155,* 261–265.

Schmitt, J., Apfelbacher, C., Heinrich, J., Weidinger, S., and Romanos, M. (2013). [Association of atopic eczema and attention-deficit/hyperactivity disorder: Meta-analysis of epidemiologic studies]. *Zeitschrift für Kinder- und Jugendpsychiatrie und Psychotherapie, 41,* 35–42.

Severance, E.G., Alaedini, A., Yang, S., Halling, M., *et al.* (2012). Gastrointestinal inflammation and associated immune activation in schizophrenia. *Schizophrenia Research, 138,* 48–53.

Shyu, C.S., Lin, H.K., Lin, C.H., and Fu, L.S. (2012). Prevalence of attention-deficit/hyperactivity disorder in patients with pediatric allergic disorders: A nationwide, population-based study. *Journal of Microbiology, Immunology, and Infection, 45,* 237–242.

Sinclair, D., Fullerton, J.M., Webster, M.J., and Shannon Weickert, C. (2012). Glucocorticoid receptor 1B and 1C mRNA transcript alterations in schizophrenia and bipolar disorder, and their possible regulation by GR gene variants. *PloS One, 7,* e31720.

Slattery, M.J., and Essex, M.J. (2011). Specificity in the association of anxiety, depression, and atopic disorders in a community sample of adolescents. *Journal of Psychiatric Research, 45,* 788–795.

Tan, B.K., Chandra, R.K., Pollak, J., Kato, A., *et al.* (2013). Incidence and associated premorbid diagnoses of patients with chronic rhinosinusitis. *The Journal of Allergy and Clinical Immunology, 131,* 1350–1360.

Tsai, J.D., Chang, S.N., Mou, C.H., Sung, F.C., and Lue, K.H. (2013). Association between atopic diseases and attention-deficit/hyperactivity disorder in childhood: A population-based case-control study. *Annals of Epidemiology, 23,* 185–188.

Tse, K., and Horner, A.A. (2008). Allergen tolerance versus the allergic march: The hygiene hypothesis revisited. *Current Allergy and Asthma Reports, 8,* 475–483.

Valicenti-McDermott, M.D., McVicar, K., Cohen, H.J., Wershil, B.K., and Shinnar, S. (2008). Gastrointestinal symptoms in children with an autism spectrum disorder and language regression. *Pediatric Neurology, 39,* 392–398.

Yaghmaie, P., Koudelka, C.W., and Simpson, E.L. (2013). Mental health comorbidity in patients with atopic dermatitis. *The Journal of Allergy and Clinical Immunology, 131,* 428–433.

Yen, C.F., Lai, C.Y., Ko, C.H., Liu, T.L., *et al.* (2014). The associations between suicidal ideation and attempt and anxiety symptoms and the demographic, psychological, and social moderators in Taiwanese adolescents. *Archives of Suicide Research, 18,* 104–116.

Yuce, M., Guner, S.N., Karabekiroglu, K., Baykal, S., *et al.* (2014). Association of Tourette syndrome and obsessive-compulsive disorder with allergic diseases in children and adolescents: A preliminary study. *European Review for Medical and Pharmacological Sciences, 18,* 303–310.

CHAPTER 7

Medical and Nutritional Approaches to Treating Self-Injurious Behavior and Aggression in Autism Spectrum Disorder

Fifteen Case Studies

John Green III, M.D., Evergreen Center, Portland, Oregon, and
Nancy O'Hara, M.D., Center for Integrative Health, Wilton, Connecticut

Introduction

Self-injurious and aggressive behaviors in people with autism and related developmental disorders (ASDs) are often viewed as by-products of the underlying disease process. Thus, such behaviors as head banging, wrist biting, eye gouging, and self-pinching, as well as head butting, biting, hitting, and lashing out at others, have been addressed as symptoms of autism per se. However, these behaviors may not be simply symptoms of autism; rather, they may be forms of nonverbal communication, dysfunctional and potentially harmful barometers of stress, or other internal states.

From this perspective, self-injurious behaviors (SIBs) in developmental disorders might be compared with nail biting, self-cutting, or addictive behaviors in neurotypical people. Such behaviors may express anxiety, depression, or major life stress, and may represent desperate attempts to change the inner landscape. In comparison, SIBs in people with communication disorders may be strong expressions of a need for change, of an intense inner experience that cannot be verbalized, of physical pain and system overload, or of a biological disturbance. In general, we have found that self-injurious behaviors may be eased or entirely alleviated by treatments or corrections that address medical problems or psychosocial stressors.

Shortly before his death, Ted Carr met with a small group of physicians, aiming to begin a study of SIBs in people with autism. We formed this group as a collaboration between Ted's behavioral approaches and our medical approaches to treating self-injury. It was so moving to feel Ted's excitement over the finding (new to him) that many children hurt themselves because of medical problems, particularly related to pain issues, and that these causes could be treated medically. Tragically, this collaboration ended prematurely with his accidental death. Remembering his dedication to helping these children, and his excitement over the new findings presented in part in this chapter, it is our hope that we may all move a step closer to solving the mystery of SIBs, arguably the most distressing aspect of autism.

There are some cases in which careful analysis of antecedents, surrounding circumstances, and the medical status of a patient fail to identify any explanation for self-harm, suggesting the behavior may be self-stimulatory, or an expression of the autism neuropathology. Nevertheless, rather like Pascal's Wager, there is less risk of harm in wrongly considering adverse behaviors in people with autism as expressive of some felt need or state to be identified and mitigated, than to wrongly attribute the behaviors to "autism," to be treated with physical, pharmaceutical, or aversive "restraints." Simply put, if we treat people with autism first as *individuals* (rather than "autistics") who are struggling with the effects of their condition, we will be better equipped to address and assist their problem behaviors.

In addition to the stresses of living with the discomforts, frustrations, and privations of autism, there are many complex medical issues that are commonly found in these patients, which may contribute directly or indirectly to self-injury through system overload. These issues include impaired pain perception (reducing nociceptive feedback—Tordjman *et al.*, 1997, 2009); autoimmune encephalopathy/pediatric autoimmune neuropsychiatric syndrome associated with *Streptococcus*; neuroinflammation/excitotoxicity (GABA/glutamate disruptions, with impaired self-regulation/impulsivity/sensory hypersensitivity); and painful disorders such as esophagitis, headache, constipation, or occult infections.

Furthermore, nutritional disturbances are common in people with ASDs. These disturbances may be caused by self-restricted diets, intestinal disorders with maldigestion and malabsorption, or nutrient dependencies associated with genetic polymorphisms, and contribute to pathological states. Thus, deficiencies of zinc, copper, iron, selenium, vitamins A, B complex, C, D, and E, or amino acids may result in immune deficiency or dysregulation, leading to opportunistic infections, allergy, autoimmunity, or impaired control of inflammatory processes. Deficits of magnesium, B6, B1, folate, or protein may result in reduced availability of methylation and trans-sulfuration by-products, including melatonin, epinephrine, dopamine, myelin, acetylcholine, carnitine, creatine, cysteine, taurine, sulfate, and glutathione, and also multiple epigenetic functions. Resultant effects may include sleep problems, poor energy production, impaired detoxification, chronic inflammation, intestinal motility disturbances, mood and attention disorders, and impaired self-regulation.

For a person with autism, being afflicted with even a few of the above-described conditions commonly found in ASD will cause significant suffering. In the context of chronic pain, sensory overload, malaise, obsessions, sympathetic overdrive, anxiety, and a hypervigilant hypothalamic–pituitary–adrenal axis, self-injury may be an effective way to redirect and, in a way, control suffering.

In effect, the child with autism faces multiple demands that exceed his capacity to respond. In working to help these people, we seek to lower demands from factors such as sensory overload, infections, toxic load, allergies, pain, and general stresses. We also seek to enhance their capacity to respond to such load factors through nutritional enhancement, assisting detoxification pathways, supporting mitochondrial functions, correcting oxidative stress, improving neurotransmitter balance, balancing endocrine disturbances, and working on improving communication efficiency.

The following cases illustrate a number of potential mechanisms contributing to self-injury. The choice of successfully managed cases is not representative of overall practice experience, as many of these individuals have very persistent SIBs that require multiple angles of investigation and treatment. In some cases, chronic repetition appears to cause habituation to the target behaviors, so that they may continue in the absence of an unmet need or trigger. Also, the common finding of relative hypoalgesia (Sandman, 1991; Tordjman et al., 1997, 2009) and stoicism in people with autism may well contribute to the severity of self-induced injuries in some individuals.

Case Studies

CASE 1: Nasal Foreign Bodies and Face Fisting

Monica is a 10-year-old girl with nonverbal autism who began striking her face and eyes violently with her fists 2 years prior to being seen in clinic. These self-attacks occurred multiple times per day, resulting in nosebleeds, black eyes, and a chronically swollen face. The behavior appeared to occur at random times, without provocation, except that attempts to restrain her resulted in violent hitting and kicking. There was no prior history of self-injury, though she had always been an intense and active child who became impatient easily. Prior treatments with risperidone, lorazepam, guanfacine, and fluoxetine produced sedation but very little reduction in SIBs. The mother had observed a moderate degree of improvement with marijuana, but, as it was illegal at that time and the source was illicit, she stopped this treatment prior to Monica's first visit. Exploring the possibility that pain was driving her behaviors, a week-long course of hydrocodone/acetaminophen was given, with significant improvements noted from the first day, and return of the behaviors the day after these drugs were discontinued. As she was not noticeably sedated by this intervention, it was suspected that pain might be driving the behaviors. An

X-ray of her sinuses revealed foreign bodies deep in her nasal cavity (a dime and a deciduous tooth), which she had apparently inserted in the distant past. These were removed, and she promptly ceased hitting herself and others.

In this case, the initial perspective and treatment approach were based on the notion that her SIBs were a manifestation of her autism, related perhaps to anxiety or to obsessive/compulsive rituals. This led to long delays in diagnosis, as she was subjected to months of ineffective drug trials. In retrospect, it is clear that her behavior was expressive of pain in her face, indicating an unmet need to have her pain identified and treated.

CASE 2: Head Banging with Multiple Complex Factors

In many cases, there is a complex set of circumstances involved in SIBs, and finding a solution may require a multi-pronged approach, including vigorous use of pharmacology. Angela, a 22-year-old woman with moderate autism, began bashing her head on walls and on the floor, with no prior history of SIBs. The SIBs began 1 day after she was extensively exposed to remodeling dust from concrete-grinding in her basement. Analysis of the dust showed lead content of 9000 ppm and mercury content of 1 ppm. Prior to this regression, she had a mild expressive language deficit but could carry on fairly complex conversations. Her favorite activities were drawing, including making illustrated cartoon stories that were quite intricate and evocative, often including themes of healing. She was learning to drive successfully, and loved roller-skating with a friend. Her SIBs were severe, unpredictable, and without discernible triggers.

She had a remote-past history of obsessive/ritualistic behaviors and had been treated with luvoxamine from age 11 to age 14 years, with partial response. The family noted further improvements with cyclic succimer (DMSA) treatments, and she was able to discontinue the luvoxamine without incident after approximately 1 year of succimer therapy. For the 8 years prior to the onset of head banging, she had taken only a multiple vitamin and a probiotic. When the head bashing began, her parents took her to Emergency Care, where she was treated with lorazepam, which was continued, though there was only a slight impact on the SIBs.

Due to severe recurring episodes, she had multiple Emergency and Urgent Care visits; clonazepam was added, with small improvement in the SIBs. Under the care of a neurologist, she continued on lorazepam and clonazepam, and a number of medication trials were performed. Risperidone aggravated her behaviors and was promptly discontinued. Zyprexa had no effect on the SIBs and caused facial swelling, so it was discontinued. Celexa was not helpful. Depakote was without benefit. Trileptal caused agitation and was stopped. Gabapentin produced a small reduction in head banging and was continued.

She came to our clinic on lorazepam 6 mg per day, gabapentin 200 mg twice a day, and clonazepam 3 mg per day. She related that she had "cobwebs" in her brain—bad thoughts that she wanted to get rid of (which she was never able to articulate clearly), and she asked for help to restore her ability to draw. Prior to the onset of these behaviors, she was a gifted though stylistic artist, could communicate quite complex thoughts, would write and illustrate stories, and enjoyed roller-skating and other outings with her family. Her SIBs would abate when on outings and intensify at home, school, or in the clinic. She had a long history of mild constipation.

Her head bashing had caused frontal bossing over a 4- to 5-cm area and, though reduced, was still occurring many times per hour in episodic fashion. Because of the severity of her self-injury, it was elected to first try aripiprazole, which produced a substantial reduction in severity and frequency of episodes. She required a large dose, 30 mg per day, which was associated with substantial sedation, drooling, social withdrawal, muffled and diminished speech, and cessation of her artwork. Attempts to reduce the dose of either benzodiazepine produced prompt increases in head banging. Elimination of gabapentin was accomplished without aggravation.

Though her head banging had been reduced to a lower severity and frequency by these medications, she was strongly sedated, and her communication was reduced to grunts and a few words. In the clinic office, she would still on occasion strike her head with moderate force on the hardwood floor or the corner of the desk. She would stop temporarily when reminded, only to resume within 1–2 minutes. A chelation challenge test for lead and mercury showed insignificant levels (1 year after exposure occurrence), and blood lead was <1. Head magnetic resonance imaging showed no abnormalities. Kidney, ureter, and bladder X-ray was unremarkable.

Because of her past response to succimer, she received a treatment trial, given 2 days each week. Due to the lack of behavioral response, and normal blood lead and provoked urine metals, this was discontinued. With the aim of replacing the benzodiazepines with less-sedating medication, a memantine trial was given, without response, followed by baclofen, amantadine, low-dose lithium, and inositol, each without benefit. Subsequently, trials with celecoxib and a pulse of prednisone failed to impact her SIBs, which continued to be partially controlled on the combination of lorazepam, clonazepam, and aripiprazole. She was trained to use a helmet, which she would often request before hitting her head, but she began hitting her eyes when the helmet was in place, causing damage to her lens and retina, which was very distressing to her because of her love of art. The eye hitting cleared when her dose of calcium was increased, the helmet was discontinued, and eye surgery was performed to improve her vision. On this regimen, her communication was very suppressed, she stopped feeding herself, began drooling, her artwork ceased, and social exchanges were virtually nonexistent.

Because of her ongoing constipation, high fecal lysozyme, and her limited response to medications, she was placed on a starch-free, low-sugar diet, with regular cleansing enemas. Within 1 week on this program, her SIBs ceased entirely for the first time in 2 years.

While continuing on this dietary and bowel regimen, the aripiprazole dose was reduced gradually from 30 mg daily to 5 mg daily, and she has been tapered completely off lorazepam and clonazepam. Each dose reduction was associated with a few days of resumed head banging, followed by improvements in artistic expression, creativity, and communication, and she began feeding herself and taking care of her own hygiene.

Angela's case illustrates the need for a comprehensive approach to the problem of self-injury, as she has required both pharmaceutical and medical interventions to regulate the severe self-damaging behaviors. At this point, she is back to creating and illustrating complex stories, is skating weekly with a friend, and her traumatic frontal bossing has resolved. It is clear that the aripiprazole is an important part of her regimen, as is the diet and the bowel regimen, as small changes in these factors may still produce aggravations.

Some people with autism are aggressive only against themselves, which is generally associated with more severe impairment or lack of awareness. In these cases, it is as if those around them do not exist, in a way, or as if their distress is so deep or vague that they cannot reach out for help. Many children are selectively aggressive toward family members (most often the mother), but not toward outsiders, instead biting or slapping or pinching themselves when outside of the home. This selectivity suggests a sort of inner hierarchy of responses, geared to the situation and context. However, in some cases, people with high-functioning autism hurt only themselves and are never aggressive toward others, perhaps understanding and respecting the notion that it is not acceptable to hurt others. Angela's case illustrates this phenomenon.

CASE 3: Allergic Rhinitis and Face Pounding

Allergies may be a trigger for SIBs, as in the case of Russell, who has severe allergic rhinitis and nonverbal autism. When the grass pollen season begins, he predictably becomes agitated and lashes out against caregivers and teachers;

or he bites his knuckles and hits his face. With vigorous symptomatic treatment of his allergies, using montelukast, antihistamines, and nasal steroids, these behaviors abate and are easy to manage with redirection and distraction.

CASE 4: Sulfur Pathway Disruptions and Self-Injury

Oxidative stress and the resulting excitotoxicity may trigger SIBs in some children. For example, William is a child with moderately severe autism who presented at age 4 years with head bashing, very limited language, striking stoicism about pain, and difficulty engaging socially. He would often seek out the edges of walls or furniture to hit his head, producing deep bruising and, at times, lacerations. Laboratory testing showed very low reduced glutathione, with elevation of the oxidized fraction, low blood cysteine, and blood nitrotyrosine level more than three times normal. When he received an intravenous infusion of glutathione, his SIBs stopped for the following week, returning gradually after that. He was tried on glutathione as a suppository and transdermal lotion without similar benefit, and so was started on N-acetyl cysteine (NAC), a precursor to glutathione. Though his response was not as prompt or dramatic as the response to IV glutathione, his SIBs diminished in severity within a few days and ceased entirely within a few weeks. Six months after initiating NAC, his family tried stopping it, and after about 1 week, he began tapping his head on corners. This behavior cleared within days of resuming the supplement.

In William's case, the labs provide a rationale for his positive response to NAC, in that his glutathione was depleted and oxidized (indicative of oxidative stress), his cysteine was low (showing deficiency, which contributes to oxidative stress and decreased glutathione synthesis), and nitrotyrosine was elevated, a marker for inflammation and oxidative stress. We know that cysteine can improve these problems directly, and that it also can compete against glutamate (through using the same transport mechanism), which is "excitotoxic." By reducing glutamate effects, cysteine can produce a general calming of the nervous system, as in William's case. Also, we are providing further supports for William's cysteine and glutathione, through enhancing his intake of animal protein, supplying generous doses of B vitamins (especially B6, B12, and folinic acid) with magnesium, and using spices and herbal remedies (such as curcumin from turmeric, broccoli-sprout extract, and grape-seed extract) to reduce inflammation.

CASE 5: Plumbism with Aggression toward Self and Others

Lead overload can cause hyperactivity and aggressive behaviors (James *et al.*, 2009; Mielke and Zahran, 2012; Needleman *et al.*, 1996; Swedo *et al.*, 1998), most likely through excitotoxic effects. Katrina is a 7-year-old girl with mild regressive autism who is able to communicate in short sentences, is learning to read, is able to engage in some playground games with other children, and is mildly hyperactive. She has meltdowns that may be triggered by transitions or slight frustrations. In these situations, she attempts to scratch whomever is nearby, and if blocked, she scratches her own face and arms until they bleed. Her lab testing showed low glutathione and elevated nitrotyrosine, similar to William, but less severe. Her blood lead was 4 (action level is 5 or greater). We did a chelation challenge to help evaluate body burden of stored lead, and her post-challenge urine output rose to 32, compared with 2 on the pre-challenge urine test. Also, we were interested to note that she was much calmer for 2 days after the DMSA challenge. As this time frame is inadequate to significantly reduce the lead burden, we interpreted the transient improvements as being related to the inherent antioxidant effects of DMSA, along with its positive effect on cysteine and glutathione.

She was started on a program of cyclic DMSA, given Friday through Sunday each week. The family reported that her aggressive and injurious behaviors diminished each week, with her best days being Mondays and her worst days being Thursdays. We elected to halve the dose of DMSA and give it Sunday through Thursday, and on this regimen her behaviors subsided. After 3 months on this schedule, as her behaviors were well maintained, we reduced the DMSA to Sunday through Tuesday, with only slight aggravations noted at the end of the week. After 3 more months on this schedule, we retested and found her blood level was 1, and the challenged urine level was down to 12. She was moved to a DMSA schedule of 2 days per week, for 6 more months, with good control of the problem behaviors; we were able to discontinue the DMSA entirely after 1 year, without recurrence of significant aggression or self-injury.

In Katrina's case, her lead values were not diagnostic of lead poisoning. Our search for the source of lead turned up the fact that she had lived in a 90-year-old home for the first 18 months of her life, which was a likely source of past exposure to lead. We felt that her response to the DMSA was at least in part due to its antioxidant effects, but that the lead burden she showed was a major contributor to her oxidative stress. In the follow-up testing after 1 year of low-dose DMSA, her nitrotyrosine had dropped to just slightly elevated, and her glutathione had risen to normal, which further supported our interpretation of lead being the major contributor to her behaviors, through its excitotoxic effects.

CASE 6: Gastroesophagitis with Wrist Biting

Gastrointestinal pain is a common source of severe distress and aggressive behaviors in children with autism (McElhanon *et al.*, 2014). Donny is a 10-year-old boy with autism and moderate communication disorder. He presented with severe agitation, aggressive behaviors in school, and wrist biting which caused bleeding and scarring. With flare-ups he would scream, bite his wrist, and complain of a volcano in his throat. Medications on presentation included risperidone and *pro re nata* (i.e., when necessary) lorazepam, which reduced classroom aggression, but did not impact the wrist biting and striking out at home. A trial course of omeprazole brought substantial relief of his wrist biting and suspected pain behaviors. He would have periodic flares, even on high-dose omeprazole, and at these times would readily accept tube feedings and IV therapies. When on nasogastric drainage and feedings, his crying and wrist-biting behaviors would clear entirely, despite the discomfort of the indwelling tube. Pan-endoscopy was performed, which showed severe esophagitis and gastritis. Antifungal therapy was offered, as this has sometimes been helpful with reflux problems, and he did show partial improvements with nystatin suspension, so it was continued, along with aggressive treatment with high-dose proton-pump inhibitors (up to 90 mg per day of lansoprazole and equivalent). However, he continued to have periodic severe flare-ups, which eventually led to placement of a gastrostomy tube for continuous drip feedings. On this regimen, he has become free of SIBs and pain complaints over the past 4 months but has had to continue with the drip feedings, due to his inability to ingest sufficient calories without recurrence of symptoms.

CASE 7: Constipation and Hand Wringing in Rett Syndrome

Susie, a 12-year-old girl, has Rett syndrome. She obsessively wrings her hands and has other repetitive behaviors, such as scratching her pubic area and repeating meaningless phrases. Her hand wringing has caused articular deformities. She also has struggled with chronic constipation. Though her hand wringing does not clear entirely, we've seen a marked reduction in this behavior, and in her pubic scratching, with bowel cleansing. In fact, an increase in her hand wringing is a good predictor of a positive response to a bowel cleanse, which has been needed periodically, even if she is having daily stools on her preventive regimen.

CASE 8: Face Slapping and Scratching Responsive to Melatonin and Methyl-B12

Katie is a 4-year-old who was diagnosed with autism at age 3 years. When first seen, her language was limited to single-word requests, her sleep patterns were very disrupted, and she would often slap or scratch her mother, or her own face, when frustrated with transitions or changes in routine. She was not toilet trained and struggled with feeding herself. Pertinent lab findings included low RBC S-adenosyl-methionine (SAMe)/elevated S-adenosyl-homocysteine (SAH) and low glutathione. She was started on low-dose melatonin, to be followed by methyl-B12, given twice weekly by subcutaneous injection. The melatonin brought prompt improvement in sleep-onset issues, though middle-of-night waking was only partially mitigated. After the first injection of B12, she started sleeping through the night. After the fourth shot, she began to use pairs of words and started to accept changes and frustrations with less protestation. After 1 month on B12, the slapping and scratching behaviors stopped, she tolerated transitions and changes in routine without difficulty, she began feeding herself, and toilet training was successfully underway. Repeat labs after 4 months showed normalization of the methylation markers (SAMe and SAH) and improvement in glutathione. At 4-month follow-up, she was speaking in three-to-four-word sentences, making simple observations, sleeping through the night regularly, and remained free of slapping and scratching behaviors.

In Katie's example, the methyl-B12 treatment helped restore the sulfur pathway in her body, as has been demonstrated in the work of James and colleagues (2004, 2009). This pathway impacts neurotransmitters, energy production, detoxification, immune function, and many other bodily functions. Though we cannot readily test all of the functions, her symptomatic response and clearing of harmful behaviors demonstrated her need for this nutrient.

CASE 9: PANDAS-Associated Aggression

Cayden has pervasive developmental disorder not otherwise specified, with excellent developmental progress in an integrated classroom until age 11 years, when he developed the sudden onset of intractable and pre-emptory obsessions, emotional volatility, threats of self-destruction, impulsivity, head slapping, and extreme aggression toward his family. Labs showed a fourfold elevation of anti-DNAase antibodies and mildly elevated ASO titer, with a negative throat culture for strep. He was treated with azithromycin, and after 1 week on the antibiotic, his agitation and aggression cleared entirely. After 3 weeks, his obsessions became mild and manageable. The dose was reduced at 1 month to 250 mg every other day, and within 2 weeks the parents noticed that his aggressive behaviors, slapping, and obsessions began to reappear. The azithromycin dose was switched to daily again, with complete settling of these symptoms. After 6 months on daily azithromycin, his symptoms again began to flare. At that time he was switched to cefuroxime, and his behaviors again subsided in a matter of days. He remained on antibiotics for 2 years, with repeated attempts to wean him resulting in reappearance of his initial symptoms. At this point, his insurance carrier granted consent for IV gamma globulin treatments. After the first round of gamma globulin, he successfully stopped the cefuroxime, and he was able to discontinue the IVs after the third round, remaining free of SIBs and aggression in the 1-year follow-up.

CASE 10: PANDAS/PANS with Severe Head Banging

Lyle, a 10-year-old boy with nonverbal autism, was placed in a 24-hour residential program because of severe aggression and head banging, both occurring without recognized triggers, and ongoing for more than 1 year prior to institutionalization. In this setting, he was treated with intensive behavioral therapies aimed at reining in his aggression and SIBs but was poorly controlled at best. He developed an upper respiratory infection, which was treated with amoxicillin. After 3 days on amoxicillin, the staff noted an unprecedented and complete cessation of head banging, with a marked calming of his violent behaviors towards others. These behaviors, however, resumed within 3–4 days of completing his course of amoxicillin, though his respiratory symptoms had cleared. Because of this recurrence of symptoms, he was placed on cefuroxime, aiming for broader antimicrobial coverage. Again, within 3 days he became manageable, with complete clearing of his problem behaviors over the succeeding 2 weeks. Cefuroxime has been continued for 4 months, and his behavioral improvements have been sustained until the past 2 weeks, when he began to show more agitation and mild aggression towards himself and his caregivers. Careful investigation into his care situation revealed that he had been successfully avoiding taking nearly half of his doses of cefuroxime. Reimplementation of a 100%-compliance regime restored peace to him and the staff in approximately 1 week, and his stabilization has been sustained for the succeeding 2 months.

In 1998, Swedo and associates first described a syndrome of acute onset of a neuropsychiatric syndrome with features similar to those of Cayden and Lyle. This syndrome was titled "pediatric autoimmune neuropsychiatric disorder associated with streptococcal infections" (PANDAS; or PANS, pediatric acute onset neuropsychiatric syndrome), for the involvement of *Streptococcus*, and has more recently been referred to as "pediatric autoimmune neuropsychiatric disorder," because of the involvement of other microbial or immune triggers, leading to inflammatory encephalopathy. Symptoms included agitation, obsessive/compulsive behaviors, tics, deterioration of motor functions, and anxiety. The presumptive pathogenesis is through molecular mimicry of group A beta hemolytic *Streptococcus* with the individual's basal ganglia, analogous to the cross-reactive immune response to strep seen in rheumatic fever and post-streptococcal glomerulonephritis. The resulting immune inflammatory response is thought to generate an autoimmune encephalopathy. Treatment is targeted against the *Streptococcus* bacteria, with ongoing antibiotics. In some cases, children require other immune-modulatory therapies, such as steroids, intravenous gamma globulin, or plasmapheresis.

CASE 11: PANS and Self-Injurious Behaviors

Ty was a 14-year-old with moderate autism—he was verbal, interactive, and calm, with some perseverative behaviors. But then in December 2012 and January 2013, Ty had a severe upper respiratory tract infection and sinus infection. In January, he developed an acute onset of extreme OCD and SIBs, picking his skin and nails, as well as biting his skin until it bled. He also developed sleeplessness—only sleeping 2–3 hours each night—enuresis, and daytime wetting.

Blood work showed high IgM and IgG mycoplasma titers, but otherwise strep titers, Lyme western blot and co-infections, thyroid function including antibodies, liver and kidney function, testosterone levels, and inflammatory markers were all within the normal range. Throat and sinus cultures were also negative.

Ty was placed on azithromycin with improvement in SIB, daytime wetting, and enuresis. His sleep was still restless and he continued to have residual skin picking. There was some additional improvement with immune support, including aloe and curcumin. He continued to take a prophylactic dose of azithromycin over the next year.

In December 2013, he developed another sinus infection and behavior again worsened, including more severe SIB, biting and ripping skin, as well as aggression and somatic symptoms (enuresis, daytime wetting, and sleeplessness). All of the repeated blood work (as above) was normal including mycoplasma titers. However, his CaM kinase testing was markedly elevated (206; normal <110). Strep and other infection-triggered antibodies increase calcium/calmodulin-dependent (CaM kinase) protein kinase in PANS. There is also high reactivity against dopamine receptors. This elevation is a pathognomonic marker of PANS, an acute-onset behavioral change due to strep and other infectious and metabolic changes.

Despite multiple antibiotic changes including penicillin, amoxicillin-clavulanate, clindamycin and ciprofloxacin, multiple natural agents (5-HTP, NAC, rhodiola, ashwagandha, GABA, and theanine), multiple anti-inflammatories (curcumin, aloe, essential fatty acids, and steroids), multiple selective serotonin reuptake inhibitors, anxiolytics and antipsychotics (including Zoloft, propanolol, clonidine, Abilify, and risperidone), multiple therapeutic and behavioral interventions, and one psychiatric hospitalization, there was no change.

In March 2014, Ty was truly suffering with extreme OCD, very little sleep, and severe anxiety. He was literally climbing the walls. At that time, IV immunoglobulin, an intervention found to be highly successful in children with PANS/PANDAS, was not approved. Thus, to try to quell his overwhelming symptoms and provide some immune support, we trialed helminth therapy (see below). Within one dose, he was calmer, sleeping well with no agitation, SIB, or aggression, and he showed a marked decrease in anxiety and a marked improvement in interactions.

It is widely recognized that autoimmune, allergic, and other inflammatory diseases are pandemic in Western cultures. These diseases are not found in pre-industrial societies, and were not observed prior to the industrial revolution in any country. Thus, these diseases are not due to any "natural" condition of humanity, but rather are due to environmental factors, such as using toilets, wearing shoes, living indoors with lack of vitamin D exposure, Caesarian section births, and the lack of breast feeding (to list a few). Given these factors, our immune systems are compromised, leading to multiple autoimmune diseases (including insulin-dependent diabetes mellitus, arthritis, inflammatory bowel disease, and PANS/PANDAS, as well as asthma, allergies, attention deficit hyperactivity disorder, and autism). These factors are detailed in peer-reviewed literature (Bilbo *et al.*, 2011; Parker and Ollerton, 2013), especially the loss of diversity from the ecosystem of the human body, a condition termed "biome depletion." This state can be described as the loss of many species of flora that normally coexist with the human body. This biome-depleted state affects all post-industrial humans during and after fetal development; it remains the strongest challenge for modern medicine to overcome in the field of immunology, and stands as the most well-established cause of autoimmune diseases.

"Helminths and their eggs probably are the most potent stimulators of mucosal Th2 responses" (Elliott *et al.*, 2000, p.1848). This intervention induces an immune response and begins to reconstitute our microbiomes and thus our immune systems. "Biome reconstitution includes the controlled and population-wide reintroduction (i.e., domestication) of selected species that have been all but eradicated from the human biome in industrialized society and holds great promise for the elimination of pandemics of allergic, inflammatory and autoimmune diseases" (Parker and Ollerton, 2013, p.89). The organism used in Ty and other such patients for the purpose of exercising their immune systems is known as an HDC (*Hymenolepis diminuta* cysticercoid). HDCs are known to increase IL-10 (a regulatory cytokine) and decrease TNF-alpha (a pro-inflammatory cytokine), thus decreasing inflammation and supporting appropriate immune function. The HDCs are raised in grain beetles (*Tenebrio molitor*), which are normally found in the human food supply as a harmless contaminant in a wide variety of grains. The grain beetles, in turn, subsist strictly on materials prepared for human consumption (a blend of oatmeal and brewer's yeast). Thus, all potential contaminants accompanying the cultivation and isolation of HDCs from grain beetles are those products already consumed by humans in post-industrial culture, making this a safe and highly effective intervention for autoimmune disease and biome reconstruction.

In the past year, Ty has been maintained on monthly HDCs and has continued to do well, with minimal and controllable OCD and anxiety, no somatic symptoms, and no intercurrent illnesses; he has been interactive and compliant. When his parents have missed an HDC dose, they have noticed marked worsening in OCD, anxiety, and SIB. We plan to continue HDCs as long as behavioral and immune improvements continue.

CASE 12: Monilial Triggering of Genital Self-Abrading

Some children with SIBs respond to nystatin, another antifungal, which does not inhibit the P450 enzyme system. Sylvia is a 9-year-old girl with autism, limited expressive language, troubled bedtime behavior consisting of unexplained giggling and agitation, mild constipation, obsessive/compulsive tendencies regarding her style of playing and artwork, and almost-mutilating scratching and rubbing of her genital area, leading to excoriation and bleeding. She did not have a vaginal discharge or typical yeast changes in the perineal area. Ketoconazole treatment brought prompt improvements in the scratching and bedtime behaviors, with recurrence about 2 weeks after completing the 3-week course. She was then treated with vigorous doses of probiotics plus oral nystatin, along with a diet low in sugar and yeast products. This produced gradual improvements in her scratching and rubbing over the succeeding month, and also in her constipation and in her bedtime routines. After 3 months of continuous nystatin, careful diet, and probiotics, her bedtime, constipation, and scratching problems remained clear. She was then able to switch to an intermittent program of nystatin given 2 weeks per month (without symptom recurrence when not taking nystatin) and is successfully weaning off it entirely. In this case, the positive response to both ketoconazole and nystatin points to direct antifungal effects as the primary mechanism of benefit in her treatment.

CASE 13: Loss of Communication System Resulting in Severe Self-Facial Beating

Steven is a 14-year-old boy with autism who speaks only a few words and has depended on signing to meet his needs. He functioned successfully in an intensive private-school program, wherein his teachers and aides were well versed in signing. When his program lost funding from the public school system and he was moved to a public special-education classroom, he began to manifest severe SIBs and also outward aggression. He would violently strike his nose against his knee, or jump up and down violently, almost like a threatening ape. Several staff people were injured trying to contain him, and two men were brought into the classroom to contain his dangerous behaviors. Exploring the causes of his behavior, his mother brought him for a visit to his previous school. He ran to the door smiling and kissed one of his previous aides on the cheek. The recognition that his violence was related to losing his communication system and being physically restrained led his mother into a long battle with the school system to return him to the expensive private school, and she eventually prevailed. During the months of waiting, he failed to respond to risperidone, aripiprazole, benzodiazepines, memantine, and baclofen, and he had to be removed from school.

When he finally was able to return to his previous school, he again walked in beaming. Marked improvements were noted immediately, though he would very occasionally have an outburst of hurting himself at school (and never at home). We suspect that he has a form of post-traumatic stress related to many months of communication loss and being forcefully restrained. Reflecting on his case, it seems that he was enraged at being misunderstood and by being physically restrained; anger cannot be treated effectively by medications—rather, the causes need to be addressed.

CASE 14: Pyrroluria with Aversive Measures Leading to Self-Slashing

Alexander was diagnosed with autism at age 4 years. At that time, he had rudimentary language (single-word requests, naming objects), very impaired social skills, poor eye contact, and selective auditory and tactile sensitivity.

Also, he was hyperactive and oppositional, oblivious to danger, and had severe tantrums, throwing objects or his own body violently on the floor. Desperate to control his behaviors, the parents resorted to heavy-handed disciplinary techniques, including deprivation, aversive measures, and actually spanking him. These measures were minimally effective.

At age 5 years, he began biting his wrist, and several times grabbed a kitchen knife and deliberately cut his arm. At that point the parents started medical interventions. His diet was changed to exclude gluten and dairy products, with reduced sugars and the elimination of food additives, followed by a notable reduction in his tantrums within 1 week. As his urinary kryptopyrrole was more than twice normal, he was treated with high-dose vitamin B6, plus magnesium and zinc supplements. Kryptopyrrole is a metabolite of heme, involved in oxygen transport. Elevation of this metabolite in the urine represents a defect in this metabolism. Kryptopyrrole causes urinary wasting of zinc and vitamin B6, and may lead to disruptions in serotonin production, which is dependent on adequate B6. In people with pyrroluria, treatment with these nutrients tends to improve focus, self-regulation, and mood.

Over the succeeding 2 weeks, his hyperactive and oppositional behaviors showed marked improvements. As his behaviors improved, the family ceased their draconian disciplinary tactics. He stopped biting his wrists and there were no more incidents with knives. He began to respond to verbal requests and became able to sit and listen to bedtime stories. When the parents ran out of B6 at one point, his hyperactivity resurfaced without a return of the SIBs. Reintroduction of B6 restored his focus and attention. Over the succeeding 2 months, his sensory problems abated and he was clearly much more comfortable in his body and his world.

In overview, addressing the food triggers and the pyrroluria helped him with receptivity, communication, focus, and self-regulation. As his function improved and the parents stopped punishing his behaviors, he stopped hurting himself. Was his self-injury a result of being punished aggressively, or did he stop hurting himself because treatment had raised his awareness and comfort level enough that he could stop sending distress signals such as self-biting and cutting? His self-injury did not end until the punishments stopped, almost 2 months after the described improvements had begun. From this, we felt that the treatments made him more comfortable and much easier to live with, so that the family could learn new ways of correcting him, and the self-injurious behaviors cleared.

CASE 15: Self-Pinching and Bruising in a Perfectionistic Boy Struggling with Math Challenges

Gabriel has been emerging from autism, with residual issues of severe shyness, concrete communication patterns, and obsessions about dinosaurs and his artistic representations of them. He has shown extraordinary artistic abilities, especially in sculpture with clay, and demands perfection in his work.

At age 11 years, after he started middle school, he was brought to clinic literally covered with bruises, confluent spots 2–3 cm in diameter, and areas of petechiae. A workup for coagulopathy was entirely unrevealing. Careful re-examination showed that the bruises were absent on his back and more densely distributed over his upper body, which led to the suspicion that they were self-induced. We learned that he was having a very hard time with math in middle school, though he did not mention this to his parents, who staunchly believed that his bruises were caused by some disease process. We met with him in private and asked him about pinching himself, which he denied, though he hung his head while responding in few words. We talked about having high expectations that cannot always be met, and about making mistakes, which is sometimes the best way to learn and grow. The parents agreed to move him to a simpler math class. Though there was no acknowledgment from him, his bruising stopped within a few weeks. In retrospect, his self-injury appeared to be a result of his perfectionistic tendencies and his sense of failure in math. In this case, acknowledging his stress, reassuring him about his struggles in math (that mistakes are common and are okay), and changing his class were sufficient interventions to mitigate his pinching behaviors.

Conclusion

In conclusion, it is important to relate to people with autism first as people, as individuals struggling with a difficult illness causing multisystem disruptions. In these people, harmful behaviors, such as self-injury or aggression, are often triggered by pain (constipation, infection, inflammation, headache), invasive or violent experiences (illustrated by our cases, such as Alexander's severe discipline, or another patient's experience of sexual abuse by a care provider, leading to genital hitting), disruption of a biochemical pathway, or overload (caused by sensory issues, school demands, social issues, perfectionism). It is appropriate to diligently search for treatable or correctable triggers of self-injury in people with autism. Successfully modifying these triggers might save them from unnecessary and potentially damaging physical or pharmacological restraints.

References

Bilbo, S.D., Wray, G.A., Perkins, S.E., and Parker, W. (2011). Reconstitution of the human biome as the most reasonable solution for epidemics of allergic and autoimmune diseases. *Medical Hypotheses, 77,* 494–504.

Elliott, D.E., Urban, J.F., Argo, C.K., and Weinstock, J.V. (2000). Does the failure to acquire helminthic parasites predispose to Crohn's disease? *Federation of American Societies for Experimental Biology, 14*(12), 1848–1855.

James, S.J., Melnyk, S.B., Fuchs, G., Reid, T., *et al.* (2009). Efficacy of methylcobalamin and folinic acid treatment on glutathione redox status in children with autism. *American Journal of Clinical Nutrition, 89*(1), 425–430.

James, S.J., Melnyk, S.B., Jernigan, S., Janak, L., Cutler, P., and Neubrander, J.M. (2004). Metabolic biomarkers of increased oxidative stress and impaired methylation capacity in children with autism. *American Journal of Clinical Nutrition, 80*(6), 1611–1617.

McElhanon, B., McCracken, C., Karpen, S., and Sharp, W. (2014). Gastrointestinal symptoms in autism spectrum disorder: A meta-analysis. *Pediatrics, 133*(5), 872–883.

Mielke, H.W., and Zahran, S. (2012). The urban rise and fall of air lead (Pb) and the latent surge and retreat of societal violence. *Environment International, 43,* 48–55.

Needleman, H.L., Riess, J.A., Tobin, M.J., Biesecker, G.E., and Greenhouse, J.B. (1996). Bone lead levels and delinquent behavior. *Journal of the American Medical Association, 275*(5), 363–369.

Parker, W., and Ollerton, J. (2013). Evolutionary biology and anthropology suggest biome reconstitution as a necessary approach toward dealing with immune disorders. *Evolution, Medicine, and Public Health, 2013*(1), 89–103.

Sandman, C.A. (1991). The opiate hypothesis in autism and self-injury. *Journal of Child and Adolescent Psychopharmacology, 1*(3), 237–248.

Swedo, S.E., Leonard, H.L., Garvey, M., Mittleman, B., *et al.* (1998). Pediatric autoimmune neuropsychiatric disorders associated with streptococcal infections: Clinical description of the first 50 cases. *American Journal of Psychiatry, 155*(2), 264–271.

Tordjman, S., Anderson, G.M., Botbol, M., Brailly-Tabar, S., *et al.* (2009). Pain reactivity and plasma β-endorphin in children and adolescents with autistic disorder. *PLoS One, 4*(8), e5289.

Tordjman, S., Anderson, G.M., McBride, P.A., Hertzig, M.E., *et al.* (1997). Plasma beta-endorphin, adrenocorticotropin hormone, and cortisol in autism. *Journal of Child Psychology and Psychiatry, 38*(6), 705–715.

CHAPTER 8

Dietary and Nutrition Intervention to Address Self-Injurious Behavior in Autism

Thoughts from Five Years of Clinical Care

Kelly M. Barnhill, MBA, CN, CCN, The Johnson Center for
Child Health and Development, Austin, Texas

Introduction

Self-injurious behavior (SIB) is often seen in children diagnosed with autism spectrum disorder (ASD). This behavior often includes head banging and hand biting. Many parents and professionals are at a loss for both the underlying cause of this behavior and also effective treatment and intervention to minimize or eradicate it. Yet if you have a conversation with any parent of a child with autism, you are more than likely to hear about "dietary intervention" and perhaps even something called the "gluten- and casein-free diet" (GFCF) in that exchange. Numerous parent reports have indicated an improvement in general well-being, including SIB, following nutritional and dietary intervention. Regardless of a family's choice in addressing a dietary approach, most families are aware of this type of intervention.

Changing diets to address associated symptoms of autism, including SIB, is not a new idea. Researchers and clinicians have been considering dietary therapy for autism for over 50 years, as well as a variety of other diseases and disorders. As more information and research has emerged over the past 20 years, more and more families have considered dietary change or management as a potential intervention to address concerning behaviors. Dietary approaches that can be useful in addressing SIB include: allergy-elimination diets, limited-carbohydrate-intake diet plans, the Feingold diet, and a diet that eliminates gluten and casein proteins (the GFCF diet). While these approaches continue to be used clinically by many practitioners, little research substantiating efficacy has been published to date. This chapter reviews the rationale for dietary intervention and discusses a variety of recommended dietary plans to address SIB on a clinical basis.

Nutritional Status and Dietary Considerations

In general, very few children in the United States are at risk of malnutrition. As a result, nutrition is not typically prioritized in pediatric well-baby/child care beyond infancy. Specific subsets of the population with significant concern are those with underlying medical conditions, those who are homeless, and those living in rural areas (Casey *et al.*, 2001). These children are, in fact, typically tracked through a variety of appropriate systems: children with chronic health concerns are triaged to dietetic care either through primary care pediatrics or a specialty clinic. Children in rural communities and those who are homeless are more often served through social services in which dietetic care is a component—free or low-cost school meals, government programs, and shelter care.

Children with autism may, in fact, fit into the underlying medical condition category, though very little work has been done to evaluate the true status and needs of this population (Geraghty, Depasquale, and Lane, 2010; Zimmer *et al.*, 2012; Lane *et al.*, 2014). Early work in nutrition and autism was published in the 1980s, indicating that children with autism were more likely to have disordered eating, cravings or food jags, and pica (Raiten and Massaro, 1986). Work published between 2005 and 2015 has expressed concern for decreased calcium intake and absorption, particularly in the presence of a casein-free diet (Hediger *et al.*, 2008). Several good review articles have also been published in recent years: some data on the diets of children with ASD have not shown significant differences compared with typical peers; others show more rigidity and pickiness in food choices (Sharp *et al.*, 2013).

While we do not have accurate data and a uniform recommended course of action for assessment and intervention with children diagnosed with ASD, we are learning more and more about factors that suggest this is a population that is nutritionally at risk. Data published in the past 15 years show that children with autism suffer gastrointestinal reflux, maldigestion, malabsorption, gastrointestinal inflammation, and growth issues more frequently than typical peers (Horvath and Perman, 2002). Unfortunately, a gastroenterology referral with a new autism diagnosis when gastrointestinal symptoms are present is rarely offered, despite the new standard of care that was recommended in a GI Consensus Statement published in 2010 (Buie *et al.*, 2010). This comprehensive paper's key recommended statement included: "Individuals with ASDs deserve the same thorough diagnostic workup for gastrointestinal symptoms as should occur for other patients." For most of us who regularly consult with and treat children with ASDs and ongoing gastrointestinal concerns, referral for gastrointestinal assessment, appropriate evaluation, and commensurate treatment still remains rare in the standard of current care.

One factor complicating the accurate assessment and diagnosis of any gastrointestinal concern is the child's inability to effectively communicate pain. Children who are nonverbal or have limited verbal abilities but are experiencing gastrointestinal pain can often present with symptoms such as applying pressure to the abdomen, night waking with crying and yelling, hyperactive behavior prior to and just after a bowel movement, and more. Parents report that children lean over chair arms and coffee tables, wake at 2 a.m. screaming uncontrollably but not in an apparent night terror, and bounce or run around just prior to a bowel movement. Burping, flatulence, diarrhea, constipation, bloating, oily or greasy stools, grainy stools, and bloody or mucous stools are all also physical signs and characteristics that are indicative of potential gastrointestinal concerns that can cause pain. The behaviors noted above can simply be a child's response to both managing and communicating pain.

Rationale for Assessment and Intervention

First, it is becoming increasingly clear that many people with autism are at risk of nutritional insufficiency for the reasons noted above. It has been shown that many children with autism have multiple underlying nutritional deficiencies. This could be a result of self-restricted diets, abnormal digestion, poor absorption, or an inability to utilize the nutrients effectively. Research has not uncovered all of the answers, and it is likely that this is a multisystemic concern. We now know that the health of the brain, the immune system, and the gastrointestinal system are tightly linked to nutritional status, and involvement between and among these systems is common. These nutrient risk factors impact growth, cognitive function, and developmental abilities both short and long term. For this reason alone, we should be assessing each child presenting with an ASD and particularly those with behavioral and health concerns as soon as possible at baseline diagnosis.

Additionally, those with ASDs can be allergic or sensitive to foods for a variety of reasons. These food allergies, intolerances, and sensitivities play a role in gastrointestinal symptoms, including gastroesophageal reflux, abdominal discomfort, and abnormal stool patterns. It has been documented that chronic gastrointestinal inflammation from foods can impair digestion and absorption, an impairment which negatively impacts growth (Christie *et al.*, 2002). However, as research and clinical experience indicates, foods can also trigger an immune response that can cause problems in other body systems, including the peripheral nervous system and brain. Chemicals, additives, and preservatives found in many foods can act directly on the brain to alter behavior.

Finally, professionally guided dietary change with the support of a qualified clinician is a reasonable approach to addressing nutritional and gastrointestinal concerns. Appropriately applied diet plans do not detract from a child's health and well-being in any way, and can enhance health significantly. From a clinical perspective, trialing a reasonable diet plan for a period of 60–90 days while taking accurate data and also observational reports can have a profound impact on a child's overall health and well-being, which can in turn positively impact the child's behavior.

Standardized assessment and appropriate treatment and care for those children requiring intervention is of primary importance for the reasons mentioned above: First, knowledgeable care and professional nutritional intervention are critical to optimal development, growth, and learning. Second, children with autism frequently lack appropriate expressive language to adequately communicate their pain and needs, leaving them completely unable to verbalize information regarding any gastrointestinal concerns. Providing treatment and intervention to meet the child's nutritional needs often then improves the child's health status, thus allowing for greater cognitive and developmental gains, and a decrease in confounding behaviors such as sleep disturbance and SIB.

Allergy-Elimination Diets

Food allergies, intolerances, and sensitivities are an often overlooked cause of behavior problems. Some children may present with red ears, red cheeks, or dark circles under their eyes. They may have dry, flaky skin, rosacea, or eczema. They may have a consistently runny nose or a dry, scratchy cough. These can be signs of food responsiveness—whether it is a true allergy, an intolerance, or a sensitivity. The most common dietary components which appear to dramatically affect a number of children are dairy, corn, soy, and wheat products, and food additives, colors, and preservatives. Symptoms associated with food responsiveness are often fairly common complaints, including diffuse headaches, tantrums, nausea, stomachaches, distractedness, and what many clients describe as "being zoned out." Such forms of pain are often associated with SIB. For example, head pain may be associated with head banging. As we have noted, many of these children lack adequate expressive language skills and are simply unable to communicate information regarding how they feel. Parents, caregivers, and teachers are then completely unaware that the child is not feeling well. Parents often report that their children are distracted, irritable, having tantrums, defiant, and clearly unhappy. Observation coupled with an accurate food diary account of intake can lead to uncovering potential food responsiveness. Children can then be tested if food allergies, intolerances, or sensitivities are suspected. If the child tests positive for certain foods, these items should be eliminated from the diet. Research indicates that children with ASD have food allergies, intolerances, and sensitivities more often than typical peers (Jyonouchi et al., 2004). While these are not true allergies, meaning they are not IgE-mediated histamine-based allergies leading to events such as hives and anaphylaxis, they are still concerning. These non-IgE-mediated food intolerances and sensitivities have been documented as adversely affecting growth, total food intake, learning, behavior, and functioning (Jyonouchi et al., 2004). Exposure to these offending foods can cause all of the behavioral symptoms (irritability, SIB, sleep disturbance, hyperactivity) and physical symptoms (burping, gastroesophageal reflux disease, bloating, flatulence, constipation, diarrhea) which can then lead to poor growth status, decreased cognitive abilities, and developmental concerns.

Clinical signs which are associated with food allergy, intolerance, and sensitivity include:

- complete avoidance of certain food groups, or an abundance of certain foods in the diet

- decreased food intake, a child who rarely seems to eat a full meal, a child who "picks" at their food

- night waking, poor sleep status

- dry skin, eczema, rosacea

- gastrointestinal symptoms including burping, reflux, flatulence, constipation, and diarrhea

- hyperactivity, excessive silliness

- irritability

- frequent runny nose, itchy ears

- dark circles under the eyes, often called "allergic shiners"

- frequent colds or upper respiratory infections.

An appropriate intervention in these circumstances is to eliminate any trigger foods, either permanently (in the case of processed additives, colors, and preservatives) or temporarily (in the case of foods that have become inflammatory to the child's system but can be tolerated once again). This allergy-elimination-diet approach is designed specifically to remove foods, for a period of time, to which a child may be responding negatively. The premise is that removing certain trigger foods will allow the body's systems time to rest and recuperate, and ultimately allow the child to eat these foods again, provided they are healthy, in the future. During a standard elimination diet, foods are typically removed for 3 weeks to 3 months, and then gradually reintroduced. Once symptoms have stabilized, foods are reintroduced one at a time and symptom response is evaluated. This process can be tedious, particularly for parents of young children, but it does yield good results. Our clinical experience has shown that children tend to respond to any elimination protocol within 5–7 days.

What Do We Tell Parents?

Here are some things we should tell parents:

- Meal planning is a must!

- Eat and cook very simple meals initially—and this can easily be maintained over the course of any elimination.

- Try cooking in bulk for one afternoon to have food options available for your children throughout the week.

- Choose healthy dietary components—organic if possible, grass-fed beef, free-range chicken and eggs, healthy whole fats.

With an allergy-elimination diet, it is imperative that a clinician look at both eliminating trigger foods and also replacing these foods with healthy, caloric, and nutrient-dense alternatives. In short, experience shows that the foods added back into the child's diet play as large a role in success as the foods that are removed. For example, removing corn chips and replacing those with unfortified rice chips likely only exacerbates the problem for this child, whether on a short- or long-term basis. But adding nutritious root chips, such as yam, beet, and parsnip, or kale chips, as a substitute crunchy snack is a win–win situation. Transitioning to a new plan through eliminating current dietary components and replacing those with options that respect the child's preferences but also maximize calorie and nutrient intake is advised.

Feingold Diet/Phenol- and Salicylate-Free Diet

Another clinical intervention that can address SIB is some form of the Feingold diet/ phenol- and salicylate-free diet. This is essentially a specific allergy-elimination diet, excluding all foods containing certain dietary components. In short, the Feingold approach excludes foods that contain highly phenolic compounds which are broken down and absorbed in the digestion process. As mentioned above, children with food intolerances or sensitivities may present with SIB, excitability, excessive silliness, irritability, and hyperactivity in response to food consumption. When children who are sensitive eat highly phenolic foods such as pure chocolates, some fruits, and many food dyes, adverse reactions can occur. Most often, parents report bright red cheeks or ears, sometimes even on one but not both sides of the face.

This diet avoids foods with the highest phenolic contents, including artificial and some natural food colorings, flavorings, and preservatives. As discussed earlier, to determine if a child suspected of phenol intolerance is reacting negatively to phenols, a strict elimination diet needs to be implemented and tracked. Accidental or scheduled exposure to phenol-containing foods with monitoring for adverse reaction will be the test of this sensitivity.

Information highlighting concerns with artificial compounds is being published on a regular basis. A recent study on pediatric intake of artificial colors was published in 2013. The authors bring to light a number of issues which many of us may not know. First, the United States currently allows nine artificial food colors (AFCs) in the food industry; all are made from petroleum, and Red 40, Yellow 5, and Yellow 6 are commonly consumed by children (Stevens *et al.*, 2013). This study suggests that AFCs may be linked to impulsivity and hyperactivity in children. Additionally, studies show that children with and without attention deficit hyperactivity disorder (ADHD) react to doses of as little as 50 mg. We know that some children are more sensitive to these chemicals than others, and this research tells us this sensitivity can be linked to immune system response, differences in the absorption of nutrients, and even genetics. And interestingly, they report behavior changes with AFC are seen when consumed in combination with foods containing milk and wheat. In 2012, the amount of AFC certified by the U.S. Food and Drug Administration (FDA) daily as a tolerable upper limit was 68 mg/per capita per day. Clearly, further research needs to be done to investigate tolerable upper intakes for children in general and ones that have an increased sensitivity.

In that same study, Stevens and his coauthors report that Red 40 is found in baked goods, candy, cereal, and beverages. The brighter the red, the more Red 40 a drink or food item is likely to contain. Red 40 is also used to make most orange and purple colors. Children between 6 and 12 years of age consume an average of 35 mg/day of this color. One alternative, a natural way to add red to any food, is through the use of beets. Beets add a lot of color without drastically changing flavor.

Yellow 5 is commonly used to dye baked goods, candy, cereal, and beverages a bright yellow color. Small amounts can be absorbed in the mouth. On average, children consume between 13 and 15 mg/day. Saffron and turmeric powder are great substitutes for yellow AFC. These spices have distinct flavors, so add very small amounts at a time. Yellow 6 is more orange than Yellow 5. It can be found in baked goods, sausage casing, cereal, and cosmetics. The FDA's acceptable daily intake is 3.75 mg/kg per day, which is 59.25 mg/day for a child that weighs 35 lbs. Children between 6 and 17 years of age consume an average of 14 mg/day. Alternatively, carrot juice is great for turning your food orange, and carrots are naturally sweet.

Unfortunately, for strict phenol avoidance and adherence to this diet, many fruits, vegetables, and some spices are also excluded from consumption. To manage exposure to certain foods and balance the need for a wholesome, nutrient-dense diet with the negative effects of phenol/salicylate exposure, clinicians recommended several options for interventions. To include healthy foods in the diet and minimize adverse reactions to exposure, research suggests that boosting phenol metabolism through increased sulfation can be beneficial. One route to increase sulfur status is the regular use of Epsom salt baths. Another option is the use of digestive enzymes specifically targeted at breaking down phenolic compounds with each meal containing these substances. In this way, a child can consume purple grapes or red-skinned apples for nutrient support without the detrimental effects of phenols.

The Gluten- and Casein-Free Diet Plan

The gluten- and casein-free (GFCF) diet plan is another form of specialized dietary elimination protocol. A number of studies have been published in the past decade looking at this particular dietary approach. Unfortunately, study design, number of participants, and outcome measures have impacted the power of each of these analyses, and the question of whether the elimination of dietary gluten and casein is beneficial remains unanswered. However, from an anecdotal perspective only, many parents often observe and report changes in sleep patterns, gastrointestinal symptoms, rashes, eczema, and eye contact within days of implementing a quality GFCF diet. A current study is underway at Massachusetts General Hospital to evaluate the impact of gluten and casein elimination on children with autism, but those results are likely still a year away from publication. Beyond that, it appears that no other large-scale work evaluating this approach is underway. In the interim, families and clinicians continue to apply this approach to address a child's symptoms. Why?

There are concerns with removing both gluten and casein protein from a child's diet without accurate information on dietary intake and without proper professional advice, particularly if the child is a selective eater or self-limits to few foods. For example, removing casein protein could create deficiencies in both calcium and vitamin D intake for children if milk products are the only source of these nutrients. Similarly, removing all gluten could eliminate dietary sources of B vitamins that are typically found in fortified foods such as breads and cereals. Appropriate dietary counseling is necessary to ensure these nutrients are adequately replaced in the diet with other foods or nutritional supplements. Working with a professional to assess current intake and needs and create a solid plan moving forward allows parents to provide a balanced intake for their child and also accurately assess the impact of this dietary change on the child's symptoms.

The GFCF diet was one of the first popularized "special" diets for children diagnosed with autism. Families who are committed to dietary change have been opting for this approach consistently since the early 1990s. More than 15 years ago, the first research work evaluating this dietary intervention was published, and while inconclusive, it did not deter parents from adhering to this diet. Over the past decade, it has become common to also avoid soy protein when eliminating gluten and casein proteins. Clinical experience revealed that children who responded negatively to gluten and casein often had a negative response to soy protein as well. This became more obvious as parents substituted soy milk for cow's milk in the diet, with an initial positive response, and then a gradual or sudden decline in dietary change benefit. There are several obstacles to success on this dietary intervention plan that can be addressed and mitigated with proper professional guidance. The identification of any potential macro- and micronutrient deficiencies through the elimination of casein and gluten protein and the inclusion of foods which are not in themselves inflammatory or inappropriate are the most important keys to success.

Grain-Free Specific Carbohydrate Diets

Another specialized form of an elimination protocol is the specific carbohydrate diet (SCD). The SCD approach was developed initially to address symptoms of celiac disease in the mid twentieth century. It calls for strict avoidance of disaccharides and polysaccharides, including all grains, their derivative sweeteners, certain starches, and cane sugar products. The premise is to allow only simple carbohydrates that are easily absorbed with minimal digestion into the diet. The hope is that these simple carbohydrates will be quickly digested and then absorbed in the small intestine. This will then allow them to be utilized by the body quickly and appropriately, and they will not be sitting in the gastrointestinal tract for long periods of time. Decreased bowel transit time with foods that are not as readily absorbed can increase difficulties with bowel status. The SCD approach posits that these unhealthy carbohydrates ferment and feed unwanted and undesirable bacteria and fungus found in the gastrointestinal tract, disrupting an appropriate happy medium among the various components of the microbiota. With this dietary protocol, the goal is to allow the gut tissue to heal, bowel flora to normalize, and digestion and absorption processes to improve. In practical terms, learning and implementing SCD is somewhat more difficult than other dietary approaches. In addition to monitoring for micro- and macronutrient needs and deficits, clinicians must also gauge ratios of intake, as children can quickly become protein heavy and carbohydrate starved without their favorite breads and chips.

SCD has not been well studied to date, though several case reports and studies have been published in recent years. Research work is ongoing, evaluating its use across a number of different diagnoses, including autism with gastrointestinal symptoms and Crohn's disease. Nevertheless, families continue to implement this approach based on easily accessible guidance and anecdotal information. Recent research work does support this as a reasonable intervention: work has shown that children with ASD have disaccharidase digestive enzyme insufficiencies which would be involved in the breakdown of larger carbohydrate molecules (T. Buie, H. Winter, and R. Kushak, unpublished). As with all other dietary approaches, it is strongly recommended that SCD be implemented and monitored by an appropriately trained and skilled professional.

Conclusion

Many children with autism present with significant SIBs and other aberrant behaviors as a response to certain foods. These sensitivities can contribute significantly to gastrointestinal symptoms, including gastroesophageal reflux, abdominal discomfort, and abnormal stool patterns. Food can also trigger an immune response that can cause problems elsewhere in the body, including the brain. In addition, it has been shown that many children with autism have multiple underlying nutritional deficiencies. This might be a result of self-restricted diets, abnormal digestion, poor absorption, or an inability by the body to utilize the nutrients effectively. Since the health of the brain and the immune system are so tightly linked to nutritional status, it is critical that each child is evaluated carefully by an experienced clinician to best serve the child's medical needs. The therapeutic intervention discussed earlier can be effective at reducing SIB when carefully monitored to confirm that the child's nutritional needs are met. This is safe, effective, and reasonable foundational care for children with an ASD and SIB, and it can be a critical part of symptom reduction and treatment success.

References

Buie, T., Campbell, D.B., Fuchs, G.J. III, Furuta, G.T., *et al.* (2010). Evaluation, diagnosis, and treatment of gastrointestinal disorders in individuals with ASDs: A consensus report. *Pediatrics, 125*(Suppl. 1), S1–S18.

Casey, P.H., Szeto, K., Lensing, S., Bogle, M., and Weber, J. (2001). Children in food-insufficient, low-income families. *Archives of Pediatric & Adolescent Medicine, 155*(4), 508–514.

Christie, L., Hine, R.J., Parker, J.G., and Burks, W. (2002). Food allergies in children affect nutrient intake and growth. *Journal of the American Dietetic Association, 102*(11), 1648–1651.

Geraghty, M., Depasquale, G.M., and Lane, A.E. (2010). Nutritional intake and therapies in autism: A spectrum of what we know. Part 1. *Infant, Child, & Adolescent Nutrition, 2*(1), 62–69.

Hediger, M.L., England, L.J., Molloy, C.A., Yu, K.F., *et al.* (2008). Reduced bone cortical thickness in boys with autism or autism spectrum disorder. *Journal of Autism and Developmental Disorders, 38,* 848–856.

Horvath, K., and Perman, J. (2002). Autism and gastrointestinal symptoms. *Current Gastroenterology Reports, 4*(3), 251–258.

Jyonouchi, H., Geng, L., Cushing-Ruby, A., and Zimmerman-Bier, B. (2004). Mechanisms of non-IgE mediated adverse reaction to common dietary proteins (DPs) in children with autism spectrum disorder. *Journal of Allergy and Clinical Immunology, 113*(2), S208.

Lane, E., Geraghty, M.E., Young, G.S., and Rostorfer, J.L. (2014). Problem eating behaviors in autism spectrum disorder are associated with suboptimal daily nutrient intake and taste/smell sensitivity. *Infant, Child, & Adolescent Nutrition, 6*(3), 172–180.

Raiten, D.J., and Massaro, T. (1986). Perspectives on the nutritional ecology of autistic children. *Journal of Autism and Developmental Disorders, 16*(2), 133–143.

Sharp, W.G., Berry, R.C., McCracken, C., Nuhu, N.N., *et al.* (2013). Feeding problems and nutrient intake in children with autism spectrum disorders: A meta-analysis and comprehensive review of the literature. *Journal of Autism and Developmental Disorders, 43*(9), 2159–2173.

Stevens, L.J., Kuczek, T., Burgess, J.R., Stochelski, M.A., Arnold, L.E., and Galland, L. (2013). Mechanisms of behavioral, atopic, and other reactions to artificial food colors in children. *Nutrition Reviews, 71*(5), 268–281.

Zimmer, M., Hart, L.C., Manning-Courtney, P., Murray, D.S., Bing, N.M., and Summer, S. (2012). Food variety as a predictor of nutritional status among children with autism. *Journal of Autism and Related Disorders, 42*(4), 549–556.

CHAPTER 9

Sensory Processing Disorder and Self-Injurious Behaviors

Lucy Jane Miller, Ph.D., OTR/L, and Karen Misher, MFA, Sensory Processing Disorder Foundation, Greenwood Village, Colorado

When I got the call from my husband (he had cut his finger badly) that I should come home, I knew I needed to hurry home from the baby shower. He was home alone with our 7-year-old twins, both on the autism spectrum.

I arrived at the house to find both boys naked, one in full-blown distress screaming for a hot dog and the other happily sitting on the couch dining on a full bag of chips. Neither was terribly aware of their father sitting on the kitchen floor looking pale and holding his finger in the sink. The chaotic distress they felt was related to their disrupted lunch preparation, rather than an awareness of their father's issue.

I scooped all three up (with some hot dogs) and drove us to the local urgent care center, which was thankfully empty of other people when we arrived.

It was that empty waiting room and a promise that they'd have Rob all stitched up in 20 minutes that eased my own anxiety, while the boys ran around inside. They had a kids' section with a TV, some books, and a few blocks. "It'll be fine," I silently whispered. Xander was happily jumping about and doing his normal repetitive "dancing" that tells me he is in a good mood. His body language tells me most of what I need to know—which is lucky since he rarely uses spoken language. He was doing his jiggy-dance, jumping a little, and then he popped onto a chair to look out the huge plate-glass window at the cars going by.

Next thing I knew, "Wham! Wham! Wham!" Xander banged his head so hard and so fast on that window that I had no time to react. He touched his forehead, so I knew it was a bruising. No crying, no stress, no real cause for that self-injurious act. I at once swung around to catch the horrified look on the receptionist's face. "We'll wait in the car. Just let my husband know we are outside..."

Karen Mischer

Introduction

Empirical evidence related to the role of sensation in self-injurious behaviors (SIBs) is growing, due to decades of phenomenological reports identifying sensory issues in individuals with autism spectrum disorder (ASD) and other disorders (Baranek *et al.*, 2006; Devine, 2014; Egelhoff and Lane, 2013). The purpose of this chapter is to review what is known about sensory issues in SIB and to raise additional issues for continued research.

Description and Prevalence of SIBs

As early as 1943, Kanner described sensory-related behaviors that provided both joy and distress for children with SIBs. Matson and colleagues (1996) and Baghdadli and colleagues (2003) report that 35–50% of children with ASD hit their faces or bite themselves. Dominick and colleagues (2006) and Richards and colleagues (2012) suggest that children with SIBs strike others, or body parts against other objects, at a prevalence rate that is two to three times more common than for other intellectually impaired children (Devine, 2014). Parents report that SIBs can have a negative impact on daily living activities and school functioning (Alcantara *et al.*, 2004) and are arguably the most problematic comorbid behavior for individuals with ASD (Ashburner, Ziviani, and Rodger, 2008). Peak impact forces during SIB events are estimated to be in the range of professional boxers' impact rates; individuals may hit themselves up to eight times per minute (Newell *et al.*, 1999), so the potential for trauma is high. The cost of treating SIBs is staggering, with the National Institute for Health reporting the annual cost of care at more than $100,000 per case (Consensus Statement NIH, 1989).

Fundamentally, SIB is difficult to understand. Why would someone inflict deliberate severe harm upon himself or herself? One suggestion is that these individuals are extremely under-responsive (less sensitive) to painful stimulation, since sensory under-responsivity is well documented in ASD (Baranek *et al.*, 2006). This hypothesis seems unlikely given that sensory hyper-responsiveness has been shown to correlate with SIBs (Boyd *et al.*, 2010), and also given that stereotypy is highly correlated (Bodfish *et al.*, 2000; Gal, Dyck, and Passmore, 2002; Oliver *et al.*, 2012). A spectrum from no relation to high pain sensitivity (Breau *et al.*, 2003) to comorbidity with high pain sensitivity (Symons, 2011) has been suggested. In a seminal paper, Edelson suggested sensory stimulation might be acquired by damaging the nerve structure in the skin, changing the sensory threshold for physical input, which is then operantly reinforced by caregiver concern (Edelson, 1984).

What *are* SIBs? It may help to define them: Self-injurious behavior is one particular type of restrictive, repetitive, and stereotypical pattern of behavior that was included as a core diagnostic feature of ASD in the *Diagnostic and Statistical Manual of Mental Disorders*, Fifth Edition (DSM-5), but it is not included in the diagnostic features of ASD in the DSM-5. These repetitive movements in general can serve an adaptive function (e.g., lining up cars, stacking blocks, spinning, jumping up and down, rocking, pacing, flapping hands, scripting, and so forth).

> Xander's head banging on objects moved into hitting his head with his hand, which then morphed into slapping his chest. We now see him take that into his repetitive movements, which are not done in frustration or anger, but just part of a routine. He will be playing with a toy, or watching a video, and stand up, thump his chest a few times, and go back to what he was doing. It provides some input that he needs in that moment.
>
> *Karen Misher*

But in many children behaviors can become self-injurious, turning into SIBs, in which individuals engage in actions that are harmful (e.g., head banging, self-biting, hitting oneself, and so forth). These behaviors can vary from mild to quite severe.

> My husband was away for a few days and my good friend came for the weekend with her typically developing 3-year-old daughter. We decided to put the kids in the car and just run a few errands close by. As we passed the farmers' market stand, I decided to stop quickly and grab some fresh fruit. It had not occurred to me that Xander would be upset that I had left, and that my dear friend Sarah was not prepared for his reaction.
>
> I took maybe five minutes to pick out some strawberries, while Xander's screaming quickly became hair pulling. He managed to pull out a small handful of his hair in that short time. I returned to the car to find everyone a bit traumatized. This was a very difficult thing to explain to another child and mother.
>
> *Karen Misher*

Some literature suggests a relation between intellectual ability and the occurrence and type of repetitive behaviors, such that SIBs increase with decreasing IQ (Bartak and Rutter, 1976; Carcani-Rathwell, Rabe-Hasketh, and Santosh, 2006; Gabriels *et al.*, 2005).

SIBs are distinguished from typically developing behaviors because they are developmentally and socially inappropriate. Stereotypies that occupy a large portion of the day for children with ASD can be intense, and can preoccupy the child's time. They interfere with learning and with socialization. Once children are perceived as dangerous to themselves, they may be seen as dangerous to others also (some children are actually dangerous to both themselves and others).

> Inclusion is perhaps one of the trickiest endeavors we face as parents of kids on the spectrum. My boys attend a specialized school for kids with autism, which is lucky enough to have a partnership with our neighboring private school for inclusion at playtime.

There is great scrutiny, at least initially, on the behaviors our kids exhibit. Other teachers are concerned about what they may perceive as "aggressive" behavior, though it is not directed at others. Parents of the kids that our kids with autism play with have many questions about perceived dangers.

Xander has deliberately banged his head on the slide when he was redirected from playing at the bottom while other kids slid down. Yet, when you think of other playgrounds full of young children, you realize that many young children have unusual behaviors. Typical kids push and hit one another as they navigate social relationships—while we adults try to teach them the correct way to negotiate. That is considered a normal part of learning. But with our kids with ASD, the behavior is seen in isolation and looked at under a microscope.

Karen Misher

Stereotypies may interfere with the ability of children to enjoy non-structured time as well as structured time (e.g., school). These behaviors are the most stigmatizing of all behaviors typically associated with ASD. This can make taking a child out in public difficult for parents, which can limit the participation of children in typical educational and community activities (Cunningham and Schreibman, 2008).

Neurobiological Mechanisms in SIBs

Though large-scale rigorous epidemiology studies exploring sensory modulation disorder do not exist—which thwarts our knowledge base—several key researchers have provided hypotheses related to the neurobiological mechanisms of SIBs in autism. Bahrick and Todd (2012) explore the role of multisensory integration in creating a platform for the core deficits of autism, including social reciprocity and communicative impairments as well as SIBs. Devine (2014) hypothesizes that a combination of cortical, limbic, and basal ganglia pathologies result in autistic behaviors. Both perspectives are briefly discussed below.

The neurobiological mechanisms responsible for these behaviors have not been well documented, although recently, chapters (Stein, 2012) and articles (Devine, 2014) have been published adding to our understanding of the role of sensory systems in SIBs; they also increase questions related to the role of sensation in causing, or at least exacerbating, SIBs. Additionally, the role of sensory-based treatment in remediating SIBs has been the focus of some recent studies.

Edelson (1984) suggested that self-injury might be considered an extreme form of sensory processing disorder (SPD) (e.g., skin picking or scratching), which may be one manifestation of poor body awareness. It has also been proposed that high levels of beta endorphins may be released during SIB events, resulting in a sense of euphoria (Sandman, 1988). It has been proposed that abnormalities in processing sensation, particularly auditory, visual, oral taste, smell, and touch (Bennetto, Kuschner, and Hyman, 2007; Gomes, Pedroso, and Wagner, 2008; Kern *et al.*, 2006), have a profound effect on the opioidergic system, and that increased endorphins may be released due to stress and anxiety, resulting in analgesia and reduced perception of the sensory stimuli in SIBs (Gillberg, 1995; Oswald, 1994). In a large study of 250 individuals ages 21 months to 19 years, Duerden and colleagues (2012) found that the most common factor affecting SIBs was sensory processing, which they note is "relatively understudied," explaining 12% of the variance in the data, followed by sameness (10%), IQ (4%), and social communication (3%). Functional communication, age, rituals, and compulsions did not contribute a significant source of variance.

> I have always felt that Xander gets something other than just his frustration out when he bangs his head. There are times when he also craves that same physical input—pressure to his head. He learned to do a headstand at the age of 3 years, and he will sometimes just lean his forehead into my body, or push my hand against his head. If you massage his head, he will close his eyes a bit and you can see his face relax.
>
> *Karen Misher*

In an interesting study, Breau and colleagues (2003) considered three alternative hypotheses that relate to SIBs being caused by pain. The three hypotheses were the following:

- Elevated levels of endogenous opioids result in a lack of inhibition of SIBs due to pain insensitivity.

- SIBs are due to low endogenous opioid levels and SIBs cause opioid release.

- SIB is a reaction to pain.

In a group of 101 non-verbal, severely cognitively impaired children ages 3–18 years, the typical location of self-injury was established: 48% head, 27% hand, 16% torso, and 9% arms/legs. In addition, the frequency of SIBs was noted: 41% injured themselves daily, with 27% displaying SIBs monthly or less often. The total time of SIBs was 132 minutes for children with chronic pain versus 217 minutes for children without chronic pain—a meaningful, but not significant, difference.

The findings showed that chronic pain does not have a significant effect on overall problem behavior or the degree of SIBs. However, chronic pain was related to self-injury on less body surface, the injuring of fewer body parts, and the location of the injuries, compared with children without chronic pain. Children without chronic pain tend to injure their head and hands, and to self-injure more frequently.

> I wonder at times if Xander has a headache—though not from his head banging— one that might feed into that behavior. Allergies? Sinuses? It is so hard to know when you have a child with little language.
>
> *Karen Misher*

In summary, two types of self-injury were found: (1) less frequent, associated with chronic pain, and located near the site of the pain; and (2) more frequent, directed at head and hands, and not associated with chronic pain. Thus, Breau and colleagues dismissed the first of their three hypotheses (reduced sensitivity to pain); they suggest their findings imply that children with sensory under-responsivity would likely not employ SIBs to increase arousal. In addition, evidence to accept the third hypothesis (that SIBs are related to pain) was confirmed for a subgroup. This latter group may be trying to relieve pain through stimulating the source of pain, or may be signaling the presence of pain.

Hypothesis Related to Sensory Craving

Scientists have drawn a distinction between *wanting* and *liking* something (Ratey and Hagerman, 2008). Liking is true pleasure from stimulation, whereas wanting is more a motivational state that defines a willingness to work toward a reward. The nucleus accumbens is where the hyperactivity/impulsivity of attention deficit hyperactivity disorder (ADHD) and the seeking of salient stimuli of a person with addictions overlap. The primary issue seems to be salience and motivation rather than pleasure. Cues for both pleasure and pain send dopamine coursing through the brain so we can take action (and survive). The brain has in a way "tricked" the individual to believe that obtaining the stimuli is a matter of life and death. Could this be the underlying mechanism in SIBs?

The National Institute on Drug Abuse defines addiction as a compulsion that persists in spite of negative health and social consequences. Addiction is a pervasive problem because of the structural changes it causes in the brain. After the compulsion is satisfied, the prefrontal cortex instructs the hippocampus to remember the sensation derived in detail. The associations get remembered and triggers become hardwired in the brain, so that when the individual sees, hears, or, even more directly,[1] smells a remembered trigger, the synapses in the nucleus accumbens are hardwired to respond and direct the brain to respond. In essence the brain has learned something "too well"; "…the basal ganglia [*sic*] goes on autopilot when you see/hear/smell/feel the stimuli, and the prefrontal cortex cannot override your actions even though you may know better…" (Ratey and Hagerman, 2008, p.172). Addiction thereby becomes a failure to inhibit "abnormal" stimulation rather than a choice to obtain particular stimuli.

The neuropathology of SIBs, though not well established, is not due to problems in peripheral sensory structures (acuity of seeing, hearing, touch) (Rosenhall *et al.*,

---

1   The sense of smell is the only sensation that has a pathway directly to the cortex without traversing the thalamus, and thus olfactory sensation is processed more quickly than other sensations.

1999; Scharre and Creedon, 1992). However, many other aspects of brain structure and function have been hypothesized to explain these processing issues, including:

- attention that is over-selective (Kinsbourne, 1987)

- poor balance between inhibition and facilitation in neural systems (Rubenstein and Merzenich, 2003)

- hyperarousal (Hirstein, Iversen, and Ramachandran, 2001)

- sensory modulation deficits (Ornitz, 1989)

- sensory discrimination deficits (Tecchio *et al.*, 2003)

- sensory-motor-gating problems with abnormal thresholds for detection of sensory stimuli (McAlonan *et al.*, 2002).

There are important individual differences in children with ASD, and our understanding of the neurobiology of ASD is rudimentary (Devine, 2014); nevertheless, abnormalities in cortical, limbic, and basal ganglia structures that are associated with the behavioral symptoms of SIB in a sample of adopted orphans from Romania and in a sample of children with ASD suggest that the neuropathology of these groups may be similar. Devine (2014) reports on anatomical studies of the brains of impulsive, overactive adopted children and found significant abnormalities in both neuronal activity and structural connectivity. For example, abnormally low fructose metabolism in limbic, amygdala, and orbitofrontal and infralimbic cortices has been reported (Chugani *et al.*, 2001). A low value for fractional anisotropy (FA) in a large projection connecting the amygdala to the cortex has also been found using diffusion tensor imaging (Eluvathingal *et al.*, 2006). Behrens and colleagues (2007) reported reduced FA in connections between frontal cortex and basal ganglia. These abnormalities are proposed to have a profound impact on the cognitive deficits, impulsive behaviors, and limbic disorganization of the children with SIBs.

Bahrick and Todd (2012) suggest that early identification efforts should be undertaken that can identify impairments in the first year of life, before the later-developing symptoms occur that can cause atypical developmental outcomes and have an amplified effect on the child's developmental trajectory as he or she ages. Across the first 6 months of life, infants learn to attend selectively to crucial sensory events while ignoring irrelevant information. They learn to attend to faces and voices, to follow gaze, and to engage in reciprocal communication. These characteristics convey emotional information and communicative intent. It has been noted that by 2 months of age infants can detect face–voice synchrony, while by 6 months they can perceive emotion common to face and voice (Flom and Bahrick, 2007; Lewkowicz, 2010), providing a foundation for social and communication development.

Inter-sensory redundancy is responsible for the development of these skills. Redundancy refers to the same information being available to different senses at the same time. Neural responsiveness is increased when multiple sensory systems are engaged, compared with when information is only available to one sense. Redundancy provides a framework to understand how salience hierarchies are developed. In ASD, individuals demonstrate selective attention to stimuli with redundant properties of rhythm, tempo, and intensity.

In an ongoing study Bahrick and Todd (2012) studied over 700 infants and found that infants attended to social faces (mothers speaking with infant-directed speech) more than non-social ones (objects striking a surface), and redundant (naturally synchronized audiovisual actions) versus non-redundant (silent) contexts. Younger infants had greater processing time and less disengagement than older infants. In developing infants, attention to social, audiovisual speech events occurs over non-social, uni-sensory modal events between 2 and 8 months of age. Social orienting appears to develop as a function of inter-sensory redundancy. This is consistent with a theory that inter-sensory processing and the salience of stimulation provide a fundamental basis for attending to social events.

There is a growing effort to study inter-sensory impairments in autism (Iarocci and McDonald, 2006); however, much remains to be done. A particular area of need is studying proprioceptive-visual functioning (Gergely, 2001) and the mirror neuron system that responds to both performed and observed actions (Gallese *et al.*, 2009).

As it specially relates to SIBs and repetitive behaviors in general, a wider, less precise inter-sensory processing window has been proposed. Lewis and Bodfish (1998), Richler and colleagues (2010), and Turner (1999) suggest that repeating behaviors could hone and shape the temporal binding window across multiple sensory stimuli. This would promote experience-dependent narrowing of the temporal integration window. In other words, perception-action loops may reoccur with predictable coupling of specific stimuli—that is, the sensory stimuli that occur simultaneously are bound together in a predictable pattern, making them recognizable and expected. The purpose of these loops is to create predictable patterns of self-stimulation, in typical development a cornerstone of cognitive development, linking perception and action across time and space (Bahrick and Todd, 2012). For example, when an infant shakes a rattle, he sees, feels, and hears perfectly contingent and synchronized stimulation. This stimulation serves to enhance neural connectivity and integrates the sensation with the motor output (Ghazanfar and Schroeder, 2006). Thus, individuals with ASD may be attracted to repetitive behaviors, which have more predictable and synchronous multisensory stimulation compared with the environmental stimuli, which are imprecise, and couple sensations in an unpredictable manner. This may help children with ASD compensate for a wide temporal-binding window and create simple, salient, self-generated patterns. Over time, these behaviors may facilitate narrowing of the temporal binding window, although the rate would likely be at a much slower pace than is typically experienced.

There is a wide variety of sensory symptoms in ASD. Individuals with ASD may have a variety of abnormal responses to sensory stimuli (Baranek, Foster, and Berkson, 1997; Gillberg *et al.*, 1997; Kern *et al.*, 2006, 2007; Liss *et al.*, 2006; Ornitz, Guthrie, and Farley, 1977; Tecchio *et al.*, 2003; Tomchek and Dunn, 2007; Volkmar *et al.*, 1987; Wainwright-Sharp and Bryson, 1993). One or more sensory domains may be affected: visual, auditory, touch, smell, taste, proprioception (sensations from muscles and joints), vestibular (sensations of movement through space), and interoceptive (sensations from organs, such as one's stomach). In addition, they may exhibit one or more sensory processing subtypes, including sensory over-responding, sensory under-responding, sensory craving, sensory discrimination disorder, postural disorder, and/or dyspraxia. This makes understanding SIBs in individuals with ASD quite complex. Considering that there are eight sensory systems and at least six sensory subtypes, and that a particular individual can have one, two, or any combination of sensory systems or subtypes, this suggests over 86 types (over a million) of sensory-related disorders. Although SPD is gaining worldwide acceptance, the fact that individuals with such a wide variety of symptoms are all diagnosed with the same condition (i.e., SPD) has created confusion and skepticism about the field.

Subtypes of Sensory Processing Disorder

Miller *et al.* (2007) described a nosology to define the six primary sensory subtypes. The two most commonly described sensory subtypes are included in the most recent *Diagnostic and Statistical Manual of Mental Disorders* (DSM-5; American Psychiatric Association, 2013) under autism: sensory hyper- and sensory hyposensitivity, formally called sensory over-responsivity and sensory under-responsivity, two subtypes of a larger category called sensory modulation disorder. However, it is the third subtype of sensory modulation disorder, sensory craving, that may be even more related to SIBs.

Sensory-seeking or sensory-craving behavior describes the actions of individuals who are trying to obtain *more stimulation* than is naturally available in the environment. It is perhaps the least understood SPD. Miller and colleagues (L.J. Miller, J.C. Sullivan, and S.A. Schoen, unpublished raw data), based on a large cluster analysis of 252 individuals with SPD, propose that sensory craving is indeed a separate category from other SPDs. They propose that a lack of adequate dopamine may be signaling the brain to want additional stimulation in the reward system, the nucleus accumbens. When this occurs the amygdala is also alerted as if danger were near. All the stimulation individuals crave boosts the dopamine in the nucleus accumbens.

Prevalence, Comorbidity, and SIBs

Children with autism consistently are reported to have higher overall rates of sensory issues than typically developing children. Sensory symptoms are not unique to ASD but are comorbid with a variety of other disorders such as ADHD (Ermer and Dunn, 1998), fragile X syndrome (Rogers, Hepburn, and Wehner, 2003), borderline personality disorder (Rosenthal, 2011), and others. Studies differ in their findings related to the specificity of sensory features separate from cognitive issues in ASD. For example, Rogers *et al.* (2003) found that preschoolers with ASD had more sensory symptoms than children with other developmental delays of a non-specific nature, but Stone and Hogan (1993) found no such differences.

The prevalence of SIBs is difficult to ascertain. Estimates of the prevalence of SIBs in individuals of all ages and all diagnoses range from 2 to 50% (Breau *et al.*, 2003; Symons and Thompson, 1997), with between 33 and 71% of individuals with ASD exhibiting symptoms (Baghdadli *et al.*, 2003; Murphy, Healy, and Leader, 2009). Certainly they coexist with disorders other than ASD. For example, in a recent study of 5240 children with tic disorders with and without ADHD, 10% (215 of 2153) had SIBs without ADHD and 14.7% (456 of 3094) had SIBs with ADHD. In 1628 adults with tic disorders with and without ADHD, 19% (191 of 997) had SIBs without ADHD and 28.5% (180 of 631) had SIBs with ADHD (Freeman, 2015). In a study of children and adults with obsessive-compulsive disorder and tic disorders, 11% (472 of 4295) of children without OCD and 21% (199 of 950) of children with OCD demonstrated SIB, whereas in adults 20% (222 of 1117) without OCD and 29% (149 of 511) with OCD demonstrated SIB. In a sample of children with tics and anxiety, 22% (180 of 830) had SIBs and 11% (491 of 4417) did not have anxiety but had SIBs (Freeman, 2015). This sample excluded individuals with autism, intellectual impairments, or psychosis.

Shentoub and Soulairac (1961) reported that 7–17% of young children who are typically developing exhibit SIBs that typically disappear by age 5 years. Several studies have undertaken an evaluation of risk factors for SIBs in ASD. Only one study was found that specifically evaluated the effect of SPD, particularly the need for sensory stimulation in the risk factors of SIBs (Duerden *et al.*, 2012). Duerden and colleagues (2012) found that compared with the other risks studied (cognitive ability, functional communication, social functioning, age, need for sameness, and rituals and compulsions) abnormal sensory processing was the single strongest predictor of SIBs; they recommended treatment approaches that focus on sensory processing to reduce self-harm. Baghdadli and colleagues (2003) found in a group of 222 children with ASD that parental socioeconomic status, gender, genetic or malformation syndromes, and presence of epilepsy were not risk factors, while younger age, perinatal conditions, higher degree of autism, and greater delay in daily living skills (speech, socialization, and adaptive skills) were all risk factors, with the greatest risk being lower daily living skills.

In another study of predictors of SIBs, Richman and colleagues (2013) found that high levels of impulsivity and stereotypy were significant predictors of SIBs in a sample of 617 individuals. Other characteristics that were not as predictive were negative affect hyperactivity, intellectual function, and severity of autism symptoms. McClintock, Hall, and Oliver (2003) conducted a meta-analysis of SIB risk factors. They concluded that four risks were the most salient: level of intellectual disability, communication deficits, severity of autism symptoms, and presence of genetic disorders (e.g., fragile X syndrome, Prader-Willi syndrome). Level of intellectual disability and severity of autism have been replicated by several other groups (Baghdadli *et al.*, 2003; Bodfish *et al.*, 2000; Holden and Gitlesen, 2006; McTiernan *et al.*, 2011). Other risk factors studied more recently also include ADHD diagnosis.

References

Alcantara, J.I., Weisblatt, E.J., Moore, B.C., and Bolton, P.F. (2004). Speech-in-noise perception in high-functioning individuals with autism or Asperger's syndrome. *Journal of Child Psychology and Psychiatry, 45*(6), 1107–1114.

American Psychiatric Association (2013). *Diagnostic and Statistical Manual of Mental Disorders* (5th ed.). Washington, DC: American Psychiatric Publishing.

Ashburner, J., Ziviani, J., and Rodger, S. (2008). Sensory processing and classroom emotional, behavioral, and educational outcomes in children with autism spectrum disorder. *American Journal of Occupational Therapy, 62*(5), 564–573.

Baghdadli, A., Pascal, C., Grisi, S., and Aussilloux, C. (2003). Risk factors for self-injurious behaviours among 222 young children with autistic disorders. *Journal of Intellectual Disability Research, 47*(8), 622–627.

Bahrick, L.E., and Todd, J.T. (2012). Multisensory Processing in Autism Spectrum Disorders: Intersensory Processing Disturbance as a Basis for Atypical Development. In B. Stein (Ed.), *The New Handbook of Multisensory Processing.* Cambridge, MA: The MIT Press.

Baranek, G.T., David, F.J., Poe, M.D., Stone, W.L., and Watson, L.R. (2006). Sensory Experiences Questionnaire: Discriminating sensory features in young children with autism, developmental delays, and typical development. *Journal of Child Psychology and Psychiatry, 47*(6), 591–601.

Baranek, G.T., Foster, L.G., and Berkson, G. (1997). Sensory defensiveness in persons with developmental disabilities. *Occupational Therapy Journal of Research, 17*(3), 173–185.

Bartak, L., and Rutter, M. (1976). Differences between mentally retarded and normally intelligent autistic children. *Journal of Autism and Childhood Schizophrenia, 6*(2), 109–120.

Behrens, T., Berg, H.J., Jbabdi, S., Rushworth, M., and Woolrich, M. (2007). Probabilistic diffusion tractography with multiple fibre orientations: What can we gain? *Neuroimage, 34*(1), 144–155.

Bennetto, L., Kuschner, E.S., and Hyman, S.L. (2007). Olfaction and taste processing in autism. *Biological Psychiatry, 62*(9), 1015–1021.

Bodfish, J.W., Symons, F.J., Parker, D.E., and Lewis, M.H. (2000). Varieties of repetitive behavior in autism: Comparisons to mental retardation. *Journal of Autism and Developmental Disorders, 30*(3), 237–243.

Boyd, B.A., Baranek, G.T., Sideris, J., Poe, M.D., *et al.* (2010). Sensory features and repetitive behaviors in children with autism and developmental delays. *Autism Research, 3*(2), 78–87.

Breau, L.M., Camfield, C.S., Symons, F.J., Bodfish, J.W., *et al.* (2003). Relation between pain and self-injurious behavior in nonverbal children with severe cognitive impairments. *The Journal of Pediatrics, 142*(5), 498–503.

Carcani-Rathwell, I., Rabe-Hasketh, S., and Santosh, P.J. (2006). Repetitive and stereotyped behaviours in pervasive developmental disorders. *Journal of Child Psychology and Psychiatry, 47*(6), 573–581.

Chugani, H.T., Behen, M.E., Muzik, O., Juhász, C., Nagy, F., and Chugani, D.C. (2001). Local brain functional activity following early deprivation: A study of postinstitutionalized Romanian orphans. *Neuroimage, 14*(6), 1290–1301.

Consensus Statement NIH (1989). Treatment of destructive behaviors in persons with developmental disabilities. *Journal of Autism and Developmental Disorders, 20,* 403–429.

Cunningham, A.B., and Schreibman, L. (2008). Stereotypy in autism: The importance of function. *Research in Autism Spectrum Disorders, 2*(3), 469–479.

Devine, D.P. (2014). Self-injurious behaviour in autistic children: A neuro-developmental theory of social and environmental isolation. *Psychopharmacology, 231*(6), 979–997.

Dominick, K., Davis, N., Lainhart, J., Tager-Flusberg, H., and Folstein, S. (2006). Atypical behaviors in children with autism and children with a history of language impairment. *Research in Developmental Disabilities, 28,* 145–162.

Duerden, E.G., Oatley, H.K., Mak-Fan, K.M., McGrath, P.A., *et al.* (2012). Risk factors associated with self-injurious behaviors in children and adolescents with autism spectrum disorders. *Journal of Autism and Developmental Disorders, 42*(11), 2460–2470.

Edelson, S.M. (1984). Implications of sensory stimulation in self-destructive behavior. *American Journal of Mental Deficiency, 89*(2), 140–145.

Egelhoff, K., and Lane, A.E. (2013). Brief report: Preliminary reliability, construct validity and standardization of the auditory behavior questionnaire (ABQ) for children with autism spectrum disorders. *Journal of Autism and Developmental Disorders, 43*(4), 978–984.

Eluvathingal, T.J., Chugani, H.T., Behen, M.E., Juhász, C., *et al.* (2006). Abnormal brain connectivity in children after early severe socioemotional deprivation: A diffusion tensor imaging study. *Pediatrics, 117*(6), 2093–2100.

Ermer, J., and Dunn, W. (1998). The Sensory Profile: A discriminant analysis of children with and without disabilities. *American Journal of Occupational Therapy, 52*(4), 283–290.

Flom, R., and Bahrick, L.E. (2007). The development of infant discrimination of affect in multimodal and unimodal stimulation: The role of intersensory redundancy. *Developmental Psychology, 43*(1), 238–252.

Freeman, R.D. (2015). *Tic and Tourette Syndrome: Key Clinical Perspectives.* London: MacKeith Press/Wiley.

Gabriels, R.L., Cuccaro, M.L., Hill, D.E., Ivers, B.J., and Goldson, E. (2005). Repetitive behaviors in autism: Relationships with associated clinical features. *Research in Developmental Disabilities, 26*(2), 169–181.

Gal, E., Dyck, M., and Passmore, A. (2002). Sensory differences and stereotyped movements in children with autism. *Behaviour Change, 19*(4), 207–219.

Gallese, V., Rochat, M., Cossu, G., and Sinigaglia, C. (2009). Motor cognition and its role in the phylogeny and ontogeny of action understanding. *Developmental Psychology, 45*(1), 103.

Gergely, G. (2001). The obscure object of desire: "Nearly, but clearly not, like me." Contingency preference in normal children versus children with autism. *Bulletin of the Menninger Clinic, 65*(3: special issue), 411–426.

Ghazanfar, A.A., and Schroeder, C.E. (2006). Is neocortex essentially multisensory? *Trends in Cognitive Sciences, 10*(6), 278–285.

Gillberg, C. (1995). Endogenous opioids and opiate antagonists in autism: Brief review of empirical findings and implications for clinicians. *Developmental Medicine and Child Neurology, 37*(3), 239–245.

Gillberg, C., Johansson, M., Steffenburg, S., and Berlin, Ö. (1997). Auditory integration training in children with autism. *Autism, 1*(1), 97–100.

Gomes, E., Pedroso, F.S., and Wagner, M.B. (2008). Auditory hypersensitivity in the autistic spectrum disorder. *Pro Fono, 20*(4), 279–284.

Hirstein, W., Iversen, P., and Ramachandran, V.S. (2001). Autonomic responses of autistic children to people and objects: Proceedings. *Biological Sciences, 268*(1479), 1883–1888.

Holden, B., and Gitlesen, J.P. (2006). A total population study of challenging behaviour in the county of Hedmark, Norway: Prevalence, and risk markers. *Research in Developmental Disabilities, 27*(4), 456–465.

Iarocci, G., and McDonald, J. (2006). Sensory integration and the perceptual experience of persons with autism. *Journal of Autism and Developmental Disorders, 36*(1), 77–90.

Kanner, L. (1943). Autistic disturbances of affective contact. *The Nervous Child, 2*(2), 217–250.

Kern, J.K., Trivedi, M.H., Garver, C.R., Grannemann, B.D., *et al.* (2006). The pattern of sensory processing abnormalities in autism. *Autism, 10*(5), 480–494.

Kern, J.K., Trivedi, M.H., Grannemann, B.D., Garver, C.R., *et al.* (2007). Sensory correlations in autism. *Autism, 11*(2), 123–134.

Kinsbourne, M. (1987). Cerebral-Brainstem Relations in Infantile Autism. In E. Schopler and G.B. Mesibov (Eds.), *Neurobiological Issues in Autism.* New York, NY: Plenum Press.

Lewis, M.H., and Bodfish, J.W. (1998). Repetitive behavior disorders in autism. *Mental Retardation and Developmental Disabilities Research Reviews, 4*(2), 80–89.

Lewkowicz, D.J. (2010). Infant perception of audio-visual speech synchrony. *Developmental Psychology, 46*(1), 66–77.

Liss, M., Saulnier, C., Fein, D., and Kinsbourne, M. (2006). Sensory and attention abnormalities in autistic spectrum disorders. *Autism, 10*(2), 155–172.

Matson, J.L., Baglio, C.S., Smiroldo, B.B., Hamilton, M., *et al.* (1996). Characteristics of autism as assessed by the diagnostic assessment for the severely handicapped-II (DASH-II). *Research in Developmental Disabilities, 17*(2), 135–143.

McAlonan, G., Daly, E., Kumari, V., Critchley, H.D., van Amelsvoort, T., and Suckling, J. (2002). Brain anatomy and sensorimotor gating in Asperger's syndrome. *Brain, 125*(7), 1594–1606.

McClintock, K., Hall, S., and Oliver, C. (2003). Risk markers associated with challenging behaviours in people with intellectual disabilities: A meta-analytic study. *Journal of Intellectual Disability Research, 47*(6), 405–416.

McTiernan, A., Leader, G., Healy, O., and Mannion, A. (2011). Analysis of risk factors and early predictors of challenging behavior for children with autism spectrum disorder. *Research in Autism Spectrum Disorders, 5*(3), 1215–1222.

Miller, L.J., Anzalone, M.E., Lane, S.J., Cermak, S.A., and Osten, E.T. (2007). Concept evolution in sensory integration: A proposed nosology for diagnosis. *American Journal of Occupational Therapy, 61*(2), 135–140.

Murphy, O., Healy, O., and Leader, G. (2009). Risk factors for challenging behaviors among 157 children with autism spectrum disorder in Ireland. *Research in Autism Spectrum Disorders, 3*(2), 474–482.

Newell, K.M., Sprague, R.L., Pain, M.T., Deutsch, K.M., and Meinhold, P. (1999). Dynamics of self-injurious behaviors. *American Journal on Mental Retardation, 104*(1), 11.

Oliver, C., Petty, J., Ruddick, L., and Bacarese-Hamilton, M. (2012). The association between repetitive, self-injurious and aggressive behavior in children with severe intellectual disability. *Journal of Autism and Developmental Disorders, 42*(6), 910–919.

Ornitz, E.M. (1989). Autism at the Interface Between Sensory and Information Processing. In G. Dawson (Ed.), *Autism: Nature, Diagnosis, and Treatment.* New York, NY: Guilford Press.

Ornitz, E.M., Guthrie, D., and Farley, A.H. (1977). The early development of autistic children. *Journal of Autism and Childhood Schizophrenia, 7*(3), 207–229.

Oswald, D.P. (1994). *Autism in Children and Adults: Etiology, Assessment, and Intervention.* Belmont, CA: Thomson Brooks/Cole Publishing.

Ratey, J.J., and Hagerman, E. (2008). *Spark: The Revolutionary New Science of Exercise and the Brain.* New York, NY: Little, Brown and Company.

Richards, C., Oliver, C., Nelson, L., and Moss, J. (2012). Self-injurious behaviour in individuals with autism spectrum disorder and intellectual disability. *Journal of Intellectual Disability Research, 56*(5), 476–489.

Richler, J., Huerta, M., Bishop, S.L., and Lord, C. (2010). Developmental trajectories of restricted and repetitive behaviors and interests in children with autism spectrum disorders. *Development and Psychopathology, 22*(1), 55–69.

Richman, D.M., Barnard-Brak, L., Bosch, A., Thompson, S., Grubb, L., and Abby, L. (2013). Predictors of self-injurious behaviour exhibited by individuals with autism spectrum disorder. *Journal of Intellectual Disability Research, 57*(5), 429–439.

Rogers, S., Hepburn, S., and Wehner, E. (2003). Parent reports of sensory symptoms in toddlers with autism and those with other developmental disorders. *Journal of Autism and Developmental Disorders, 33*(6), 631–642.

Rosenhall, U., Nordin, V., Sandström, M., Ahlsén, G., and Gillberg, C. (1999). Autism and hearing loss. *Journal of Autism and Developmental Disorders, 29*(5), 349–357.

Rosenthal, Z.M. (2011). Reactivity to sensations in borderline personality disorder: A preliminary study. *Journal of Personality Disorders, 25*(5), 715–721.

Rubenstein, J., and Merzenich, M. (2003). Model of autism: Increased ratio of excitation/inhibition in key neural systems. *Genes, Brain and Behavior, 2*(5), 255–267.

Sandman, C.A. (1988). β-endorphin dysregulation in autistic and self-injurious behavior: A neurodevelopmental hypothesis. *Synapse, 2*(3), 193–199.

Scharre, J.E., and Creedon, M.P. (1992). Assessment of visual function in autistic children. *Optometry & Vision Science, 69*(6), 433–439.

Shentoub, S.A., and Soulairac, A. (1961). L'enfant automultilateur: Les conduites automutilatrices dans l'ensemble du comportement psychomoteur normal. Étude de 300 cas. *La Psychiatrie de l'Enfant, 3,* 111–145.

Stein, B.E. (Ed.) (2012). *The New Handbook of Multisensory Processing.* Cambridge, MA: MIT Press.

Stone, W.L., and Hogan, K.L. (1993). A structured parent interview for identifying young children with autism. *Journal of Autism and Developmental Disorders, 23*(4), 639–652.

Symons, F.J. (2011). Self-injurious behavior in neurodevelopmental disorders: Relevance of nociceptive and immune mechanisms. *Neuroscience and Biobehavioral Reviews, 35*(5), 1266–1274.

Symons, F.J., and Thompson, T. (1997). Self-injurious behaviour and body site preference. *Journal of Intellectual Disability Research, 41*(Pt. 6), 456–468.

Tecchio, F., Benassi, F., Zappasodi, F., Gialloreti, L.E., *et al.* (2003). Auditory sensory processing in autism: A magnetoencephalographic study. *Biological Psychiatry, 54*(6), 647–654.

Tomchek, S.D., and Dunn, W. (2007). Sensory processing in children with and without autism: A comparative study using the short sensory profile. *American Journal of Occupational Therapy, 61*(2), 190–200.

Turner, M. (1999). Annotation: Repetitive behaviour in autism—A review of psychological research. *Journal of Child Psychology and Psychiatry, 40*(6), 836–849.

Volkmar, F.R., Sparrow, S.S., Goudreau, D., Cicchetti, D.V., Paul, R., and Cohen, D.J. (1987). Social deficits in autism: An operational approach using the Vineland Adaptive Behavior Scales. *Journal of the American Academy of Child and Adolescent Psychiatry, 26*(2), 156–161.

Wainwright-Sharp, J.A., and Bryson, S.E. (1993). Visual orienting deficits in high-functioning people with autism. *Journal of Autism and Developmental Disorders, 23*(1), 1–13.

CHAPTER 10

Assessment and Intervention for Self-Injurious Behavior Using Positive Behavior Support

Lauren J. Moskowitz, Ph.D., St. John's University, New York,
Caitlin E. Walsh, Ph.D., University of Colorado School of Medicine, Denver,
Colorado, and V. Mark Durand, Ph.D., University of South Florida,
St. Petersburg, Florida

Why Is Self-Injurious Behavior Important to Target?

Self-injurious behavior (SIB) is one of the most challenging and debilitating forms of problem behavior displayed by individuals with autism spectrum disorder (ASD) and other intellectual and developmental disabilities (ID/DD), with harmful physical and social consequences for the individual who exhibits SIB. Approximately 10–15% of people with ID engage in SIB (Davies and Oliver, 2013), with recent estimates as high as 19% in children with ID/DD (MacLean and Dornbush, 2012). SIB and other problem behaviors (such as aggression, property destruction, and tantrums) are important to target because they are a major barrier to a good quality of life for the individual displaying such behaviors, as well as to his family. First, problem behavior could lead to injury or serious harm for the individual or others with whom he interacts. Furthermore, problem behavior may also lead to rejection by other people; for example, if someone is banging his head on the table or hitting other people or screaming, he will most likely have a difficult time making friends or making progress on any social or educational goals. As such, problem behavior prevents full community integration; it is one of the major reasons why children are placed in segregated classrooms (Janney and Meyer, 1990); it is associated with social rejection and exclusion from neighborhood schools (Koegel, Koegel, and Dunlap, 1996); and in adulthood it is a major obstacle to successful employment (Bruininks, Hill, and Morreau, 1988). Problem behavior is also one of the leading causes of institutionalization (Bruininks *et al.*, 1988), which often leads to a loss of choice and a loss of dignity.

Second, in addition to the negative impact on the person who displays SIB, problem behavior is associated with increased stress for family members (Koegel *et al.*, 1992; Lucyshyn, Dunlap, and Albin, 2002). It can demoralize parents and other family members and contribute to feelings of hopelessness. In addition, problem behavior results in social isolation from other family members and the community (Lucyshyn *et al.*, 2002). When a child is biting himself or biting other people, for example, it makes it difficult for his parents to leave the house to go shopping or to a restaurant, or even have pleasant family activities at home. Quality of life for the individual's parents and other family members is obviously negatively impacted due to this increased stress, extreme disruption of family routines, decreased engagement in family leisure activities, and restricted family involvement in social and community life (Turnbull and Ruef, 1996; Vaughn *et al.*, 1997). In short, SIB and other problem behaviors are major barriers to education, social development, integration, employment, community adaptation, and overall quality of life, which makes it essential that we address such behavior.

How Do We Treat SIB?

There are a number of ways to address SIB that are effective, based on the principles and procedures of applied behavior analysis (ABA) and positive behavior support (PBS). ABA involves a series of techniques based on the principles of operant conditioning, which suggests that the future probability of SIB (or any behavior) is determined by its past consequences. PBS is an approach rooted in the principles of ABA that includes the development of multicomponent interventions. It is based on a comprehensive functional assessment, with the purpose of improving quality of life and reducing problem behaviors across multiple, naturalistic contexts (Carr *et al.*, 2002). ABA and PBS help parents, teachers, and practitioners to understand what causes the child's problem behavior so that they can select the best intervention strategies to address it. Although ABA and PBS share the same core principles based on operant conditioning, PBS focuses on using these principles to produce meaningful changes in the person's life; in PBS, the focus is not just on reducing SIB or other problem behaviors but on teaching new skills and improving overall quality of life.

Basic Assumptions of PBS

Before we discuss the key features of PBS, it is necessary to explain the basic laws or assumptions of behaviorism (the foundation on which ABA and PBS are based):

- **Behavior is learned.**
  The first law is that SIB and other problem behaviors are learned. Often, parents or caregivers may respond by saying something such as "That can't

be true; I didn't teach my child to bite." But that is not what we mean by "learned"; in fact, most behaviors outside of academic skills are not taught through direct instruction. Rather, what we mean is that behaviors are learned through the consequences that follow them (operant conditioning), through association/pairing (respondent conditioning), or through watching what other people do (imitation/modeling, i.e., observational learning). The first point is the key one in ABA and PBS: behaviors are learned by the consequences that follow them. For example, if I tell a joke and the consequence is that someone laughs at my joke, I have learned that I should tell that joke again; if I touch a hot stove and it burns my hand, I have learned not to touch that stove again. This is how so much of our behavior is learned, including SIB. The good news is that, if individuals learn to engage in SIB and other problem behaviors, they can also learn more positive behaviors to replace those problematic behaviors.

- **Behavior is functional.**
  If a behavior is followed by a consequence and then that behavior occurs again in the future, this means that behavior is serving some purpose or "function" for that individual. Individuals engage in SIB because it "pays off"; it is helping them get their needs or wants met in some way. In other words, SIB and other problem behaviors persist because they meet an immediate need for that individual. Most commonly, this need could be for attention from parents, peers, teachers, or staff; it could be a need or want for some preferred "tangible" item or activity (e.g., favorite food or toy, watching TV, playing on the computer); it could be the need to escape from a demand or task/activity or person or situation that is in some way aversive (disliked, boring, frustrating, anxiety provoking, or otherwise uncomfortable); or it could be the need to increase or reduce sensory stimulation or arousal. For example, if a child starts banging his head while waiting in line at the grocery store with his mother, his SIB could be fulfilling his immediate need for attention (if his mother responds to his SIB by telling him to stop banging his head), his immediate need to escape the boredom of waiting in line, or the overstimulation of the grocery store (if his mother responds to his SIB by quickly taking him out of the store). Viewed in this way, SIB can be seen as a form of communication; the individual is trying to say, for example, "I don't like this; I need a break," "This makes me anxious; I need to get out of here," or "I don't want to talk to you" (i.e., escape function); "I want you to talk to me" (i.e., attention function); "This noise is too loud" or "Biting my finger makes me feel calm" (i.e., sensory function); or "I want that ball" (i.e., tangible function), but he does not have the words to express those messages. As with the concept that behavior is learned, the advantage of the view that SIB serves a function and can be viewed as a

form of communication is that we can then teach individuals a better way to communicate that serves the same function; we can teach them to verbally or non-verbally ask for a break (i.e., escape function) or ask for someone to play with them (i.e., attention function), for example (see Chapter 11 for more information).

- **Behavior is context dependent.**
  What we mean by this is that behavior does not occur in a vacuum; it occurs in a specific context or multiple contexts. Often, when we are first interviewing a parent or teacher, they tell us that the SIB or problem behavior occurs constantly, all day long, and/or that the behavior comes "out of nowhere" or happens "for no reason." It probably feels like that because the problem behavior is so intense and/or so distressing that it seems like it is happening all the time. However, when we take a closer look at the behavior by doing a functional assessment, we see that the behavior happens more in certain contexts than in others; it happens more with certain people, in certain places, during certain times of day, and/or in certain situations than in others. Context encompasses both the immediate antecedents that directly lead to problem behavior (such as a parent saying, "Do your homework," or the malfunction of the computer) as well as the more distant "setting events" (such as fatigue or pain/illness, or being teased by a classmate) that set the stage for problem behavior to be triggered by an antecedent. It is worth noting that context can be said to include not only environmental factors, but genetic factors as well; the occurrence of SIB can only be understood in regard to the context (both genetic and environmental) in which that behavior is embedded (Langthorne and McGill, 2008). In summary, a major tenet of PBS is that problem behaviors are caused by problem contexts; to change the behavior, we must change the context. With these ideas in mind, in the following section, we discuss the key features of PBS.

Key Features of PBS

The key features of PBS are as follows:

- **It is assessment based.**
  Perhaps the most important feature of PBS is that we need to know *why* an individual is engaging in SIB (or any other problem behavior) in order to design a successful intervention plan to address it. The key to helping someone stop engaging in SIB lies in understanding what is motivating him or her at the time. Using a PBS approach, the interventions we choose are based on a careful assessment of the factors that control, cause, or contribute to the SIB. Through conducting a thorough functional behavior assessment (FBA), we can identify the situations that provoke SIB ("antecedents"), the

situations that seem to set the stage for SIB to be triggered by an antecedent ("setting events"), and what the individual may be gaining or avoiding by engaging in SIB (the "consequences" that maintain SIB). By understanding *why* the SIB is occurring (i.e., understanding its function or purpose) and the situations that set off these behaviors, we can develop intervention strategies. Based on the results of the functional assessment, we address the maintaining consequences as well as associated environmental factors that contribute to SIB. In this way, assessment is directly linked to treatment (i.e., intervention is based on the results of an FBA, which we explain how to conduct later in the chapter).

Although it may seem like common sense that we need to know why an individual is engaging in problem behavior in order to know how to treat it, this can often be a difficult concept for parents, teachers, other caretakers, and even therapists to understand. People tend to pay more attention to the "what" of a behavior rather than the "why" behind the behavior. For example, we are often asked "My child is hitting—what should I do?" or "My student is biting himself—what should I do?" and it is sometimes frustrating for parents or teachers to hear that we cannot tell them what the best course of action is for treatment without first knowing *why* the child is hitting or biting himself. We explain that it is the same as when a pediatrician cannot tell you the best course of action to treat a sore throat without knowing what is causing it.

To illustrate the importance of identifying the "why" (i.e., the function) behind the behavior, one of us was working with a boy with autism spectrum disorder (ASD), "Sam," who banged his head with his fist whenever his parents sat down next to him and started talking to him. Each time Sam engaged in head banging, his parents quickly walked out of the room and left him alone because, as soon as they walked away, he stopped head banging. Observing the situation while conducting an FBA, it became clear that the function or purpose of Sam's SIB was to escape or avoid social demands that were placed on him. Had the function of his SIB been to gain attention from his parents, their walking away when he head banged might have been a reasonable intervention strategy to choose (in combination with other positive strategies, which we discuss later). However, since the function of his SIB was to escape social interaction, walking away when he head banged was the wrong intervention strategy to use, since this reinforced his behavior. This illustrates that we cannot know the best intervention strategies to choose until we know *why* the individual is engaging in SIB. We need to know what he is gaining from that behavior, so that we can make sure he does not get those needs met through SIB, but rather through a safer, more appropriate behavior. This involves teaching a more appropriate alternative. In summary, using a PBS approach, we attempt to understand why SIB is occurring, and under what circumstances, rather than simply asking how to get rid of the behavior. This necessitates a customized approach to intervention, in which strategies are individualized.

- **It is comprehensive.**

Instead of a focus on single interventions, such as relying solely on the use of a "reward chart" (i.e., positive reinforcement), PBS involves multicomponent intervention packages that combine the most effective prevention (antecedent based), replacement (teaching), and management (consequence based) strategies. The goal of PBS is to lead to durable behavior change across the person's entire life, across multiple settings and activities and times of day, and across all individuals with whom the person typically interacts (see "systems focused" and "lifestyle focused" bullets below). To achieve this kind of broad, lasting change, it is generally necessary to include multiple interventions to change the many aspects of an individual's life that are problematic (Carr *et al.*, 2002). Once we know the functions or causes of an individual's SIB and the factors that contribute to it, we develop "prevention strategies" to prevent SIB from occurring, "replacement strategies" to teach the individual new behaviors or skills, and "consequence strategies" (also known as "response strategies" or "management strategies") to ensure that the SIB is not being reinforced or maintained in some way.

- **It is educational.**

The main goal of PBS is to teach skills, not just to reduce SIB or other problem behavior (although the assumption is that, by teaching skills, the need for problem behavior will be reduced or even eliminated). Individuals resort to engaging in problem behaviors such as SIB or aggression out of necessity, because they are lacking in skills or competencies; they do not have a better way to get their needs met. PBS involves teaching specific replacement behaviors or skills that serve the same function as the problem behavior so that the individual will use these new skills to get his needs and wants met. Depending on the situation, this may involve teaching the individual how to make choices, teaching him skills for interacting with other people (social skills), teaching him how to become more independent in daily tasks (daily living skills), teaching him skills for tolerating difficult situations such as waiting (coping skills), and, possibly most importantly, teaching him how to communicate his needs and wants (communication skills). The most well-researched and effective method for teaching a replacement skill is known as "functional communication training" (FCT; Carr and Durand, 1985), which involves teaching the individual an appropriate form of communication that serves the same function as the problem behavior (see Chapter 11 for more details).

- **It is preventive.**

   In addition to teaching skills, PBS is focused on prevention, which means modifying the circumstances that provoke problem behavior so that those circumstances are less likely to evoke that behavior. Prevention strategies are also known as "antecedent-based strategies" or "antecedent manipulations" because they involve introducing stimuli that are associated with positive behaviors as well as removing, altering, or ameliorating stimuli that are associated with problem behaviors. This proactive approach requires a shift in the way most parents, caregivers, teachers, and clinicians approach SIB and other problem behaviors, which often focuses on how to respond or react to the behavior while it is occurring, or afterward. In fact, the most effective interventions typically take place when problem behavior is *not* occurring (e.g., *before* the SIB occurs) rather than during or after it. Knowing the situations that tend to provoke SIB can help us to prevent the SIB. Some prevention strategies are short term and should ultimately be faded out, such as prompting or temporarily avoiding a trigger (e.g., seating the child away from a specific peer if that peer's crying tends to trigger SIB, or choosing a student first if waiting for his name to be called during transitions is a trigger) while the child is first learning skills to cope with the situation. However, other prevention strategies can be long-term strategies, such as using a visual schedule (much as many adults without special needs use a calendar or agenda book), incorporating choices or preferences into difficult or disliked activities (e.g., listening to a favorite song while waiting in line at the store), altering setting events (e.g., limiting TV before bedtime if fatigue contributes to SIB), or modifying the mode of task completion (e.g., allowing a child with fine-motor issues to type out his assignments rather than write them out by hand, if handwriting leads to SIB and typing is just as functional a skill). In short, PBS focuses on redesigning the environment and teaching skills so that problem behavior is no longer necessary.

- **It involves management.**

   In addition to preventing SIB and teaching the individual more appropriate skills to replace that SIB, PBS also teaches parents, caregivers, and teachers to change the consequences for SIB so that their reactions or responses are not inadvertently reinforcing SIB. Managing consequences involves controlling access to reinforcers (e.g., attention, escape) so that they are available only for positive behavior, not problem behavior. In other words, PBS teaches caregivers to ensure that the outcome for SIB is not reinforcing or maintaining the SIB, and to reinforce or strengthen positive behaviors instead. The goal is to promote desired behavior, and eliminate or at least minimize the rewards for problem behavior.

- **Its focus is on the long term.**

PBS recognizes that interventions must be developed and implemented from a longitudinal and lifespan perspective (Carr *et al.*, 2002). Although the results of intervention plans might be evident immediately, SIB and other serious problem behaviors have usually been occurring for a long period of time (sometimes the individual's entire life) and it may take more than a "quick fix" for this behavior to be changed. For example, even if we develop an intervention plan to assist a child in transitioning from preschool to elementary school and the effects of that plan are maintained throughout elementary school, we will most likely need a very different plan to assist that same child in transitioning from middle school to high school. Whereas most behavioral interventions (in research and in practice) tend to be short term, PBS recognizes that interventions often must evolve over time as challenges come up at different stages of life; new strategies will need to be added, and old strategies removed or modified (Carr *et al.*, 2002).

- **It is ecologically oriented.**

Numerous ABA studies have shown that behavioral analytic procedures are efficacious in "analog" settings (e.g., laboratories, universities) when implemented by researchers. PBS focuses on how effective behavioral interventions are in the "real world," which is known as "ecological validity." PBS holds that intervention strategies must be relevant to, and effective in, real-life settings and situations (Dunlap and Carr, 2007). We explain to parents and teachers that, as researchers and clinicians, we know that *we* can change a child's behavior in the controlled setting of our office for an hour, but that may not have any impact on the child's life for the rest of the week (e.g., when the dogs are barking and the phone is ringing and parents have to get dinner ready and cannot prompt or reinforce as frequently and consistently), at school (e.g., when the child's classmates are inadvertently reinforcing disruptive behavior by laughing when the child pours milk all over the desk), or in the community. When creating an intervention plan, we need to ensure that the intervention strategies we choose will fit within the real-life setting in which they will be implemented. Even the best technology will fail if it is applied in an uncooperative or disorganized context (Carr *et al.*, 2002) or if it is applied in a system that does not support that technology.

In addition to ecological validity, PBS is concerned with social validity, or clinical significance, which refers to how effective an intervention is perceived to be by key stakeholders such as parents and teachers (Wolf, 1978). An intervention may improve a child's SIB so that he is only banging his head 50 times per day after intervention, in contrast to 100 times per day during baseline. Although this difference may be a statistically significant improvement, it may not be a clinically meaningful improvement to the child or his family or teachers. PBS is concerned with whether the child and/or the people in the child's life perceive that the SIB has been reduced to an acceptable level and that quality of life has improved. Related to this, PBS is concerned with whether the stakeholders consider the intervention procedures to be valuable or worthy of implementation, and whether the strategies fit within the context in which they are to be implemented (i.e., goodness of fit) (Carr *et al.*, 2002).

- **It is systems focused.**
  As previously alluded to, one of the tenets of PBS is that even the best strategies for problem behavior reduction and skill enhancement will fail without considering impeding systemic factors. Meaningful change is possible only if problematic systems or environments are restructured in a way that enables change to occur and be sustained (Carr *et al.*, 2002). Therefore, a major goal of PBS is to help create systems that sustain the application of evidence-based procedures by parents, teachers, and other providers. In adhering to a PBS philosophy, we attempt to balance the needs of the individual with the needs of the broader system in which the individual participates. In considering the needs of the broader system, we evaluate whether behavior support plans take into account the cultural and personal values of families (a vision issue), responsivity to their social and emotional needs (an incentives issue), and feasibility of the plan with regard to time required, labor intensiveness, finances, and sources of support available in the community (a resources issue). In designing a PBS plan, we must consider, for example, the schedules and time constraints of parents, caretakers, and teachers and their competing demands, financial/budget constraints, their training needs, cultural expectations, the organizational structure (e.g., the amount of support a teacher gets from a principal and staff), and—perhaps most importantly—the motivation and attitudes of parents, caretakers, teachers, and other team members (e.g., whether or not they "buy into" the plan, believe the strategies will work, believe they have the ability to implement the strategies, and believe these behaviors are worth changing). Thus, it is crucial to consider contextual and systems factors during assessment and when implementing intervention.

  To illustrate, when working with Jake, a 13-year-old boy with ASD who displayed aggressive and disruptive behavior at home that primarily functioned to obtain his mother's attention, his mother Pam shared her stress as a recent widow who worked full time and had three children. She expressed that she did not have the time nor the energy to implement a positive reinforcement system, reliably use prevention strategies (e.g., prompt him to engage in prosocial activities, use a visual schedule, provide choices), or provide Jake with daily attention in the context of positive activities (e.g., engaging in 5 or 10 minutes of playing with him or reading to him each day). The fact that she had not accepted Jake's diagnosis of ASD and felt a lack of self-efficacy in her ability to manage his behavior or even interact with him (she always said, "My husband was the one who knew how to deal with him") contributed to Pam's distress. Thus, in addition to developing a behavioral intervention plan for Jake, it was also necessary to address Pam's depression using behavioral activation, cognitive restructuring, and acceptance-based work; recruit an undergraduate student to provide respite support to the family; work with Jake's younger siblings on their embarrassment and resentment of their brother with ASD; meet with Jake's teachers, principal, school social worker, and special education director to increase consistency between home and school; teach Jake to do home chores to assist his mother; and find Jake a volunteer position at a local pizza place. In short, developing a successful treatment plan to reduce Jake's problem behavior and increase quality of life required the involvement of his family system, school system, and community. An effective PBS plan must consider whether the systems in a person's life can nurture and sustain the designated interventions, just as, when we plant a tree, we need to consider whether the soil in which we are planting it can nurture the seedling and sustain the growth of that tree.

- **It is collaborative (i.e., team based).**
Given that PBS is systems based, in order to reduce SIB and improve quality of life for all involved, it is important to involve the people in the child's family system, school system, and community (e.g., friends, neighborhood, religious community, employers, and coworkers). If a child engages in SIB, only obtaining information from the child's mother, for example, during the FBA may not provide a complete picture of the various antecedents that trigger it, the setting events that make it more likely to occur, the consequences that maintain it, the child's skills, strengths, and needs, or existing resources. So it is essential to involve the child's parents, siblings, any other family members or caretakers with whom the child frequently interacts (e.g., grandparents, cousins, nanny), teachers and other school staff with whom the child interacts frequently (e.g., paraprofessionals, principal, school psychologist, custodian), friends, and anyone else who could have an impact on the child's behavior (e.g., neighbors, bus driver), as well as the child himself, in conducting a comprehensive functional assessment. Similarly, in using a PBS approach, all stakeholders are partners in developing and implementing the intervention plan (Dunlap and Carr, 2007). If only the child's mother is involved in developing the intervention and carrying it out, this will probably not lead to a lasting change in the child's behavior, and any gains the child makes in intervention may not generalize to another environment (e.g., from home to school) or to when he is with his father,

grandmother, babysitter, teacher, or others. Therefore, it is important to involve all, and of course the child himself, in the intervention planning and implementation. As Carr *et al.* (2002) noted when describing stakeholder participation as a key feature of PBS, all team members participate in building the vision, method, and success criteria relevant to defining quality of life for everyone involved. All team members must communicate and collaborate with one another so they share a common vision and goals, and so there is consistency across different environments and individuals (in how they respond to the SIB, how they prevent the SIB, and how they teach skills to replace the SIB). In other words, all team members must "buy in" to the intervention plan for it to be effective in the long term. This type of collaboration or team-based approach is more likely to lead to lasting change across multiple settings and situations in life.

- **It is lifestyle focused.**
A final feature of PBS is that the ultimate goal is to achieve broader lifestyle change and improved quality of life (Carr *et al.*, 2002), rather than just changing one or two specific behaviors. Our goal is to help the individual with a disability, as well as his family members, to live a full, meaningful life, however they define that. Using this perspective, reducing problem behavior is a secondary goal that is important chiefly because it will enable one to achieve a good quality of life. As our late advisor, Dr. Ted Carr, would say, "This table doesn't have problem behavior; this chair doesn't have problem behavior. Do I want to be this table? Do I want to be this chair? No!" The point is that most people want to be more than just a table or chair—they want more than just the *absence* of problem behavior; they want the *presence* of a good quality of life. A good quality of life might include friends, a job, volunteer work, meaningful activities, or involvement in the community for the individual with DD, and might include being able to do things together as a family (for example). Carr *et al.* (2002) defined quality of life as encompassing social relationships (e.g., friendship formation), personal satisfaction (e.g., self-confidence, happiness), employment (e.g., productivity), self-determination (e.g., personal control, choice of living arrangement, independence), recreation and leisure (e.g., enjoyable activities), community adjustment (e.g., domestic skills, survival skills), and community integration (e.g., school inclusion, opportunities for participation in community activities).

To use the example in the previous "systems focused" bullet, Jake was engaging in problem behavior to gain his mother's attention; solely teaching his mother to positively reinforce him when he was appropriately requesting attention and ignore him when he was engaging in inappropriate attention-seeking behaviors would not have been sufficient. Basically, Jake did not have a life; he did not have any other ways to obtain his mother's attention outside of behaviors such as spreading toothpaste or deodorant all over the walls, and he did not have any meaningful activities to fill up his time or give him a sense of purpose and accomplishment, so there was little incentive *not* to spread toothpaste all over the walls. Teaching Jake to exercise on the treadmill and do home chores not only helped his mother (by addressing her needs and improving her quality of life) but gave Jake other activities to do, particularly activities that increased his sense of self-efficacy and accomplishment; doing laundry and taking out the trash also provided him with opportunities to naturally recruit praise (attention) from his mother. In addition, after visiting over ten pizza places, we were able to find Jake a volunteer position at a local pizza place, which built on his strengths and interests (particularly his interest in pizza!). Teaching him to exercise, do chores, and volunteer at a restaurant added structure to his life and built a sense of competency and self-worth, which led to lasting (durable) improvements in his behavior and quality of life. Thus, developing a successful intervention plan required addressing Jake's entire lifestyle and his family's life as a whole, rather than solely focusing on getting rid of his problem behavior.

To achieve broader lifestyle change, PBS incorporates person-centered planning (PCP) and self-determination. PCP is a strengths-based approach used to improve quality of life as defined by the individual (e.g., having friends, engaging in meaningful activities, feeling accepted by community members) and his family members and other relevant stakeholders. PCP focuses on the individual as a person rather than as a disability, and focuses on his strengths and abilities rather than weaknesses and deficiencies. Using PCP, the PBS intervention plan is designed to fit with the vision of the individual and his family, by including lifestyle supports to enable his goals. If an individual's quality of life is improved, he may have less reason or need to resort to problem behavior, and thus these behaviors may be reduced or even eliminated.

Self-determination, which is a defining feature of PCP, involves giving the individual the opportunity to determine what he will do, where he will go, whom he will engage with, and how he will spend his time. The goal is to enable individuals with disabilities to be causal agents in their own lives. Some argue that SIB and other problem behaviors may not just function to obtain attention or a preferred "tangible" item/activity, or escape from something unpleasant or gain/escape sensory stimulation; problem behavior may also function to obtain a sense of control, competency, or mastery over one's environment. Often, individuals with disabilities are given little choice or control over how they spend their time and what they do with their lives; allowing them the opportunity to have a say in their own destinies and determine how they will live their lives by expressing their preferences (e.g., choosing an employment setting, choosing which tasks they learn, or choosing their recreational activities) could give them a sense of control and mastery, and thus reduce the need for SIB and other problem behaviors.

In addition to considering the values, vision, wants, and needs of the individual, it is important to consider the values, hopes, dreams, and needs of family members and other stakeholders. For example, if a family's goal is to increase their child's self-sufficiency, we could then design a system in which the child could manage his own day. This relates to the previously mentioned notion of "contextual fit"; for a behavior intervention plan to be effective, it must "fit" with the ongoing routines, values, priorities, and overall context of the settings in which the plan is to be implemented (Dunlap and Carr, 2007). The extent to which the plan fits within the given context or system will impact whether the plan will actually be implemented.

In summary, SIB is often the result of an interaction between the individual and the context in which the SIB occurs, and the SIB often persists because it is being reinforced in some way. A critical aim of PBS is to implement effective ABA procedures within a broader system of support that values the rights and needs of people with disabilities and the participation of stakeholders (Durand and Hieneman, 2008); thus, PBS is respectful and values based.

Conducting a Functional Assessment

There are specific strategies and procedures for implementing PBS. Every PBS intervention plan begins with a functional behavior assessment (FBA; briefly discussed earlier in this chapter), which is the process of gathering contextual information about an individual and his problem behavior or, in this case, SIB (Horner and Carr, 1997). The results of an FBA help to determine the function(s) or purpose(s) of SIB. The information gathered includes broad information (e.g., major life events, health factors, history of SIB) as well as specific information related to antecedents, setting events, and maintaining consequences. (These concepts are explained further later in this chapter.) Many times a behavior analyst, psychologist, or social worker will conduct the FBA; however, parents, teachers, and other care providers may be able to complete an FBA with a basic understanding of the process. It is important to note, however, that because SIB can be dangerous and even life-threatening, parents and teachers are encouraged to consult with specialized providers in the event that the behavior worsens or does not improve within a relatively short time frame (e.g., 1 month).

Type of Information Gathered to Complete an FBA

Our understanding of how and why SIB occurs can be best explained using a four-term contingency (illustrated in Table 10.1). Another way to think about the four-term contingency is that it is a method by which we define setting events, antecedents, and consequences of an individual's behavior. By understanding what antecedents trigger SIB as well as what consequences reinforce it, we can begin to make hypotheses about the function of SIB, which then directly inform the intervention strategies we select. This equation is one of the most crucial components of an FBA. Each component of the four-term contingency is described in detail below.

Table 10.1 Four-Term Contingency Helps Us to Understand Why Self-Injurious Behavior Occurs

Setting Event	Antecedent	Behavior	Consequence
The child feels tired from lack of sleep the night before.	The child's mother says, "Time for school."	The child scratches his arms and bangs his head.	The child's mother yells "Stop!" and then allows the child to go to school late.

Antecedents

Antecedents are situations, events, people, objects, or other triggers that lead directly to the occurrence of SIB and other problem behaviors. Antecedents are typically immediate, simple, and discrete events that bring about problem behavior (Durand, 1990). They tend to occur right before SIB and generally fall into one of the following categories: (1) physiological (e.g., heart beating fast), (2) cognitive/emotional (e.g., feeling anxious), (3) physical environment (e.g., too much noise, light), and (4) social/activity events (e.g., recently reprimanded, preferred activity ends) (Carr, 1977; Carr *et al.*, 2002). Examples of common antecedents include task demands (e.g., academic demands, chores at home), reprimands or corrections, transitions or changes, and being told "no." It is important to note that antecedents result in the immediate display of problem behavior. To return to the example of Sam, who banged his head with his fist whenever his parents sat down next to him and started talking to him, the antecedent in this case was the social demand of his parents talking to him.

Setting Events

Setting events include events, circumstances, or stimuli that increase the potential for SIB or other problem behaviors to occur. Setting events are usually more complex situations that increase the likelihood for problem behavior rather than immediately triggering its occurrence. They do not in and of themselves evoke problem behavior; rather, they make it more likely that problem behavior will occur once the antecedent is presented. Setting events are the reason that parents and teachers often say that problem behavior seems to "come out of nowhere," because sometimes an antecedent might lead to SIB, but at other times the same antecedent might not lead to SIB. For example, when four women with ID were presented with task demands (e.g., "it's time to brush your teeth") but were not experiencing menstrual pain (i.e., the setting event), they displayed problem behavior (SIB, aggression, property destruction, and tantrums) 0–37% of the time, whereas when they were given a demand *and* in menstrual pain, they displayed problem behavior 67–100% of the time (Carr *et al.*, 2003). Thus, setting events influence whether or not a particular antecedent (e.g., a task demand) will evoke a particular behavior. Setting events can be summarized into the same categories as antecedents (i.e., physiological, cognitive/emotional, physical environment, social/activity). Common setting events include the presence or absence of specific people, feeling crowded, having a bad day, feeling fatigued, being sick or in pain, having a preferred activity end, and difficulty sleeping. The same stimulus (such as an unfamiliar person) can serve as an antecedent for one individual (in that the individual immediately displays SIB each time he meets an unfamiliar person) and a setting event for another individual (in that the individual is more likely to display problem behavior when around an unfamiliar person, but only if that unfamiliar person asks him a question [the antecedent]). In the case of Sam, a potential setting event may be having a bad day at school during which he gets in trouble several times with the teacher, which could result in Sam being in a bad mood. His parents might not be aware that he has had a bad day when they sit down to talk to him. So the combination of his bad mood, carried over from earlier in the day, as well as his parents' social demand to engage in conversation, could lead Sam to hit his head.

Consequences

SIB is functional, often serving a purpose or as a form of communication. Knowing the consequences of SIB helps us to identify the function or purpose of its occurrence. A consequence is merely the response or event that occurs immediately after SIB; in order for it to be a maintaining consequence, it must reinforce the SIB. Punishment is also a type of consequence; however, by definition, punishment decreases behavior and therefore is not a maintaining consequence. Punishment is also not a first line of treatment for SIB, particularly when using a PBS approach. Consequences typically map directly onto the function of the behavior. Common consequences for SIB include attention, social avoidance, task avoidance or escape, tangible-seeking, sensory reinforcement, and biological reinforcement. (The focus here is on the first four categories, as the last two, sensory and biological reinforcement, are discussed further in the section on gene–environment interactions.)

Returning to Sam, his parents walked out of the room each time he engaged in SIB, resulting in a removal of the social demand to engage in conversation. Based on this information, we can guess that Sam was engaging in SIB to escape the demand from his parents to have a conversation. His parents' departure paid off for Sam, as it allowed him to avoid talking. Understanding the functionality of his SIB allows us to build a comprehensive intervention plan that can teach Sam skills while also decreasing his SIB. It is important to note that people often may not realize that a consequence is reinforcing SIB, but it still may be. For example, some individuals who engage in SIB are put in physical restraints (consequence) to protect themselves from injury; however, removing the restraints then often triggers SIB, possibly because the restraints could, over time, be a safety signal for them, indicating that no demands will be placed on them while they are in restraints (Carr, 1977). It is only when demands need to be made on the individual (e.g., he must eat or shower) that the restraints are removed, so the individual learns that demands are associated with removing the restraints, which then become an antecedent for SIB.

Methods of Conducting an FBA

Interviews and Checklists

There are several ways to collect information about antecedents, consequences, and setting events before beginning direct observation of SIB. One way is to interview people who spend time with the individual and who have observed SIB (including interviewing the individual himself if he is able to communicate). Family members and teachers are important people to interview. Questions to ask in the interview include broad questions about the person's history of SIB, any past interventions used to decrease SIB, broad factors that might contribute to SIB, specific antecedents to SIB, and maintaining consequences for SIB. The interview should uncover where, when, with whom, and during which specific activities the SIB is most likely and least likely to occur, as well as how other people typically respond to the SIB (e.g., yelling "Stop doing that!", which provides attention, or removing the demand, which provides escape), and whether the individual knows a better way to get his needs met (i.e., his skills or abilities). A common interview to use is the Functional Assessment Interview (FAI; O'Neill *et al.*, 1997). There are also several checklists that can be given to family members, teachers, and providers who know the individual very well. Examples of questionnaires that assess the consequences or functions of problem behavior are the Motivation Assessment Scale (MAS; Durand and Crimmins, 1988a, 1988b) and Questions About Behavioral Function (QABF; Matson and Vollmer, 1995). Examples of questionnaires that assess antecedents and/or setting events are the Contextual Assessment Inventory (CAI; McAtee, Carr, and Schulte, 2004) and the Setting Events Checklist (Gardner *et al.*, 1986). A major advantage of using these brief checklists is the reduction in time it takes to complete them compared with an extensive interview. Furthermore, these checklists can be given to multiple people to complete. Interviews and checklists can help us narrow down the situations in which SIB is most likely to occur so we can directly observe those situations. Interviews and checklists can also inform us about antecedents, consequences, and setting events that may have occurred outside of the direct observation (such as if a child did not get enough sleep the night before he was observed in his classroom).

Direct Observation

Although interviews and questionnaires can be helpful, they also have the potential to be inaccurate because they are subjective impressions rather than direct observations of behavior. This is why a direct observation can be so important; it often provides more detailed and accurate information about the specific antecedents and consequences of SIB, such as revealing that the individual only displays SIB when presented with a fine-motor task rather than a gross-motor task, when given a specific type of prompt, or when spoken to in a certain tone of voice (Horner and Carr, 1997).

Direct observations include informal and formal methods that are used to observe SIB as it is occurring. Formal observation methods are most useful when the problem is already identified. SIB can then be observed in the context of very structured situations to identify certain hypotheses about functions of the SIB. There are several observational tools that can be used to assist in an FBA, all of which include similar descriptions of behavior. When using an antecedent–behavior–consequence (ABC) analysis, the observer writes down specific information in each column corresponding to the *antecedents* (e.g., "brush your teeth"), *behaviors* (e.g., Johnny bites himself), and maintaining *consequences* (e.g., "okay, but you have to brush your teeth in ten minutes"). It is also important to include information about the time of day, type of activity, and individuals present during the activity or situation. Table 10.2 shows an example of a completed ABC chart. A scatter plot is one measure that may be less time intensive but can still provide crucial information about an individual's SIB; it allows the observer to tally each time period during which SIB occurs during the day, providing information about specific days and times that SIB is more likely to occur. Finally, a Functional Assessment Observation Form (FAOF) may be another measure used in direct observation (O'Neill *et al.*, 1997). The FAOF is in checklist format in which the observer can record up to 25 incidents of SIB across situations and time frames. This checklist also allows the observer to check specific antecedents and consequences that directly translate to potential functions of the behavior. A nice aspect about all of the measures above is that they can be individually tailored depending on person, context, or setting.

Table 10.2 ABC Analysis of a 9-Year-Old Male Student

Date	Time	Antecedent	Behavior	Consequence	Possible Function
3 Dec 2014	9:00 a.m.	The teacher announces it is time for math.	The student flips the chair over and pulls his hair.	The teacher removes him from class.	Escape
3 Dec 2014	9:45 a.m.	The teacher asks him to rejoin the group.	The student screams and pulls his hair.	The teacher reminds him to use safe hands.	Escape/ Attention
3 Dec 2014	10:30 a.m.	The teacher instructs him to get ready for spelling.	The student bangs his head on desk.	The teacher removes him from class.	Escape
3 Dec 2014	11:00 a.m.	The teacher instructs him to join a reading group.	The student screams, flips his chair, and pulls his hair.	The teacher, assistant principal, and school psychologist all become involved and remove him from class.	Escape/ Attention

Functions of Behavior

Once data are collected from multiple sources and multiple informants, the observer can begin to make hypotheses about the possible functions of SIB and the factors that contribute to it. To summarize, the following are the most common underlying reasons or functions for why SIB persists: (1) to escape or avoid tasks or activities, (2) to gain attention, (3) to obtain preferred tangible items or activities (e.g., food, toys, watching television), and (4) to gain or escape sensory stimulation (known as "automatic" or internal reinforcement) (Iwata *et al.*, 1994). The importance of completing a valid FBA and determining the underlying cause of SIB leads directly into how to treat it. Treatment of SIB using a PBS approach is discussed in the next section.

Designing an Intervention Plan

Developing Prevention Strategies

Prevention is the main goal in using interventions that adjust or change antecedents and setting events. If used functionally and successfully, these strategies will prevent opportunities for SIB to occur. Antecedent-based interventions essentially eliminate the need for the individual to engage in SIB by eliminating or modifying the situations that provoke or trigger it. The focus here is specifically on intervening *before* SIB occurs. These interventions tend to be fast-acting and can quickly reduce SIB, which can be very important when the behavior is dangerous or life-threatening. Questions we might ask ourselves when developing prevention strategies include: "What can we do to make the SIB unnecessary?"; "What short-term strategies might prevent the SIB?"; and "What long-term accommodations might prevent the SIB?" Note that any intervention used should be based on the hypothesis about *why* the behavior is occurring, rather than chosen randomly. If we choose strategies based only on the person's behavior rather than the function of the behavior, we will only temporarily reduce SIB, because the underlying reasons for it are still present. Furthermore, prevention strategies are always only one component of a multicomponent intervention plan. In this section we provide an overview of general prevention strategies that have been supported by research. Readers should keep in mind that there are many preventive strategies; this chapter covers the most common ones. It is meant to be a foundation for the reader to expand upon, and it is important to highlight that parents, school teams, staff, and mental health providers should work together when creating a comprehensive behavioral intervention plan, and to individualize each plan for the student or adult with ASD or DD.

USING VISUAL SUPPORTS

Visual schedules are used to increase predictability for the individual by providing information proactively about upcoming events. Visual schedules as well as visual cues (e.g., a picture of feet on the floor to convey where the child should stand) help make the environment, activity, or task more predictable, more concrete, and less overwhelming. Visual supports may also enhance a person's sense of control over their environment and promote independence, and reduce stress, uncertainty, and anxiety. There are many types of visual supports. Visual schedules depict each activity in an individual's day, thus allowing him to preview each aspect of the day and anticipate transitions. Visual schedules have been shown to be effective in reducing problem behaviors, including SIB (Lequia, Machalicek, and Rispoli, 2012). Visual schedules are most commonly used to decrease escape-motivated problem behaviors (the individual is less likely to want to escape an activity if he is prepared for it). However, they can also be used to prevent attention-motivated, tangible-motivated, and sensory-motivated problem behavior by providing the individual with visual information about when during his day he will receive attention or a preferred food, object, activity, or sensory stimulus. For example, for a 20-year-old male with ASD, Charlie, who punched his father on most days when he came home from work (the consequence was obtaining attention from his father, who went into his work office as soon as he came home on most days), simply providing him with a visual schedule that included a set playtime with his father each day dramatically reduced his problem behavior, presumably because now he knew when he was going to get attention from his father. Social Stories (Gray and Garand, 1993), which are narratives that describe a social situation and typically include pictures or other visual aids, can also help the individual to better understand what is expected of him in a given situation and identify appropriate ways to behave in a specific situation.

USING TIMERS OR COUNTDOWNS

Providing individuals with an advance warning that an activity is about to end or begin can reduce the likelihood that the antecedent (the start or end of an activity) will provoke SIB, particularly when the function of SIB is to escape a non-preferred activity or gain access to a preferred activity (Mace, Shapiro, and Mace, 1998). An advance warning provides the person with time to prepare for the transition and makes the process gradual rather than abrupt. Ways to provide advance warnings include using timers, countdowns, and/or verbal warnings (e.g., saying, "It's time to do work in two minutes," and so on, every 30 seconds for 2 minutes prior to the onset of the task). This can prevent or reduce the uncertainty and anxiety or frustration associated with transitions. Just like visual supports, these strategies help to increase predictability and give the individual a greater sense of control over his environment. Such timers and countdowns can be helpful to everyone, not just those with disabilities. After all, many metro stations have installed countdown clocks to inform passengers when the next train will be coming. This provides them with information that can influence actions (e.g., they can choose to take a taxi or walk), but, most often, it just alleviates uncertainty and anxiety.

PROVIDING CHOICES

Too often, individuals with developmental disabilities lack opportunities to make choices because of the highly structured nature of their special education programs or therapeutic interventions, and some believe that they lack the ability. The opportunity to make choices allows people to express their personal preferences concerning their environment, activities, and the people present. Furthermore, choice-making enhances a sense of control and allows the individual to learn how to become an active participant, rather than a passive bystander. Research has shown that simply allowing the individual to choose the task can reduce the aversion to non-preferred tasks and therefore reduce the likelihood of escape-motivated problem behavior including SIB (e.g., Vaughn and Horner, 1997).

Providing choices could also possibly reduce tangibly motivated problem behavior; for example, a boy who engaged in problem behavior when told he could not eat his favorite fast-food fried chicken was given a choice of two comparable but healthier fast-food restaurants. Some research has even suggested that the act of making a choice is reinforcing in and of itself, which further increases a person's motivation to participate and behave well. There are many ways to provide choices within and across activities. A student who engages in SIB to escape doing homework, for example, may be allowed to choose the sequence of academic tasks or the order in which to complete a specific academic task (e.g., math problems), where to complete the homework assignment (e.g., at the kitchen table or his bedroom desk), which materials to use (e.g., monkey pencil or starfish pencil), when to complete the task, or with whom to complete the activity.

BEHAVIORAL MOMENTUM AND EMBEDDING

The goal of behavioral momentum is to create momentum toward compliance with a non-preferred (or more difficult) task. The individual is asked to do quick and easy activities (i.e., "high-probability commands" with which the individual has a history of complying, such as "Give me five!") right before he is asked to complete a more difficult or disliked task (i.e., "low-probability commands," such as putting one's coat in the closet). This strategy works particularly well when the function of SIB is to escape or avoid task demands. Behavioral momentum has been shown to increase compliance in individuals with DD (Mace *et al.*, 1988), which often results in collateral decreases in SIB, aggression, and disruptive behavior. A great example of a behavioral-momentum exercise is singing a song or giving high fives. Similarly, embedding difficult or disliked tasks (e.g., an instructional demand) within the context of more preferred or easier tasks (e.g., a positive conversational exchange) is another way to decrease problem behavior, including SIB, particularly when the function is escape.

TASK MODIFICATIONS

When an individual is engaging in SIB to escape from task demands, task modifications such as curricular revisions are important to consider as an antecedent strategy. There are many types of task modifications; several of the main ones will be discussed here. The length of an activity can be changed so that it is more manageable for the person to complete. For example, it might be overwhelming to clear all of the dishes off the table, whereas clearing just one set of dishes may be more manageable. Then, as the individual becomes more successful in completing this easier task, expectations can be increased such that the person is required to complete more of the task. Similarly, the mode of an activity can be altered (e.g., typing instead of handwriting) or the difficulty of a task can be changed. Activities can also incorporate an individual's interests to make the task more motivating.

USING PREFERRED ACTIVITIES OR INTERESTS

Incorporating an individual's preferences or interests into disliked or unpleasant activities can increase his motivation to engage in those activities, thereby reducing escape-motivated problem behavior (Clarke *et al.*, 1995). For example, if a student enjoys music, then songs might be incorporated into tasks. Similarly, if a studentengages in SIB to get out of completing a math assignment, his favorite objects could be incorporated into the math assignment (e.g., math with counting pictures of Legos), or favorite animals (e.g., pictures of monkeys on the math assignment)or favorite characters (e.g., a Buzz Lightyear or Batman pencil or notebook that is reserved for math). It is important that there be ongoing assessment of an individual's interests, as they may change over time.

PROVIDE ALTERNATIVE SENSORY STIMULATION

The function of SIB can also be to gain or increase sensory input or stimulation, or to escape or reduce sensory stimulation. In order to prevent the person from achieving sensory input in a dangerous way (i.e., SIB), alternative means may be offered. For example, for a child who threw himself on the floor repeatedly to gain intense pressure, his treatment team designed an intervention in which he received deep pressure and access to a weighted blanket several times throughout the day.

MINIMIZING THE EFFECTS OF SETTING EVENTS

If there is a known setting event that makes it more likely for a person to engage in SIB, it is important to make sure the setting event has less of a chance of happening. We can mitigate the setting event so that it makes a given antecedent less likely to evoke SIB. For example, menstrual pain as a setting event might make task demands more likely to evoke problem behaviors, including SIB; researchers have mitigated the setting event by providing non-drug ancillary treatment, such as heating pads or hot water bottles to alleviate menstrual cramps, or a period of bed rest for fatigue (Carr *et al.*, 2003).

Important Considerations When Using Prevention Strategies

When designing antecedent-based interventions to prevent SIB, it is important to note several caveats. There may be factors other than behavior functions contributing to SIB, particularly if it does not improve after implementing several of these interventions. These other factors could include medical, physical, or health-related issues, mental health concerns, learning disabilities, or other skills deficits that should be considered when designing interventions.

Sometimes parents and teachers use prevention strategies because it is easier than teaching skills. This can be problematic, given that recent work suggests this may result in parents and teachers changing the environment to avoid difficult situations, rather than teaching the individual how to cope (e.g., communicating his needs in that situation); this could result in reduced maintenance and generalization over time (Durand, 2011a, 2011b). Some prevention strategies, such as changing a child's seat to move him away from a "triggering" peer or avoiding going shopping during crowded times of day (if crowds are an antecedent or setting event), should only be used on a temporary basis while the individual is learning skills to cope with the problematic situation. It is neither feasible nor desirable to avoid difficult situations forever, and avoidance can make the individual's problems worse as he grows older, because he never learns how to deal with them. Some prevention strategies can be used on a more long-term basis, such as a visual schedule to help enhance predictability (after all, even adults without disabilities use calendars and visual planners), but it is still important to note that events in an individual's life will not always be predictable; thus, we need to build in flexibility and teach the individual how to cope with changes to his schedule over time. In any case, teaching replacement skills is critical so that prevention strategies can be faded out once the individual learns more appropriate ways to express his needs.

Developing Replacement Behaviors and Teaching Skills

We cannot simply *remove* something that is serving a purpose without *replacing* it with a more appropriate alternative. We first must understand what purpose the SIB serves and then teach the individual a better way to get that need met. A main goal of PBS is to teach alternative skills that are more effective and socially acceptable than prior behaviors (Bambara and Kern, 2005; Carr *et al.*, 1994, 1999). Individuals who acquire skills to communicate better will be more likely to integrate into the community, will have more successful relationships, and will be more successful in school. Skill building can be categorized into three domains: (1) replacement skills, (2) coping and tolerance skills, and (3) general adaptive or life skills (Bambara and Knoster, 1998). When developing replacement strategies, questions we might ask include "What can this individual do instead?" and "What alternative behaviors or skills might replace the SIB?" The following discussion is about some of the main skill-building concepts to consider when building a comprehensive behavior intervention plan. With replacement strategies, instead of caretakers changing the environment to prevent problem behaviors, the individual is taught skills that allow him to change his own environment.

TEACHING COMMUNICATION SKILLS

Communication skills are the most researched and arguably the most important. If the individual with ASD or DD does not have a way to say that he wants his mother, teacher, or peer to pay him attention, that he does not like something or does not want to do something he is told to do, or that he wants his sister's toy, it makes perfect sense that he would resort to hitting or biting himself, or someone else. It is imperative to teach the person how to ask for those things in a better way (e.g., verbally, through sign language, through pointing to pictures, or using a voice-output device), so that he does not need to injure himself to get what he wants or needs. Functional communication training (FCT; Carr and Durand, 1985) teaches the individual to ask through language instead of SIB/problem behavior. For example, he can be taught to ask for social interaction, attention, or praise (e.g., "Am I doing good work?", "Can I play?", "Hi, what's up?", or even just "play" or "hi") to replace the SIB. If he engages in SIB to escape from some disliked or difficult or anxiety-provoking activity or situation, he can be taught to say "no," to ask for a break, to ask for help with the task, or to ask for a change in activity. If he engages in SIB to obtain tangible reinforcement, he can be taught to ask for those preferred items or activities (e.g., "want book" or "my turn please"). If he engages in SIB to gain sensory reinforcement, he can ask for an item or activity that provides sensory stimulation (e.g., "bounce please" or "swing") or ask for privacy. The communication skill that we teach the individual cannot just be any communication response; it must be a communicative response that serves the same function as the SIB. The communication skill also must work better than (or, at least, as well as) the SIB. Numerous studies have demonstrated the effectiveness of FCT in treating SIB in individuals with ASD and DD (e.g., Derby *et al.*, 1997; Durand, 1999). A separate chapter in this book on using FCT to treat SIB (see Chapter 11) goes into depth on teaching individuals communication skills using FCT, so this chapter focuses on coping and adaptive skills in order to avoid redundancy. (We encourage readers to refer to Chapter 11 to learn more about FCT and replacement skills.)

TEACHING COPING SKILLS

Coping and tolerance skills refer to any skills an individual needs to remain in a particular situation and take care of himself while handling a difficult situation that cannot or should not be changed. These skills may include "waiting" skills, self-management skills such as relaxation (e.g., deep breathing), anger-management skills, and problem-solving skills. Individuals with DD also need to learn how to tolerate unpleasant or difficult situations. For example, even if we teach Billy to request a toy and teach the main people in his environment to immediately honor that request (at least initially while he is first learning the skill), not every peer will give Billy the toy as soon as he asks for it, so we also need to teach Billy how to wait for a turn with the toy (Bambara and Kern, 2005). Coping skills and tolerance both need to be taught in a strategic, concrete manner, using visuals and step-by-step directions. It is important that these skills be scaffolded to set the individual up for success right away. This will increase motivation and give the person a sense of efficacy. Many of these skills lack inherent motivation, so it may be important to reward the individual for using his or her learned coping strategies. Furthermore, teaching these skills should be combined with teaching replacement skills (e.g., asking for a break), when possible, in order to provide the person with some control over his wants and needs.

Teaching tolerance typically involves gradually delaying reinforcement for longer and longer periods of time while also incrementally increasing demands so the individual learns to persist through more difficult situations. For example, Ashley, a young girl with autism, would bite her arms if she was not given the computer tablet right away when she got home from school. A therapist working with Ashley and her family helped structure an intervention in which Ashley would be required to wait longer periods to use the tablet. She began with only waiting a minute and slowly increased the time. During these periods Ashley would be allowed to choose a different preferred activity, such as puzzles, reading a book, or eating a snack, so that she could be productively engaged while waiting (Carr *et al.*, 1994). Eventually Ashley was able to complete less preferred activities (e.g., completing a few items of homework) before using the tablet. It is important to note that, when an individual is first learning a communication skill (e.g., asking for a break), that skill must be immediately reinforced (e.g., by giving him a break right away) every time. However, over time, we must gradually increase the demands before reinforcement (e.g., "Break? Okay, do one more problem, and then you can take a break"; then the next day, "Do these two first, and then you can take a break"; and so forth).

Teaching coping strategies or self-management skills also requires structured approaches that slowly increase expectations for the individual. There are many self-management strategies. One common strategy that has been shown to be effective in various research studies is relaxation training, using deep breathing or progressive muscle relaxation (Mullins and Christian, 2001; Moree and Davis, 2010). (See Chapter 13 for more information about relaxation skills.) Another self-regulation skill is coping self-talk (e.g., "I can do it"). (See Chapter 12 for more information about coping self-talk.) Individuals can be taught how to increase their awareness of emotions and triggers that lead them to engage in SIB. Similarly, social-problem solving is a strategy that involves teaching the student to identify a problem and generate various solutions to it. It is important that, with each of these strategies, an adult takes the lead in teaching, rehearsing, and prompting the individual to use the strategy appropriately. As with functional communication skills, the great part about self-management skills is that, once they have been learned, the individual is no longer dependent on teachers, parents, or staff and can use these skills independently when alone or with new "untrained" people.

TEACHING ADAPTIVE SKILLS

Adaptive skills are broader in nature and include general life skills (e.g., daily living skills such as getting dressed or brushing teeth), academic competence, general communication abilities, social skills, organizational skills, and leisure activities. They address areas of skills deficits that may cause the person to engage in SIB, so the person may complete functional tasks more independently. For example, if we teach a student how to complete subtraction problems, that removes the need for him to engage in SIB to obtain assistance with the problems, or to escape from doing the math assignment (Bambara and Kern, 2005). Although providing choices can be considered a prevention or antecedent-based strategy, teaching the skill of choice-making can be considered an adaptive skill. Skills that lead to a fulfilling and meaningful life include recreational activities (e.g., attending sports events, going to church) as well as functional tasks (e.g., grocery shopping, eating at a restaurant). Providers working with families should discuss with them which areas are most important for the individual, and work to prioritize the necessary skills. If the individual is pursuing meaningful activities, this may reduce his need to engage in SIB. After all, any of us might resort to problem behavior (even if not SIB) if we spent all day every day engaged only in tasks or activities that were incredibly difficult, boring, frustrating, or anxiety-provoking (and over which we had no control), and were not engaged in any activities that were rewarding or meaningful.

Consequence-Based Strategies to Reduce SIB

Using a PBS approach, a treatment team designs an intervention plan that focuses on replacement or teaching strategies as well as the use of antecedent-based strategies. Once SIB starts to occur, there are very few immediate responses that effectively stop or decrease the behavior in the moment other than interruption or restraint. However, neither of these approaches contributes to long-term reductions and can at times be dangerous. There are, however, several response or consequence-based strategies that can strategically be used that will help decrease SIB over time. Essentially, management strategies are used to alter the consequences for SIB and other problem behaviors so that they no longer lead to desired results for the individual, and "positive behaviors" (e.g., replacement behaviors) lead to desired results instead. In other words, consequence strategies include making sure that the SIB is not effective (by not reinforcing the SIB) and that we reinforce alternative skills instead. Developing consequence strategies involves asking ourselves "How can we respond differently to SIB and reinforce replacement skills?" as well as "What consequences can we use to decrease SIB and increase replacement behaviors?" The goal of using consequence-based strategies is to prevent SIB from worsening and to provide natural consequences or consequences that have a close relationship with the behavior or that help the individual understand rules about engaging in appropriate behavior. Although consequence-based strategies are important, a PBS plan should not include consequence strategies *only*, since that would make the plan reactive rather than instructive and proactive (Bambara and Kern, 2005).

Although it is beyond the scope of this chapter, we will briefly mention that there has been an ongoing ethical debate about the use of aversive and/or punitive strategies in treating SIB. These strategies (e.g., restraint, shock, food aversion) tend to further stigmatize the individual and do not address the underlying reason for why he is engaging in SIB. It is also important to keep in mind the values of PBS as outlined in this chapter, that is, the focus is on treating the underlying function or reason for why SIB is occurring, and always includes teaching, prevention, and strategies as a first line of treatment.

INSTRUCTIONAL APPROACHES

Instructional approaches include strategies that help the person engage in an alternative behavior or redirect the person away from engaging in SIB. Common strategies include praise and redirection. Praise can be offered specifically to the individual for engaging in safe behaviors (e.g., waiting calmly) or can be given to other people in close proximity to the individual who are engaging in appropriate behaviors (e.g., praising other children in a class who are waiting calmly). Praise is most effective when the target individual values praise. Redirection refers to a prompt given to the person engaging in SIB to engage in a more appropriate behavior (e.g., prompting the child to ask for help using a help card). The prompt should directly state what is expected.

DIFFERENTIAL REINFORCEMENT

Differential reinforcement procedures increase alternative or more appropriate behaviors by providing reinforcement when the individual engages in appropriate behavior, while withholding reinforcement when he engages in SIB/problem behavior. Differential reinforcement of other behavior (DRO) involves providing reinforcement whenever an individual is not engaging in SIB (i.e., engaging in any behavior other than SIB). For example, if a child's SIB functioned to gain attention, a DRO would consist of providing the child with attention every 5 minutes during which he has not displayed the SIB, while ignoring the SIB if and when it occurs. Differential reinforcement of incompatible behavior (DRI) would involve reinforcing a behavior that is physically incompatible with SIB (e.g., a child holding onto the handles of a shopping cart while pushing it) rather than SIB (e.g., the child biting his hand). Finally, differential reinforcement of alternative behavior (DRA) involves providing reinforcement for an alternative behavior or skill that is dissimilar to SIB (though not necessarily physically incompatible with SIB), while not providing any reinforcement for SIB. For example, a child who hits himself every time he is required to wait in line at the grocery store (in order to escape having to wait) might be reinforced for calmly looking at a magazine while in the check-out line and would not be taken out of the line if he begins to hit himself. When using differential reinforcement it is very important that the individual have the necessary skills that will be reinforced in his repertoire. If the child in the above example was not able to look at a magazine, then he would need to be taught other strategies (e.g., playing on the tablet, looking at pictures) before he could be reinforced for an alternative behavior.

EXTINCTION

Extinction involves completely removing reinforcement from a previously reinforced behavior, which causes the behavior to decrease. Planned ignoring is an example of extinction when the function of a behavior is to gain attention. If the function of SIB is to escape from a task or activity, extinction involves not terminating the task contingent upon SIB. It is important to note that the short-term effect of extinction is usually worsening of the behavior (i.e., extinction burst); therefore, it is extremely important to consider the severity of the behavior before implementing extinction for SIB. For very severe SIB, extinction should be used carefully and in conjunction with other methods (e.g., teaching the person skills to get what he needs). The long-term effect of extinction is that the behavior gradually decreases because the person learns that his behavior is no longer effective for gaining his desired outcome (e.g., attention). Sometimes reinforcing a replacement behavior (such as a student raising his hand) will not be effective on its own if the problem behavior (e.g., calling out) is still being reinforced rather than extinguished. However, if the SIB is so severe that it would be dangerous to use extinction, reinforcing alternative behavior can still be effective on its own if the reinforcement for the alternative behavior is more powerful than the reinforcement for the SIB (Athens and Vollmer, 2010).

Putting It All Together

For a PBS plan to be most effective, it should include (a) prevention strategies to mitigate setting events and modify or alter antecedents, (b) teaching replacements for problem behavior, and (c) altering consequences so that SIB is no longer reinforced and appropriate behaviors are reinforced instead. For example, let us say that an FBA reveals that a child sometimes bangs her head when her favorite toy is out of reach (antecedent) and her mother responds to this SIB by giving her the toy (consequence), and that her favorite toys being out of reach is more likely to lead to SIB if she has not had access to them for a while (setting event), since that makes the consequence of getting her toy even more valuable (Horner and Carr, 1997). A multicomponent PBS plan would address all these elements by immediately scheduling play time with the preferred toys (altering the setting event), placing the toys within the child's reach (removing or altering the antecedent), teaching the child to request her toys (teaching a replacement skill), and giving her the toys only when she appropriately requests the toys rather than when she bangs her head (altering consequences) (Horner and Carr, 1997). To return to the example of menstrual pain as a setting event for escape-motivated problem behavior in response to task demands, Carr and colleagues (2003) designed an intervention in which they

(a) mitigated the setting event of pain/discomfort by providing ancillary medical intervention (e.g., heating pads for cramps); (b) altered the antecedent by providing preferred activities such as drinking hot tea prior to presenting task demands (non-contingent reinforcement), asking the women which tasks they wanted to do first (providing choices), and interspersing task demands within the context of positive interactions or activities (embedding); and (c) taught the women to request a break from task demands, or seek assistance (teaching a replacement skill, i.e., FCT). This multicomponent intervention reduced problem behaviors including SIB to near-zero levels. The plan did not include consequence strategies; for some individuals such a plan might be more effective if it included consequence strategies such as reinforcing the women for task completion (positive reinforcement) and extinction. In summary, these examples illustrate the comprehensive nature of a PBS plan.

Long-Term Support and Lifestyle Changes

In addition to developing prevention, replacement, and management strategies, a PBS plan also must include lifestyle changes. After all, SIB and other problem behaviors may continue to persist (in spite of smaller antecedent changes, or skills taught) because broader issues in the individual's life, educational or vocational program, or social network are interfering. To foster lasting change, a PBS plan must address how the effects of intervention will be maintained over time and generalized to new situations, as well as address broader systemic issues. This could include increasing the individual's level of independence; providing respite for caretakers; helping the individual to engage in community activities with family members (e.g., going out to eat at a restaurant, seeing a play or movie, going to church or synagogue, going bowling, visiting relatives); helping the individual to develop social relationships, find a job, join a club or afterschool activity, and/or learn new hobbies; and above all, identifying areas in which the individual can make a valuable contribution to his family, school, workplace, or community (Bambara and Kern, 2005). For example, we encouraged one of the individuals with ASD with whom we worked to volunteer at an animal shelter and another individual with DD to volunteer at a nursing home, as this capitalized on their respective interests in animals and talking to the elderly, and allowed them to make meaningful contributions. The plan could also include identifying responsibilities that the individual can take on in the home, school, workplace, or community. For example, the intervention plan for a 13-year-old boy with ASD involved helping the first-grade students to the bus with their backpacks, a responsibility he chose that made him feel very proud.

From Functional Assessment to Behavior Support Plan: Joey's Case Example

Joey is a 10-year-old boy with ASD and ID. He is in fourth grade and is in a classroom for children with severe special needs. Joey had recently begun displaying more dangerous behaviors that included throwing chairs, tipping filing cabinets, and engaging in SIB (e.g., self-biting, banging his head, scratching his face) and aggression toward others (e.g., kicking). A consultation was requested in order to develop a comprehensive behavior intervention plan to reduce Joey's SIB, as that is the behavior that occurs most frequently and is the most dangerous.

The Functional Behavior Assessment

Joey was observed in his classroom and at home. His parents and main special education teacher, Ms. Swanson, also completed the Contextual Assessment Inventory (CAI) and the Motivation Assessment Scale (MAS). Based on these questionnaires, we learned that Joey typically engages in SIB when he is asked to participate in group activities and when he is required to read new material. We also learned that the SIB is more likely to occur when he has difficulty communicating his wants and needs as well as when he is in the presence of disliked staff. We then structured the classroom observation in order to observe times when Joey would be asked to join group activities, read, and interact with less-desired staff. At home, we observed Joey during a typical routine when he gets home from school. We also assessed Joey's strengths and his interests and learned that Joey has a special interest in music, animals, and puzzles. He enjoys being with his family and his siblings. Furthermore, Joey is very good at (and enjoys) fixing things around the house and he tends to be the "go-to" person when something breaks. An ABC chart was completed during the observation at school (see Table 10.3).

The main hypothesis is that Joey engages in SIB (biting his finger or his hand and banging his head) when he is asked to participate in group activities and when he is required to read new material (antecedents) because, when he does, he is allowed to escape the task or activity (consequence). This is more likely to occur when he is in the presence of disliked staff members and when he has difficulty communicating (setting events).

Table 10.3 Joey's ABC Chart

Time	Antecedent	Behavior	Consequence	Possible Function
10:15 a.m.	Joey is asked to read the instructions on a new worksheet.	Joey bites his fingers repetitively.	Joey is told "safe hands" and another peer is asked to read.	Escape and Attention
10:45 a.m.	Ms. Leigh (Joey's paraprofessional) asks Joey to join a reading group.	Joey attempts to kick the teacher and scratches his face.	Joey is taken out of the class to a separate room for reading.	Escape
11:15 a.m.	Ms. Leigh approaches Joey's desk.	Joey yells, tips his chair over, and bites his arms.	Ms. Swanson (Joey's teacher) walks to another child's desk.	Escape
11:35 a.m.	Ms. Swanson instructs Joey to join a small math group.	Joey bangs his head on his desk.	The teacher and several aides go over to Joey and tell him "safe hands" while removing him from the small group.	Escape and Attention

Joey's Positive Behavior Support Plan
PREVENTION PLAN

The following is a prevention plan for Joey:

- **Increase predictability.**
  Break down tasks visually. Let Joey know how much time is required for him to complete activities that are difficult for him (reading, group work). Use brief instructions and visual cues as much as possible. Written instructions along with pictures on the board or on paper may help Joey understand what he is expected to do and decrease unnecessary verbal input.

- **Use priming.**
  Have Joey preview new material one-on-one with a teacher before giving him a new assignment to complete alone or in a group.

- **Incorporate interests and preferences.**
  Incorporate Joey's special interest in music, animals, and/or puzzles into reading new material (e.g., reading a story about animals) or participating in group activities (e.g., listening to music or singing with a group).

- **Encourage choice-making.**
  Increase opportunities to make requests and choices. Incorporate choice-making throughout Joey's day, in particular in the context of non-preferred tasks such as reading new material or participating in group activities (e.g., choice between two different new reading materials matched on generic content, choice in where he can sit in the group, choice in *how* he can complete a non-preferred task).

- **Schedule less-desirable activities followed by more motivating activities to encourage task completion.**

- **Use embedding.**
  Intersperse difficult activities (e.g., reading new material) with easy tasks (e.g., reading older, more familiar material).

- **Promote rapport-building.**
  Focus on building positive relationships between Joey and the adults who work with him. Rapport-building strategies may include having the disliked staff members present Joey with his favorite food or toys and engage with him around his preferred activities (e.g., puzzles, listening to music) for brief, positive periods of time without academic demands. Staff members should give Joey his favorite items and activities non-contingently, meaning that Joey does not have to do anything in order to receive these reinforcers. If they keep pairing themselves with Joey's favorite things, the disliked staff members will come to trigger approach rather than escape (Magito McLaughlin and Carr, 2005).

REPLACEMENT/SKILL-BUILDING

To promote replacement/skill-building:

- Teach Joey to request breaks (e.g., "break, please") from disliked or difficult activities, or ask for help with difficult activities (i.e., promote FCT). Initially, honor all communicative requests for break and help. Over time, gradually fade breaks and assistance.

- Teach Joey coping strategies to calm down during difficult situations (e.g., counting to 10, deep breathing, taking a water break).

- Teach Joey to participate in group activities, as part of the reason he avoids these activities may be because he lacks the skills to participate.

RESPONSE/CONSEQUENCE STRATEGIES

Response/consequence strategies are as follows:

- Develop a reward plan for Joey that reinforces him for appropriate behavior (e.g., asking for help, asking for a break). A reinforcement inventory should be completed to assess the kinds of rewards that Joey would like the most. Capitalize on his special interests.

- It is also important to match the reward to the function of Joey's behavior. If he is trying to escape task demands, a possible reward may be leaving class 5 minutes early for lunch if he completes five out of seven reading comprehension questions, or a "get-out-of-one-assignment free" that he can earn on Fridays if he completes his assignments from Monday through Thursday.

- In a crisis situation, when Joey's SIB is at its worst, the most important response is to secure safety, and de-escalation of his behavior.

LIFESTYLE CHANGES

Lifestyle changes could include the following:

- Expand on some of the activities Joey already likes, to include others that are related. He really loves music. His family may pursue having him join a music class or club or taking him to concerts in their hometown. Joining a class or club could help achieve a goal that is important to his family: making friends.

- Increase age-appropriate activities. For example, Joey likes puzzles, so he may enjoy doing puzzles with others and taking turns finding pieces. He might also play interactive games with peers on the Nintendo Wii (e.g., Wii tennis or bowling).

- Joey enjoys spending time with his family. They should participate in activities in the community that they can all enjoy together (e.g., going out to a restaurant, going to the zoo, seeing a movie), and share interests, such as listening to music together or singing a song together in the car.

- Joey's parents may benefit from respite services, which would provide them with time for self-care and also allow him to build positive relationships with other adults.

References

Athens, E.S., and Vollmer, T.R. (2010). An investigation of differential reinforcement of alternative behavior without extinction. *Journal of Applied Behavior Analysis, 43*(4), 569–589.

Bambara, L., and Kern, L. (2005). *Individualized Supports for Students with Problem Behaviors: Designing Positive Behavior Plans.* New York, NY: Guilford Press.

Bambara, L., and Knoster, T. (1998). Designing positive behavior support plans. *Innovations* (No. 13). Washington, DC: American Association on Mental Retardation.

Bruininks, R.H., Hill, B.K., and Morreau, L.E. (1988). Prevalence and Implications of Maladaptive Behaviors and Dual Diagnosis in Residential and Other Service Programs. In J.A. Stark, F.J. Menolascino, M.H. Albarelli, and V.C. Gray (Eds.), *Mental Retardation and Mental Health: Classification, Diagnosis, Treatment, Services.* New York, NY: Springer-Verlag.

Carr, E.G. (1977). The motivation of self-injurious behavior: A review of some hypotheses. *Psychological Bulletin, 84,* 800–816.

Carr, E.G., Horner, R.H., Tunbull, A.P., Marquis, J.G., *et al.* (1999). *Positive Behavior Support for People with Developmental Disabilities: A Research Synthesis.* Washington, DC: American Association on Mental Retardation.

Carr, E.G., Dunlap, G., Horner, R.H., Koegel, R.L., *et al.* (2002). Positive behavior support: Evolution of an applied science. *Journal of Positive Behavior Interventions, 4*(1), 4.

Carr, E.G., and Durand, V.M. (1985). Reducing behavior problems through functional communication training. *Journal of Applied Behavior Analysis, 18,* 111–126.

Carr, E.G., Levin, L., McConnachie, G., Carlson, J.I., Kemp, D.C., and Smith, C.E. (1994). *Communication-Based Intervention for Problem Behavior: A User's Guide for Producing Positive Change.* Baltimore, MD: Paul H. Brookes Publishing.

Carr, E.G., Smith, C.E., Giacin, T.A., Whelan, B.M., and Pancari, J. (2003). Menstrual discomfort as a biological setting event for severe problem behavior: Assessment and intervention. *American Journal on Mental Retardation, 108,* 117–133.

Clarke, S., Dunlap, G., Foster-Johnson, L., Childs, K.E., *et al.* (1995). Improving the conduct of students with behavioral disorders by incorporating student interests into curricular activities. *Behavioral Disorders, 20*(4), 221–237.

Davies, L., and Oliver, C. (2013). The age related prevalence of aggression and self-injury in persons with an intellectual disability: A review. *Research in Developmental Disabilities, 34*(2), 764–775. doi:10.1016/j.ridd.2012.10.004

Derby, K.M., Wacker, D.P., Berg, W., DeRaad, A., *et al.* (1997). The long-term effects of functional communication training in home settings. *Journal of Applied Behavior Analysis, 30*(3), 507–531. doi:10.1901/ jaba.1997.30-507

Dunlap, G., and Carr, E.G. (2007). Positive Behavior Support and Developmental Disabilities: A Summary and Analysis of Research. In S.L. Odom, R.H. Horner, M. Snell, and J. Blacher (Eds.), *Handbook of Developmental Disabilities.* New York, NY: Guilford.

Durand, V.M. (1990). *Functional Communication Training: An Intervention Program for Severe Behavior Problems.* New York, NY: Guilford.

Durand, V.M. (1999). Functional communication training using assistive devices: Recruiting natural communities of reinforcement. *Journal of Applied Behavior Analysis, 32*(3), 247–267. doi:10.1901/jaba.1999.32-247

Durand, V.M. (2011a). *The Concession Process: A New Framework for Understanding the Development and Treatment of Challenging Behavior in Autism Spectrum Disorders.* Washington, DC: American Psychological Association.

Durand, V.M. (2011b). *Optimistic Parenting: Hope and Help for You and Your Challenging Child.* Baltimore, MD: Paul H. Brookes Publishing.

Durand, V.M., and Crimmins, D.B. (1988a). *The Motivation Assessment Scale.* Topeka, KS: Monaco & Associates.

Durand, V.M., and Crimmins, D.B. (1988b). Identifying the variables maintaining self-injurious behavior. *Journal of Autism and Developmental Disorders, 18,* 99–117.

Durand, V.M., and Hieneman, M. (2008). *Helping Parents with Challenging Children: Positive Family Intervention. Facilitator's Guide.* New York, NY: Oxford University Press.

Gardner, W.I., Cole, C.L., Davidson, D.P., and Karan, O.C. (1986). Reducing aggression in individuals with developmental disabilities: An expanded stimulus control, assessment, and intervention model. *Education and Training of the Mentally Retarded, 21,* 2–12.

Gray, C.A., and Garand, J.D. (1993). Social Stories: Improving responses of students with autism with accurate social information. *Focus on Autistic Behavior, 8*(1), 1–10.

Horner, R.H., and Carr, E.G. (1997). Behavioral support for students with severe disabilities: Functional assessment and comprehensive intervention. *Journal of Special Education, 31,* 84–104.

Iwata, B.A., Duncan, B.A., Zarcone, J.R., Lerman, D.C., and Shore, B.A. (1994). A sequential, test-control methodology for conducting functional analyses of self-injurious behavior. *Behavior Modification, 18,* 289–306.

Janney, R.E., and Meyer, L.H. (1990). A consultation model to support integrated educational services for students with severe disabilities and challenging behaviors. *Journal of the Association for Persons with Severe Handicaps, 15*(3), 186–199.

Koegel, L.K., Koegel, R.L., and Dunlap, G. (1996). *Positive Behavioral Support: Including People with Difficult Behavior in the Community.* Baltimore, MD: Paul H. Brookes Publishing.

Koegel, R.L., Schreibman, L., Loos, L.M., Dirlich-Wilhelm, H., *et al.* (1992). Stress profiles for mothers and fathers of children with autism. *Journal of Autism and Developmental Disorders, 22,* 205–216.

Langthorne, P., and McGill, P. (2008). A functional analysis of the early development of self-injurious behavior: Incorporating gene–environment interactions. *American Journal on Mental Retardation, 113,* 403–417.

Lequia, J., Machalicek, W., and Rispoli, M.J. (2012). Effects of activity schedules on challenging behavior exhibited in children with autism spectrum disorders: A systematic review. *Research in Autism Spectrum Disorders, 6*(1), 480–492. doi:10.1016/j.rasd.2011.07.008

Lucyshyn, J.M., Dunlap, G., and Albin, R.W. (2002). *Families and Positive Behavior Support: Addressing Problem Behavior in Family Contexts.* Baltimore, MD: Paul H. Brookes Publishing.

Lucyshyn, J.M., Horner, R., Dunlap, G., Albin, R.W., and Ben, K.R. (2002). Positive Behavior Support with Families. In J. Lucyshyn, G. Dunlap, and R. Albin (Eds.), *Families and Positive Behavior Supports: Addressing Problem Behavior in Family Contexts*. Baltimore, MD: Paul H. Brookes Publishing.

Mace, A.B., Shapiro, E.S., and Mace, F.C. (1998). Effects of warning stimuli for reinforcer withdrawal and task onset on self-injury. *Journal of Applied Behavior Analysis, 31*(4), 679–682.

Mace, C.F., Hock, M.L., Lalli, J.S., West, B.J., *et al.* (1988). Behavioral momentum in the treatment of noncompliance. *Journal of Applied Behavior Analysis, 21*(2), 123–141.

MacLean, W.E., and Dornbush, K. (2012). Self-injury in a statewide sample of young children with developmental disabilities. *Journal of Mental Health Research in Intellectual Disabilities, 5*(3–4), 236–245. doi:10.1080/19315864.2011.590627

Magito McLaughlin, D., and Carr, E.G. (2005). Quality of rapport as a setting event for problem behavior: Assessment and intervention. *Journal of Positive Behavior Interventions, 7*(2), 68–91.

Matson, J.L., and Vollmer, T. (1995). *User's Guide: Questions About Behavioral Function (QABF)*. Baton Rouge, LA: Scientific Publishers.

McAtee, M., Carr, E.G., and Schulte, C. (2004). A contextual assessment inventory for problem behavior: Initial development. *Journal of Positive Behavior Interventions, 6*(3), 148–165.

Moree, B.N., and Davis III, T.E. (2010). Cognitive-behavioral therapy for anxiety in children diagnosed with autism spectrum disorders: Modification trends. *Research in Autism Spectrum Disorders, 4,* 346–354.

Mullins, J.L., and Christian, L. (2001). The effects of progressive relaxation training on the disruptive behavior of a boy with autism. *Research in Developmental Disabilities, 22*(6), 449–462. doi:10.1016/S0891-4222(01)00083-X

O'Neill, R.E., Horner, R.H., Albin, R.W., Sprague, J.R., Storey, K., and Newton, J.S. (1997). *Functional Assessment and Program Development for Problem Behavior: A Practical Handbook* (2nd ed.). Pacific Grove, CA: Brooks/Cole.

Turnbull, A.P., and Ruef, M. (1996). Family perspectives on problem behavior. *Mental Retardation, 34,* 280–293.

Vaughn, B.J., Dunlap, G., Fox, L., Clarke, S., and Bucy, M. (1997). Parent–professional partnership in behavioral support: A case study of community-based intervention. *Journal of the Association for Persons with Severe Handicaps, 22,* 185–197.

Vaughn, B.J., and Horner, R.H. (1997). Identifying instructional tasks that occasion problem behaviors and assessing the effects of student versus teacher choice among these tasks. *Journal of Applied Behavior Analysis, 30*(2), 299–312. doi:10.1901/jaba.1997.30-299

Wolf, M.M. (1978). Social validity: The case for subjective measurement or how applied behavior analysis is finding its heart. *Journal of Applied Behavior Analysis, 11*(2), 203–214. doi:10.1901/jaba.1978.11-203

CHAPTER 11

Using Functional Communication Training to Treat Self-Injurious Behavior

*V. Mark Durand, Ph.D., University of South Florida, St. Petersburg, Florida,
and Lauren J. Moskowitz, Ph.D., St. John's University, New York*

Introduction

Self-injurious behaviors (SIBs) (face slapping, self-biting, head banging, severe scratching, and so forth) among individuals with developmental disabilities, including autism spectrum disorder (ASD), are of great concern to family members, educators, and other professionals. As other chapters in this book attest, a variety of perspectives exist as to why these individuals hurt themselves. In the late 1970s, an important review of the research on what motivates individuals with developmental disorders to hurt themselves suggested that many of these behaviors could be occurring because they result in some form of reinforcement (Carr, 1977). In other words, over time some individuals may learn, for example, to hit or bite themselves for some positive outcome or to escape from an unpleasant situation. As will be seen, this social role for SIB does not preclude the influence of biological or physical influences which can, in some circumstances, interact with social influences (e.g., Edelson, 1984). This chapter describes these non-medical or non-biological causes of SIB and functional communication training (FCT), a treatment that has been proven to reduce or eliminate these types of difficulties.

Suppose a young boy cries and screams when he is asked to come to the dinner table. Sometimes his parents give in, and let him eat in the living room in front of the television; other times they persist with the request despite him becoming upset. This is likely to cause the boy to intensify his resistance, and one time, he flops to the floor and hits his head. The potential harm alarms his parents and they comfort him and let him eat away from the dinner table. These outcomes—comforting, and escaping the dinner table—are likely to increase the chance that in these and similar situations in the future (e.g., when being asked to brush his teeth, which he also dislikes) the boy will escalate his behavior as before, and he will hit his head on the floor again. Wanting him to not hurt himself will make his parents more likely either to give in or to avoid these contentious requests altogether.

This type of process has been validated in hundreds of research studies. For example, there is evidence that some individuals hurt themselves to escape unpleasant situations (e.g., Carr, Newsom, and Binkoff, 1980). When some children are presented with a difficult task in school, they might slap their face or bite themselves to get the teacher to stop requesting them to participate. And there is evidence that teachers learn to withdraw these types of requests—even if they are not consciously aware of it—when students hit themselves (Taylor and Carr, 1992). Other children and adults appear to engage in SIB to gain the attention of others, to get things (e.g., food, toys), or to engage in activities (e.g., watching television during meals). Teachers, parents, and others often respond in ways that they believe are supportive (e.g., providing loving attention when a child is upset and hurting himself), which unfortunately can reinforce this pattern of behaving. In this way, the SIB comes to serve a function or purpose for the child: when he hits his head on the floor, he gets things that he wants, or gets out of doing things that are unpleasant for him (e.g., Edelson, Taubman, and Lovaas, 1983).

SIB as Communication

Based on the premise that SIB and other behavior problems serve a function or purpose, a behavioral approach to the treatment for SIB was developed in the mid 1980s, designated as functional communication training (FCT) (Carr and Durand, 1985; Durand, 1990, 2012). FCT relies on the deceptively simple notion that behavior problems can be viewed as a form of communication (Durand, 1990). Looking at problem behavior as communication is not an entirely new concept. Writers as early as Plato observed that the crying seen in infants may be an attempt to get parents to fulfill their desires (Plato, circa 348 BC/1960, p.174). The French philosopher Rousseau also observed that crying may have communicative properties (Rousseau, 1762/1979, p.77). Family systems theorists have long relied on the idea that non-verbal behavior has communicative properties (e.g., Haley, 1963). Furthermore, developmental psychologists have systematically studied the communicative nature of non-verbal behavior in young children (e.g., Bates, Camaioni, and Volterra, 1975).

The fact that non-verbal behavior, such as SIB, might constitute communication is of particular interest to people who work with individuals having ASD. Workers in this field have proposed that behaviors such as aggression and SIB observed among persons with severe disabilities may be similar to non-verbal forms of communication (Carr and Durand, 1985). Personal experience often supports this view of behavior problems. Observing a student who has severe disabilities engaging in SIB brings with it a sense of frustration—an inability to comfort or respond in a satisfactory way. Parents, teachers, and other caregivers frequently report that they wish the students could just "tell us what they want."

We have used the concept of communication as a metaphor in our work (Durand, 1986). It has proven useful to compare SIB to other forms of non-verbal communicative behavior. What are the implications for adopting a communicative metaphor as a model of SIB? One effect of this view of SIB is the suggestion that these behaviors are not just responses that need to be reduced or eliminated. Instead, looking at behavior problems in this way reminds us that we need to find out what is causing them and what these individuals are sometimes trying to tell us through their behaviors. Such a view respects the person's right to communicate, while suggesting alternatives that may serve the same purpose. This perspective also reminds us that attempting to eliminate these behaviors through some reductive technique (such as punishment or reinforcing the absence of SIB) would leave these individuals with no way of expressing their needs and desires. You could anticipate that other maladaptive behaviors would take their place (also called "symptom substitution" or "response co-variation") as an effort to get the desired outcome.

Introduction to Functional Communication Training

FCT specifically teaches communication to reduce challenging behaviors such as SIB (Durand, 1990). This strategy includes assessing the variables maintaining the behavior to be reduced and providing the same consequences for a different behavior. It is assumed that if individuals can gain access to desired consequences more effectively with the new response, they will use this new response and will reduce their use of the undesirable response. Applying this logic to SIB, we are able to teach individuals more acceptable behaviors that serve the same function as their self-injury. So, for example, we could teach people to ask for attention by saying, "Am I doing good work?" This would allow them to gain teacher or parent attention in this appropriate way rather than in an inappropriate way such as through slapping their face. What follows is an example of an intervention for one young boy that illustrates the procedures involved in FCT (Durand, 1999).

CASE STUDY: Using FCT to treat Michael's Self-Injurious Behavior

Michael was a 6-year-old boy who had received diagnoses of ASD and severe intellectual disability. His parents and teachers expressed distress because when he became frustrated he would slap his face repeatedly, hard enough to cause red marks. He would also occasionally bang his head on the floor or a desk, which they feared would cause brain damage. Michael had no functional language skills and therefore had no reliable way to communicate with others. A number of behavioral interventions (e.g., time out from positive reinforcement, restraint) and medical (e.g., Risperdal/risperidone) had been used in an attempt to reduce his SIB, but with no significant success.

The first step in designing an intervention plan for Michael involved assessing why he was engaging in his SIB—also known as conducting a functional behavior analysis (FBA). A preliminary assessment used the Motivation Assessment Scale (MAS) (Durand and Crimmins, 1988), a rating scale that assesses the functions of someone's problem behaviors. The MAS was completed by his teachers and parents and suggested that his behaviors were being maintained by escape from task demands. In other words, he seemed to be trying to avoid certain school and home activities that may have been unpleasant to him. This was supported by observations of his behavior in a variety of different academic and home situations (FBA), which showed that his SIB increased in frequency and intensity when he was presented with difficult tasks, and that his SIB typically resulted in the task demands being withdrawn.

Because Michael's behaviors seemed to be serving an escape function (i.e., they often led to the termination of tasks), we decided to implement FCT by teaching him an alternative response. Instruction began with his teacher at school. Since requesting help on difficult tasks was the most appropriate reaction to these situations and the resulting assistance provided by teachers and his parents should make the tasks easier for him to complete, we taught him to use the phrase "I need help" when he could not complete his work. Because his language skills were so limited, we decided to teach him to use an assistive communicative device (a computer tablet with an assistive communications app) that he could use to express himself. We began the intervention by introducing a task that we knew would be difficult for him and then prompted him to use the tablet to request help. For example, one of Michael's tasks involved assisting with meal preparation. The teacher would prompt him in this task for several minutes, introduce a step in the task that she knew would be difficult for him (e.g., spreading peanut butter), and then verbally and physically prompt him to press the icon on the device. After he pressed the pad and it played the phrase programmed into it ("I need help"), his teacher used graduated guidance (e.g., holding his hand to spread the peanut butter) to help him. Following the assistance, he was prompted to continue working until the task was complete. Once Michael was successful with prompts, this assistance was faded until only the work itself prompted Michael to use his device. Fading occurred in steps. Initially his teacher would just point to the device. If he did not press the icon she would take his hand and move it toward the device but let his hand go. Once he reliably pressed the icon this way, she only touched his hand. Quickly he learned to press the icon on his tablet without any assistance or prompting when the difficult work was presented to him. Other situations throughout his day that tended to elicit SIB were also identified, and his teacher made his device available so he could ask for help in a variety of situations (e.g., opening doors, putting on his coat, putting away task materials). Within several weeks Michael was using the tablet appropriately to ask for help, and SIB was reduced dramatically within the classroom.

Michael's mother was present during some of these instructional sessions, and she was encouraged to use the tablet at home as well. Despite having seen Michael successfully use the device at school and receiving help from the teacher about how to set up challenging situations to help prompt him to use his device properly, his mother reported no similar success at home. We conducted some training sessions at home, but she said his SIB was still occurring at about the same rate. After some discussion it became clear that Michael's mother was resistant to placing even simple demands on him at home. Her fear that Michael might hurt himself resulted in her rearranging situations at home to avoid problems. For example, rather than asking him to sit at the dinner table for meals, she allowed him to sit on the living room floor watching videos when he ate. One of the goals discussed between Michael's mother and his teacher was getting him to put away any toys or other objects when he was finished with them. Michael often resisted this, but at school he used his tablet to ask for help and was now more compliant. At home, however, Michael's mother continued to put his things away herself. In fact, she had a rather large list of "rules of the house" that the family had to follow in order to avoid placing Michael in situations that might upset him. Despite all of these extensive efforts, SIB was still triggered occasionally, and was a constant source of anxiety for his mother.

We decided that Michael's mother was a good candidate for "optimistic parenting," a procedure we developed for parents whose difficulty implementing behavioral interventions at home was the result of cognitive obstacles rather than (or in addition to) a lack of knowledge about how to intervene with their child (Durand, 2011; Durand *et al.*, 2013). We began by asking his mother to write down a problem situation at home with Michael (e.g., brushing his teeth) and then also write down what she was thinking at the time (e.g., "Oh, no, this is going to be a battle," "I hope he doesn't hurt himself," "Will he be like this forever?"). We found that she had thoughts that were common to many families who have children like Michael. She became highly anxious because she was thinking he would hurt himself. This anxiety led her to avoid situations that might be helpful for Michael's communication. We also found that she believed he would never change and that living with him would always be like "walking on eggshells." It is important to recognize that she kept thinking this would always be a problem despite having witnessed his progress at school. Note that this type of thinking—seeing problems as permanent—is one characteristic of people who have what is referred to as pessimistic attributional styles (Seligman *et al.*, 1979). In other words, even in the face of contradictory evidence, she still believed things would not get better and might get worse. Furthermore, seeing him do better at school only made her feel worse about herself—believing she was not capable of doing this work with him, and that she must be a bad mother.

What we have learned in our work in this area is that a significant number of parents and other caregivers harbor these and similar thoughts (e.g., "My child is hitting himself in public and other people are judging me to be a bad parent, and that my child is strange"). They also commonly believe that SIB is part of their child's disorder (e.g., "He slaps his face because he has autism"). These thoughts contribute to an increase in anxiety, which will make the adult avoid any difficult situation, and the belief that nothing will change causes the adult to give up trying out a new technique to improve SIB. We have the parents practice examining these interfering thoughts, so that in the next phase of optimistic parenting we can help change this unhelpful way of looking at their child and SIB.

Once Michael's mother was becoming comfortable identifying her interfering thoughts, we adapted and implemented techniques from Seligman's version of cognitive behavior therapy—"learned optimism" (Seligman, 1991)—to help her. First, we went through a *disputation* process to challenge the validity and usefulness of these thoughts. For example, Michael's mother reported, "My whole family is looking at me and thinking I'm a terrible parent." We were able to point out that most of her family thought she was working very hard with Michael and doing her best as a parent given Michael's difficulties. We also discussed that the situations that triggered his SIB made her feel bad about herself as a mother, and made her anxious and panicky when anticipating other similar situations. We pointed out that thinking these thoughts actually interfered with her ability to put limits on Michael, which was counterproductive. In other words, these interfering thoughts not only were not completely true— they were not useful to her as a parent.

An additional technique used in optimistic parenting is *substitution*. This exercise teaches parents to practice new thoughts that make them feel more optimistic and confident about their own abilities and about their child's progress. First we pointed out how much time, effort, and emotional energy she spent on her son, and that this was a sign of a very caring and committed parent. We also pointed out that his SIB was capable of improving, as seen in his progress with his teacher at school. We taught her to practice saying to herself, "I am a great mom, and with help I can help Michael behave better!" We particularly encouraged this self-talk as she was about to try to get him to communicate for assistance using his tablet in difficult situations. Finally, we used one more technique—*distraction*—which was practiced for those times when Michael's behavior would put her in a particularly bad mood. The idea for this technique was to have Michael's mom put a more positive spin on problem situations. For example, she came up with an idea to use when he resisted tooth brushing. She said, "I started to sing a song with Michael about brushing his teeth. We saw this in a movie [*Pee-Wee's Big Adventure*]. This made us both smile and refocused me on a fun thing."

Once she was skilled at being aware of her own thoughts and countering them with her newfound skills, we had her practice introducing the tablet into some situations at home. With some training, Michael's mother was able to get him to use the tablet to ask for help just as he did in school. For example, we had her work on teaching Michael to put away a few toys on a floor that was carpeted, since it would reduce the likelihood of injury if he hit his head. Quickly she made progress getting him to put one toy in a box, then two, and then more. If he asked for help she would guide his hand. Gradually we introduced the tablet into other situations, and he quickly learned that—just like at school—he could get help if he asked. Michael's mom reported that he seemed more at ease in difficult situations because he was making the connection that pressing the icon on his device would result in his receiving help in frustrating situations at home.

Michael's case illustrates a number of important features of FCT, including the need for a functional assessment, as well as specific communication training techniques. In addition, no intervention will be successful if not implemented, and this case also showed how to help others introduce FCT when there are significant cognitive obstacles.

We next turn to a more complete discussion of the necessary components of FCT as an intervention for challenging behavior.

Steps for Using FCT
Assess the Function of the Behavior

To assess the function of a problem behavior, the antecedents and consequences of that behavior must be identified. It is recommended that two or more functional assessment techniques be used to determine what variables are maintaining SIB (e.g., MAS, direct observation, manipulating aspects of the environment). SIB is often found to serve one or more of the following three functions: (1) to avoid or escape non-preferred stimuli (e.g., difficult demands; non-preferred staff); (2) to access preferred stimuli (e.g., toys, attention); or (3) to increase or decrease sensory stimulation (Durand and Crimmins, 1988). Once the purpose of a targeted behavior is understood, individuals can be taught to request the variables previously obtained by SIB.

Select the Communication Modality

Once the function of SIB is identified, the type of response to encourage from the individual needs to be determined. If the individual already has some facility in a mode of communication (e.g., verbal, ACC, sign language), that mode should be considered for FCT. Usually, if an individual has been unsuccessful in learning to communicate effectively after extensive verbal language training, an alternative mode should be used. In Michael's case we taught him how to ask for assistance using the vocal output function of a computer tablet; others use picture books, in which an individual can point to a picture that represents what he or she wants.

Create Teaching Situations

As a next step, the environment is arranged to create opportunities for communication (e.g., putting out Michael's toys and asking him to put them away). This use of incidental teaching (McGee, Morrier, and Daly, 1999)—that is, arranging the environment to establish situations that elicit interest and that are used as teaching opportunities—is an important part of successful communication training. Using the person's interest in some interaction, whether it be a desire to stop working on a difficult task or to elicit the attention of an adult, is a very powerful tool in teaching generalized communication.

As soon as possible and where appropriate, training trials are interspersed throughout the individual's day. For Michael, his teacher set up a variety of potentially frustrating situations for him and quickly prompted him to ask for help with his device. Generalization and maintenance of intervention effects might be facilitated by using the criterion environment (i.e., where you want the person to communicate) as the training environment. In addition, obstacles to maintenance can be immediately identified when teaching in the criterion environment (e.g., the interventionist can determine whether the consequences being provided in that setting are going to maintain the new response).

Prompt Communication

Teaching individuals to communicate as a replacement for their SIB requires a range of sophisticated language training techniques (Durand, Mapstone, and Youngblade, 1999). A multi-phase prompting and prompt-fading procedure is used to teach the new communicative response. Prompts are introduced as necessary (e.g., guiding the hand, verbally providing help, or just gesturing to use a device), and then faded as quickly as possible. One procedure we used with Michael was to teach him to request assistance (e.g., "I need help"). For other individuals whose SIB functions to avoid or escape an unpleasant situation, requesting a brief break from a task may be more appropriate. For those whose SIB is occurring to get attention, we teach some message that is likely to result in attention from others but that is not annoying (e.g., "Is this right?" while pointing to their work in school, as opposed to "Come here"). Obviously, if the person's SIB is occurring to get something they want (e.g., a drink of water), we prompt that request ("Water, please").

Fade Prompts

We recommend pulling back prompts through fading them as soon as possible (e.g., responding with a full physical prompt each time after he requests help on five occasions, then fading to a partial physical prompt) so that the individual does not become dependent on prompts to use his communication skill (Durand, 1990). When necessary, fading can involve going from a full physical prompt to partial prompts (e.g., just touching the hand), to gestural prompts (e.g., motioning to encourage use of the hands), to, finally, only the verbal prompt (e.g., "Point to the picture"). We also recommend using delayed prompting as another method of fading (Halle, Baer, and Spradlin, 1981; Schwartz, Anderson, and Halle, 1989). For example, with Michael, after several trials, his teacher would intersperse a trial with a delayed prompt (e.g., waiting approximately 5 seconds) to see if he responded without the next level of prompt. Typically we find that SIB improves most dramatically as soon as the person begins to make requests without prompts.

Teach New Communicative Responses

Once SIB is reduced in the targeted settings, intervention continues by introducing new forms of communication (e.g., requests for food, music, work) while at the same time reintroducing work demands or expanding the settings in which requests are made, and introducing new people into the training program (e.g., assistant teachers, bus monitor, siblings).

Environmental Modification

Recommendations are often made concerning environment and curriculum changes. Therefore, when students who participate in this program are observed to engage in SIB when directed to participate in non-functional or age-inappropriate activities (e.g., stringing beads), we recommend that they no longer be required to work on these tasks. Instead, we suggest alternatives that might be more useful and engaging.

Address Obstacles

If implementation is not successful with some caregivers (in Michael's case, his mother), then directly addressing obstacles is important. Sometimes additional education or coaching on teaching communication skills is necessary. Supports may be necessary at times (e.g., a temporary aide in a classroom while training is occurring). Importantly, cognitive obstacles, such as pessimism, should be assessed. Research suggests that optimism training for parents (Durand *et al.*, 2013) or teachers (Steed and Durand, 2013) can be used to successfully overcome thoughts that the person cannot improve his or her behavior and that the teacher or parent is not able to help.

Evidence Base for FCT

FCT is one of the most frequently used approaches to reduce a variety of challenging behaviors, including SIB, in people with ASD and other developmental disabilities (Durand, 2012; Harvey *et al.*, 2009; Petscher, Rey, and Bailey, 2009; Walker and Snell, 2013). The types of challenging behaviors that appear to be appropriate targets for FCT in addition to SIB include aggression (e.g., Bailey *et al.*, 2002), tantrums and property destruction (e.g., Durand and Carr, 1992), elopement (e.g., Lang *et al.*, 2009), inappropriate sexual behavior (e.g., Fyffe *et al.*, 2004), and bizarre vocalizations (e.g., Durand and Crimmins, 1987; Wilder *et al.*, 2001). The research on SIB is extensive. Numerous studies document the effectiveness of FCT to significantly reduce SIB in a variety of individuals (e.g., Bird *et al.*, 1989; Durand, 1993; Kemp and Carr, 1995; Moore *et al.*, 2010). FCT exceeds the American Psychological Association's criteria for empirically supported treatments to be designated as a well-established treatment for challenging behavior in children with intellectual and developmental disabilities, including ASD (Chambless *et al.*, 1996; Task Force Promoting Dissemination of Psychological Procedures, 1995; Wong *et al.*, 2014).

Conclusion

In conclusion, a great deal of research has demonstrated that we can reduce or eliminate SIB by assessing the function or purpose of the individual's SIB, and teaching him an alternative form of communication that serves the same function. It is noteworthy that, under certain circumstances, FCT may be most effective when implemented as one intervention strategy in a more comprehensive intervention plan (see Chapter 10). The notion that SIB or other problem behaviors serve a function or purpose means that individuals with ASD or a developmental disability often resort to SIB because they do not have a better way to get their needs or wants met; hitting themselves or biting themselves is the reliable way to get someone to pay attention, to leave them alone, to self-soothe (i.e., increase or decrease arousal), or to get someone else to give them whatever they want in order to make the SIB stop because it is so upsetting to watch. If we want to reduce or stop the SIB, we need to give individuals a better way to get their needs or wants met by teaching them alternative behaviors or skills. Most often these skills are communication skills, as in FCT, but sometimes we need to teach other skills, such as relaxation or coping skills (see Chapter 13), social skills, academic skills, daily living skills, or self-management skills.

The advantages of FCT are its portability and its potential to generalize across multiple people, settings, and situations, and over time. A specific benefit of FCT over other interventions is that, if an individual is taught to ask for what he wants or needs from other people, then the individual is able to recruit reinforcers from other people (i.e., known as "recruiting natural communities of reinforcement"—Stokes, Fowler, and Baer, 1978) without an interventionist having to train other people on how to respond to the individual.

References

Bailey, J., McComas, J.J., Benavides, C., and Lovascz, C. (2002). Functional assessment in a residential setting: Identifying an effective communicative replacement response for aggressive behavior. *Journal of Developmental and Physical Disabilities, 14*(4), 353–369.

Bates, E., Camaioni, L., and Volterra, V. (1975). The acquisition of performatives prior to speech. *Merrill-Palmer Quarterly, 21*(3), 205–226.

Bird, F., Dores, P.A., Moniz, D., and Robinson, J. (1989). Reducing severe aggressive and self-injurious behaviors with functional communication training. *American Journal on Mental Retardation, 94*(1), 37–48.

Carr, E.G. (1977). The motivation of self-injurious behavior: A review of some hypotheses. *Psychological Bulletin, 84*(4), 800–816.

Carr, E.G., and Durand, V.M. (1985). Reducing behavior problems through functional communication training. *Journal of Applied Behavior Analysis, 18*(2), 111–126.

Carr, E.G., Newsom, C.D., and Binkoff, J.A. (1980). Escape as a factor in the aggressive behavior of two retarded children. *Journal of Applied Behavior Analysis, 13*(1), 101–117.

Chambless, D.L., Sanderson, W.C., Shoham, V., Bennett Johnson, S., *et al.* (1996). An update on empirically validated therapies. *The Clinical Psychologist, 49*, 5–18.

Durand, V.M. (1986). Self Injurious Behavior as Intentional Communication. In K.D. Gadow (Ed.), *Advances in Learning and Behavioral Disabilities* (Vol. 5). Greenwich, CT: JAI Press.

Durand, V.M. (1990). *Severe Behavior Problems: A Functional Communication Training Approach.* New York, NY: Guilford Press.

Durand, V.M. (1993). Functional communication training using assistive devices: Effects on challenging behavior and affect. *Augmentative and Alternative Communication, 9*(3), 168–176.

Durand, V.M. (1999). Functional communication training using assistive devices: Recruiting natural communities of reinforcement. *Journal of Applied Behavior Analysis, 32*(3), 247–267.

Durand, V.M. (2011). *Optimistic Parenting: Hope and Help for You and Your Challenging Child.* Baltimore, MD: Paul H. Brookes Publishing.

Durand, V.M. (2012). Functional Communication Training to Reduce Challenging Behavior. In P. Prelock and R. McCauley (Eds.), *Treatment of Autism Spectrum Disorders: Evidence-Based Intervention Strategies for Communication and Social Interaction.* Baltimore, MD: Paul H. Brookes Publishing.

Durand, V.M. and Carr, E.G. (1992). An analysis of maintenance following functional communication training. *Journal of Applied Behavior Analysis, 25*, 777–794.

Durand, V.M., and Crimmins, D.B. (1987). Assessment and treatment of psychotic speech in an autistic child. *Journal of Autism and Developmental Disorders, 17*, 17–28.

Durand, V.M., and Crimmins, D.B. (1988). Identifying the variables maintaining self-injurious behavior. *Journal of Autism and Developmental Disorders, 18*, 99–117.

Durand, V.M., Hieneman, M., Clarke, S., Wang, M., and Rinaldi, M. (2013). Positive family intervention for severe challenging behavior I: A multi-site randomized clinical trial. *Journal of Positive Behavior Interventions, 15*(3), 133–143.

Durand, V.M., Mapstone, E., and Youngblade, L. (1999). The Role of Communicative Partners. In J. Downing (Ed.), *Teaching Communication Skills to Students with Severe Disabilities within General Education Classrooms.* Baltimore, MD: Paul H. Brookes Publishing.

Edelson, S.M. (1984). Implications of sensory stimulation in self-destructive behavior. *American Journal of Mental Deficiency, 89,* 140–145.

Edelson, S.M., Taubman, M.T., and Lovaas, O.I. (1983). Some social contexts of self-destructive behavior. *Journal of Abnormal Child Psychology, 11,* 299–312.

Fyffe, C.E., Kahng, S., Fittro, E., and Russell, D. (2004). Functional analysis and treatment of inappropriate sexual behavior. *Journal of Applied Behavior Analysis, 37*(3), 401–404.

Haley, J. (1963). Strategies of Psychotherapy. In J. Haley (Ed.), *The Therapeutic Paradoxes.* New York, NY: Grune and Stratton.

Halle, J.W., Baer, D., and Spradlin, J. (1981). Teachers' generalized use of delay as a stimulus control procedure to increase language use in handicapped children. *Journal of Applied Behavior Analysis, 14,* 389–409.

Harvey, S.T., Boer, D., Meyer, L.H., and Evans, I.M. (2009). Updating a meta-analysis of intervention research with challenging behaviour: Treatment validity and standards of practice. *Journal of Intellectual and Developmental Disability, 34*(1), 67–80.

Kemp, D.C., and Carr, E.G. (1995). Reduction of severe problem behavior in community employment using an hypothesis-driven multicomponent intervention approach. *Journal of the Association for Persons with Severe Handicaps, 20*(4), 229–247.

Lang, R., Rispoli, M., Machalicek, W., White, P.J., *et al.* (2009). Treatment of elopement in individuals with developmental disabilities: A systematic review. *Research in Developmental Disabilities, 30*(4), 670–681.

McGee, G.G., Morrier, M.J., and Daly, T. (1999). An incidental teaching approach to early intervention for toddlers with autism. *Journal of the Association for Persons with Severe Handicaps, 24,* 133–146.

Moore, T.R., Gilles, E., McComas, J.J., and Symons, F.J. (2010). Functional analysis and treatment of self-injurious behaviour in a young child with traumatic brain injury. *Brain Injury, 24*(12), 1511–1518.

Petscher, E.S., Rey, C., and Bailey, J.S. (2009). A review of empirical support for differential reinforcement of alternative behavior. *Research in Developmental Disabilities, 30*(3), 409–425.

Plato (circa 348 BC/1960). *The Laws* (A.E. Taylor, Trans.). London: J.M. Dent.

Rousseau, J.J. (1762/1979). *Emile* (A. Bloom, Trans.). New York, NY: Basic Books.

Schwartz, I.S., Anderson, S.R., and Halle, J.W. (1989). Training teachers to use naturalistic time delay: Effects on teacher behavior and on the language use of students. *Journal of the Association for Persons with Severe Handicaps, 14*(1), 48–57.

Seligman, M. (1991). *Learned Optimism.* New York, NY: Knopf.

Seligman, M., Abramson, L.Y., Semmel, A., and Von Baeyer, C. (1979). Depressive attributional style. *Journal of Abnormal Psychology, 88*(3), 242–247.

Steed, E.A., and Durand, V.M. (2013). Optimistic teaching: Improving the capacity for teachers to reduce young children's challenging behavior. *School Mental Health, 5*(1), 15–24.

Stokes, T.F., Fowler, S.A., and Baer, D.M. (1978). Training preschool children to recruit natural communities of reinforcement. *Journal of Applied Behavior Analysis, 11,* 285–303.

Task Force Promoting Dissemination of Psychological Procedures (1995). Training in and dissemination of empirically-validated psychological treatments: Report and recommendations. *Clinical Psychology: Science and Practice, 48,* 3–23.

Taylor, J.C., and Carr, E.G. (1992). Severe problem behaviors related to social interaction. 1: Attention seeking and social avoidance. *Behavior Modification, 16*(3), 305–335.

Walker, V.L., and Snell, M.E. (2013). Effects of augmentative and alternative communication on challenging behavior: A meta-analysis. *Augmentative and Alternative Communication, 29*(2), 117–131.

Wilder, D.A., Masuda, A., O'Connor, C., and Baham, M. (2001). Brief functional analysis and treatment of bizarre vocalizations in an adult with schizophrenia. *Journal of Applied Behavior Analysis, 34,* 65–68.

Wong, C., Odom, S., Hume, K., Cox, A., *et al.* (2014). *Evidence-Based Practices for Children, Youth, and Young Adults with Autism Spectrum Disorder.* Chapel Hill, NC: University of North Carolina, Frank Porter Graham Child Development Institute, Autism Evidence Based Practice Review Group.

CHAPTER 12

Assessment and Intervention for Self-Injurious Behavior Related to Anxiety

Lauren J. Moskowitz, Ph.D., and Alexis B. Ritter, M.S., St. John's University, New York

Introduction

Individuals with autism spectrum disorder (ASD) and other developmental disabilities (DD) engage in self-injurious behavior (SIB) for a variety of reasons or purposes. The most common reasons why they engage in SIB are to escape something that is aversive, to get attention, to get something "tangible" that they want (such as a favorite food, toy, or activity), or for internal reasons (to gain some sort of sensory stimulation or escape some painful or uncomfortable sensory stimulation). (See Chapters 10 and 11 for more information about these different reasons or "functions" of SIB.) Although most applied behavior analytic literature has traditionally focused on individuals engaging in SIB and other problem behaviors to "escape from demands" (i.e., escape from a disliked or non-preferred task), more researchers and clinicians are starting to recognize that individuals with ASD and DD may engage in these behaviors to escape from anxiety.

Although the difference between escaping from a task demand and escaping from an anxiety-provoking situation may at first glance appear to be only a semantic distinction, there are important intervention implications. Conceptualizing SIB as arising due to fear or anxiety rather than non-compliance, disobedience, anger, or irritability may lead to very different interpretations and attributions by parents, teachers, and therapists. After all, wouldn't you feel a little bit more compassionate toward someone if he told you he was afraid to do something that you wanted him to do, rather than that he just did not want to do it? Recognizing anxiety in individuals with ASD and DD can help parents, teachers, and clinicians choose intervention strategies to reduce or prevent SIB by targeting the real cause: anxiety. This chapter provides some background information about anxiety as it relates to

SIB, discusses how to assess anxiety-related SIB, and outlines intervention strategies to prevent, replace, or respond to SIB associated with anxiety.

What Is Anxiety?

Originally, Wolpe's (1958) conception of anxiety included three components: (1) a subjective mental state inferred from verbal reports of the experienced level of anxiety, (2) behavioral avoidance of anxiety-provoking stimuli or situations, and (3) autonomic nervous system arousal. Although anxiety is still thought to be a construct including cognitive, behavioral, and physiological components (Barlow, 2002), the construct of anxiety has expanded to also encompass affective components (Davis and Ollendick, 2005). Specifically, anxiety involves *affective* or "emotional" states (e.g., subjective fear and panic experienced), *cognitions* (e.g., beliefs, thoughts, and images, such as worrying, "I'm going to get hurt"), *behaviors* (e.g., physically escaping or avoiding the situation, such as running out of the room, whining, crying, or pacing), and associated *physiological arousal* (e.g., heart racing, palms sweating, or muscles tightening) (Barlow, 2000). For our purposes in this chapter, we combine the thoughts and feelings, because both are subjective, internal components that are not easily measured by outside observers. Thus, we define anxiety here as encompassing three components: cognitive/affective (i.e., subjective), behavioral, and physiological.

Recent research has shown that anxiety, as a specific form of emotional distress, appears to be more prevalent in individuals with ASD and DD compared with the general population (Gotham, Brunwasser, and Lord, 2015; White *et al.*, 2009). In fact, approximately 40% of youth with ASD (van Steensel, Bögels, and Perrin, 2011) and 50% of adults with ASD (Lugnegård, Hallerbäck, and Gillberg, 2011) meet the criteria for at least one anxiety disorder, and as many as 80% of children with ASD present with clinically significant symptoms of anxiety (Muris *et al.*, 1998). Moreover, children with ASD who also experience anxiety demonstrate more severe ASD symptoms, including greater impairments in social functioning, more restrictive, repetitive movements, and more perseverative interests than children with ASD who do not experience anxiety (Bellini, 2004; Rudy, Lewin, and Storch, 2013). Individuals with DD may experience lower rates of anxiety than individuals with ASD, as international samples suggest that 9–27% of individuals with DD have comorbid anxiety disorders (Davis, Saeed, and Antonacci, 2008). However, the prevalence rates of anxiety in individuals with both ASD and DD are likely underestimates, given how difficult it is to assess anxiety in these populations.

Anxiety in ASD and DD: Why Is It Often Overlooked?

Despite the fact that clinicians have long asserted that individuals with ASD experience high levels of anxiety (e.g., Attwood, 2000; Kanner, 1943, 1951), and that researchers have increasingly called for and developed treatments that address anxiety-related symptoms in ASD (e.g., Sofronoff, Attwood, and Hinton, 2005; White *et al.*, 2009), as Groden and colleagues noted, behavioral researchers have been reluctant to use the concept of anxiety to either describe or explain behavior when discussing those with ASD and DD (Groden *et al.*, 1994). This may be because the thoughts, feelings, and physiological arousal that are part of the construct of anxiety often cannot be directly observed in the same way that overt behaviors can be observed (Groden *et al.*, 1994). Furthermore, in neurotypical individuals (i.e., those without ASD or DD), anxiety is usually assessed by asking the individuals—and, for youth, their caretakers—to report on their thoughts, feelings, and physiological symptoms. Given that individuals with DD and ASD often cannot articulate their emotional states, the traditional assessment of anxiety using paper-and-pencil self-reports or interviews may be difficult or even impossible (Hagopian and Jennett, 2008). After all, communication in ASD is universally impaired to some degree; approximately 50% of individuals with ASD are functionally non-verbal, and those who have verbal language often have difficulty describing their mental states, mental experiences, and daily life experiences (Leyfer *et al.*, 2006), and tend not to signal their emotional states to others (Rogers, 1998).

In addition to the limitations of self-report due to the communication deficits of individuals with ASD, anxiety can also be difficult to assess because the actual expression of anxiety in individuals with ASD and DD may differ from the expression of anxiety in neurotypical individuals, making it more difficult for caretakers or providers to identify the symptoms of anxiety. In general, individuals with ASD may express their anxiety in idiosyncratic ways, such as, for one person, plugging his ears; for someone else, using the perseverative phrase "C'mon everybody!"; or, for a third person, humming in a very specific way that escalated in volume and speed. In fact, unlike neurotypical individuals, research suggests that those with ASD are more likely to express fear and anxiety through externalizing or "acting out" behaviors such as SIB, aggression, and tantrums (White *et al.*, 2009). So, for example, while a neurotypical child who is given a difficult assignment in class may express anxiety by freezing up, a child with ASD who is given a difficult task may express anxiety by banging his head on the desk. Thus, like other emotional states, anxiety is often overlooked or unrecognized because it may be expressed differently from the way neurotypical people usually express anxiety.

Conceptualizing Anxiety and SIB Functionally

As previously discussed, in applied behavior analysis (ABA), it is traditionally held that people with ASD and DD engage in SIB and other problem behaviors for one of four main "functions" or reasons: (1) to escape or avoid a task demand, person, or situation, (2) to gain attention, (3) to access tangible items (e.g., food, toy) or activities (e.g., playing computer), or (4) to gain or escape internal or sensory reinforcement.

For some with ASD and DD, in certain situations, these four functions could be re-conceptualized as reducing anxiety in some way:

- Instead of engaging in SIB to escape from or avoid an activity just because it is boring, frustrating, or disliked (i.e., escape-demand), they could be trying to escape or avoid a task or situation because it is frightening or anxiety-provoking (i.e., escape-anxiety).

- Instead of engaging in SIB just to gain attention, they could be trying to gain comfort or reassurance (to reduce anxiety).

- Instead of engaging in SIB just to obtain a preferred tangible item or activity, they could be trying to obtain a comfort object or a self-soothing activity (to reduce anxiety).

- Instead of engaging in SIB just to obtain sensory stimulation or escape or avoid unpleasant sensory stimulation, they could be trying to reduce feelings of physiological arousal that are associated with anxiety (similar to a neurotypical individual biting his nails to calm himself).

While there may be at least four reasons why anxiety could contribute to SIB, it is not always the case that an individual simply feels anxious and then displays SIB. Although it sometimes happens that anxiety may directly and immediately lead to it (e.g., the person is feeling anxious and thus bites himself to reduce the anxiety), at other times the presence of anxiety may not lead to SIB unless another event, demand, or stressor "sets off" the individual (e.g., the person is feeling anxious and thus, when asked to do homework, he is more likely to bite himself). Therefore, it has been proposed that there are two ways (or pathways) by which the presence of a biological factor, such as anxiety, can result in SIB (Carr and Smith, 1995):

- Anxiety can serve as a direct antecedent (known as "discriminative stimulus") that occasions or leads to SIB. For example, an antecedent could be that Johnny's mother says, "It's time to get on the school bus," and then Johnny immediately starts biting his hand. In this situation, Johnny's fear of getting on the school bus directly and immediately evokes the SIB. It is noteworthy that an antecedent only leads to SIB or other problem behavior if it is reinforced. For instance, in the previous example, if his mother responds to Johnny biting his hand by saying, "Okay Johnny, you don't have to take the bus; I will drive you to school," then Johnny learns that engaging in SIB results in a "payoff" (i.e., he gets out of taking the school bus). Thus, the antecedent "It's time to get on the school bus" serves as a trigger because Johnny has learned that, in the presence of that antecedent, engaging in SIB will help him get his needs met (i.e., he gets to escape or avoid an anxiety-provoking situation).

- In other cases, anxiety may not serve as the direct antecedent or trigger for problem behavior, but instead serves as a "setting event," meaning that it sets the stage for problem behavior to be evoked by a different antecedent. A "setting event" can influence whether or not an antecedent will evoke problem behavior by making the antecedent more or less aversive to the individual. Setting events can include activities and routines (e.g., transitions, noisy or crowded environment), social and interpersonal factors (e.g., lack of attention, being recently teased), and biological factors (e.g., illness, pain, discomfort, fatigue). In illustration, consider another child named Billy who occasionally shows SIB when his parents ask him to board the school bus. On some days, his parents ask him to board the school bus (antecedent) and he complies (response), which results in his parents praising him (consequence). However, on other days, his parents ask him to board the bus (antecedent) and he bites his hand (response), which results in his parents withdrawing the demand and driving him to school instead (consequence). In this situation, Billy's SIB seems to come out of the blue, since some days he gets on the bus without a problem, but other days he bites his hand when asked to board the bus. However, further assessment reveals that Billy is experiencing anxiety on the mornings he shows SIB. In this scenario, anxiety is the setting event, increasing the aversiveness of the antecedent (i.e., makes boarding the bus more aversive), and increasing the reinforcement value of escaping from boarding the bus. Thus, on days in which Billy is both anxious (setting event) and asked to board the bus (antecedent), he is more likely to exhibit SIB and be allowed to avoid boarding the bus (consequence of negative reinforcement). On days when Billy is not anxious, the antecedent of boarding the bus is not as aversive, his parents' praise has a greater reinforcement value than escape, and Billy is more likely to comply. As illustrated in this example, a biological or internal variable, such as anxiety, can be a setting event, substantially increasing the likelihood of SIB.

If anxiety is a setting event, this means that, when the person is anxious and a certain antecedent is presented (e.g., a difficult task, a demand, a new person, a non-preferred person), that stimulus will likely result in SIB, whereas in the absence of anxiety (the setting event), SIB might *not* result when the person is presented with the same antecedent. Using this conceptualization, SIB that is reported by parents and teachers to be unpredictable and to have "come out of nowhere" may actually be precipitated by an internal physiological antecedent or setting event, such as arousal or anxiety (e.g., interoceptive cues or somatic sensations including heart racing, muscles tightening, or intrusive mental images), or by an external antecedent or setting event that causes anxiety (e.g., change in routine, unpredictability, transitions, interruption of stereotyped routine, a new person, loud noise, or crowds). Research has demonstrated that biological or internal variables, such as fatigue (e.g., O'Reilly, 1995), menstrual pain (e.g., Carr *et al.*, 2003), allergies (e.g., Kennedy and Meyer, 1996), physical illness (e.g., Carr and Owen-DeSchryver, 2007), and anxiety (e.g., Moskowitz *et al.*, 2013), can be setting events or antecedents for problem behavior.

You may be asking why it is so important to determine the exact reason for the SIB and the exact manner in which anxiety may contribute to it. Research suggests that it is important to determine *why* problem behavior is occurring in order to most effectively treat it. This is known as a functional assessment. Specifically, research demonstrates that interventions based on functional assessments of the factors controlling problem behavior (including the consequences, antecedents, and setting events) are about *twice* as likely to succeed as those that are not (Carr *et al.*, 1999). Therefore, using functional assessment to inform intervention has become a best practice in the field of developmental disabilities. The function of an individual's problem behavior directly influences the type of intervention strategies that should be chosen, as well as the intervention strategies that should *not* be chosen. This means that SIBs that function to reduce or escape anxiety may require different intervention strategies from SIBs that serve to escape demands, gain attention, gain tangibles, or gain/escape sensory stimulation. For example, if a child is engaging in SIB to escape doing homework because he dislikes it, intervention strategies might include making the homework assignment more interesting in order to compete with the reinforcement value of escaping from the homework. However, if the child is engaging in SIB to escape doing homework because he is becoming anxious while doing homework, simply making the homework more fun and interesting may not be enough to counteract his anxiety; the child may need to be taught a replacement communication skill (e.g., asking for a break, asking for help) or a replacement coping behavior (e.g., deep breathing, listening to a soothing song) that calms him down. Now that we have outlined the major reasons why individuals with ASD and DD who experience anxiety may engage in SIB, the remainder of this chapter focuses on assessing the presence of anxiety-related SIB and the specific reasons for that anxiety. We then outline intervention strategies that appropriately target the identified reasons.

Assessment

Assessment that specifically identifies the functions or reasons for SIB and other problem behavior is called a functional behavior assessment (FBA). An FBA involves identifying the ABCs of the behavior. The A is the antecedent, or what occurs *before* the person displays SIB/problem behavior (this refers to the antecedents that occur immediately before SIB as well as the setting events that make SIB more likely to occur in the presence of specific antecedents). The B is the specific behavior itself (e.g., SIB), including what the behavior looks like. The C is the consequence, or what occurs immediately *after* the individual exhibits SIB—the consequence tells us the function(s) that the SIB is serving for that individual in that situation. Chapter 10 covers FBAs in more depth, but we provide a brief description here in order to illustrate how an FBA could reveal that an individual's SIB or aggressive behavior may be related to anxiety.

Step 1: Describing the Problem Behavior

The first step in an FBA is to identify and describe the behavior that is problematic or that you want to change. For instance, if a person is displaying SIB, we would describe what that behavior looks like (e.g., biting his hand, banging his head on the table, or hitting his head with the palm of his hand). Once we have defined the specific behaviors that are problematic in a way that is objective, observable, and measurable (so that all observers could agree if the behavior was occurring or not), we begin to keep track of the behavior, including how frequently it occurs, how long it lasts, and how intense it is.

For the purposes of identifying SIB that is specifically related to anxiety, it becomes important to differentiate SIB and other problem behaviors from anxious behaviors. Problem behaviors, including SIB or aggressive behaviors, may be easier to identify, especially since they are more overt or obvious and often the reason that the FBA is being conducted in the first place. However, it may be much more difficult to identify and clearly describe an individual's anxious behaviors, especially if they are milder or subtler "precursor behaviors" that precede SIB, and are less problematic than the SIB or aggression that comes afterward. Often, researchers and clinicians may conflate a SIB or problem behavior and anxious behavior with one another, or describe SIB as evidence that the individual is anxious (e.g., "We think he is anxious because he bites himself"). However, the SIB in and of itself does not necessarily mean that the individual is anxious, as he could be engaging in SIB for a variety of reasons other than anxiety (e.g., because he is feeling tired, overstimulated, or otherwise distressed). Thus, rather than saying "We think he is anxious because he bites himself," it would be more helpful to identify specific anxious behaviors that are being displayed (e.g., trembling, shaking) in addition to the SIB or problem behavior, in order to say "We think he is anxious because he is trembling or shaking, and that anxiety leads him to bite himself."

In general, the same behaviors may not indicate anxiety in all people with ASD/DD, or even within the same individual at different times. Therefore, it is important that parents, teachers, and providers become more skilled at identifying the unique behaviors that may indicate anxiety so that they can recognize when it might be preceding SIB and aggressive behaviors. Parents, teachers, and providers can specifically assess the three components of anxiety—physiological, cognitive/ affective, and behavioral—in trying to establish whether anxiety is the reason (or one of the reasons) for the SIB. It is important to conduct a multi-method assessment when assessing for the presence of anxiety because, although any behavior on its own does not necessarily indicate anxiety (e.g., someone may cry because he is feeling afraid, sad, or ill), multiple sources of converging data may support the theory that the behavior is a sign of anxiety (Moskowitz *et al.*, 2013). The first two components of anxiety—physiological and cognitive/affective—are very important to consider but, as discussed earlier in this chapter, may be difficult to identify in individuals with ASD/DD in particular.

PHYSIOLOGICAL COMPONENT OF ANXIETY

Physiological responses associated with anxiety include heightened autonomic responses such as increased heart rate, respiratory rate (rapid breathing), blood pressure, larger pupil size, higher skin conductance (sweating), and lower parasympathetic activity (e.g., respiratory sinus arrhythmia). While these physiological symptoms accurately indicate the presence of anxiety and are useful for clinical researchers to measure (see Moskowitz *et al.*, 2013), it usually is not realistic for parents, teachers, or providers to attempt to measure them. However, there are increasingly affordable, non-intrusive, portable monitors that parents, teachers, or clinicians could use to assess the physiological component of anxiety (e.g., heart activity, breathing, or skin conductance) (Goodwin, Velicer, and Intille, 2008). In lieu of such a device, it is still possible to assess observable symptoms that indicate physiological arousal, such as visible muscle tension, rapid breathing, sweating, or trembling. (See "Physical/Physiological Symptoms Associated with Anxiety" in the comprehensive list of behavioral indicators in Appendix D.)

COGNITIVE/AFFECTIVE COMPONENT OF ANXIETY

Cognitive/affective components of anxiety include subjective thoughts and/or feelings of fear, anxiety, nervousness, worry, or dread, which—for neurotypical individuals—are usually identified through the use of interviews and ratings scales. Informant reports including parent-report questionnaires, such as the Screen for Anxiety and Related Emotional Disorders—Parent Version (SCARED-P; Birmaher *et al.*, 1999), and parent interviews such as the Anxiety Disorders Interview Schedule—Parent Version (ADIS-IV-P; Silverman and Albano, 1996), can be used to get at that "subjective" component of anxiety (e.g., from the SCARED-P: "People tell me that my child looks nervous"). Interviews generally provide more information than questionnaires. Although these measures can be helpful for some, parents of children with ASD and DD are not always aware of their children's anxious thoughts and feelings. This is especially true for children who may have difficulty communicating their thoughts and feelings, and/or express them in unusual ways. In our clinical and research experience, although we initially attempted to use parent reports such as the SCARED as a proxy for the cognitive and affective components of anxiety, we ended up not using it because some parents said that they were unable to accurately answer many of the items. For instance, while parents generally were able to accurately rate items that were objective, observable, behavioral indicators, such as "My child follows me wherever I go," they had more difficulty rating subjective items such as "My child worries about other people liking him," or "My child worries about being as good as other kids," because they were not sure what their children were thinking. Thus, when in doubt, they rated such questionable items as a zero ("not true or hardly ever true"), which possibly underestimated their children's anxiety. Thus, for individuals with ASD and DD, particularly for those who have intellectual disabilities (ID; i.e., IQ below 70), informant questionnaires and informant interviews may need to be modified. For example, Cordeiro and colleagues (2011) modified the ADIS-IV-P for the parents of people with fragile X syndrome (ages 5–33 years; mean IQ = 67; range of IQ 30–117) by eliminating the screening-question criteria, which allowed for a diagnosis of social phobia in those who exhibited clinically significant impairment as a result of social phobia symptoms but were unable to verbalize or explain "a worry that they might do something embarrassing." Similarly, Leyfer *et al.* (2006) modified the Kiddie Schedule for Affective Disorders and Schizophrenia (KSADS; Kaufman *et al.*, 1997) to create the Autism Comorbidity Interview—Present and Lifetime Version (ACI-PL). The ACI-PL has modified questions that consider the unique presentation of depressive and anxiety symptoms in children with ASD ages 5–17 years, and distinguishes impairment due to comorbid disorders from impairment due to ASD (Leyfer *et al.*, 2006). The ACI-PL appears to be reliable and valid for diagnosing specific phobias and OCD in children with high-functioning autism, but not for other anxiety disorders or ID (Leyfer *et al.*, 2006).

Research has demonstrated the utility of some informant-based rating scales, such as the Child and Adolescent Symptom Inventory—4th Edition Revised (CASI-4R; Gadow and Sprafkin, 2002; Lecavalier *et al.*, 2014) and the worry/depressed subscale of the Autism Spectrum Disorders—Comorbidity for Children (ASD-CC; Matson *et al.*, 2009), in identifying anxiety in children with ASD, but not for those children with ASD who also have ID (Rieske *et al.*, 2013). However, there are several global measures of emotional and behavioral problems (including anxiety) that have been developed for individuals with ID. Specifically, the Diagnostic Assessment for the Severely Handicapped (DASH; Matson, Gardner, and Coe, 1991) and DASH-II (Matson, 1995) have been validated with individuals with severe and profound ID. However, the validity of the DASH-II anxiety subscale in categorizing individuals with and without anxiety is mixed; only behavioral symptoms associated with anxiety could be reliably assessed in individuals with ID (Matson *et al.*, 1997). Also, the Anxiety, Depression, and Mood Scale (ADAMS; Esbensen *et al.*, 2003) was designed as an observationally based informant-rating scale of symptoms related to anxiety, depression, and mania in those with ID ages 10–79 years. While the ADAMS appears to be a reliable and valid instrument for screening OCD, its use with other anxiety disorders may be limited (Hagopian and Jennett, 2008). Additionally, the Baby Infant Screen for Children with Autism Traits—Part 2 (BISCUIT—Part 2; Matson *et al.*, 2011) can be used to assess anxiety and other comorbid psychopathology in 17- to 37-month-old children with developmental disabilities, and the Developmental Behavior Checklist (DBC; Einfeld and Tonge, 1995) reliably measures anxiety in children with intellectual disabilities (Hastings *et al.*, 2001).

In addition to informant reports, to assess the subjective (cognitive/affective) component of anxiety, self-reports can also be used. However, as previously discussed, many with ASD are non-verbal, and those who are verbal often have difficulty describing their mental experiences. The self-report scales most commonly used to assess anxiety in neurotypical children include the Multidimensional Anxiety Scale for Children (MASC; March *et al.*, 1997), the Revised Children's Manifest Anxiety Scale (RCMAS; Reynolds and Richmond, 1978), the State-Trait Anxiety Inventory for Children (STAIC; Spielberger, 1973), and the Screen for Anxiety and Related Emotional Disorders—Child Version (SCARED-C; Birmaher *et al.*, 1999). Some evidence suggests that scales such as the MASC may not measure the same constructs in anxious children who have ASD as those who do not have ASD (White *et al.*, 2015). However, the SCARED and the Revised Children's Anxiety and Depression Scale (RCADS; Chorpita, Moffitt, and Gray, 2005; Sterling *et al.*, 2015) may be valid tools for assessing anxiety in children with ASD (Stern *et al.*, 2014), at least for those children with an IQ ≥70, and there is also preliminary research that the RCMAS may be valid for children with ASD whose IQ ≥70 (Mazefsky, Kao, and Oswald, 2011). However, anxiety self-report scales typically require a second- or third-grade reading level; it is likely that the majority of self-reports would not be appropriate for many children with ASD, especially those with ID, without appropriate modifications. There is some evidence that self-reports that are modified for children with ID can be reliable and valid. Several scales for neurotypical children have been modified for children with ID, such as the Fear Survey Schedule for Children—Revised (FSSC-R; Gullone, King, and Cummins, 1996; Ollendick, 1983) and the Fear Survey for Children with and without Mental Retardation (FSCMR; Ramirez and Kratochwill, 1990). Modifications include asking questions both verbally and visually, using simpler language, limiting the number of words, and providing pictures of response options (i.e., a visual scale of facial expressions of fear) (Hartley and MacLean, 2006). Therefore, these self-report scales may be used to gain as much information as possible about the child's anxiety from the child's perspective, but they should not be used as the only source of information. Children and adolescents with ASD or DD can also be given structured or semi-structured clinical interviews such as the ADIS-IV-child version (ADIS-IV-C; Silverman and Albano, 1996). Youth with ASD generally show good diagnostic agreement on the ADIS-IV-C with parents and clinical consensus, at least for those children with an IQ ≥70 (Ung *et al.*, 2014). For individuals with ID, interviews such as the ADIS-C may need to be modified (similar to the aforementioned example of how the ADIS-P was modified). Clinician-rated measures, such as the Pediatric Anxiety Rating Scale (PARS; RUPP, 2002), may be used to supplement information gathered from parent and self-report rating scales. Research has demonstrated that clinician ratings on the PARS are consistent with parent and child ratings on other measures, including the ADIS-IV-C/P (Storch *et al.*, 2012).

With everyone, not just those with ASD or DD, the identification of physiological and cognitive components of anxiety is often difficult because anxiety is such an internal and subjective experience. Even as adults, it is difficult to ascertain when someone is "worrying" or "nervous," unless we see physical expressions or verbal affirmations of those internal feelings. For instance, we may only know that someone is nervous because he is pacing back and forth, biting his nails, or saying that he feels nervous. Therefore, it may often be easier and perhaps more valid to describe the specific anxious behaviors that occur just before the individual exhibits self-injurious or aggressive behavior.

BEHAVIORAL COMPONENT OF ANXIETY

A comprehensive list of behavioral indicators or signs of anxiety was created by Moskowitz *et al.* (2013) from multiple sources (see Appendix D). The list of behavioral descriptors was originally derived from a variety of sources, including the Cues for Tension and Anxiety Survey Schedule (CTASS; Cautela, 1977), the Affex Facial Coding System for Negative Facial Expressions (Izard, Dougherty, and Hembree, 1989), the Behavioral Relaxation Scale (BRS; Poppen, 1988), behavioral indicators from Lesniak-Karpiak, Mazzocco, and Ross (2003), Richards and colleagues (2009), and Sullivan, Hooper, and Hatton (2007), as well as from our clinical observations. However, the list may not include all behaviors that individuals with ASD or DD display when they are anxious, nor does it necessarily apply to each person with ASD. Although the items on the list appear to be the most concrete, observable, behavioral descriptors of anxiety available to date (in contrast to other scales that include inferred mental states), it is still possible that these behaviors could be associated with another internal state (e.g., anger or frustration, excitement, pain, or illness), could be context dependent (e.g., the same behaviors could indicate different emotional states depending on the context), or could be idiosyncratic (e.g., could indicate anxiety in one individual with DD but not in another). As a result, it is likely that identifying idiosyncratic markers of anxiety that are particular to each individual might be the most reliable, valid, and clinically useful method of assessing anxiety. For instance, for a child, Joey, who became anxious whenever his parents left the house, we defined "anxious behaviors" (or indicators of anxiety) as: inquiring about parents' whereabouts (e.g., asking Mom "Where are you going?"), verbalizations about Mom (e.g., "Mommy!"; "I want Mommy"), running to the front door, standing by the front door, eyebrows raised and downturned, and corner of mouth downturned. For another child, Tommy, who exhibited a fear of the Happy Birthday song, we defined anxious behaviors as: clinging (holding onto or grabbing onto mother), crying or tearfulness, freezing (lack of movement except respiration), eyes wide open or eyes rapidly darting back and forth, cowering, frowning (turning down of the mouth), eyebrows sloping down in an inverted V shape, and specific vocalizations (noise indicating fear or anxiety, e.g., whimpering, whining, moaning). These anxious behaviors are often the ones that go unrecognized in individuals with ASD or DD, but a thorough FBA should reveal the presence of these behaviors, and may often show that these behaviors are consistently occurring along with or prior to the SIB and/or aggressive behaviors.

The behavioral components of anxiety that reliably precede the occurrence of problem behavior are considered precursor behaviors. Identifying precursor behaviors can alert parents, teachers, or providers to the probability that a more severe SIB or problem behavior is about to occur so that they may intervene proactively to prevent it from occurring (Langdon, Carr, and Owen-DeSchryver, 2008). It is important to note that some of the behavioral indicators of anxiety for an individual with ASD may mimic their ASD symptoms. For instance, although inappropriate vocalizations or repetitive movements are often characteristic of individuals with ASD, some may also exhibit idiosyncratic vocalizations or movements specifically when they are anxious. Similarly, some may not express different behaviors when they are anxious; rather, they may exhibit more extreme versions of the ASD-like behaviors they already exhibit (Rudy *et al.*, 2013). The purpose of the FBA is to identify these nuanced behaviors in order to inform interventions.

Step 2: Measure the Behavior, the Antecedents, and the Consequences

After the SIB or other problem behaviors have been identified and clearly defined, it is necessary to identify the function(s) of the problem behaviors. This can be done using a combination of questionnaires such as the Motivation Assessment Scale (MAS; Durand and Crimmins, 1988), informant interviews such as the Functional Assessment Interview (FAI; O'Neill *et al.*, 1997), and, most importantly, direct observation. (See Chapters 10 and 11 for more information about conducting an FBA.) The purpose of direct observation is to track the SIB and anxious behaviors while also tracking the antecedents (what occurs right before the behaviors start) and the consequences (what occurs right after the behaviors). This information is important for knowing how to address these behaviors. This is the phase of the FBA in which we are specifically looking for the role that anxiety may play in self-injurious and aggressive behavior. Although existing measures, such as the MAS and FAI, do not assess the role of anxiety or mention anxiety, they can help inform whether the SIB broadly functions to escape or avoid something, gain attention, gain a tangible item or activity, or address sensory needs. If we determine the broader function of the SIB and identify the presence of anxiety using the multi-method assessment described above, we can determine the specific role that anxiety plays. For example, if the MAS and/or FAI suggest that the SIB is broadly escape motivated, and then we establish the presence of anxiety from converging sources, we can conclude that the SIB serves to escape an anxiety-provoking situation (i.e., social interaction, transition). Similarly, if the MAS and/or FAI suggest that SIB is broadly attention motivated and we establish the presence of anxiety, then the SIB may serve to obtain comfort or reassurance to reduce anxiety. (It is noteworthy that Joosten, Bundy, and Einfeld [2009] added four items to the MAS designed to assess anxiety as a function and found that the stereotypic and repetitive behavior of children with ASD and ID was motivated more by anxiety than sensory seeking, whereas the reverse was true for children with just ID. Providers may add these additional items to the MAS if they so choose: (1) resistance to change, (2) being easily upset, (3) presence of tantrums, fearfulness, and tenseness, and (4) agitation and irritability—although three of the four items are subjective adjectives rather than concrete, observable behaviors.)

ANTECEDENTS

To determine the antecedents of SIB, or what sets the stage for the behavior, it is important to assess the "Ws" that precede the behavior: *Who* is around? *What* demands are being placed on the child or in what activities is the child engaged? *Where* does the behavior occur? *When* (what time of day) does it occur? (Durand and Hieneman, 2008). As previously mentioned, this can include antecedents that immediately evoke anxiety and SIB (e.g., a feared object, such as a spider or Santa, or a feared activity, such as others singing happy birthday) as well as setting events that make the individual more anxious (e.g., transition, change in routine) and thus set the stage for SIB to be triggered by a given antecedent. For example, consider a child named Bobby who engages in SIB when he is in a novel environment (a setting event that increases anxiety) and a new person attempts to initiate conversation by asking him a question (the antecedent, a social demand). In this example, the combination of the setting event (new environment) and antecedent (social demand) leads Bobby to feel anxious and engage in SIB to escape the anxiety-provoking situation. It is important to identify the context because the process of labeling one's state of affective arousal as "anxiety" or any other emotion is highly influenced by the situational context in which the arousal occurs (Bandura, 1988). (For example, if one's heart were racing while exercising, the arousal would not likely be interpreted as anxiety, whereas if one's heart were racing while taking an exam, the arousal might be interpreted as anxiety because of the context in which the arousal occurs.)

Informant-report scales such as the Contextual Assessment Inventory (CAI; McAtee, Carr, and Schulte, 2004) can be used to identify contexts (setting events and/or antecedents) that evoke SIB and other problem behaviors, and informant-report scales such as the Stress Survey Schedule (SSS; Groden *et al.*, 2001) can be used to identify situations that evoke anxiety. However, it is important to note that the possible stressors listed on standardized measures such as the SSS (e.g., vacuum cleaner, remote-control robot) may be anxiety-provoking, stressful, and/or physiologically arousing to one individual with ASD or DD, but not to another. For example, the idiosyncratic fears and anxieties of some with whom we have worked—such as a fear of right or left turns while riding in a car (Moskowitz *et al.*, 2013)—would not be found in any standardized measure.

CONSEQUENCES

The final step of the FBA is to record the consequences of the problem behavior. How do the other people surrounding the person respond to his SIB? Does the expression of it result in his being removed from the anxiety-provoking situation, being given comfort or reassurance, or being given a soothing tangible reinforcer? It is important to recognize what consequences in particular lead to the cessation of the SIB, because those consequences are the ones that are most likely to point to the function of the behavior. For instance, during the FBA for Tommy, who was afraid of the song "Happy Birthday," we discovered that he stopped exhibiting SIB if his mother stopped singing it. Therefore, it became clear that the function of his SIB was to escape the anxiety-provoking activity (i.e., singing "Happy Birthday").

In addition to identifying the consequence for the SIB itself, it is important to identify the consequence for anxious behaviors, which is typically the same consequence but may not always be. For example, for Ed, a boy with mild ID who also had a diagnosis of obsessive-compulsive disorder (OCD), his obsession or fear was that he might be sick, and his compulsion or ritual was to engage in reassurance-seeking behavior by following his mother around for several hours per day while asking her if he was healthy (e.g., "Are you sure that I don't have a sore throat?"). His mother typically responded by telling him that he was healthy (e.g., that he did *not* have a sore throat). In this instance, the most typical consequence for Ed's anxious behavior was reassurance from his mother. However, sometimes his mother did not answer him because she was tired of answering the same questions. In those instances when she did not answer him, he generally escalated his behavior in that he would yell the same questions while engaging in SIB. In response to his SIB, his mother typically answered his questions ("You don't have a sore throat") to make him stop injuring himself. Thus, the consequence or function for both Ed's anxious behavior and SIB was reassurance from his mother, but his anxious behavior only escalated into problem behavior (SIB) when it was not reinforced by reassurance from his mother.

After all of the data have been collected for the FBA, the patterns of antecedents, behaviors, and consequences will suggest the function(s) of the SIB as well as the antecedents and possible setting events that contribute to it. Once the factors controlling the SIB are identified, we can then implement interventions by altering setting events, antecedents, or consequences, and/or by teaching replacement behaviors.

Intervention

As previously discussed, the FBA should inform the selection of intervention strategies. There are three categories of interventions that can be implemented following the functional assessment: prevention strategies (antecedent-based and setting-event-based strategies), replacement strategies, and response- or consequence-based strategies. The prevention, replacement, and consequence-based strategies we describe are integrated from the best-practice features of applied behavior analysis and positive behavior support (e.g., Carr *et al.*, 2002) as well as evidence-based treatments for childhood anxiety disorders from the cognitive behavioral therapy (CBT) literature for neurotypical individuals, particularly children (e.g., Albano and Kendall, 2002).

Prevention Strategies

Prevention strategies aim to prevent the anxiety from developing, or at least prevent the anxiety from leading to SIB. This includes changing the environment in order to alter the antecedents and setting events that lead to anxiety. Below are examples of prevention strategies that can be used to prevent the onset of anxiety, minimize the likelihood of anxiety, or reduce the intensity or impact of anxiety in individuals with ASD or DD.

INCREASING PREDICTABILITY

Research has demonstrated that increasing predictability reduces problem behavior in individuals with ASD and DD. For example, Flannery and Horner (1994) found that problem behavior was lower in predictable conditions (when the steps of an upcoming familiar or unfamiliar task were described and modeled) and conversely was higher when the upcoming tasks were unpredictable. Although Flannery and Horner did not conceptualize the reduction in problem behavior as being due to a reduction in anxiety per se, other research has found that the ability to predict aversive events also attenuates anxious responses (Grillon, 2008). Thus, one prevention strategy entails providing information proactively to reduce anxiety (Lucyshyn *et al.*, 2007); this can be done using visual schedules, Social Stories, priming, or advanced warnings.

Visual Schedule

A visual schedule is one way to reduce the unpredictability associated with transitions by informing individuals about the upcoming sequence of events (Mesibov, Browder, and Kirkland, 2002). Visual schedules can incorporate pictures to aid in the individual's understanding of what is coming next. Reinforcement can also be embedded into the visual schedule, so that individuals know that, if they complete the anxiety-provoking activity, they will be able to engage in a preferred activity immediately afterward. For example, one boy, Ryan, who had fragile X syndrome, became anxious when his mother asked him to run errands, particularly during the transition from one errand site to another. We created pictures to represent the most common errands that Ryan's mother needed to conduct (e.g., grocery store, bank, dry cleaner, post office) (Moskowitz, Carr, and Durand, 2011). To ensure the predictability of Ryan's transitions, we used those pictures to construct a visual schedule of the settings to which Ryan had to transition. Before entering the car, Ryan was presented with a portable board that contained pictures and words representing the locations he would be traveling to in the community as well as anchor pictures of his home on each end of the schedule. Ryan's mother reminded him where they were going while pointing to his visual schedule when they first entered the car in the driveway, when they reentered the car after the first errand, and when they reentered the car after the second errand, and referred to the visual schedule any time Ryan asked where they were going. Each time an errand was completed, she prompted Ryan to remove each Velcro errand picture.

Social Stories

Another strategy for increasing predictability is reading the child a Social Story prior to the anxiety-provoking event. Social Stories are individualized narratives that visually depict the sequence of events involved in a routine or situation and describe appropriate behavior relevant to the situation, thereby decreasing unpredictability and providing a model for socially acceptable behavior (Gray and Garand, 1993). These stories are intended to adopt the perspective of the individual for whom the story is written. Social Stories can be used for a multitude of purposes such as explaining new situations or changes in routine, describing situations in a way that is non-intimidating, teaching adaptive skills, and dealing with challenging behaviors, including emotional expression, aggression, or obsessive behavior. Since some individuals with ASD and DD exhibit anxiety when routines are changed or when entering a novel or unfamiliar situation, providing advance information about this type of situation can reduce anxiety and provide alternative coping strategies to deal with such a situation (Gut and Safran, 2002). For Ed, who constantly asked his mother if he was sick, we:

- created a picture book for him in which we normalized anxiety (i.e., "Everyone feels worried or afraid or anxious sometimes—kids and grownups too")

- explained that anxiety has a function or purpose (i.e., "If a lion is chasing you, it is okay to feel afraid, because your fear will make you run from the lion")

- described the nature of Ed's anxiety and how he responds to that anxiety (i.e., "When I feel bad and anxious, I want to go find Mom and ask her a question")

- explained the concept of ritual prevention (i.e., "To fight my anxiety, I will try not to ask Mom these questions and Mom will try not to answer my questions")

- explained the concept of habituation (i.e., "At first, when Mom says, 'I don't know,' or 'I can't tell you,' I feel scared. But after a while, I'm less scared. Then, after a while longer, I'm not scared anymore").

Priming

A third strategy for increasing predictability is through priming, in which the individual is able to preview future events on a one-to-one basis under relaxed conditions so that these events become more predictable (Wilde, Koegel, and Koegel, 1992). Video priming is one way to do this. Seeing a video allows a person to experience many of the cues (e.g., sight, sound, movement) that may cause anxiety, which is not often possible with verbal descriptions or pictorial representations (Schreibman, Whalen, and Stahmer, 2000). The use of video also allows for priming with children who are non-verbal or limited in their ability to comprehend verbal descriptions. For example, for Mike, for whom transitions from one classroom to another were an anxiety-provoking setting event, his teachers video-recorded the school setting to show the environment as Mike would see it when progressing through the transition. The video showed him exiting the classroom, walking through the halls and up the stairs, entering the lunch room, and finally his favorite toy sitting on the lunch table (to show that he would receive this reinforcer upon completing the transition successfully). Mike viewed the video every night for 2 weeks in order to make the transitions at school highly predictable, which reduced his anxiety and resulting problem behavior.

Providing Advanced Warning

Advanced warnings to signal upcoming transitions or changes in routine can help make the transitions or changes more predictable. These advanced warnings can be verbal and/or visual. In particular, visual representations of time, such as the Time Timer™, can help decrease problem behavior in individuals with ASD and DD by providing time to prepare for the upcoming anxiety-provoking situation (e.g., Dettmer *et al.*, 2000). Timers and/or countdowns can be used to make the transition a more gradual process, so the anxiety-provoking situation is not encountered abruptly. In illustration, Mike used an hourglass timer so he could visually see the time passing and see how much time he had left until it was time to leave his classroom. It was also helpful for his teachers to prompt him to look at the timer and give him several countdowns (e.g., "You have 2 minutes left until we leave the bumble-bee room…you have 1 minute left…you have 30 seconds left…10-9-8-7-6-5-4-3-2-1—it's time to go!").

PROVIDING CHOICES (CHOICE-MAKING)

Allowing individuals to choose activities and reinforcers is another prevention strategy that has been demonstrated to increase task engagement while minimizing escape-motivated problem behaviors (Shogren *et al.*, 2004). Providing a choice allows someone to become an active participant in the anxiety-provoking situation, rather than a passive, helpless bystander. Offering choices prior to or during an aversive activity could help reduce SIB and other problem behaviors regardless of whether the activity is anxiety-provoking versus simply disliked. However, choice-making may be especially important for individuals who are experiencing anxiety. After all, many researchers have suggested that a sense of unpredictability and uncontrollability is at the heart of anxiety, and that developing coping responses that impart a sense of control can buffer anxiety (Barlow, 2000). Given that SIB and other problem behaviors can be a way of exerting control over one's life (Wehmeyer, 1999), providing opportunities for choice-making may provide those with ASD and DD, especially those who are anxious, with a sense of control over their environment (Dattilo and Rusch, 1985), thus reducing anxiety and allowing them to attain their wants and needs in more appropriate ways. In illustration, Ryan, who became anxious while running errands, was given the opportunity to choose several preferred items (e.g., "blankie," sticker book) to pack in a "car bag" that he could bring with him while running errands. In addition, at the end of each errand, Ryan was allowed to choose a positive reinforcer, which was either a preferred item (e.g., a snack or small object to purchase in the grocery store) or a preferred activity (e.g., "swiping" his credit card at the store). Furthermore, when creating the visual schedule, whenever possible, Ryan's mother attempted to provide him with a choice of which place he wanted to go first (e.g., first the post office, then the bank) (Moskowitz *et al.*, 2011). As another example, Cale and colleagues (2009) found a substantial reduction in problem behavior when they provided students with ASD with a choice between their feared stimulus (e.g., math worksheets with pictures of sea creatures) and alternative stimuli that did not contain the feared stimulus but were matched on content (e.g., math worksheets without sea creatures). This allowed the children to avoid the feared stimulus without compromising the instructional goal. However, it is often not possible nor desirable to avoid the specific anxiety-provoking stimuli or situations, which is where exposure comes in.

GRADUATED EXPOSURE

The power of stimuli to evoke fear reactions can be reduced by exposing individuals to their feared stimuli (Kendall, 1994). Most researchers would agree that engaging in exposure is necessary for a positive outcome when treating anxiety, and that exposure to the feared stimuli is a crucial element of all CBT for anxiety in neurotypical individuals (Kendall *et al.*, 2005). Exposure has also been shown to reduce anxiety in children with ASD (e.g., Lehmkuhl *et al.*, 2008), as well as fear and problem behavior including SIB in children with DD (e.g., Davis *et al.*, 2007). During the graduated-exposure procedure, an individual remains in the presence of a feared stimulus or situation (e.g., birthday candles, spider) until the situation no longer brings about the anxious physiological, cognitive, or behavior symptoms. With graduated exposure, approach behaviors (i.e., when the individual approaches the feared stimulus or just remains in the feared situation) are positively reinforced while fearful or avoidant responses are eliminated, as the individual is gradually exposed to increasing proximity, intensity, or amounts of the feared stimulus or situation. For example, a boy with ASD, Sam, was afraid when his parents turned on the blinker and made a left or right turn while riding in the car. We exposed him to this feared situation in gradually more challenging steps. Sam first engaged in activities that we predicted would provoke relatively low levels of anxiety: he listened to audio recordings of the sound of blinkers and then watched Internet videos of cars making left and right turns. He then engaged in an activity that we predicted might evoke moderate levels of anxiety: Sam and his parents practiced listening to the real blinker in their car when the car was stationary (parked in their driveway), first with the car door open and then with the door closed. Finally, he engaged in activities that we predicted would evoke high levels of anxiety because they all involved riding in the car. We moved up the exposure hierarchy from right and left turns that were thought to be less anxiety-provoking (e.g., a small intersection on a side street with a stop sign) to more anxiety-provoking (e.g., major intersections with traffic lights).

COUNTERCONDITIONING AND GENERALIZED REINFORCEMENT

Counterconditioning involves pairing an anxiety-provoking stimulus or situation with an item or activity that produces an emotional state that is *incompatible* with anxiety (i.e., an item or activity that induces a relaxed, positive state). For example, Luscre and Center (1996) used anti-anxiety stimuli (e.g., hand-held mirror, music, Play-doh) to elicit a positive response in children with ASD and help counter a fear response to dental examinations. In illustration, for Sam, riding in the car was paired with his most highly preferred and otherwise inaccessible positive stimulus, an audio recording of Dr. Seuss' book *The Sneetches*. While listening to *The Sneetches*, Sam's anxious behaviors substantially decreased, and his problem behaviors were eliminated on car rides, even during left and right turns. Counterconditioning has not proved more effective than standard exposure in the treatment of fear in humans. However, anecdotally, our clinical observations suggest that pairing the anxiety-provoking stimuli with equally potent or even more powerful "perseverative" stimuli (e.g., *The Sneetches*) served to counteract individuals' fearful or anxious responses in a way that exposure to the feared stimulus alone (without pairing it with anti-anxiety stimuli) may not have been able to accomplish, or at least may not have been able to accomplish as quickly. Thus, clinically, we often tend to use counterconditioning with individuals with ASD or DD, especially with those who display severe SIB or aggression, because waiting for them to get used to (i.e., habituate to) the feared stimulus through exposure alone may be too dangerous when there is serious problem behavior. When the individual only displays anxious behaviors and no problem behavior, or mild problem behavior, and/or when the individual has an average or above-average cognitive ability, we are more likely to use standard exposures (exposing the individual to the anxiety-provoking situation *without* anti- anxiety stimuli) instead of counterconditioning (exposing the individual to the anxiety-provoking situation while pairing it with anti-anxiety stimuli). Although using anti-anxiety stimuli would be considered as distraction or "safety signals" in the CBT literature and would thus be contraindicated for neurotypical individuals with anxiety, it is possible that this may not be as true for those with ASD and DD, who often lack the cognitive capacity to understand that their anxiety will eventually decline (i.e., they will habituate) if they simply remain in the situation for long enough, without having to do anything at all.

Another way to conceptualize counterconditioning is as "generalized reinforcement," in which the anxiety-provoking stimulus or situation is paired with a wide variety of highly preferred tangible, activity, and social reinforcers, such as candy, books, and the singing of favorite songs. This pairing establishes the anxiety-provoking situation itself as a generalized reinforcer (Skinner, 1953), so that the formerly anxiety-producing situation becomes an antecedent for approach rather than escape or avoidance through SIB. For instance, Magito McLaughlin and Carr (2005) trained staff members who had a "poor rapport" with the participants with ASD and ID to non-contingently present strongly preferred positive reinforcers (e.g., pretzels), which strengthened participants' approach behavior toward the staff members. It is noteworthy that this strategy is often most effective if we pair the anxiety-provoking situation with not only the most highly preferred stimulus, but one that is otherwise inaccessible. For instance, if the child is afraid of his mother leaving the house, the child would be allowed to watch his favorite video while the parent is gone, but the child would *not* be allowed to watch this video at any other time of the day, in order to maximize the reinforcing power of the video (i.e., we are manipulating the setting event of satiation/deprivation). This turns the anxiety-provoking situation into one that is generally associated with positive feelings instead of negative feelings of worry or dread.

INCORPORATING PERSEVERATIVE INTERESTS

Incorporating an individual's preferences or interests into a "disliked" or "unpleasant" activity is another antecedent intervention that has been shown to effectively reduce escape-maintained problem behavior (Clarke *et al.*, 1995). To counteract anxiety, it may be especially helpful to incorporate not just the individual's interest but a perseverative interest. Obsessive or "perseverative" interests refer to an object, activity, or topic with which the individual is intensely preoccupied. Studies have shown that using perseverative behaviors as reinforcers is superior to using food reinforcers (Charlop, Kurtz, and Casey, 1990), and that providing obsessions as reinforcers when individuals are *not* displaying problem behavior is the most effective at reducing inappropriate behaviors (Charlop-Christy and Haymes, 1996). For instance, for a child whose perseverative interest is trains, that child would be allowed to play with a train when exposed to a feared situation. Alternatively, many with ASD naturally use self-stimulatory and perseverative behaviors to reduce their anxiety. Therefore, it is often very effective to use these perseverative behaviors as the reward for getting through an anxious situation without exhibiting SIB or aggression. For instance, if a child who is afraid of school enters the school without engaging in SIB, he may be allowed to flap his hands repetitively or repeat the names of all the U.S. presidents for 3 minutes. In addition to using perseverative objects or activities as reinforcers *after* the anxiety-provoking activity has been completed (see "Positive Reinforcement" under the consequence-based strategies below), perseverative interests can also be incorporated into the anxiety-provoking activity itself (e.g., telling a child who is obsessed with Harry Potter to rehearse the mantra "I can be brave like Harry Potter" when confronted with a feared situation) or be paired non-contingently with the anxiety-provoking activity (see "Counterconditioning and Generalized Reinforcement" above). For an individual who engages in SIB to escape a situation that is anxiety-provoking, it is possible that pairing it with a strongly preferred item or activity (such as pretzels) may not be enough to counteract the anxiety; in such instances, it may be that the most perseverative item or activity is the only thing strong enough to counteract the anxiety.

It is important to emphasize that these strategies can be used in combination with one another to target both the setting events and/or the antecedents. For example, in the case of Bobby, who displayed SIB when he was in a novel environment and someone asked him a question, we mitigated the setting event (new environment) by showing him videos or photos of the new setting he would be entering so that the setting would be more familiar to him and less anxiety-provoking. To address the antecedent (social demand of Bobby being asked a question), we incorporated his obsessive or perseverative interest in subways into the social demand. The new social partner asked him questions about subways (the topic with which he was most preoccupied), which eased his anxiety over being asked questions. Gradually, the new social partner asked increasingly more non-subway questions interspersed among subway-related questions (known as embedding or activity interspersal). This illustrates how assessing the setting events and antecedents that contribute to anxiety can allow us to alter or modify both variables, thus preventing anxiety from occurring or at least reducing the intensity of anxiety. (See Chapter 10 for other prevention strategies, such as embedding, behavioral momentum, and curricular modification.)

Replacement Strategies

The previous strategies target the setting events and antecedents that lead to SIB in the hopes of preventing the behavior from occurring in the first place. However, sometimes predicting and controlling the environmental factors that may or may not result in SIB and aggression is difficult to accomplish. In addition, people in the person's life (such as teachers or parents) may not always be able or willing to modify the environment to prevent anxiety and problem behavior from occurring. Furthermore, over-reliance on prevention strategies in the absence of teaching skills often results in parents, teachers, and providers simply avoiding difficult situations rather than teaching how to cope with those situations. Thus, it becomes important to teach skills for coping with anxiety-provoking situations so that they can be used in any environment, independent of trained staff or caretakers. The goal of replacement strategies is to teach alternative behaviors or skills that serve the same function(s) as the problem behavior (and are more effective and efficient than the problem behavior) so that they can replace the problem behavior. The following interventions can be used to replace SIB and other problem behaviors with more adaptive, coping behaviors.

FUNCTIONAL COMMUNICATION TRAINING

Functional communication training (FCT; Carr and Durand, 1985) is discussed in more detail in Chapter 11, but we address it briefly here in order to discuss how it can be used in the context of anxiety-induced problem behaviors. SIB and other problem behaviors can be viewed as a form of communication, especially in those individuals with communication deficits who do not have a better way to get their needs and wants met. Thus, if we can determine the function or communicative "messages" of the behavior problems (e.g., "This makes me anxious—I want to get out of here!" or "I want you to comfort me"), we can teach them to communicate the same message in a more appropriate way, which would render their problem behavior unnecessary (Durand and Moskowitz, 2015). This is known as FCT, which involves assessing the function(s) of an individual's SIB or problem behavior and then teaching functionally equivalent communicative responses that serve the same purpose. If SIB functions to escape anxiety, FCT can be used to teach the individual to ask for assistance or a break from the anxiety-provoking activity. Those whose SIB serves the purpose of gaining comfort or reassurance could be taught to ask for a hug or reassurance (e.g., "Am I doing good work?" [Carr and Durand, 1985], for example). Those whose SIB serves a tangible or sensory function can be taught to request a calming object or activity. Individuals can be taught to communicate via verbal requests, sign language, gestures (i.e., hand raising, pointing), or assistive technology such as a voice-output device.

In the early stages of teaching an individual to use a communicative response, it is important that we initially reinforce him by giving him what he is asking for every time he asks for it; if the reinforcer is too difficult to obtain, the individual might resort to SIB to gain his reinforcer, rather than using his new communication skill (Durand and Moskowitz, 2015). However, over time, reinforcement often must be faded from a continuous to intermittent schedule or by making the individual wait for increasingly longer amounts of time before he receives the reinforcer (e.g., "You want a break? Okay, do one more and then you can take a break"). This is especially true in the case of anxiety, since we want individuals to be exposed to the anxiety-provoking situation for long-enough periods of time until they can habituate (i.e., graduated exposure); if they are constantly asking for a break from the anxiety-provoking situation, they will probably not habituate. In illustration, a boy with ASD named Wesley became very anxious whenever another child would cry, and responded by hitting, scratching, or biting the other child. We gradually exposed Wesley to the sounds and sights of crying, progressing from audio recordings to video recordings of children crying, to real-life adults crying, to children in the clinic and siblings crying, and ultimately to the real children in his class crying. While experiencing the audios and videos, Wesley was taught to ask for a break by handing us a "break card" while saying, "I want a break." Each time he handed us a break card, we stopped the audio or video and allowed him to leave the room for a time-limited break. Gradually, we reduced the number of break cards available so that Wesley was exposed to the crying for increasingly longer periods of time. (Instead of reducing the number of break cards, we also could have gradually increased the time Wesley had to wait until he could take a break.)

RELAXATION TRAINING

In addition to replacing the SIB or problem behavior with a form of communication, we can also replace problem behavior that functions to reduce anxiety with relaxation skills that serve the same function. Relaxation skills—including deep breathing, progressive muscle relaxation (PMR), and guided imagery—can allow enough reduction in anxiety so that additional interventions can be successful. (See Mullins and Christian [2001] for an example of PMR with an adolescent with ASD and ID [who was taught an abbreviated version of PMR from Cautela and

Groden, 1978], and Lindsay and colleagues [1994] for an example of behavioral relaxation training with adults with ID. Chapter 13 discusses relaxation training in more detail.)

Interestingly, a study by Hirstein, Iversen, and Ramachandran (2001) found that most of the children with ASD in their study had abnormally high electrodermal activity and appeared to use "calming" self-stimulation activities (e.g., immersing their hands in dry beans, being wrapped in a heavy blanket, deep-pressure massage) to calm hyper-responsive sympathetic activity. However, they also found a subgroup of children who showed either a complete absence of skin conductance responses (SCRs) or SCRs produced only by extreme activities, such as SIB. Hirstein *et al.* suggested that this subgroup of children may engage in SIB or risk-taking behavior to produce *more* autonomic activity. Thus, it may be that many individuals with ASD engage in calming or relaxing activities or behaviors when their arousal level becomes too high in order to bring it down to a manageable level, whereas others may engage in SIB or other high-intensity behavior if their arousal levels are too low in order to bring them up to an optimal level. In addition to highlighting the importance of conducting an FBA to determine the unique functions of SIB (e.g., increasing or decreasing arousal) for each person, this research suggests that, for those who experience high levels of arousal, it may be especially important to teach relaxation skills to bring their arousal (one component of anxiety) down to a manageable level.

TEACHING COPING SKILLS

Another type of replacement skill that can be taught in order to reduce anxiety is coping skills, such as "coping self-statements" or "coping self-talk" (e.g., Kendall, 1994), that individuals can use while they are feeling afraid. Coping statements have been found to decrease the reported anxiety seen in desensitization (Hayes *et al.*, 1983) and are usually part of multi-component CBT intervention programs for neurotypical children (e.g., *Coping Cat*; Kendall and Hedtke, 2006) as well as children with high-functioning ASD (e.g., *Facing Your Fears*; Reaven *et al.*, 2012). Coping statements, such as "I've handled this before and I will handle it again," or simpler statements such as "I can be brave!", are often used before exposures to help reduce anticipatory anxiety and/or during exposures to help reduce anxiety. Similarly, children with OCD are often taught to use "boss-back" talk to boss back their OCD, such as "My brain is just stuck right now, I don't have to do this [the ritual]," or "Can't catch me this time, OCD" (March and Mulle, 1998).

For instance, Ed, who constantly sought reassurance from his mother regarding whether he was sick, was taught coping skills through his Social Story: "Sometimes I need help coping with this bad feeling. So here are some things I can do when I feel anxious. When I feel worried or anxious, I can tell myself, 'This is just my anxiety talking. I am not really sick.'"

It is noteworthy that, in the previous section, we conceptualized "graduated exposure" and "counterconditioning" as prevention strategies because they are methods for reducing the aversiveness of the feared context or stimulus (similar to interspersing easy tasks with difficult tasks or providing toys when a child has to wait). However, graduated exposure and counterconditioning can also be conceptualized as replacement strategies in that the individual is taught a replacement behavior (e.g., an approach response, or remaining in the feared situation) to replace avoidance behavior (e.g., running away).

Consequence Strategies

Although prevention strategies are aimed to prevent SIB from occurring in the first place and replacement strategies are designed to replace it, consequence-based strategies need to be in place in case SIB occurs anyway. As previously stated, the way the people around the person respond to the SIB or problem behavior will be directly related to whether or not he learns that the problem behavior will be effective. Therefore, consequence-based strategies (also known as "response" or "management" strategies) are used to alter the consequences for the problem behavior, so that SIB no longer leads to desired results for the individual. Consequence-based strategies include making sure that the SIB or problem behavior is not effective (i.e., that we do not reinforce the SIB or anxious behavior) and that we reinforce alternative skills or "positive" behaviors (e.g., approach behavior) instead. Essentially, the rewards for positive behavior should either exceed or at least be equal to the rewards for engaging in anxious behavior or SIB/problem behavior.

POSITIVE REINFORCEMENT

Positive reinforcement "occurs when a behavior is followed immediately by the presentation of a stimulus and, as a result, occurs more often in the future" (Cooper, Heron, and Heward, 2007, p.36). As applied to anxiety, the individual receives positive reinforcement (e.g., labeled praise, a highly preferred item) contingent upon approaching the anxiety-inducing stimulus or remaining in the feared situation, which increases the likelihood that he will display such "brave" behavior in the future. For example, although Tommy, who was afraid of the Happy Birthday song and birthday cake, was initially provided with a highly preferred, perseverative item (Sesame Street pop-up toy) non-contingently as soon as we started singing happy birthday, when the birthday cake and birthday song were presented for a third time, we prompted an approach response by instructing him to approach the birthday cake (the feared stimulus) and attempt to blow out the candles in order to receive his reinforcer. If he responded by approaching the birthday cake for the preferred item and making any attempt to blow out the candles, we immediately delivered the item and provided positive feedback. If he did not approach the cake, we presented a general cue (e.g., "Tommy, do you want to play with this?" while showing him the Sesame Street pop-up toy or CD player) to encourage an approach response. Following each successful approach response, we gradually increased the cake's proximity to Tommy. If he spontaneously approached the birthday cake and attempted to blow out the candles, he immediately received positive feedback along with the preferred item. Prior to using this strategy, approaching the feared setting or object only resulted in increased levels of anxiety and/or SIB or problem behavior. However, if the child only receives his most highly preferred item when approaching the feared stimulus, he will learn that approaching the feared stimulus results in a reward, while avoiding the feared stimulus results in no reward.

DIFFERENTIAL REINFORCEMENT

When using differential reinforcement procedures, we heavily reinforce non-injurious behavior in order to strengthen it, while withholding or delaying reinforcement following SIB in an attempt to weaken it (Favell, McGimsey, and Schell, 1982). Parents, teachers, and providers can respond to brave and anxious behavior by providing labeled praise for brave or approach responses (assuming attention or praise is reinforcing) and selectively ignoring anxious or avoidant responses and SIB or aggression. One type of differential reinforcement procedure is differential reinforcement of other behavior (DRO), in which we provide reinforcement following periods of time in which no SIB occurs; that is, reinforcement is provided whenever a specified period of time has passed in which any behavior *other* than SIB has occurred. Thus, the individual receives reinforcement for refraining from SIB. In differential reinforcement of incompatible behavior (DRI), we provide reinforcement for specific appropriate behaviors that are physically incompatible with SIB. For example, if a child bites his finger repeatedly, we could provide the child with reinforcement for drawing pictures on a piece of paper (which the child is physically incapable of doing while biting his finger) (Carr *et al.*, 1990). Another differential reinforcement procedure is differential reinforcement of alternative behavior (DRA), in which reinforcement is provided for a specific alternative behavior or skill that enhances an individual's social competence, such as a communication skill (see FCT above; also known as differential reinforcement of communication, or DRC), or other socially useful behaviors such as leisure skills, vocational skills, and self-help skills (Carr *et al.*, 1990). Although differential reinforcement procedures may be most effective in combination with other techniques and may not be able to completely eliminate SIB on their own, they are nevertheless an essential component of most treatments to reduce SIB (Favell *et al.*, 1982).

Just as differential reinforcement can be applied to SIB, it can also be applied specifically to anxious behaviors in that we can provide relatively more reinforcement for approaching a feared stimulus than for running away (i.e., DRI), more reinforcement for specific "brave" behaviors such as relaxation strategies, communication, or positive self-statements (i.e., DRA), or more reinforcement for any behavior that is non-anxious (i.e., DRO). For example, Ed's mother awarded him a sticker for every 30 minutes that he engaged in "brave behavior" (i.e., doing anything *other* than asking his mother questions about his health, such as "Mom, am I sick?"). The stickers counted toward larger prizes from his reward menu. The DRO system helped to prevent him from ritualizing (e.g., asking reassurance-seeking questions), which is a critical component of exposure-and-ritual prevention, the most evidence-based approach for treating OCD in neurotypical individuals.

As another example, for Joey (the boy who became anxious when his parents left the house), his family members were coached to promote his brave behaviors by differentially responding to his brave versus anxious behavior. Prior to intervention, it was observed that his anxious behaviors were not only negatively reinforced by escape or avoidance (i.e., his parents occasionally decided *not* to leave the house if Joey became anxious enough), but also positively reinforced by reassurance and comfort. For instance, Joey received attention when he displayed anxious behavior regarding his parents leaving, whereas he generally did not receive any attention when he was sitting quietly while they left, talked about leaving, or while they were away. Therefore, during intervention, his family members were coached to provide Joey with attention and praise for brave or courageous behavior that was incompatible with anxious behavior (DRI, e.g., sitting in a chair in the living room versus standing by the front door watching to see his parents' car) or when he was behaving in a calm and/or quiet manner (i.e., DRO, not displaying anxious behavior) while minimizing attention for his anxious behavior.

EXTINCTION

Extinction refers to withholding reinforcement following a behavior that has been previously reinforced. Of course, the nature of extinction depends on the nature of the reinforcement. If the individual's SIB and/or anxious behavior are reinforced by attention, then extinction consists of ignoring the behavior. However, if the SIB is reinforced by being allowed to escape or avoid an anxiety-provoking situation, then extinction involves preventing escape ("escape extinction"). Thus, with extinction, the SIB must result in no differential consequences, meaning that the other people in the person's life (e.g., parent, teacher, employer) must respond as though the SIB has not occurred (Favell *et al.*, 1982). For instance, for Joey, the child who was afraid of his parents leaving the house, this meant that, for intervention, his parents had to leave regardless of whatever behaviors Joey displayed. Similarly, for Tommy, the child who was afraid of the Happy Birthday song, escape extinction meant finishing the song in its entirety even if Tommy displayed anxious or problem behaviors during the song. In the case of SIB that is motivated to gain comfort or reassurance, extinction means not providing that comfort or attention if the child displays SIB. For instance, if a child is comforted by his mother's hug, the mother only hugs the child if the child is making an effort to display calm behaviors. It is only natural that most parents would want to do anything to stop their child from hurting themselves or someone else; however, the long-term elimination of these behaviors requires that parents do not reinforce their children's anxious or problem behaviors. If the child's behaviors no longer get them what they want, or get them out of something they *do not* want, they will stop exhibiting those behaviors and only display behaviors that are actually effective. Practically, it is not always safe to implement extinction procedures for severe SIB, and extinction for SIB should almost always be just one component of a treatment package (Sturmey, 2008), with the emphasis on replacement, prevention, and reinforcement-based strategies.

Conclusion

As Howlin (1998) commented when discussing problem behavior in children with ASD:

> Imagine for a moment how any [typical] person might react to a world in which they are able to understand almost nothing of what is happening around them; in which they are thrown daily into an ever-changing and unpredictable environment; where they lack even the rudimentary verbal skills necessary to make their needs known; where they have no access to the internalized, imaginative facilities that are so crucial for dealing effectively with anxiety, uncertainty, and distress. (Howlin, 1998, p.309)

As she notes, most neurotypical individuals would quickly resort to engaging in problem behavior, such as SIB, to cope with this situation. As such, many individuals with ASD and DD engage in SIB or other problem behavior *because* they are anxious and do not know how to cope with this anxiety, or because problem behavior *is* their way of coping with anxiety.

The purpose of this chapter was to present ways in which anxiety might contribute to SIB and other problem behaviors in individuals with ASD and DD. Although we presented a general overview of how to look for anxiety-related SIB while conducting an FBA, and presented several prevention, replacement, and response strategies for reducing SIB that is functionally related to anxiety, we want to emphasize the importance of individualizing these approaches. Each individual with ASD or DD has unique reasons for experiencing anxiety and engaging in SIB as well as idiosyncratic manifestations of anxious and self-injurious behaviors. Clinically, we understand the challenges presented by SIB and the desire for parents, caretakers, and clinicians to eradicate these behaviors as quickly as possible. However, especially for SIB that may be related to anxiety, we urge parents, caretakers, and clinicians to exhibit "brave behavior" themselves, and carefully consider the functions of these behaviors and the specific intervention strategies that may permanently eliminate the behaviors, while instilling long-lasting coping strategies.

References

Albano, A.M., and Kendall, P.C. (2002). Cognitive behavioural therapy for children and adolescents with anxiety disorders: Clinical research advances. *International Review of Psychiatry, 14,* 129–134.

Attwood, T. (2000). Strategies for improving the social integration of children with Asperger syndrome. *Autism, 4,* 85–100.

Bandura, A. (1988). Self-efficacy conception of anxiety. *Anxiety, Stress, & Coping, 1,* 77–98.

Barlow, D.H. (2000). Unraveling the mysteries of anxiety and its disorders from the perspective of emotion theory. *American Psychologist, 55,* 1247–1263.

Barlow, D.H. (2002). *Anxiety and Its Disorders: The Nature and Treatment of Anxiety and Panic* (2nd ed.). New York, NY: Guilford Press.

Bellini, S. (2004). Social skills deficits and anxiety in high-functioning adolescents with autism spectrum disorders. *Focus on Autism and Other Developmental Disabilities, 19,* 78–86.

Birmaher, B., Brent, D.A., Chiappetta, L., Bridge, J., Monga, S., and Baugher, M. (1999). Psychometric properties of the Screen for Child Anxiety Related Emotional Disorders Scale (SCARED): A replication study. *Journal of the American Academy of Child and Adolescent Psychiatry, 38,* 1230–1236.

Cale, S.I., Carr, E.G., Blakeley-Smith, A., and Owen-DeSchryver, J.S. (2009). Context-based assessment and intervention for problem behavior in children with autism spectrum disorder. *Behavior Modification, 33,* 707–742.

Carr, E.G., Dunlap, G., Horner, R.H., Koegel, R.L., *et al.* (2002). Positive behavior support: Evolution of an applied science. *Journal of Positive Behavior Interventions, 4,* 4–16, 20.

Carr, E.G., and Durand, V.M. (1985). Reducing behavior problems through functional communication training. *Journal of Applied Behavior Analysis, 18,* 111–126

Carr, E.G., Horner, R.H., Turnbull, A.P., Marquis, J.G., *et al.* (1999). *Positive Behavior Support for People with Developmental Disabilities: A Research Synthesis.* Washington, DC: American Association on Mental Retardation.

Carr, E.G., and Owen-DeSchryver, J.S. (2007). Physical illness, pain, and problem behavior in minimally verbal people with developmental disabilities. *Journal of Autism and Developmental Disorders, 37,* 413–424.

Carr, E.G., Robinson, S., Taylor, J.C., and Carlson, J.I. (1990). *Positive Approaches to the Treatment of Severe Behavior Problems in Persons with Developmental Disabilities: A Review and Analysis of Reinforcement and Stimulus-Based Procedures* (Monograph No. 4). Seattle, WA: Association for Persons with Severe Handicaps.

Carr, E.G., and Smith, C.E. (1995). Biological setting events for self-injury. *Mental Retardation and Developmental Disabilities Research and Reviews, 1,* 94–98.

Carr, E.G., Smith, C.E., Giacin, T.A., Whelan, B.M., and Pancari, J. (2003). Menstrual discomfort as a biological setting event for severe problem behavior: Assessment and intervention. *American Journal on Mental Retardation, 108,* 117–133.

Cautela, J. (1977). *Behavior Analysis Forms for Clinical Intervention.* Champaign, IL: Research Press Co.

Cautela, J., and Groden, J. (1978). *Relaxation: A Comprehensive Manual for Adults, Children and Children with Special Needs.* Champaign, IL: Research Press.

Charlop, M.H., Kurtz, P.F., and Casey, F. (1990). Using aberrant behaviors as reinforcers for autistic children. *Journal of Applied Behavior Analysis, 23,* 163–181.

Charlop-Christy, M.H., and Haymes, L.K. (1996). Using obsessions as reinforcers with and without mild reductive procedures to decrease inappropriate behaviors of children with autism. *Journal of Autism and Developmental Disorders, 26,* 527–546.

Chorpita, B.F., Moffitt, C.E., and Gray, J. (2005). Psychometric properties of the Revised Child Anxiety and Depression Scale in a clinical sample. *Behaviour Research and Therapy, 43,* 309–322.

Clarke, S., Dunlap, G., Foster-Johnson, L., Childs, K., *et al.* (1995). Improving the conduct of students with behavioral disorders by incorporating student interests into curricular activities. *Behavioral Disorders, 20,* 221–227.

Cooper, J.O., Heron, T.E., and Heward, W.L. (2007). *Applied Behavior Analysis* (2nd ed.). Upper Saddle River, NJ: Pearson Education.

Cordeiro, L., Ballinger, E., Hagerman, R., and Hessl, D. (2011). Clinical assessment of DSM-IV anxiety disorders in fragile X syndrome: Prevalence and characterization. *Journal of Neurodevelopmental Disorders: Advancing Interdisciplinary Research, 3*(1), 57–67.

Dattilo, J., and Rusch, F. (1985). Effects of choice on leisure participation for persons with severe handicaps. *Journal of the Association for Persons with Severe Handicaps, 10,* 194–199.

Davis, E., Saeed, S.A., and Antonacci, D.J. (2008). Anxiety disorders in persons with developmental disabilities: Empirically informed diagnosis and treatment. Reviews of literature on anxiety disorders in DD population with practical take-home messages for the clinician. *Psychiatric Quarterly, 79*(3), 249–263.

Davis, T.E., Kurtz, P.F., Gardner, A.W., and Carman, N.B. (2007). Cognitive-behavioral treatment for specific phobias with a child demonstrating severe problem behavior and developmental delays. *Research in Developmental Disabilities, 28,* 546–558.

Davis, T.E., and Ollendick, T.H. (2005). Empirically supported treatments for specific phobia in children: Do efficacious treatments address the components of a phobic response? *Clinical Psychology: Science & Practice, 12,* 144–160.

Dettmer, S., Simpson, R.L., Myles, B.S., and Ganz, J.B. (2000). The use of visual supports to facilitate transitions of students with autism. *Focus on Autism and Other Developmental Disabilities, 15*(3), 163.

Durand, V.M., and Crimmins, D.B. (1988). *The Motivation Assessment Scale.* Topeka, KS: Monaco & Associates.

Durand, V.M., and Hieneman, M. (2008). *Helping Parents with Challenging Children: Positive Family Intervention. Parent Workbook.* New York, NY: Oxford University Press.

Durand, V.M., and Moskowitz, L.J. (2015). Functional communication training: Thirty years of treating challenging behavior. *Topics in Early Childhood Special Education, 35*(2), 116–126.

Einfeld, S.L., and Tonge, B.J. (1995). The Developmental Behaviour Checklist: The developmental and validation of an instrument for the assessment of behavioural and emotional disturbance in children and adolescents with mental retardation. *Journal of Autism and Developmental Disorders, 25,* 81–104.

Esbensen, A.J., Rojahn, J., Aman, M.G., and Ruedrich, S. (2003). The reliability and validity of an assessment instrument for anxiety, depression and mood among individuals with mental retardation. *Journal of Autism and Developmental Disorders, 33,* 617–629.

Favell, J.E., McGimsey, J., and Schell, R. (1982). Treatment of self-injury by providing alternate sensory activities. *Analysis and Intervention in Developmental Disabilities, 2,* 83–104.

Flannery, K., and Horner, R. (1994). The relationship between predictability and problem behavior for students with severe disabilities. *Journal of Behavioral Education, 4,* 157–176.

Gadow, K.D., and Sprafkin, J. (2002). *Child Symptom Inventory—4: Screening and Norms Manual.* Stony Brook, NY: Checkmate Plus.

Goodwin, M.S., Velicer, W.F., and Intille, S.S. (2008). Telemetric monitoring in the behavior sciences. *Behavior Research Methods, 40,* 328–341.

Gotham, K., Brunwasser, S.M., and Lord, C. (2015). Depressive and anxiety symptoms trajectories from school-age through young adulthood in samples with autism spectrum disorder and developmental delay. *Journal of the American Academy of Child and Adolescent Psychiatry, 54,* 369–376.

Gray, C.A., and Garand, J.D. (1993). Social Stories: Improving responses of students with autism with accurate social information. *Focus on Autistic Behavior, 8,* 1–10.

Grillon, C. (2008). Models and mechanisms of anxiety: Evidence from startle studies. *Psychopharmacology, 199,* 421–437.

Groden, J., Cautela, J., Prince, S., and Berryman, J. (1994). The Impact of Stress and Anxiety on Individuals with Autism and Developmental Disabilities. In E. Schopler and G.B. Mesibov (Eds.), *Behavioral Issues in Autism.* New York, NY: Plenum Press.

Groden, J., Diller, A., Bausman, M., Velicer, W., Norman, G., and Cautela, J. (2001). The development of a stress survey schedule for persons with autism and other developmental disabilities. *Journal of Autism and Developmental Disorders, 31,* 207–217.

Gullone, E., King, N.J., and Cummins, R.A. (1996). Fears of children and adolescents with mental retardation: A psychometric evaluation of the Fear Survey Schedule for Children—II (FSSC-II). *Research in Developmental Disabilities, 17,* 269–284.

Gut, D.M., and Safran, S.P. (2002). Cooperative learning and Social Stories: Effective social skills strategies for reading teachers. *Reading & Writing Quarterly, 18,* 87–91.

Hagopian, L.P., and Jennett, H.K. (2008). Behavioral assessment and treatment of anxiety in individuals with intellectual disabilities. *Journal of Developmental and Physical Disabilities, 20,* 467–483.

Hartley, S.L., and MacLean, W.E. (2006). A review of the reliability and validity of Likert-type scales for people with intellectual disability. *Journal of Intellectual Disability Research, 50,* 813–826.

Hastings, R.P., Brown, T., Mount, R.H., and Cormack, K.M. (2001). Exploration of psychometric properties of the Developmental Behavior Checklist. *Journal of Autism and Developmental Disorders, 31*(4), 423.

Hayes, S.C., Hussian, R.A., Turner, A.E., Anderson, N.B., and Grubb, T.D. (1983). The effect of coping statements on progress through a desensitization hierarchy. *Journal of Behavior Therapy and Experimental Psychiatry, 14*(2), 117–129.

Hirstein, W., Iversen, P., and Ramachandran, V.S. (2001). Autonomic responses of autistic children to people and objects. *Proceedings of Biological Sciences, 268,* 1883–1888.

Howlin, P. (1998). Practitioner review: Psychological and educational treatments for autism. *Journal of Child Psychology and Psychiatry, 39,* 307–322.

Izard, C.E., Dougherty, L.M., and Hembree, E.A. (1989). *A System for Identifying Affect Expressions by Holistic Judgments (Affex)*. Newark, DE: University of Delaware.

Joosten, A., Bundy, A., and Einfeld, S.L. (2009). Intrinsic and extrinsic motivation for stereotypic and repetitive behavior. *Journal of Autism and Developmental Disorders, 39,* 521–531.

Kanner, L. (1943). Autistic disturbances of affective contact. *Nervous Child, 2,* 217–250.

Kanner, L. (1951). The conception of wholes and parts in early infantile autism. *The American Journal of Psychiatry, 108,* 23–26.

Kaufman, J., Birmaher, B., Brent, D.A., Rao, U., *et al.* (1997). Schedule for affective disorders and schizophrenia for school-age children: Present and lifetime version (K-SADS-PL). Initial reliability and validity data. *Journal of the American Academy of Child and Adolescent Psychiatry, 36*(7), 980–988.

Kendall, P.C. (1994). Treating anxiety disorders in children: Results of a randomized clinical trial. *Journal of Consulting and Clinical Psychology, 62,* 100–110.

Kendall, P.C., and Hedtke, K.A. (2006). *The Coping Cat Program Workbook* (2nd ed.). Ardmore, PA: Workbook Publishing.

Kendall, P.C., Robin, J.A., Hedtke, K.A., Suveg, C., Flannery-Schroeder, E., and Gosch, E. (2005). Considering CBT with anxious youth? Think exposures. *Cognitive and Behavioral Practice, 12,* 136–150.

Kennedy, C.H., and Meyer, K.A. (1996). Sleep deprivation, allergy symptoms, and negatively reinforced problem behavior. *Journal of Applied Behavior Analysis, 29,* 133–135.

Langdon, N.A., Carr, E.G., and Owen-DeSchryver, J.S. (2008). Functional analysis of precursors for serious problem behavior and related intervention. *Behavior Modification, 32*(6), 804.

Lecavalier, L., Wood, J., Halladay, A., Jones, N., *et al.* (2014). Measuring anxiety as a treatment endpoint in youth with autism spectrum disorder. *Journal of Autism and Developmental Disorders, 44*(5), 1128–1143. doi:10.1007/s10803-013-1974-9

Lehmkuhl, H.D., Storch, E.A., Bodfish, J.W., and Geffken, G.R. (2008). Brief report: Exposure and response prevention for obsessive compulsive disorder in a 12-year-old with autism. *Journal of Autism and Developmental Disorders, 38,* 977–981.

Lesniak-Karpiak, K., Mazzocco, M.M., and Ross, J.L. (2003). Behavioral assessment of social anxiety in females with Turner or fragile X syndrome. *Journal of Autism and Developmental Disorders, 33,* 55–67.

Leyfer, O.T., Folstein, S.E., Bacalman, S., Davis, N.O., *et al.* (2006). Comorbid psychiatric disorders in children with autism: Interview development and rates of disorders. *Journal of Autism and Developmental Disorders, 36*(7), 849–861. doi:10.1007/s10803-006-0123-0

Lindsay, W.R., Fee, M., Michie, A., and Heap, I. (1994). The effects of cue control relaxation on adults with severe mental retardation. *Research in Developmental Disabilities, 15*(6), 425–437.

Lucyshyn, J.M., Albin, R.W., Horner, R.H., Mann, J.C., Mann, J.A., and Wadsworth, G. (2007). Family implementation of positive behavior support for a child with autism: Longitudinal, single-case, experimental, and descriptive replication and extension. *Journal of Positive Behavior Interventions, 9,* 131–150.

Lugnegård, T., Hallerbäck, M., and Gillberg, C. (2011). Psychiatric comorbidity in young adults with a clinical diagnosis of Asperger syndrome. *Research in Developmental Disabilities, 32,* 1910–1917.

Luscre, D.M., and Center, D.B. (1996). Procedures for reducing dental fear in children with autism. *Journal of Autism and Developmental Disorders, 26,* 547–556.

Magito McLaughlin, D., and Carr, E.G. (2005). Quality of rapport as a setting event for problem behavior: Assessment and intervention. *Journal of Positive Behavior Interventions, 7,* 68–91.

March, J., and Mulle, K. (1998). *OCD in Children and Adolescents: A Cognitive-Behavioral Treatment Manual*. New York, NY: Guilford Press.

March, J., Parker, J., Sullivan, K., Stallings, P., and Conners, C. (1997). The Multidimensional Anxiety Scale for Children (MASC): Factor structure, reliability and validity. *Journal of the American Academy of Child and Adolescent Psychiatry, 36,* 554–565.

Matson, J.L. (1995). *The Diagnostic Assessment for the Severely Handicapped—Revised (DASH-II)*. Baton Rouge, LA: Scientific Publishers.

Matson, J.L., Gardner, W.I., and Coe, D.A. (1991). A scale for evaluating emotional disorders in severely and profoundly retarded persons: Development of the Diagnostic Assessment for the Severely Handicapped (DASH) scale. *The British Journal of Psychiatry, 159,* 404–409.

Matson, J.L., LoVullo, S.V., Rivet, T.T., and Boisjoli, J.A. (2009). Validity of the Autism Spectrum Disorder—Comorbid for Children (ASD-CC). *Research in Autism Spectrum Disorders, 3*(2), 345–357.

Matson, J.L., Mahan, S., Fodstad, J.C., Worley, J.A., Neal, D., and Sipes, M. (2011). Effects of symptoms of co-morbid psychopathology on challenging behaviours among infants and toddlers with autistic disorder and PDD-NOS as assessed with the Baby and Infant Screen for Children with aUtIsm Traits (BISCUIT). *Developmental Neurorehabilitation, 14*(3), 129–139. doi:10.3109/17518423.2011.557029

Matson, J.L., Smiroldo, B.B., Hamilton, M., and Baglio, C.S. (1997). Do anxiety disorders exist in persons with severe and profound mental retardation? *Research in Developmental Disabilities, 18*(1), 39–44.

Mazefsky, C.A., Kao, J., and Oswald, D.P. (2011). Preliminary evidence suggesting caution in the use of psychiatric self-report measures with adolescents with high-functioning autism spectrum disorders. *Research in Autism Spectrum Disorders, 5*(1), 164–174.

McAtee, M., Carr, E.G., and Schulte, C. (2004). A contextual assessment inventory for problem behavior: Initial development. *Journal of Positive Behavior Interventions, 6,* 148–165.

Mesibov, G.B., Browder, D.M., and Kirkland, C. (2002). Using individualized schedules as a component of positive behavioral support for students with developmental disabilities. *Journal of Positive Behavior Interventions, 4,* 73–79.

Moskowitz, L.J., Carr, E.G., and Durand, V.M. (2011). Behavioral intervention for problem behavior in children with fragile X syndrome. *American Journal on Intellectual and Developmental Disabilities, 116*(6), 457–478.

Moskowitz, L.J., Mulder, E., Walsh, C.E., McLaughlin, D., *et al.* (2013). A multimethod assessment of anxiety and problem behavior in children with autism spectrum disorders and intellectual disability. *American Journal on Intellectual and Developmental Disabilities, 118*(6), 419–434.

Mullins, J., and Christian, L. (2001). The effects of progressive relaxation training on the disruptive behavior of a boy with autism. *Research in Developmental Disabilities, 22,* 449–462.

Muris, P., Steerneman, P., Merckelbach, H., Holdrinet, I., and Meesters, C. (1998). Comorbid anxiety symptoms in children with pervasive developmental disorders. *Journal of Anxiety Disorders, 12,* 387–393.

Ollendick, T.H. (1983). Reliability and validity of the Revised Fear Survey Schedule for Children (FSSC-R). *Behavior Research and Therapy, 21,* 685–692.

O'Neill, R.E., Horner, R.H., Albin, R.W., Storey, K., Newton, J.S., and Sprague, J.R. (1997). *Functional Assessment and Program Development for Problem Behavior.* Pacific Grove, CA: Brooks/Cole.

O'Reilly, M.F. (1995). Functional analysis and treatment of escape-maintained aggression correlated with sleep deprivation. *Journal of Applied Behavior Analysis, 28,* 225–226.

Poppen, R. (1988). *Behavioral Relaxation Training and Assessment.* Elmsford, NY: Pergamon.

Ramirez, S.Z., and Kratochwill, T.R. (1990). Development of the Fear Survey for Children with and without Mental Retardation. *Behavior Assessment, 12,* 457–470.

Reaven, J., Blakeley-Smith, A., Leuthe, E., Moody, E., and Hepburn, S. (2012). Facing your fears in adolescence: Cognitive-behavioral therapy for high-functioning autism spectrum disorders and anxiety. *Autism Research and Treatment,* 1–13. doi:10.1155/2012/423905

Research Units on Pediatric Psychopharmacology Autism Network (RUPP) (2002). The Pediatric Anxiety Rating Scale (PARS): Development and psychometric properties. *Journal of the American Academy of Child and Adolescent Psychiatry, 41*(9), 1061–1069.

Reynolds, C.R., and Richmond, B.O. (1978). What I think and feel: A revised measure of children's manifest anxiety. *Journal of Abnormal Child Psychology, 6,* 271–280.

Richards, C., Moss, J., O'Farrell, L., Kaur, G., and Oliver, C. (2009). Social anxiety in Cornelia de Lange syndrome. *Journal of Autism and Developmental Disorders, 39,* 1155–1162.

Rieske, R.D., Matson, J.L., Davis, T.E., Konst, M.J., Williams, L.W., and Whiting, S.E. (2013). Examination and validation of a measure of anxiety specific to children with autism spectrum disorders. *Developmental Neurorehabilitation, 16*(1), 9–16. doi:10.3109/17518423.2012.705909

Rogers, S.J. (1998). Neuropsychology of autism in young children and its implications for early intervention. *Mental Retardation and Developmental Disabilities Research Reviews, 4,* 104–112.

Rudy, B.M., Lewin, A.B., and Storch, E.A. (2013). Managing anxiety comorbidity in youth with autism spectrum disorders. *Neuropsychiatry, 3*(4), 411–421.

Schreibman, L., Whalen, C., and Stahmer, A.C. (2000). The use of video priming to reduce disruptive transition behavior in children with autism. *Journal of Positive Behavior Interventions, 2,* 3–11.

Shogren, K.A., Faggella-Luby, M.N., Jik Bae, S., and Wehmeyer, M.L. (2004). The effect of choice-making as an intervention for problem behavior: A meta-analysis. *Journal of Positive Behavior Interventions, 6,* 228–237.

Silverman, W.K., and Albano, A.M. (1996). *The Anxiety Disorders Interview Schedule for DSM-IV: Child and Parent Versions.* San Antonio, TX: Psychological Corporation.

Skinner, B.F. (1953). *Science and Human Behavior.* New York, NY: Free Press.

Sofronoff, K., Attwood, T., and Hinton, S. (2005). A randomized controlled trial of a CBT intervention for anxiety in children with Asperger syndrome. *Journal of Child Psychology and Psychiatry, 46,* 1152–1160.

Spielberger, C. (1973). *Manual for the State-Trait Anxiety Inventory for Children.* Palo Alto, CA: Consulting Psychologists Press.

Sterling, L., Renno, P., Storch, E.A., Ehrenreich-May, J., *et al.* (2015). Validity of the Revised Children's Anxiety and Depression Scale for youth with autism spectrum disorders. *Autism, 19*(1), 113–117. doi:10.1177/1362361313510066

Stern, J.A., Gadgil, M.S., Blakeley-Smith, A., Reaven, J.A., and Hepburn, S.L. (2014). Psychometric properties of the SCARED in youth with autism spectrum disorder. *Research in Autism Spectrum Disorders, 8*(9), 1225–1234.

Storch, E., Wood, J., Ehrenreich-May, J., Jones, A., *et al.* (2012). Convergent and discriminant validity and reliability of the Pediatric Anxiety Rating Scale in youth with autism spectrum disorders. *Journal of Autism and Developmental Disorders, 42*(11), 2374–2382. doi:10.1007/s10803-012-1489-9

Sturmey, P. (2008). *Behavioral Case Formulation and Intervention: A Functional Analytic Approach.* London: John Wiley & Sons.

Sullivan, K., Hooper, S., and Hatton, D. (2007). Behavioural equivalents of anxiety in children with fragile X syndrome: Parent and teacher report. *Journal of Intellectual Disability Research, 51,* 54–65.

Ung, D., Arnold, E., De Nadai, A., Lewin, A., *et al.* (2014). Inter-rater reliability of the Anxiety Disorders Interview Schedule for DSM-IV in high-functioning youth with autism spectrum disorder. *Journal of Developmental and Physical Disabilities, 26*(1), 53–65.

van Steensel, F.J.A., Bögels, S.M., and Perrin, S. (2011). Anxiety disorders in children and adolescents with autistic spectrum disorders: A meta-analysis. *Clinical Child and Family Psychology Review, 14*(3), 302–317.

Wehmeyer, M.L. (1999). A functional model of self-determination: Describing development and implementing instruction. *Focus on Autism and Other Developmental Disabilities, 14,* 53–61.

White, S.W., Lerner, M.D., McLeod, B.D., Wood, J.J., *et al.* (2015). Anxiety in youth with and without autism spectrum disorder: Examination of factorial equivalence. *Behavior Therapy, 46*(1), 40–53.

White, S.W., Oswald, D., Ollendick, T., and Scahill, L. (2009). Anxiety in children and adolescents with autism spectrum disorders. *Clinical Psychology Review, 29*(3), 216–229.

Wilde, L., Koegel, L.K., and Koegel, R.L. (1992). *Increasing Success in School Through Priming.* Santa Barbara, CA: University of California.

Wolpe, J. (1958). *Psychotherapy by Reciprocal Inhibition.* Stanford, CA: Stanford University Press.

CHAPTER 13

A Stress-Reduction Approach to Addressing Self-Injurious Behavior in Individuals with Autism

June Groden, Ph.D., Leslie Weidenman, and Cooper R. Woodward,
The Groden Center, Providence, Rhode Island

> The battle for self-control over an intense undesired habit consists of an endless series of skirmishes, in which our urges and our better angels clash several times each day.
>
> *Matthew D. Lieberman* (2013, p.210)

Introduction

Jane was 13 years old when she was referred to The Groden Center. She had been unsuccessfully treated for severe self-injury by at least three other organizations, regularly biting her arm and hand to the point of tearing flesh away—and then she would not tolerate topical treatments or bandages. At the time of referral, self-injury attempts occurred nearly 60 times per week, and her teachers at her previous placement reported that there "wasn't anything to do" about it.

Sylvester was 27 years old. He had blinded himself in both eyes through self-injurious behavior (SIB) while he was a longtime resident at a state institution. He was well on his way to damaging his hearing by bringing his fists to his ears and pounding on them. Staff at the institution attributed his self-injury to developmental disability, and while they would interrupt and try to redirect the behavior, that did not seem to do any good.

These are examples of two of the individuals who were referred to The Groden Center, a treatment and educational program for children and adults with an autism spectrum disorder (ASD), other pervasive developmental disabilities, and severe problem behaviors. The outcome of the treatment for these two persons is presented later in the chapter.

SIB is a form of repetitive behavior that has the potential to cause harm or even permanent damage to the person engaging in it. It is often seen in individuals with ASD and other significant behavioral disorders, with wide-ranging topography. Some frequently observed forms of SIB include head hitting, biting, scratching, skin picking, eye poking, pinching, and head banging. This chapter focuses on self-injury, which is one of the most dangerous and difficult problem behaviors to treat in this population. We present a personalized approach for treating those who engage in SIB, and highlight the benefits of including self-control and stress-reduction procedures in the treatment package. Although the treatment packages may have similar components, each one will vary depending on the outcome of the assessments and the needs of the individual. The ultimate goal is to reduce or eliminate the SIB, and to teach the individual self-control so he or she can maintain the treatment results without the assistance of caregivers.

The procedures described in this chapter are based on specific definitions of behavior, functional assessment, supporting scales, and technology to assess stress. We also discuss how this information can be used as a whole to positively address both antecedent supports and consequence packages. In other words, our goals are to augment information on function using a stress perspective, and describe how to create complementary tailored interventions that foster self-control and stress reduction for the persons we support.

The Stress Perspective

Although the role of stress is apparent in many self-reports from people with high-functioning autism, there is surprisingly little research in this field. Those with autism who can report their feelings verbally have stated the following:

> No one really understands what the emotional suffering of a person with autism is like. It is the confusion that results from not being able to understand the world around me, which, I think, causes all the fear. This fear then brings a need to withdraw. (Jolliffe, Landsdown, and Robinson, 1992, p.12)

Others report that they are "very nervous about everything, fear[ing] people and social activity greatly" (Volkmar and Cohen, 1985, p.49), and that "the real world [was] terrifying. Stress showed in my speech, my actions, my relationship with others" (Grandin and Scariano, 1986, p.79). There have been many books and papers written by persons with high-functioning autism expressing their stress and anxiety, but it is still one of the most overlooked problems.

Stress has been defined as the physiological reaction of the body to life situations that can be happy (eustress) or unhappy (distress). It is a demand placed on the individual that disturbs homeostasis (Selye, 1956). It is difficult to develop an intervention, since pinpointing and describing the behavior in terms of stress is ambiguous. For that reason we prefer to use the term *stressor*, which can be operationally defined, targeted, and measured for the purpose of designing assessments and treatments. A stressor is any stimulus or circumstance that compromises physical or psychological well-being and that requires an adjustment on the part of the individual (Lazarus and Folkman, 1984). Cohen *et al.* (2011, p.258) state:

> The consequence of stressors for individuals is known as *the stress response*, of which there are emotional, cognitive, behavioral, and physiological correlates. Many variables have been found to moderate the severity of psychological and physiological responses to stressors. Among them are a stressor's severity (amount of impact a stressor will have), temporal factor (length of time before a stressor occurs), event probability (likelihood of the stressor occurring), novelty (prior experience with the stressor), duration (how long the stressor will last), ambiguity (relating to prediction of a stressor's severity, temporal factor, event probability, novelty, and duration) and whether one's responses can affect an outcome (Paterson and Neufeld, 1989; Turner, 1994).

We also are suggesting in this chapter that stress plays a large part in the initiation and maintenance of SIB, as well as other challenging behaviors. The inherent perspective here emphasizes how the characteristics of autism make this population more vulnerable to stressors. Areas in which challenges or deficits are frequently seen include:

- deficits in communication and socialization skills

- problems in executive function (i.e., the ability to be goal directed, future oriented, and have strong cognitive abilities thought to be mediated by the frontal cortex) (Duncan, 1986)

- challenges in planning and organization

- difficulties with flexibility, inhibition, and self-monitoring (Prior and Hoffmann, 1990; Prior and Ozonoff, 1998; Rumsey and Hamburger, 1988)

- hardiness (i.e., the ability to accept challenge and have commitment, confidence, and self-control)

- medical conditions (i.e., high incidence of seizures)

- differences in sensory perception and sensory regulation.

Given these challenges specific to persons with autism, the role of stress may have particular implications that need to be considered. We will be discussing the relationship between stress and SIB, describing multimodal assessments to identify stressors, and examining interventions that can be incorporated into a treatment package based on the findings of the stress assessments.

We also suggest that SIB might sometimes be a maladaptive coping response to circumstances that cause stress and arousal. We call this a maladaptive coping model (Groden, Baron, and Groden, 2006, p.19) in which, under stressful situations, persons with poor coping strategies, like many individuals with ASD, do not have sufficient buffers (e.g., a social network of friends, ability to articulate concerns and needs, assertiveness, self-control, and so forth) to manage their stress. As an alternative, they display maladaptive behaviors such as self-injury. A failure to consider the role of stress might lead to the implementation of negative consequences, which would then increase the stress and begin a vicious cycle. In addition, when SIB responses, such as biting, head hitting, and eye poking, are displayed, opportunities to use adaptive coping behaviors are diminished. As an example, a child who wants to play with a favorite toy may lack the communication skills necessary to express this need and instead may use hand biting and screaming to attract the attention. Such behavior often leads to negative responses from caregivers and others who do not consider the stress perspective, which in turn leads to an increase in stress and completes a loop of accumulating stress and anxiety (Groden *et al.*, 2006, p.19). The following sections describe the multimodal assessment and treatment procedures that incorporate the understanding of the relationship between stress and SIB with a focus on stressors.

Multimodal Assessment of SIB

Any behavior could be conceived of as the result of a complex interplay of both external factors (cues, setting events, antecedents, motivating operations, learning histories, and so forth) and internal factors (cognitions, emotions, attributions, psychological states, physiological conditions, and so forth). Given the numerous influences on behavior, how can we assess both these external and internal factors? There are many tools available to help in the assessment. Some tools focus primarily on the external factors, others on the internal factors, and a third group addresses both. We discuss several tools that we find particularly useful in gathering information about the individual and the target behaviors.

For assessing external factors, the literature is replete with articles that detail a broad technology that has been developed to determine the function(s) of target behaviors such as self-injury (Iwata *et al.*, 1994). Understanding the function a behavior serves is essential to developing effective treatments. (A full review of the literature is beyond the scope of this chapter and is available from multiple sources [Betz and Fisher, 2011; Campbell, 2003; Hanley *et al.*, 2014]. Our focus is on a direct observation method of functional assessment, as well as rating scales and surveys that glean information about factors that influence behavior.) Horner and colleagues (2002) state: "Functional assessment increases the likelihood of intervention success. The use of functional assessment procedures is the strongest covariate with intervention success. The more precise the assessment, the more likely the intervention will result in intervention success" (p.429). The critical step is to ensure that the information gleaned from the assessments is used in the planning of the interventions.

Assessing internal factors with any accuracy in individuals with ASD and limited cognitive functioning may be challenging, yet those who spend significant amounts of time with them may be able to provide relevant insight. Typically this type of information is collected through interviews with caretakers, examination of behavioral trends or patterns, use of technology and sophisticated equipment (e.g., heart-rate monitors, skin sensors, and other medical testing devices), and/or via surveys designed to rate behavioral markers of cognitive or emotional states or trends (e.g., Brief Psychiatric Rating Scale [Overall and Gorham, 1962]; Repetitive Behavior Scale [Lam and Aman, 2007]; the Stress Survey Schedule for Individuals with Autism and Other Pervasive Developmental Disabilities [Groden *et al.*, 2001a]). All of these avenues may provide important information that taken together can provide insight into a person's internal state.

Direct Observation

The method of direct observation widely used at The Groden Center is one that was developed by Dr. Gerald Groden and is called detailed behavior analysis. It is a type of descriptive functional analysis that utilizes the Detailed Behavior Report (DBR), the Detailed Behavior Report Summary (DBRS), and the Detailed Behavior Analysis and Intervention Recommendations (DBAIR). A full description of the procedure can be found in *Understanding Challenging Behavior* (Groden, Stevenson, and Groden, 1996).

The DBR form is shown in Figure 13.1 and depicts the information recorded each time a target behavior occurs. DBRs are completed by parents, teachers, staff, or other caregivers who observe the behavior. The form begins with a detailed description of the behavior, a rating of its severity, and its duration.

> Original: GC Client's File
> Copy: Unit/Residence
> Saturday Program
> If restraint is used, attach Addendum and also copy for:
> Quality Assurance, GC Director of Office Administration
> If there is injury, attach Accident/Health Incident report

The Groden Center, Inc
Detailed Behaviour Report (DBR)

STUDENT/CLIENT: Jane B.		STAFF: C.L.	
CLASSROOM/PROGRAM 1C		HOW RECORDED: (Continuous)/Sample:	DATE & TIME **DBR COMPLETED** 3/10/2008

BEHAVIOR

TARGET BEHAVIOR (describe in detail)	SIB – Bit her arm with force; broke skin lightly	
SEVERITY RATING	(5)(severe) 4 3 2 1 (mild)	DURATION 8 Seconds
PRECURSORS (body state, thoughts, emotions, verbalizations)	Loud vocals, tense facial expression	

ANTECEDENTS

General

SCHEDULE	DATE: 3/10	DAY OF WEEK: Monday	TIME OF DAY: 1:20pm
LOCATION	Classroom		

ACTIVITY (be specific; include transition or waiting as an activity type)

TYPE: Leisure; on preferred game on computer

LENGTH ENGAGED: 8 m.   Beginning / Middle /(End)   MASTERED: Yes /(No)

MOVEMENT: High /(Low)   CLIENT CHOICE: Yes /(No)   RELEVANCY TO CLIENT: High /(Low)

Specific

PERSONAL / SOCIAL / PHYSICAL

(Sequence of who was doing and/or saying what to whom)

STAFF INVOLVED: C.L., B.P., F.N.

OTHER CLIENTS INVOLVED: None

TONE OF INTERACTION: Calm

ENVIRONMENTAL CHARACTERISTICS: Room generally quiet, minimal distractions.

Jane was enjoying leisure game on the computer and it was time for work. Staff told her that computer would be done in 1 minute, and after 1 minute, said "Time to do some work".

SETTING EVENTS	Stomach pain earlier in the day.

CONSEQUENCES

Describe sequence of events that followed behavior's occurrence. Include what staff did and what client did.

Blocked further attempt to bite arm. Prompted a deep breath and relaxation. Re-introduced the demand and showed her what we would be doing and what she could earn.

PERCEIVED FUNCTION(S) OF BEHAVIOR *To be completed by Clinical Team*	*Circle the most likely reason for, or function of the target behavior. In the Notes area, describe details.* Medical/physical Attention/social Tangibles (Escape/avoidance) Sensory *Notes:*

Behavioral Programming   Copyright © 1994 The Groden Center, Inc.   12/2009

Figure 13.1 Sample of a Completed Detailed Behavior Report (DBR)

Next, any precursor behaviors that preceded the target behavior are recorded. For example, prior to biting his own arm, perhaps the person vocalized or had a tense facial expression. This information is essential in developing markers when staff might intervene to help the person reduce stress levels, prior to the target behavior. The DBR also includes a description of the general and specific antecedents or stressors, the setting in which the behavior occurred, the time, location, and the individuals involved. At The Groden Center, all staff are trained to pay particular attention to this section, as it offers important information as to the function of the behavior. Finally, a section on the consequences of the target behavior is completed. This includes a section in which the recorder is asked to hypothesize the possible functions the behavior may be serving—for example, whether its occurrence enables the individual to escape or avoid something, acquire something tangible, gain social attention, or perhaps provide some intrinsic or automatic reinforcement.

After completing DBRs on a number of occurrences of the target behavior, the data are transferred to the Detailed Behavior Report Summary (DBRS). The DBRS, shown in Figure 13.2, condenses the information obtained from multiple events onto a single sheet to facilitate the analysis of the behavior. On the form, the clinician sees what time(s) of day the behavior occurred most often, under what conditions it happened, the topography of the behavior, the consequences of the behavior, and the recorder's impressions of the function(s) of the behavior for each incident. This enables the clinician analyzing the data to identify trends and begin to develop hypotheses and interventions. This information is transcribed onto the Detailed Behavior Analysis and Intervention Recommendations (DBAIR) (see Figure 13.3) and interventions are formulated.

The reader will notice that the final form begins with the basic hypothesized function and then leads the clinical team through a thinking process. Keeping function in mind, specific antecedent and contextual information is reviewed, and proactive or preventative strategies are proposed by the team. These can be as simple as environmental alterations, or include more complex strategies such as cognitive-picture-rehearsal scenes (which are discussed later in this chapter), but the focus is on individualized, tailored, and creative interventions that support appropriate behavior. The next consideration of the clinical team is in creating interventions that teach functionally equivalent replacement behaviors, and finally, creation of reactive strategies that are designed to manage the behavior when it occurs.

Groden, Cove, & Halcyon Centers, Inc.

Detailed Behavior Report Summary (DBRS)

Client	Jane B.	Target Behavior	SIB	# DBRs	10
Unit/Residence	1C	Period Covered: from	3/5/08	to	3/21/08

Purpose: This form is used to organize and summarize DBR information.
1. Number the DBRs in chronological order for the targeted behavior.
2. Write the specified behavior descriptor, antecedent, and consequence in the left columns under each category.
3. In the right columns, record the number of the DBR next to the corresponding behavior descriptor, antecedent, and consequence.

SEVERITY RATING		DURATION		ACTIVITY	LOCATION
1.					
2.		<15 sec.	1,2,3,4,5,10		
3.	3,7	15 sec ->min	6,7,8,9	Computer 7,8,9	
4.	4,5,10				Classroom 1-3,6-10
5.	1,2,6,8,9			Group game 1,2	

DAY OF WEEK		TIME: *List in hour blocks.*			Gym 4,5
Monday	1,2,7,8			Lunch 3,6,10	
Tuesday	3,4,5,6	9-10	4,5		
Wednesday		10-11	1,2	In gym/bowling 4,5	
Thursday		11-12	3,6,10		
Friday	9,10	12-1	7,8,9		
Saturday		1-2	---		
Sunday					

STAFF	CLIENTS	SETTING EVENTS	
CL	None 7,8,9	Stomach pain	7
BP	NN, PL, FC 1,2,3,6		
FN	10	Bus late	3,6
	4 & 5		
SPECIFIC ANTECEDENTS		Missed meds	7
Directed to transition	1,2,4,5	PRECURSORS	
Directed to work	7,8,9,3,6,10	Loud vocals	7,8,2
		Tense face	7,8,2
		Stomp feet	2,6,4

SPECIFIC CONSEQUENCES		POSSIBLE FUNCTION(S) OF BEHAVIOR
		Medical/Physical: (7 ?)
Blocked		**Attention:**
		Tangible:
Prompted relaxation	All	**Escape/avoidance:** 1,2,3,4,5,6,7,8,9,10
		Sensory:
Re-introduced request		**Notes:**
		Upcoming classroom change

OTHER HYPOTHESES/JOINT STIMULI:
Visiting classroom she will be moving to.

Figure 13.2 Sample of a Completed Detailed Behavior Report Summary (DBRS)

The Groden Center, Inc.

Detailed Behavior Analysis and Intervention Recommendations (DBAIR)

Client	Jane B.	Behavior	SIB	# DBRs 10
Unit/Residence 1C		Period Covered: from 3/5/08		to 3/21/08

Instructions: Complete the form from information identified on the DBRS.
1. List in order of frequency the precursors, antecedents, setting events, and consequences that occurred most often (at least 20% of time).
2. Indicate the number of times the antecedent/consequence occurred.
3. Indicate the possible effects and reasons for the effects on the client.
4. Recommend possible intervention strategies that correspond to the characteristics of the stimuli, precursors, and skill deficits.

ANTECEDENT(S)	#	REASONS BEHAVIOR FOLLOWS	INTERVENTIONS(S)
Directed to transition Directed to work	1,2,4,5 7,8,9,3,6,10	Attempted to remain on preferred task and avoid requested task.	- Give 2 minute warning - Prompt relaxation prior to making request - Cognitive Picture Rehearsal for these situations
SETTING EVENT(S)		REASONS BEHAVIOR FOLLOWS	INTERVENTION(S)
Stomach pain Late bus Missed meds	7 3,6 7	- Discomfort - Alteration of schedule/stress - Alters mood (presumably)	- Check for discomfort - Contact bus company - Remind of importance—parent
ANTECEDENTS FOR POSITIVE BEHAVIOR		POSSIBLE REASONS	INTERVENTION(S)
Jane transitioned calmly from gym for tangible in room	n/a	Tangible strong enough reinforcer	Use tangibles to reinforce calm transitioning
PRECURSOR(S)		POSSIBLE PREDICTOR?	INTERVENTION(S)
Loud vocals Tense face Stomp feet	7,8,2 7,8,2 2,6,4	(Yes)	- Prompt relaxation at precursor level - Remind of learning
PROGRAM (P) & NON-PROGRAM (NP) CONSEQUENCES Blocked Prompted relaxation Re-introduced request	All	REINFORCING QUALITIES? No Perhaps—delay? No	INTERVENTION(S) Prompt deep breath only; not entire relaxation sequence
FUNCTION(S)		SKILL DEFICIT(S)?	INTERVENTION(S)
Escape/Avoidance	All	Yes → How to appropriately request a delay?	Train use of "delay card" for 1 time/1 minute delay of requests when used

Behavioral Programming   Copyright © 1994 The Groden Center, Inc.   9/2003

Figure 13.3 Sample of a Completed Detailed Behavior Analysis and Intervention Recommendations Form (DBAIR)

Rating Scales and Interviews

In addition to the descriptive analysis of the DBR, there are numerous surveys and scales that assess various aspects of external factors related to function. For example, the Motivation Assessment Scale (MAS) (Durand and Crimmins, 1992) is a widely used survey tool that asks respondents to rate the accuracy and applicability of various situational contexts or stressors related to problem behavior. These responses are then scored, and this information can augment the descriptive approach of the DBR analysis. Typically, tools such as the MAS are completed by a number of persons familiar with the individual; hypotheses as to the function of the behavior are better identified with input from a variety of sources. Another form of functional assessment in survey format is the Functional Assessment Interview (FAI) (O'Neill *et al.*, 1997). In contrast to the ratings of the MAS, the FAI asks informants familiar with the individual a variety of open-ended questions related to settings, contexts, antecedents, stressors, and consequences surrounding the behavior of interest. Taken as a group, a descriptive functional analysis (such as the DBR analysis) along with a variety of survey tools that tap into function of behavior (such as the MAS and FAI) can be combined to provide guidance as to the actual purpose of behavior. At The Groden Center, we have found that while staff often feel that they can identify the function without these tools, they are often surprised to compare their impressions to those derived from the collection of actual data!

The Stress Survey Schedule for Individuals with Autism and Other Pervasive Developmental Disabilities

One tool that is particularly relevant to this discussion is the Stress Survey Schedule for Individuals with Autism and Other Pervasive Developmental Disabilities (SSS) (Groden *et al.*, 2001a). Cohen and colleagues state, "Curiously, the known characteristics of ASD that would increase the likelihood of challenging behaviors are not part of many functional analysis assessments" (Cohen *et al.*, 2011, p.248). The SSS does address this issue. The purpose of the SSS is to provide educators, therapists, and parents with a tool to increase awareness of environmental stressors that affect the lives of persons with autism. Such a tool can be used to create programming aimed at modifying stress reactions in the population of persons with autism and in similar populations, thereby enhancing the quality of their lives and their overall physical and emotional well-being. It asks people familiar with the individual to rate the relevance of various potential stressors. If the individual is capable, he can complete the survey independently. A portion of the SSS is shown in Figure 13.4. It identifies situations that cause stress responses, from which treatment procedures can be developed to address these stressors.

The Groden Center, Inc.

The Stress Survey Schedule for Persons with Autism and Developmental Disabilities (p. 2)

Please rate the intensity of the stress reaction to the following events by filling in the appropriate circle:

	None to mild	Mild to Moderate	Moderate	Moderate to severe	Severe
24. Receiving a reprimand	1	2	3	4	5
25. Transitioning from preferred to non-preferred activity	1	2	3	4	5
26. Being told "no"	1	2	3	4	5
27. Receiving criticism	1	2	3	4	5
28. Having something marked incorrect	1	2	3	4	5
29. Being interrupted while engaging in a ritual	1	2	3	4	5
30. Receiving hugs and affection	1	2	3	4	5
31. Having to engage in not-liked activity	1	2	3	4	5
32. Waiting in line	1	2	3	4	5
33. Being unable to communicate needs	1	2	3	4	5
34. Waiting at a restaurant	1	2	3	4	5
35. Going home (from school, to visit parents)	1	2	3	4	5
36. Waiting for transportation	1	2	3	4	5
37. Being unable to assert oneself with others	1	2	3	4	5
38. Needing to ask for help	1	2	3	4	5
39. Participating in group activity	1	2	3	4	5
40. Having a change in staff, teacher, or supervisor	1	2	3	4	5
41. Losing at a game	1	2	3	4	5
42. Waiting for reinforcement	1	2	3	4	5
43. Feeling crowded	1	2	3	4	5
44. Someone else making a mistake	1	2	3	4	5
45. Receiving tangible reinforcement	1	2	3	4	5
46. Waiting for food	1	2	3	4	5
47. Waiting for routine to begin	1	2	3	4	5
48. Having a conversation	1	2	3	4	5
49. Receiving verbal reinforcement	1	2	3	4	5

Figure 13.4 Page 2 of the Stress Survey Schedule for Persons with Autism and Other Developmental Disabilities

Groden *et al.* (2001b) conducted a factor analysis of the SSS and identified eight stress components: changes, anticipation/uncertainty, social/environmental interactions, pleasant events, sensory stimuli, unpleasant events, food-related stress, and rituals. These stress dimensions are related to the problems of SIB. An analysis was conducted at The Groden Center using 180 completed stress surveys. The items most frequently rated as moderate to severe or severe included (1) receiving a reprimand, (2) being told "no," (3) being in the vicinity of noises or disruption by others, (4) transitioning from a preferred to a non-preferred activity, and (5) having to engage in a non-preferred activity (Goodwin *et al.*, 2007). These items are also prevalent in the DBR functional analysis when assessing SIB.

Utilizing the SSS, we can (a) use it as part of the assessment in order to create treatment, (b) have teachers, parents, and staff become aware of stressors in the environment, (c) identify stressors such that programs can be instituted before the stressors that lead to self-injury occur, and (d) do further research in the area of stress.

Using Technology in Assessment

Various forms of technology-based assessments have been used with persons with autism and other developmental disabilities, including computer-aided instruction, touch screens, voice-output devices, virtual reality, video-based instruction, and others. However, we focus on two areas specifically related to the role of stress and self-injury. First, advances in technology, such as heart-rate recording or electrodermal responses, have allowed us to access information on physiological states that simple observation or paper and pencil tools could not. This is significant because persons with autism may not demonstrate the external indicators of stress that a typically developing person might (e.g., nervousness, a wide-eyed look, flushing, crying, or trembling), thus limiting behavioral markers or precursors. The physiological information can alert us to when the individual is in an aroused state as the result of experiencing stressors in the environment, giving staff an indicator of the opportunity for preventative intervention such as relaxation. Advances have also given rise to improved ways to record self-injury, a problem behavior that is often challenging to accurately track and represent. Because these non-intrusive sensors enable us to record specific movement, a clear parameter for when the behavior took place is created.

HEART RATE

The autonomic nervous system (ANS) is one way to measure the impact of stress. In the presence of a stressor, physiological systems necessary for mobilizing a response are activated, initiating widespread changes in the cardiovascular system, the immune system, the endocrine glands, and brain regions involved in emotion and memory (Sapolsky, 1998). Heart rate provides a robust measure of arousal and is the most commonly used ANS measure of stress. Skin conductance also has been used effectively for this purpose. A study by Groden *et al.* (2005) explored the feasibility of measuring cardiovascular responses to environmental stressors in persons with autism and other developmental disabilities. The study found that participants tolerated the heart monitor well and complied with task instructions. The protocol was found to be useful for examining stressors.

Using the same protocol, Goodwin *et al.* (2006) used heart rate as a measure of sympathetic nervous system activity to compare arousal responses to the presentation of potentially stressful situations in five persons with autism and five matched, typically developing individuals. Findings showed that the group with autism showed significant heart-rate responses to stressors only 22% of the time, and the typically developing group showed significant responses 60% of the time. It was hypothesized that the diminished cardiovascular reactivity to potential stressors in the group with autism may be related to their high basal heart rate. An important finding revealed that the participants with autism showed mean heart-rate responses approximately 20 beats per minute higher during baseline and also during nearly every potentially stressful situation. It could be interpreted that some individuals with autism are in a general state of high autonomic arousal.

Heart rate is a non-invasive physiological measure that can provide information about stress levels and arousal for individuals with ASD. It is particularly helpful for those with low verbal and cognitive abilities who are unable to complete self-report measures about their stress. Heart-rate assessment can be an important measure for persons exhibiting SIB. If an individual can show increased arousal levels before a self-injurious event, preventative procedures can be put in place to extinguish the self-injury. At the present time, there are many corporations and institutions that are developing wearable technology to indicate heart rate that is observable and can be used in home, school, and community environments. This would be an important step forward to facilitate the inclusion of a heart-rate measure to the study, assessment, and treatment of SIB.

AUTOMATED ASSESSMENT OF SIB

Accurate assessment of SIB is essential to good treatment, but it can be challenging given a number of factors. First, the behavior may not be continuously displayed, meaning that there may be long periods when it is not exhibited. This means that staff charged with collecting frequency data may spend long periods of time waiting to observe the behavior. It is easy for staff to become distracted by other responsibilities, and when the behavior is displayed, it may take place very quickly, making accurate data collection difficult. Adding another observer may increase accuracy, but this doubles staffing requirements. Second, SIB often has various levels of severity, and staff may have a difficult time agreeing as to whether or not the behavior even took place. This situation can be improved with complete and accurate operational definitions, but even with the best definition the observer may find himself asking, "Do we count that?" In the example of hand hitting, this behavior can be a light tap that is not very concerning, slightly harder hitting of a surface, or it can be so severe that bones in the hand can be broken. Adding levels of behavioral definitions or a severity scale to the behavioral presentation can clarify what behavior is being demonstrated, but it also can further complicate the accurate collection of frequency data.

One recent use of technology addresses these problems through the automatic assessment of SIB. Plotz *et al.* (2012) used sensors worn on the body to more accurately assess movement related to a number of problem behaviors, including aggression, disruption, and SIB. These researchers used devices called "data loggers," which continuously recorded tri-axial acceleration signals that indicated movement. The data loggers were attached to the wrist or ankle by sensor straps. Using computational assessment, the researchers were able to categorize the three behaviors of interest effectively, and collect accurate frequency data.

The study by Albinali, Goodwin, and Intille (2012) shows another example of automated assessment of behavior. They used wireless accelerometers placed on both wrists and the chest to detect a range of stereotypical motor movements. Although stereotypical behavior is not necessarily injurious, SIB is clearly related to this domain. Recognition accuracy (i.e., the accuracy of the equipment for recording the target behavior) was found to be 88.6%. More recently, Goodwin *et al.* (2014) compared recognition results for two different automated recognition systems and concluded that adaptive algorithms were needed to accurately measure stereotypical motor movements using this type of technology. As this technology moves forward, the advantages of these new types of assessment are clear. Not only are fewer staff needed to observe and assess the behavior, the accuracy of data is as good as human observers, and there is no question as to whether or not the behavior took place.

Intervention

Before beginning interventions and as part of assessment, a thorough medical and dental evaluation is necessary to rule out any physiological components to the SIB. The purpose of conducting a comprehensive assessment is to gather information about a problem behavior in order to devise an effective and appropriate intervention. Developing an intervention must take into account all the information gleaned from the assessment process concerning why a problem behavior occurs and what the conditions are that maintain it. This can lead to an intervention package that approaches the problem from all angles, and includes strategies for both long-term and short-term gains. These gains include the:

- identification of antecedents and environmental conditions that can be altered to prevent or minimize the chances of the behavior occurring

- development of reactive strategies to manage the behavior safely when it occurs

- establishment of consequences that promote desired alternative behaviors for the individual and reduce the likelihood that the target behavior will occur

- creation of skill development programs needed to address any deficits identified during the assessment that contribute to the occurrence of the target behavior (typically in the areas of communication and socialization)

- development of self-control strategies to help the individual manage identified stressors.

Coping with Stress

It is not the amount or kind of stress that has the most impact; it is how we deal with stress that is the important factor. Coping strategies play a critical role in well-being when someone is faced with challenges, negative events, and stress (Westman, 2004). Lazarus (1993) defines coping as an individual's efforts to change thinking or overt behavior to manage stress. Coping is also by definition how a person responds to stressful situations, and coping changes in accordance with the situational context. Although in the past coping was seen mainly as a reactive strategy to be used once stress had been experienced, more recently it has come to be seen as a proactive strategy that one can apply before stress occurs (Hobfoil, 2001). Aspinwall and Taylor (1997) viewed proactive coping as one of the missing links in stress and coping research, maintaining that the processes through which people anticipate potential stressors and act in advance to prevent them can be seen as proactive behavior. Thus, to the extent that individuals reduce or modify impending stressful events, proactive behavior can eliminate a great deal of stress before it occurs.

Strategies to Reduce Stress

Lennart Levi of the World Health Organization presented a useful depiction of stress responses at the International Conference on Stress Management (Levi, 1995). As illustrated in Figure 13.5, he considered three important variables: demand, control, and support.

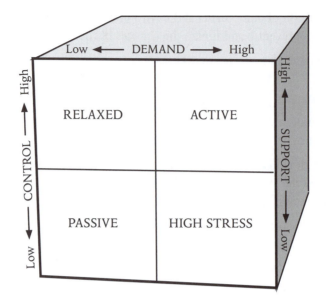

Figure 13.5 Demand–Control–Support Model (Adapted from Levi, 1995)

As depicted, most stress occurs in the conditions of high demand, low support, and low control. Conversely, low demand, high support, and high control produce a relaxation condition or low-stress condition. "Demand" is any force, pressure, or strain placed on the individual. "Support" refers to significant others, including family members, friends, and teachers who help buffer the adverse mental and physical effects of stress-inducing situations. "Control" is the capacity to make active responses during stressful situations and is closely associated with a sense of mastery over the environment. The key is to identify ways to foster low demand, provide high support, and teach high control in the lives of people with SIB. Below are some of the strategies to foster these variables.

PRODUCING LOW DEMAND
Producing low demand comprises the following:

- **Informed choice-making.**
  Giving the person with autism the opportunity to make choices at the appropriate developmental level. The intrinsic reinforcement of obtaining the choice one has made can lead to personal satisfaction and a sense of well-being that may reduce the occasion for stress.

- **Visual supports.**
  Current best practices abound with examples of individualized visual supports, such as schedules, calendars, reinforcement boards, and rule cards. Gestures and body language are often visual supports, as are furniture

arrangements, object placement, and the common everyday signs and symbols we all use (Hogdon, 1995).

- **Establishing routines.**
  A person with autism feels more comfortable when they have knowledge of what is expected of them. Since communication is such a large deficit in the population with autism, they often find it hard to follow instructions and change tasks. Procedures that can establish acceptable routines are helpful in these situations.

- **Schedules.**
  Schedules are a specific type of visual support and can be in picture form, written on paper, or on tablets, smart phones, and so forth. When an individual participates in developing their own schedule, it allows a feeling of control, which helps to reduce stress. The advantage of a schedule is that it allows the person to visually see what happens in time and space. They can then predict what happens next, reducing the stress of not knowing what to expect.

- **Errorless learning.**
  This procedure has an emphasis on positive reinforcement for each response, because each response is preceded by the necessary prompts to make it the correct response. The high level of positive reinforcement provided by errorless teaching contributes to self-confidence and feelings of pride, which are effective buffers in coping with stress.

- **Skill-building at developmental levels.**
  The more abilities a person has, the more they are able to make choices and choose alternatives.

PROVIDING HIGH SUPPORT

High support can come from many places. Supportive families, school personnel, peers, work situations, and a safe environment all can contribute to dealing with stress effectively for persons with SIB. The negative physical and psychological effects of stress can be greatly reduced by having supportive relationships. Procedures to build high support include non-contingently increasing the general level of reinforcement, building support networks, joining social groups, and having multiple experiences with success. An important concept is to build "islands of competence" by nurturing and building special interests and capabilities that can be appreciated by others. For example, at The Groden Center we developed a photography program in which many of the students excelled; they were highly reinforced by having photography shows, selling their pictures, and receiving praise from many people in the community.

TEACHING HIGH CONTROL

A number of studies show that a sense of control reduces psychological problems and physical illness and buffers the negative effects of stressors (Turner and Roszell, 1994). Below are examples of procedures that help promote high control. Special emphasis is placed on the procedures of relaxation and cognitive picture rehearsal. Specific examples of how to develop and use these procedures are discussed.

Changing Attributions

"Attribution is the explanation of causes of behavior that can affect an individual's coping style and programmatic decision-making. Attribution can be viewed from the perspective of both the individual with autism and the caregivers" (Groden *et al.*, 2006, p.27). There is a good deal of evidence in favor of the general proposition that an individual's attribution style influences how he responds to life events (Rutter, 1983). If people feel they can control their fate and make positive attributions, they are more likely to use self-control, self-reinforcement, positive imagery, positive assertions, and other practices, leading to a better future (Groden *et al.*, 2006). Evidence clearly suggests that antecedent reappraisals for both internal and external threat and danger before the fact has a salutary effect on the later expression of negative emotion (Barlow, Allen and, Choate, 2004); therefore, it is important to identify stressors and change attributions before the event occurs.

Positive Assertions

Positive assertions are statements describing a person's strengths and abilities. At The Groden Center, with input from teachers, parents, and the children and adults themselves, we develop a list of strengths from which a number of positive assertion statements are developed. Clients practice reading their assertions every day. If they are non-verbal or non-readers, the teacher or staff member reads the list for each child. Positive assertions are sometimes shown in picture form. Statements such as "I share with my friends," "I am good at basketball," or "I help my mother" are individualized. The purpose of practicing positive assertions daily is to increase self-esteem. People high in self-esteem are more likely to use active, problem-focused coping responses related to the demand itself. People low in self-esteem are likely to use more passive, avoidant, emotion-focused coping (Thoits, 1995). In designing interventions for persons with SIB, it is important to focus on positive changes and skill-building, not only the deceleration of the self-injury.

Relaxation and Cognitive Picture Rehearsal

As part of the high control strategies, we focus on two key procedures to reduce stress: relaxation and cognitive picture rehearsal (CPR). The two have common characteristics in that they incorporate self-control procedures and are easily combined with many other interventions. They are pervasive procedures in that they can be used before a SIB occurs, during the episode, and following the behavior. Both can function as adaptive behaviors that are incompatible with challenging behaviors, including self-injury (Baron, Groden, and Cautela, 1988). These procedures can be used in any setting, including school, home, or workplace, whenever a stressful situation occurs. They are positive, preventative strategies in which the learner actively reduces stress by engaging in a familiar routine that, through practice, becomes inherently reinforcing. Special emphasis is given to the role and value of self-control to reduce the stress in the lives of individuals with autism and to increase the use of proactive and adaptive coping techniques.

RELAXATION

Cautela and Groden's book, *Relaxation: A Comprehensive Manual for Adults, Children, and Children with Special Needs* (1978), is a guide for caregivers, teachers, clinicians, and parents, and is an adaptation of Jacobson's (1938) progressive relaxation procedures to fit the needs of persons with autism and other developmental disabilities. Relaxation enables the individual to remain in control in stressful situations and is incompatible with most maladaptive behaviors. This procedure also can become part of a daily routine and help decrease general stress and anxiety.

Prior to beginning the program, a readiness assessment is completed to determine if the individual should follow the basic or advanced relaxation protocol. The results indicate the appropriate step at which to begin the program. Initially, relaxation involves discrimination training, that is, learning the difference between what the muscles feel like when they are tense and when they are relaxed. In identifying the feeling of tight and relaxed muscles, the learner can begin to focus on the nature of a relaxed muscle and eventually use this knowledge to recognize for themselves when they are tense; they can then learn to relax those muscle areas (see Figure 13.6). More time should be spent on the relaxing aspect of the program than the tension. When the learner can successfully discriminate between tight and relaxed muscles, tightening the muscles is put on a maintenance schedule (about once a week), and only the relaxation part of the procedure along with deep breathing is practiced. It is important for generalization that the concept of "relax" be fully understood. Relaxation is first taught in a sitting position, then standing, and then walking in different environments. This enables the individual to generalize the procedure to a range of settings and in different positions. It is the feeling of relaxed muscles and deep breathing that contribute to the effectiveness of the program.

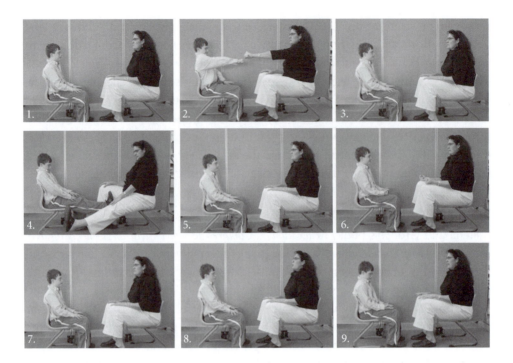

Figure 13.6 Student Learning the Relaxation Procedure
(From Groden *et al.*, 2011, p.249)

For persons with autism and other developmental disabilities, simply learning to perform self-control responses to reduce stress is not enough. For effective coping, learning to *use* self-control responses in various life contexts is necessary (Lazarus, 1993). After mastering the relaxation response, the individual is taught to identify situations in which stress occurs, and then to use relaxation to reduce stress. It is preferable to identify stressors *before* they occur and to prompt the relaxation at that time. This often leads to prevention of the SIB. In order to accomplish this, it is suggested that the learner first practice the relaxation procedure for special needs. After they understand the relaxation response, they are taught to recognize situations in which stress occurs. This information is gleaned from the many assessments described above.

At first the therapist or caregiver prompts the individual to relax when they anticipate that an anxiety-provoking situation or a stressor is about to occur. For example, if the person finds it difficult to make a transition from one activity to another, the teacher might say, "We are now finishing math—math is all done." She would then have the student check his schedule to show completion of the math activity and to see what is next; in this case, gym class. She would then say, "It is time for gym." She would have the student take a deep breath, relax his hands (or whatever part of his body is involved in the self-injury), keep his arms relaxed at his side, and walk in a relaxed manner toward the gym. He would then receive reinforcement (e.g., check on his contract, verbal praise, small edible, pat on his back, and so forth). Building in appropriate reinforcement for relaxation is essential to ensure that the skill is retained and will become a part of the individual's repertoire. Which reinforcers to use and the schedule of reinforcement needed depends on the individual.

Our ultimate goal in teaching relaxation is to shape the individual to use it independently as a means of self-control. We begin shaping independence by gradually fading out the teacher or therapist's prompts. Depending on the individual's age, cognitive ability, and developmental level, the next step might be having the teacher say, "We are now going to gym—what do you do?" The student would be expected to say, "I will relax my hands, take a deep breath, and walk toward the gym in a relaxed manner." If the student is non-verbal, he would demonstrate the response. When the student has mastered this phase, the goal will shift again to require increased independence. This might involve the teacher announcing it is time for gym, then pausing and waiting for the student to say on his own, "I will take a deep breath, relax my hands, and walk toward the gym in a relaxed manner." A relaxed manner is taught to mean that there is no pushing, hitting others, banging the walls, engaging in self-injury, and so forth. It functions as an all-inclusive method and is an alternative to a number of inappropriate behaviors.

Although relaxation procedures, such as meditation, yoga, and progressive relaxation, are taught in a number of clinics, schools, and institutions, it is rare to see them taught as self-control procedures. We feel that this is an important step in getting the full benefits of the program. While it is helpful to learn to relax and to do it daily, adding the self-control feature serves to greatly improve the quality of life for those who use it. It also can complement other procedures that reduce self-injury to ensure the continuation of the success of the program. If, for example, an individual learns to use assertive responses and communicates his needs rather than use self-injury, he can use the relaxation response first by taking a deep breath, relaxing his body, and then stating his needs in a positive manner.

In summary, the individual first learns the relaxation procedure, stressors are then identified, and the relaxation procedures are incorporated into the individual education plan, or a general service plan, and included in schedules or daily routines at home. Initially, the teacher, parent, or caregiver cues the relaxation response *before* stressful situations. Following accomplishment of this step, the person should be able to self-cue the relaxation response when needed. In our experience, there are some who do not reach this self-cueing goal, but all have been able to learn the relaxation response and respond to cues when prompted. The focus is on helping the individual to identify both the bodily signs of stress and the situations that elicit stress.

COGNITIVE PICTURE REHEARSAL

The major assumption that underlies cognitive picture rehearsal (CPR) is that people with autism, regardless of their cognitive functioning, are capable of imagery and can be taught to use it as a tool for coping with stressful events. When an individual is imagining, they are responding to the absence of an external stimulus as if the stimulus were present. For example:

- When asked to imagine a frustrating situation (not being able to do an assignment), she feels anger similar to the anger that would be felt if the situation occurred externally.

- If asked to imagine swimming, he can experience similar exhilaration and muscular sensations as if he were swimming.

- When asked to imagine approaching a feared object, she has psychological arousal similar to the physiological arousal that would occur if actually approaching the feared stimulus.

The CPR programs we will be discussing were originally based on the imagery work of Cautela and Kearney (1993). During our early years of using this procedure, we found that many of the children and adults with autism, because of their excellent rote memory and good visual imagery, did very well with this procedure. However, as we expanded the program to more persons with deficits in cognitive functioning, we found that they needed the visual support of pictures to help with the imagery; we now primarily use CPR.

CPR is an instructional strategy that uses repeated practice of a sequence of behaviors by presenting the sequence to the person in the form of pictures and an accompanying script. Although it is widely recognized that those with autism have strengths in the area of visualization, there is very little literature to show its use in therapeutic endeavors with this population. CPR incorporates established psychological procedures to increase appropriate behavior or decrease maladaptive behavior (Groden *et al.*, 2009). The sequence of pictures for a CPR scene is based on an individual client's requirements, and may be presented as line drawings, Boardmaker™ pictures, or photographs. They may or may not be accompanied by words. They may be presented flashcard style; laid out on a table left to right, like a reading program; presented in story book form; or made portable and carried in a credit card folder, or on a computer, tablet, or smart phone. Therapists may be creative in the construction of these pictures. Some have made them three dimensional, using Velcro stick-on pictures; others have cut pictures from magazines. The visual display of these scenes appears to be most helpful to those clients who learn better by looking at material than by using only their auditory pathway, are unable or have difficulty in attending to an internal scene presentation, or are unable to provide verbal feedback to the clinician about their level of involvement.

Designing a Cognitive Picture Rehearsal Program

Below are the main components involved in creating a CPR sequence, based on the information gained from the multimodal assessments.

COMPONENT 1: PRIORITIZE THE IDENTIFIED STRESSORS

It is not possible to implement treatment for all the stressors identified in the assessment process at the same time. The following factors are important to consider when prioritizing the stress responses to address first:

- Intensity of the stress reaction: if the response to the stressor evokes a severe self-injurious episode, it should get a high priority.

- Interference with daily life: if the stressor occurs frequently and interferes with adaptive living (i.e., making transitions), it should be given a priority even if the intensity is not high.

In using this procedure, daily practice with at least two repetitions is important. It is therefore not realistic to present too many picture rehearsal programs, and this entails careful prioritization.

COMPONENT 2: IDENTIFY THE BEHAVIOR ASSOCIATED WITH THE STRESSOR

An important part of developing a CPR scene is pinpointing the specific form the target behavior takes in the presence of the particular stressors. That way, appropriate alternative behaviors can be described and included in the CPR scene. When describing the behavior, it is vital that it be defined operationally to ensure that it can be measured accurately, and that reliable data are obtained.

COMPONENT 3: WRITING AND SEQUENCING THE SCRIPT

This is a critical component of the intervention. CPR for persons with special needs was developed in 1978 by Groden and Cautela. Years later, other programs using scripts and stories were developed. Many of those scripts are behavioral rehearsals in that they describe the steps needed but are not based on psychological principles. Script-based procedures can be powerful when the scripts are based on effective practices. The four procedures that we find most helpful in dealing with SIB are positive reinforcement for alternative behavior, cognitive restructuring, positive psychology principles, and relaxation (defined and discussed earlier). Positive reinforcement is when the behavior to be increased is followed by a consequence or event that results in an increase in the probability of that behavior. Cognitive restructuring is "the process of replacing maladaptive thought patterns with constructive thoughts and beliefs. Any behavior therapy that results in notable shifts in an individual's perception and thought processes" (The Free Dictionary,

2003–2015). "Positive psychology is an umbrella term for the study of positive emotions, positive character traits, and enabling institutions" (Seligman *et al.*, 2005, p.410). We have primarily incorporated the traits of resilience, optimism, humor, kindness, and self-efficacy into the scripts that we use (Groden *et al.*, 2011).

The pictures and script in a CPR scene are sequenced carefully. The first pictures show an antecedent event, situation, and/or environment. The next series of pictures describe the desired behavior that replaces the behavior targeted for change, and the last pictures end with a reinforcing event. The subject of these pictures is personalized and based on information obtained from the multiple assessments described earlier.

The CPR scene shown in Figure 13.7 was developed for an individual with ASD for whom going to birthday parties was found to be a stressor. Through the assessment process, it was learned that birthday cake was a reinforcer, even though attending parties was very challenging for him; he exhibited head hitting both when he arrived at a party and during the event. A CPR scene was devised that incorporated an appropriate alternative behavior to head hitting (keeping his hands relaxed and by his sides), cognitive restructuring (thinking about the fun things that will happen at the party, imagining having a good time and feeling happy), and reinforcing events (eating birthday cake, seeing balloons). Negative thoughts such as "I hit my head" are not included in the script since that would give practice in imagining and thinking about an undesirable behavior. The anxiety feeling is mentioned briefly and kept to a minimum, followed immediately by the introduction of appropriate alternative behavior. This particular scene is short, containing only six cards. The length of a scene and the complexity of the script are determined by the ability of the individual to attend and to comprehend language.

The scene would be practiced before going to an actual birthday party. Scenes can be adapted to include details regarding a specific birthday party. For example, if a friend also was attending a party, the friend could be incorporated into the script as another positive event to think about or as a supportive figure. When relaxation is included in the scene, it is important that the person know the procedure and have practiced and used it often. When using CPR, generally the script is read first by the therapist, parent, or caregiver, and then again by the individual. If the person for whom the scene was developed is non-verbal or has limited verbal skills, participation could be pointing to the pictures as the scene is reviewed a second time, turning the cards after the script is read, or filling in a word/word approximation in a part of the script. To help them fully imagine the scene, questions can be asked such as what kind of cake it was and what it tasted like, and they can be asked to show how their hands should be kept when they are anxious. These questions are asked to gauge comprehension of the scene. Verbal or tangible reinforcement can be provided to the learner for participating in the session. It is important to have many trials of the scene. In order to change a behavior, at least 100 trials are necessary.

Figure 13.7 Cognitive Picture Rehearsal Scene: Birthday Party
The Picture Communication Symbols © 1981–2010 by Mayer-Johnson LLC. All Rights Reserved Worldwide. Used with permission. Boardmaker™ is a trademark of Mayer-Johnson LLC.

Like many interventions, CPR and relaxation are not procedures that are effective immediately. It takes many trials before the individual can benefit, so it is helpful to put in place short-term measures that prevent the behavior from taking place, perhaps causing dangerous and life-threatening injury. The procedures that are helpful in these cases are (a) blocking or redirecting the response, and (b) prosthetics that prevent the response from occurring or causing damage. Blocking is a procedure in which the caregiver, staff, teacher, or parent intervenes during the self-injury and uses their own body or an object to come between the part of the body being injured and the person's body part doing the injuring. Often, as a complementary intervention, redirection prompts the individual to engage in an alternate behavior, also interrupting the SIB. Prosthetics are materials that are specifically suited to the type of self-injury being performed. Examples of these include soft or padded materials that would go on or wrap around the arm for a person who bites his arm, or soft helmets or caps to interrupt hitting of the head. These apparatuses are gradually reduced in size until they are no longer needed and the longer-term stress-reduction procedures or other interventions take effect. Unfortunately, there are many cases in which the self-injury was not initially prevented and the person suffered lasting and permanent damage.

Case Studies

Many clients have been referred to The Groden Center since its inception in 1976. Our approach of combining functional assessment with a stress perspective has resulted in effective treatment and more independent living for many clients. Below is a continuation of the two case studies introduced at the beginning of this chapter.

CASE 1: Combining Functional Assessment and Self-Control Strategies for the Reduction of SIB in a Young Girl

Jane was 13 years old when she was referred to The Groden Center day and residential program. She was non-verbal and diagnosed with ASD and associated severe/profound intellectual disability; she was healthy otherwise and able to ambulate independently. Jane did have some limited use of pictures to communicate but generally did not make use of the system that had been prepared for her. She had been unsuccessfully treated for severe self-injury by at least three school- and home-based organizations, had been hospitalized repeatedly, and prescribed a number of medications in an attempt to reduce her SIB. Jane's self-injury took the form of regularly biting her arm and hand to the point of tearing flesh away, and at the time of referral, her SIB averaged 60 occurrences per week. This behavior left open wounds for extended periods, as Jane would not tolerate topical treatments or bandages. The teachers and aides from her previous placements reported that the behavior occurred without obvious context or antecedent, so there "wasn't anything to do" about it.

Jane began at The Groden Center in 2007, when the first functional behavioral assessment of her SIB hypothesized that escape or avoidance of non-preferred activities was maintaining this behavior. This behavior was observed to take place when Jane was approached by staff and given a direction to take part in a task she did not want to do. Typically these included work tasks, or transitions to other areas in the building or outside of the building. Initial interventions included reinforcement for any instance of cooperation with these non-preferred activities and related activities (such as helping to clean up after snack or lunch); the Center's occupational therapist provided redirection to an alternate item to bite in response to precursor behavior (loud vocals); and the therapist waited for Jane to engage in the non-desired task while keeping her safe. Jane was not allowed to escape or avoid the task presented, but she could delay it with the appropriate use of a break card. As a short-term precaution, Jane was given soft arm guards to wear during school hours, and alternately, protective sleeves were also made available to limit skin damage. Additional training in communication skills was put in place, so Jane could better indicate her wants and needs through the use of pictures.

In addition to these contingencies that were based on the functional assessment information, the DBR analysis was used to generate stress reduction and self-control strategies tailored to Jane's particular situation. Jane took part in relaxation training in the classroom and at the residential program, and began learning what it meant to "relax." Staff created CPR scenes based on the identified antecedents, training adaptive responses to known environmental stressors. Specifically, Jane's scenes included staff approaching her and requesting engagement in work, and Jane taking a deep breath and telling herself that work was fun and she liked spending time with staff. The scene indicated that when she relaxed and engaged cooperatively in work tasks, specific reinforcers that had been shown to work for her resulted. Similarly, CPR scenes were developed for transitions to other areas of the building (an example is shown in Figure 13.8). Cognitive-restructuring strategies suggested to Jane that these activities were exciting and interesting, and that good things happened when she took part in them cooperatively. Jane had no difficulty taking part in viewing the CPR scenes and usually enjoyed this process. This typically took place after taking part in the relaxation procedure in the morning and at other times during the day, especially prior to typical antecedent situations such as transitions.

Figure 13.8 Cognitive Picture Rehearsal Scene: Transition
The Picture Communication Symbols © 1981–2010 by Mayer-Johnson LLC. All Rights Reserved Worldwide. Used with permission. Boardmaker™ is a trademark of Mayer-Johnson LLC.

The complement of contingencies and strategies (Treatment 1) resulted in an initial dramatic decrease in rates of SIB. Short-term interventions kept Jane safe, while the longer-term interventions were given time to take effect. As can be seen in Figure 13.9, rates of SIB decreased from her intake period through the following 2 years, into early 2009. At that time, an increase in SIB took place and a second DBR analysis was completed. In this analysis, a secondary functional hypothesis was added to escape/avoidance, in that Jane was found to engage in SIB when she was denied access to a tangible item, when she had to wait for that item, or when she did not receive a tangible reinforcer. With this information, treatment strategies were revised (Treatment 2), staff were instructed not to allow access to the item when Jane engaged in this behavior, and communication training was assessed for training in appropriate requesting. However, sometimes even if Jane asked appropriately, staff needed to say "no" to certain requests. Given this situation, additional CPR scenes were implemented to help her respond appropriately to this new set of stressors. Specifically, when she was denied access to an item, she was prompted to take a deep breath as instructed in her relaxation sequence, and an alternate cognition was suggested: "I don't mind not having that right now. I know I can have some later."

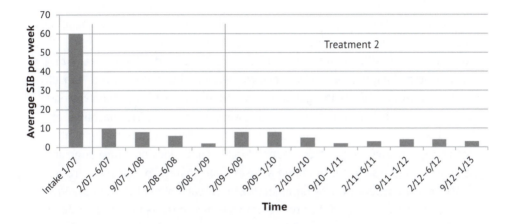

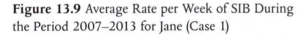

Figure 13.9 Average Rate per Week of SIB During the Period 2007–2013 for Jane (Case 1)

With appropriate contingencies, protective gear, and targeted CPR scenes in place, behavior rates continued to fall through 2011. The severity of the incidents of behavior also decreased, as rated on the DBRs that were collected. It is noted that, on a number of occasions, attempts were made to fade the protective gear, but these were unsuccessful given the low rate but high damage potential of this particular behavior. It is noted in the graph that a slight increase in SIB was recorded in early 2012, and a third functional assessment was consistent with what had already been found in the first two assessments. A consultation with the parents and the psychiatrist who was treating Jane resulted in blood work that found no significant medical issues. Staff continued to work with the treating psychiatrist, and a change in medication helped to further reduce rates of SIB in the following months. When Jane graduated from The Groden Center, she was demonstrating very low rates of SIB and associated behaviors, and was able to prompt a relaxation response independently. She was able to cooperatively take part in non-preferred tasks and transitions, and she was able to accept "no" when it was necessary. Jane was quickly accepted into an adult program. Her rates of SIB are represented in Figure 13.9.

CASE 2: Protective and Antecedent-Based Supports for the Treatment of Severe SIB in an Adult Man

Sylvester entered a Groden Network program in June 1987 at the age of 31 years. He was six feet tall and weighed about 220 pounds. He had been living in a state hospital where at the age of 27 years he had blinded himself during a major self-injurious episode. He had a history of being abused both by his biological family and while a resident in an institution. At the time of entry into the Groden Network program, Sylvester's SIB consisted of severe head banging (requiring treatment for hemorrhaging in both eyes); punching himself (with both hands, closed fists) in the face, eyes, ears, head, and genital area; biting himself; scratching the back of his neck with enough intensity to make himself bleed; and hitting his head against walls. The behavior of punching his ears was so severe that he was in danger of losing his hearing. The baseline rate for SIB was 23 times a week. In addition to his self-injury, other maladaptive behaviors included aggression (defined as hitting, kicking, and punching others); tearing his clothes (defined as using both hands to tear his shirt and pants near the zipper); throwing objects within reach; verbal threats (defined as threatening to hit himself or others); threatening gestures (with open hand or fist in the direction of others); incontinence; disruptive behavior in a vehicle; inappropriate verbalizations; and non-compliance.

When Sylvester was referred to the Groden Network in 1987, the following psychotropic medications were already prescribed: Serax, Corgard, and Thorazine. The state hospital also had a standing order to administer chloral hydrate when necessary. Upon program entry, the chloral hydrate was discontinued; however, all other medications were maintained.

Protective Strategies
In order to protect Sylvester from further self-injury, to prevent him from becoming deaf, and to prevent him from hurting the other residents and staff, protective strategies were put into place. State law allowed only holding as an acceptable physical intervention. A two-point control hold for 30 seconds was implemented that involved holding his arms down by his sides to prevent SIB. Sylvester's size and strength were such that it took four and sometimes five staff to implement the procedure when he first entered the program. A soft helmet to protect his ears also was recommended by his physician.

Sylvester's long history of SIB with the extreme result of blinding himself, his age and his size, the numerous severe maladaptive behaviors, and his history of being abused created an enormous challenge to providing an appropriate and effective treatment program. The demand, control, and support model described earlier became an integral part of the philosophy behind the design of his program. Assessments conducted of Sylvester's behavior included direct observation, the use of the DBR system, interviews with staff who worked with Sylvester at the state hospital, and a review of the hospital records.

Low Demand, High Support, and High Control Interventions

In welcoming Sylvester into our residential program, our first goal was to make him comfortable and to provide a warm and safe environment. His room was furnished with a comfortable bed appropriate for his size and a reclining lounge chair. Consultants from the state were enlisted to teach him how to navigate the house and to train staff to accommodate his blindness. A unique pattern of interacting was discovered during the assessments. The clinical team learned that all requests and conversations with Sylvester had to contain certain words and sequences or they became antecedents to SIB and aggression. An example of this is that when he asked for a glass of water the staff would need to say, "Here's your wicked slow glass of water." If Sylvester did not hear that phrase, he would stamp his feet and begin to engage in SIB. A detailed intervention treatment plan was written for Sylvester, and everyone working with him was trained to implement it. A key element of the plan was that Sylvester was reinforced frequently for using appropriate, alternative behaviors to SIB. Reinforcers were derived from the reinforcement surveys, direct observation, and input from Sylvester. One of Sylvester's most powerful reinforcers was cigarette smoking. When he entered the program he was a heavy smoker. Although we wanted to help him quit smoking for health reasons, we felt it would have been extremely difficult for him to quit "cold turkey." In order to cut down on his cigarettes, we made smoking contingent on appropriate behavior. A behavioral contract was designed with Sylvester's input and he understood the contingencies. He received checks on a contract and he was able to earn his cigarette, a treat of his choice, or a trip out to a restaurant for lunch or dinner at a location of his choosing. A schedule for the day was instituted and Sylvester had many choices in the schedule. He also was taught to tell staff when he preferred to be alone in his room and when he did not want to engage in conversation. He could say, "I don't want to talk about it now."

A large part of Sylvester's treatment program focused on teaching him self-control procedures. He practiced the relaxation protocol daily. Given his visual disability, the CPR procedure had to be modified. A number of scenes were developed for Sylvester that consisted of scripts with lots of rich detail.

To practice a scene, staff would read the script to Sylvester and then have him repeat it. He also was taught to use the procedures that he practiced in the scripts when confronted with the stressors in his daily life. These procedures were very effective with Sylvester. The staff reported that he used the alternative behaviors (appropriate communication, "being polite," expressing his needs and concerns by using appropriate assertiveness) the way he had practiced in the scenes. The scenes were maintained and changed as new stressors were identified.

Three examples of Sylvester's scenes are shown below. The first two scenes focus on practicing self-control in the face of generic stressors. The third scene was written to address Sylvester's problem behavior when traveling in the van. Also shown are a couple of the positive assertions that were developed for Sylvester. These were reviewed daily following his relaxation and CPR practice sessions.

- Scene 1: "Something is bothering me."

    1. Something is bothering me.

    2. I will put my hands and feet right down, very softly, and hold them there.

    3. I feel comfortable.

    4. I say, "I did it!"

    5. Now I imagine a nice cup of coffee. It tastes so good. I smile and go back to my schedule.

- Scene 2: "I am beginning to feel upset."

    1. I begin to feel upset.

    2. I say, "That upset feeling is like a bubble, and I want to kiss that bubble goodbye."

    3. I say to myself "STOP" and the bubble pops.

    4. I take a deep breath and relax, and I kiss the bubble goodbye.

    5. Now I feel so calm and relaxed.

    6. I imagine having a nice lunch at my favorite restaurant, Johnny's Diner.

    Note: This procedure is called the self-control triad (Cautela and Kearney, 1993). It combines thought-stopping (Cautela and Kearney, 1993), relaxation, and positive reinforcement.

- Scene 3: Riding in the van (a fantasy scene that Sylvester enjoys).

    1. I imagine I am in the van.

    2. I imagine a beautifully colored butterfly flying away, just as I am about to do.

    3. It travels many miles over land and sea.

    4. The sun, rain, wind, and snow feel soothing and cool against its wings.

    5. It lands at the beach on a vanilla seashell and the ocean is cream soda.

    6. I love watching the butterfly flutter by.

    7. That butterfly is soooo happy that it made the trip.

Positive Assertions

The following are samples from Sylvester's list, which is updated periodically:

    1. I am a smart man and I can do many things. I can deliver the mail and I can make iced coffee (etc.).

    2. I am a likeable man;_____ likes me and _____ likes me. (Names of staff, fellow housemates, or persons in the community are inserted into the blanks.)

    3. I use my words in a nice way to tell staff what I want.

Sylvester's Intervention Plan

The intervention plan for Sylvester was designed to prevent self-injury and other challenging behaviors and to promote adaptive behaviors. It outlines the appropriate way for staff to interact with Sylvester, reinforces the use of relaxation techniques and other appropriate coping skills, and provides an appropriate response from staff to ensure safety when Sylvester's behaviors present a risk to himself and others. The intervention plan is described on an Intervention Description Form (IDF), shown in Table 13.1.

The IDF details exactly how staff are to interact with Sylvester and how they are to respond to identified antecedent events, stressors, and target behaviors. The phrases and coping strategies included on the IDF correspond to CPR scenes and positive assertions that he would practice on a daily basis. All staff are trained to implement the plan consistently. Since the wording of sentences, tone of voice, and the placement of objects in the environment are known antecedents for SIB and other disruptive behaviors, carrying out this program exactly as written has contributed a great deal to the deceleration of Sylvester's target behaviors. In addition to his behavioral treatment plan, Sylvester is followed closely by a psychiatrist and takes the following medications: Depakote, Klonopin, Trazodone, Risperdal, and Cogentin.

Table 13.1 Sylvester Case Study Intervention Description Form

(Directions: List the setting events, antecedents, and behaviors for which an intervention has been planned. Describe the intervention strategies that are implemented for each situation listed.)

Setting Events, Antecedents, Behavior(s)	Intervention Name(s)	Description of Intervention Strategies
Waking in the middle of the night	Reminders	Give Sylvester the opportunity/reminders to go to the bathroom *before* going to bed.
Time alone with no interactions	Staff Interaction	Offer Sylvester a choice of positive activities to engage in throughout the evening and day.
Others saying something he doesn't like; others talking too loudly, quickly, or slowly	Staff Guidance, CPR Script	Reinforce Sylvester when he lets staff know, verbally, that he wants/wanted them to say something differently or that he did not like something they said. Encourage Sylvester to state it in a positive tone before reinforcing.
		Engage Sylvester in the statement "If someone says something the wrong way, you can say to that person…" Sylvester will usually fill in the rest and then go through self-control procedures.
Others not saying something that he wants them to say (ritualistic interactions)	Staff Guidance, Planned Ignoring	If Sylvester appears upset because he is not getting the response he wants, say something like "I don't understand," "Tell me what you want to say/do," or "Help me out Sylvester."
		If he keeps trying to get someone to repeat something and is getting louder and more demanding, tell him, "You can say it if you want, *but I don't have to.*" Walk away from him and do not interact with him until he stops (30 seconds).

Someone talking too much, asking too many questions, or asking questions to which he does not know the answer	Staff Direction, Reinforcement	If Sylvester asks you to leave or says he does not want to talk, thank him for telling you and leave or stop trying to converse with him. (If he says it in an angry tone, ask him to say it another way—he will almost always respond by asking you politely to leave—and always respond to this request.)
		When a staff person converses with Sylvester, he thinks before he responds, creating a delay of 5 seconds or more. Wait for his response. He is probably not ignoring you. Do not repeat the question or ask another one until he has had ample time to respond. (Sylvester may rock or shake his head from side to side while he is thinking. He may occasionally change his answer several times before responding.) Be patient.
Others bumping into him	Staff Guidance, Reinforcement, Staff Direction, CPR Script	Sylvester should be verbally praised for "trailing" as he moves around his environment. ("Great job finding the wall, Sylvester.") Staff do not need to say anything when he bumps into something (i.e., when he fails to "trail"), since this is a natural consequence and it usually does not upset Sylvester when he bumps into an object rather than a person.
		Allow Sylvester to be as independent as possible as he moves around. Allow him to open doors for himself. It is sometimes confusing and stressful for him when someone opens a door for him, particularly if they do not tell him they are doing so.
		Ensure that Sylvester has as much space as possible in crowded situations and that people are conscious of trying not to bump into him.
		If someone does bump into him it is usually better to say "Sylvester, I didn't mean to bump you" or "Excuse me," paired with an apology such as "It was an accident." Always use a matter-of-fact voice projecting the idea that it is no big deal.
		Sylvester has learned to say "Could you please move?" when he knows that others are in his way (he has an excellent sense of this). When he asks, staff should help clear the area for him and then let him know when "the coast is clear."

cont.

Setting Events, Antecedents, Behavior(s)	Intervention Name(s)	Description of Intervention Strategies
Others handing him something or taking something out of his hand too quickly	Staff Guidance, Staff Direction, CPR Script	Always tell Sylvester exactly what is being handed to him including the type of container (i.e., paper cup, plastic cup, soda in a can, etc.).
		Medication time and meal time can be stressful for Sylvester as they involve interactions (i.e., handing him something, putting an item down on the table in front of him, the sounds associated with touching a surface near him, etc.). The best way of communicating the presence and position of an object to Sylvester is to lightly tap it on the table/counter when placing it down, without making a loud noise. Sylvester understands and accepts this practice.
		At times, Sylvester tenses his body and has very pronounced body movements when taking something from the table. It is best to give him a reminder such as "I know you can keep your hands relaxed" before presenting the item. Staff also can suggest to Sylvester that he relax his hands or holds his hands on his lap until they are ready with the item (i.e., medications, popcorn, etc.).
		For items that need to be handed to him or when there is no table, staff will say, "Here's your wicked slow _____, Sylvester." Sylvester may extend his hand out in front of him, either flat or cupped. Staff should place a hand below his as they put the item in his hand since he will sometimes drop his hand rapidly after he has the item in his hand.
		If Sylvester does not extend a hand, staff will extend their hand, holding the item steady, and Sylvester can independently track the item. Allow Sylvester to fumble, as needed, until he locates the item, unless he requests assistance. If unsure, staff should tell Sylvester that they need to hand him _____, and ask Sylvester how he wants it. He may say something like "In my hand, wicked slow."

Someone helping him when he doesn't need help; not being able to find something; someone correcting him	Staff Guidance, Staff Direction, Positive Assertions	Allow Sylvester to be as independent as possible. If he looks like he needs help with something, allow him the chance to ask for your assistance as needed. Sylvester does well with asking for help, even though it may appear he is becoming frustrated.
		Sylvester will generally ask for help when he needs it, but he will sometimes moan instead of asking for help. Staff should matter-of-factly ask, "What's the matter, Sylvester?" Generally, Sylvester will then ask appropriately.
		Avoid giving Sylvester assistance such as opening a door for him or getting something for him when he knows where it is. This often causes more confusion and anxiety for him than assistance.
		Sylvester knows his way around the house and knows how to scan his environment with his hands to find objects. Some verbal assistance, such as, "The door is to your left," may be acceptable to him, but there should be no further verbal instruction.
		Sylvester usually remembers where he left his belongings. It is important to ensure that his possessions are put back in their usual spot.
		In general, give Sylvester reminders like "I know you will remember to ___ " or "You do such a good job at ___," in order to get him to do a step he missed or to go back and do something correctly.
Someone interrupting him when he is intently engaged in an activity/motor movements, etc.	Staff Interaction	Check to see what Sylvester is doing before verbally interacting with him.
		Avoid interrupting him when he is intently engaged in something.
		If it becomes necessary to interrupt him, wait until there is a pause in his verbalizations or movements and start by just calling his name in a calm, low voice.
		Wait for him to respond before interacting.

cont.

Setting Events, Antecedents, Behavior(s)	Intervention Name(s)	Description of Intervention Strategies
Threats and gestures	Evasion, Verbal Direction, Relaxation, Reinforcement	If Sylvester threatens aggression or SIB, tell him, "You know your program, Sylvester." Remind him of what he is working toward. Then cue him to relax using his preferred phrase "Now it is not time for relaxation?" If he responds and uses relaxation, verbally praise him by saying, "Congratulations—good job, Sylvester, getting yourself back in control."
		If he does not respond, repeat the sequence.
Stomping feet, yelling, crying	Verbal Direction, Relaxation, Reinforcement	If Sylvester exhibits precursors to his target behaviors, remind him of what he is working toward. Then cue him to relax using his preferred phrase "Now it is not time for relaxation?" If he responds and uses relaxation, verbally praise him. "Good job, Sylvester, getting yourself back in control."
		If he does not respond, repeat the sequence.

Note: Having the staff say "Now it is not time for relaxation?" is the way that Sylvester wants it said.

Current Status

Sylvester is fully ambulatory and has good mobility skills. He is able to adjust readily to new environments when given initial training on space and furniture location. He moves with his hands out in front of him and with staff support (light touch to the forearm). Sylvester has good communication skills, although he demonstrates a processing delay of up to 5 seconds. As long as he is not given too many questions or directions at the same time, he is able to respond appropriately. Sylvester does not initiate interactions with his peers, but he is capable of making his needs and wants known to staff, asks questions to obtain information, is able to relate experiences in a meaningful manner, and shares his sense of humor. He exhibits ritualistic verbal routines requiring others to respond to him in a specific manner. It is hypothesized that this is one way he establishes a connection and comfort level with staff—those who "know him" respond with the routine reply.

Sylvester's target behaviors of incontinence, ripping his clothes, and severe maladaptive behaviors during transport on the van have all been extinguished from his repertoire. He still has his hearing. His SIB and other maladaptive behaviors, while not fully extinguished, have been reduced considerably in frequency and intensity. He has had only one two-point hold in 6 years and exhibits an average of 2.3 SIBs per week. That is down from the 23 incidents per week he exhibited at entry. When SIB does begin to occur, Sylvester can be verbally redirected to more appropriate behavior. He is able to find enjoyment in his daily routine and interact with others.

This case study is a good example of how a treatment that focused on an insightful assessment and personalized treatment can make a vast difference in the life of an older person with severe self-injury. His treatment consisted of the use of relaxation and CPR, medication, and interventions based on a thorough assessment. He was destined for a solitary life with very little to look forward to or enjoy. He has learned to communicate in an effective way to ensure that staff understand his needs. The provision of a reliable and structured daily schedule has provided him the comfort and security of his routines such that he has become more independent in his choice-making and in the activities of daily living.

He is now a member of the community, eats at his favorite restaurants, delivers mail to the company facilities, goes on vacation with his housemates, engages in humorous interactions, enjoys his room and comfortable chair, enjoys his favorite foods, goes for short walks, takes trips to the beach, and goes to the movies and other community events. These are activities that the rest of us take for granted, and certainly 20 years prior they seemed like a very remote possibility for Sylvester.

Discussion

In this chapter, treatment of SIB in individuals with autism was approached from the perspective that stress contributes to the occurrence and maintenance of the behavior. From that concept, the development of any given treatment plan requires more than just a functional assessment of the target behavior. Along with thorough physical and dental evaluations, the stressors that affect the individual and his behavior also must be assessed. A multimodal assessment strategy was detailed that includes functional assessment of the behavior using direct observation, rating scales, interviews, the Stress Survey Schedule for Individuals with Autism and Other Pervasive Developmental Disabilities (Groden *et al.*, 2001a), and physiological measures. One of the advantages of looking at self-injury from the point of view of stress and anxiety is that it can change our attributions about why the behavior occurs. In addition to asking "What is the purpose of the behavior?" another question becomes "What are the stressors that provoke the behavior?" The stress perspective allows us to focus on specific antecedents that are stressors for the individual. The outcome of such assessments leads to intervention methods designed to reduce the stress and anxiety as well as to reduce the frequency and intensity of the SIB. In the case studies presented, stress-reduction procedures, such as relaxation and CPR, were used successfully in conjunction with a variety of behavioral and medical procedures to treat significant SIB in individuals with ASD.

Relaxation and Cognitive Picture Rehearsal

Relaxation and CPR procedures have been discussed in detail as two of the key interventions we use to reduce stress. These procedures are always used in combination with evidence-based academic curricula, communication programs, social skills training, vocational training (for children over 14 years of age), occupational therapy, physical therapy, physical education, programs to teach adaptive living skills, recreational programs, and community learning experiences. All these programs are geared toward the appropriate developmental and cognitive levels and age of each individual.

In an applied setting, it is difficult to parcel out the effects of each of these components. In our analysis of the treatment programs for the children and adults whom we support at The Groden Center, we have found that there is always a package of interventions that is appropriate for each person. It is noteworthy that every person in The Groden Center learns the relaxation response and has a CPR program that is incorporated into all the above programs across many environments. We have been fortunate in that we could follow many of the children into adulthood and observe their use of relaxation and CPR in community employment situations. Job coaches, or the individuals themselves, identify their stressors at work (i.e., transitioning from one task to another, loud noise, using the staff cafeteria) and

CPR scenes are developed. When the stressors occur, the persons with autism appropriately initiate relaxation responses or say the CPR script to themselves.

A limitation of the relaxation and CPR program is the amount of time required before the interventions are successful. Variables such as the duration, intensity, and topography of the SIB, the length of time the SIB has taken place, and the age of the individual all contribute to the prognosis. Strategies need to be implemented during the learning period for the stress-reduction procedures. Although it may take time for the individual to master and use the procedures effectively, it is time well spent. Once relaxation and CPR can be used for self-control, whether self-initiated or staff-cued, the individual has a powerful tool to reduce stress in many situations, and to prevent or minimize SIB.

Generalization

Generalizing a response learned in one setting to another can be difficult for those with autism; therefore, it is necessary to practice appropriate responses in many different environments and situations. Stressors also change in different environments, so assessment should include as many different settings as possible. Fortunately, persons with autism are now being included in typical classrooms, employment situations, and community and family activities. It is important to keep in mind that, with inclusion, we also see the addition of many stressors in which transitions, social experiences, and new skills are needed. Programs to reduce stress are beneficial in addressing these needs.

Self-Control

Self-control complements all procedures and teaches an individual that he has the power to effect change. Self-control is not limited to the procedures under the rubric of behavior therapy, but is an adjunct to all interventions. By learning self-control, attributions change from "I can't help myself" to "I can do something about this." Self-control procedures can be used to address numerous challenges—for example, engaging in an appropriate, alternative response to self-injury, complying with a medication regimen, or perhaps finishing a difficult assignment. Self-control also can complement programs to teach positive attributions, being optimistic, and becoming resilient. When self-control procedures as described in this chapter are used, an important outcome is prevention. By identifying the SIB, learning the stressors, using antecedent interventions, and encouraging self-control, SIBs can be prevented.

Conclusion

In treating individuals with ASD who engage in SIB, we emphasize the need for multiple assessments of the behavior itself as well as the stressors that have an impact on the behavior's strength and severity. Although we acknowledge that we cannot eliminate all sources of stress for anyone, and that the characteristics of autism add to stress in the lives of persons with ASD, we can reduce the impact of it by including stress-reduction procedures such as CPR and relaxation in individual treatment plans. SIB may be a maladaptive strategy for coping with arousal and stress—how one copes with stress is the important variable. In taking a perspective that there is a relationship between stress and SIB, we hope to change attributions, focus on stressors in the environment, and implement adaptive coping skills that can lead to the prevention of SIB and a higher quality of life.

Future Trends

The explosion in the prevalence rates of autism has occurred worldwide. This has ignited research in the fields of psychology, behavior analysis, education, and medicine. Since Kanner identified autism in 1943, there have been many advances in the treatment and education of persons with autism. The following are further areas to be explored in the area of SIB:

- the incorporation of stress-reduction programs into schools, treatment centers, the home, and community

- the addition of stress assessments added to the body of assessments for individuals with SIB

- research into different types of stressors related to different types of SIB

- research on specific stressors that affect children and adults with SIB at different stages of development

- investigation of biological setting events

- the examination of biobehavioral responding (i.e., synchrony and dysynchrony between observable behavior and heart-rate measures) to contribute to classification and to help increase diagnostic clarity by identifying subgroups of SIB for individuals who have qualitatively different response patterns and differential stressors

- the addition of physiological measures to assessment and ongoing treatment (i.e., heart rate and heart-rate variability, electrodermal responses, cortisol levels) that provides accurate, continuous, and efficient measurement, eliminates human error, adds covert behavior to behavioral analysis, and can look at internal states as context

- the integration of internal and external factors in our conceptualization of problem behaviors and the creation of intervention packages

- the adoption of current gains in technology to better access internal states and stressors, better identify precursor behavior or related physiological changes, or measure SIB more accurately (in other words, how can we make this technology more accessible for use in applied settings?)

- the development of wearable technology that can show arousal levels in individuals with SIB before the SIB response is emitted.

In conclusion, although there have been many advances in the field in recent years, there is still a lot to be done. Hopefully with more national attention focused on this problem, there will be more funding and grants available for further research and application.

> Since 1976, the Groden Center programs have been focused on removing not only environmental, educational, and vocational barriers, but also the barriers that come from external control by others. We assume that people with autism, like all human beings, can learn self-control and reduce the impact of stress in their lives. (Groden *et al.*, 2006, p.30)

The population with developmental disabilities has been subjected to many years of programs that primarily use external controls, but these procedures have to be established and maintained during a person's lifetime. We feel it is important to teach behaviors that give power to the person, reduce the effects of stress, and teach individuals with SIB to manage their own behavior and learn self-control. Self-control is freedom from the burden of external control and is fostered through personalized treatment and support. Dr. Lennart Levi's words (online interview, The American Institute of Stress) sum up our view of the importance of designing treatment to fit the individual: "My priority has always been to try to adjust the 'shoe'…to the 'foot'…and not just the other way round."

Acknowledgments

The authors of this chapter thank Linda Ollari for her continual support and help with organizing the logistical aspects of our work. We also thank Jacqueline Rastella and Matthew Dondey for their assistance in collecting information on case studies. And thanks to Andrea DeBarros for her assistance in research. As always, we are forever grateful for the hard work, trust, and cooperation of the staff, parents, children, and adults in our Groden Network programs.

References

Albinali, F., Goodwin, M., and Intille, S. (2012). Detecting stereotypical motor movements in the classroom using accelerometry and pattern recognition algorithms. *Pervasive and Mobile Computing, 8,* 103–114.

Aspinwall, L., and Taylor, S. (1997). A stitch in time: Self-regulation and proactive coping. *Psychological Bulletin, 121,* 417–436.

Barlow, D., Allen, L., and Choate, M. (2004). Towards a unified treatment for emotional disorders. *Behavior Therapy, 35,* 205–230.

Baron, G., Groden, J., and Cautela, J. (1988). Behavioral Programming: Expanding Our Clinical Repertoire. In G. Groden and G. Baron (Eds.), *Autism: Strategies for Change.* Lake Worth, FL: Gardner Press.

Betz, A., and Fisher, W. (2011). Functional Analysis: History and Methods. In W.W. Fisher, C.C. Piazza, and H.S. Roane (Eds.), *Handbook of Applied Behavior Analysis.* New York, NY: Guilford.

Campbell, J. (2003). Efficacy of behavioral interventions for reducing problem behavior in persons with autism: A quantitative synthesis of single-subject research. *Research in Developmental Disabilities, 24,* 120–138. doi:10.1016/S0891-4222(03)00014-3.

Cautela, J., and Groden, J. (1978). *Relaxation: A Comprehensive Manual for Adults, Children, and Children with Special Needs.* Champaign, IL: Research Press.

Cautela, J., and Kearney, A. (1993). *Covert Conditioning Casebook.* Pacific Grove, CA: Brooks/Cole Publishing Company.

Cohen, I., Yoo, J., Goodwin, M., and Moskowitz, L. (2011). Assessing Challenging Behaviors in Autism Spectrum Disorders: Prevalence, Rating Scales, and Autonomic Indicators. In J. Matson and P. Sturmey (Eds.), *International Handbook of Autism and Pervasive Developmental Disorders.* New York, NY: Springer.

Duncan, J. (1986). Disorganization of behavior after frontal lobe damage. *Cognitive Neuropsychology, 3,* 271–290.

Durand, M., and Crimmins, D. (1992). *The Motivation Assessment Scale Administration Guide.* Topeka, KS: Monaco & Associates.

Goodwin, M., Groden, J., Velicer, W., and Diller, A. (2007). Brief report: Validating the Stress Survey Schedule for Persons with Autism and Other Developmental Disabilities. *Focus on Autism and Other Developmental Disabilities, 22*(3), 183–189.

Goodwin, M., Groden, J., Velicer, W., Lipsitt, L., *et al.* (2006). Cardiovascular arousal in individuals with autism. *Focus on Autism and Other Developmental Disabilities, 21*(2), 100–123.

Goodwin, M., Haghighi, Q.T., Akcakaya, M., Erdogmus, D., and Intille, S. (2014). *Moving Toward a Real-Time System for Automatically Recognizing Stereotypical Motor Movements in Individuals on the Autism Spectrum Using Wireless Accelerometry.* Ubicomp 2014, Seattle, Washington.

Grandin, T., and Scariano, M. (1986). *Emergence: Labeled Autistic.* Novato, CA: Arena Press.

Groden, J., Baron, M., and Groden, G. (2006). Assessment and Coping Strategies. In M. Baron, J. Groden, G. Groden, and L. Lipsitt (Eds.), *Stress and Coping in Autism.* New York, NY: Oxford University Press.

Groden, J., Cautela, J., Diller, A., Velicer, W., and Norman, G. (2001a). *The Stress Survey Schedule for Individuals with Autism and Other Pervasive Developmental Disabilities.* Providence, RI: The Groden Center.

Groden, J., Diller, A., Bausman, M., Velicer, W., Norman, G., and Cautela, J. (2001b). The development of a Stress Survey Schedule for Persons with Autism and Other Developmental Disabilities. *Journal of Autism and Developmental Disorders, 31*(2), 207–217.

Groden, J., Goodwin, M., Baron, M.G., Groden, G., *et al.* (2005). Assessing cardiovascular responses to stressors in individuals with autism spectrum disorders. *Focus on Autism and Other Developmental Disorders, 20*(4), 244–252.

Groden, J., Kantor, A., Woodard, C., and Lipsitt, L. (2011). *How Everyone on the Autism Spectrum, Young and Old Can... Become Resilient, Be More Optimistic, Enjoy Humor, Be Kind, and Increase Self-Efficacy: A Positive Psychology Approach.* London: Jessica Kingsley Publishers.

Groden, J., LeVasseur, P., Diller, A., and Cautela, J. (2009). *Coping with Stress Through Picture Rehearsal: A How-To Manual for Working with Individuals with Autism and Developmental Disabilities.* Providence, RI: The Groden Center.

Groden, G., Stevenson, S., and Groden, J. (1996). *Understanding Challenging Behavior: A Step-by-Step Behavior Analysis Guide.* Providence, RI: The Groden Center.

Hanley, G., Jin, C., Vanselow, N., and Hanratty, L. (2014). Producing meaningful improvements in problem behavior of children with autism via synthesized analyses and treatments. *Journal of Applied Behavior Analysis, 47,* 16–36.

Hobfoil, S. (2001). The influence of culture, community, and the nested-self in the stress process: Advancing conservation of resources theory. *Applied Psychology, 50,* 337–421.

Hogdon, L. (1995). *Visual Strategies for Improving Communication.* Troy, MI: Quirk Roberts Publishing.

Horner, R., Carr, E., Strain, P., Todd, A., and Reed, H. (2002). Problem behavior interventions for young children with autism: A research synthesis. *Journal of Autism and Developmental Disabilities, 32*(5), 423–446.

Iwata, B., Pace, G., Dorsey, M., Zarcone, J., *et al.* (1994). The functions of self-injurious behavior: An experimental–epidemiological analysis. *Journal of Applied Behavior Analysis, 27,* 215–240.

Jacobson, E. (1938). *Jacobson Progressive Relaxation.* Chicago, IL: University of Chicago Press.

Jolliffe, T., Landsdown, R., and Robinson, T. (1992). Autism: A personal account. *Communication, 3*(2b), 12.

Kanner, L. (1943). Autistic disturbances of affective contact. *Nervous Child, 2,* 217–250.

Lam, K., and Aman, M. (2007). The Repetitive Behavior Scale—Revised: Independent validation in individuals with autism spectrum disorders. *Journal of Autism and Developmental Disorders, 37*(5), 855–866.

Lazarus, R. (1993). Coping theory and research: Past, present, and future. *Psychosomatic Medicine, 55,* 234–247.

Lazarus, R., and Folkman, S. (1984). *Stress, Appraisal, and Coping.* New York, NY: Springer-Verlag.

Levi, L. The American Institute of Stress. *Occupational Stress Part 2: An interview with Dr. Lennart Levi.* Available at www.stress.org/occupational-stress-part-2, accessed on 23 February 2014.

Levi, L. (1995). *Global Review and State of the Art Approaches in Stress Management and Prevention.* Fifth International Conference on Stress at the Workplace: Health and Productivity. Noordwijkerhout, The Netherlands.

Lieberman, M. (2013). *Social: Why Our Brains Are Wired to Connect.* New York, NY: Crown Publishers.

O'Neill, R., Horner, R., Albin, R., Sprague, J., Storey, K., and Newton, J. (1997). *Functional Assessment and Program Development for Problem Behavior.* Pacific Grove, CA: Brooks/Cole Publishing.

Overall, J., and Gorham, D. (1962). The Brief Psychiatric Rating Scale. *Psychological Reports, 10,* 799–812.

Paterson, R., and Neufeld, R. (1989). The Stress Response and Parameters of Stressful Situations. In R. Neufeld (Ed.), *Advances in the Investigation of Psychological Stress.* Oxford: John Wiley & Sons.

Plotz, T., Hammerals, N., Rozga, A., Reavis, A., Call, N., and Abowd, G. (2012). *Automatic Assessment of Problem Behaviors for Individuals with Developmental Disabilities.* UbiComp 2012, Pittsburgh, Pennsylvania.

Prior, M., and Hoffmann, W. (1990). Neuropsychological testing of autistic children through an exploration with frontal lobe tests. *Journal of Autism and Developmental Disorders, 20,* 581–590.

Prior, M., and Ozonoff, S. (1998). Psychological Factors in Autism. In F. Volkmar (Ed.), *Autism and Pervasive Developmental Disorders.* New York, NY: Cambridge University Press.

Rumsey, J., and Hamburger, S. (1988). Neuropsychological findings in high-functioning autistic men with infantile autism, residual state. *Journal of Clinical and Experimental Neuropsychology, 10,* 201–221.

Rutter, M. (1983). Stress, Coping, and Development: Some Issues and Some Questions. In N. Garmezy and M. Rutter (Eds.), *Stress, Coping, and Development in Children.* New York, NY: McGraw-Hill.

Sapolsky, R. (1998). *Why Zebras Don't Get Ulcers.* New York, NY: W.H. Freeman.

Seligman, M., Steen, T., Park, N., and Peterson, C. (2005). Positive psychology progress: Empirical validation of interventions. *American Psychologist, 60*(5), 410–421.

Selye, H. (1956). *The Stress of Life.* New York, NY: McGraw-Hill.

The Free Dictionary (2003–2015). *Cognitive restructuring.* Available at http://medical-dictionary.thefreedictionary.com/cognitive+restructuring, accessed on 13 February 2015.

Thoits, P. (1995). Stress, coping, and social support processes: Where are we? What next? *Journal of Health and Social Behavior (Extra Issue),* 53–79.

Turner, J. (1994). *Cardiovascular Reactivity and Stress: Patterns of Physiological Response.* New York, NY: Plenum Press.

Turner, R., and Roszell, P. (1994). Psychosocial Resources and the Stress Process. In W. Avison and I. Gotlib (Eds.), *Stress and Mental Health: Contemporary Issues and Prospects for the Future.* New York, NY: Plenum Press.

Volkmar, F., and Cohen, D. (1985). The experience of infantile autism: A first person account by Tony W. *Journal of Autism and Developmental Disabilities, 15,* 47–54.

Westman, M. (2004). Strategies for coping with business trips: A qualitative exploratory study. *International Journal of Stress Management, 11*(2), 167–176.

BIOLOGICAL CONTRIBUTORS TO SELF-INJURIOUS BEHAVIOR

Body Area	Specific Behavior(s)	Possible Contributors	Chapter
Head	Head banging	Sinusitis, seasonal allergies	6
Head	Head hitting, head banging	Pain from migraine headache, ear infection	2
			3
			6
			7
			8
Nose	Hitting face area	Allergic rhinitis, foreign object in nasal cavity	6
			7
Mouth	Hitting, pressing	Dental pain	2
Ears	Hitting, pressing	Otitis media (ear infection)	2
			6
Hair	Trichotillomania	Low cholesterol	1
Abdomen	Hitting or pressing against abdomen	Constipation, bloating	2
			7
			8
Genitals	Excessive rubbing of genitals	Yeast overgrowth, constipation	7
Skin	Excessive skin picking	Calluses on fingers and hands from hand biting, pruritus, eczema, atopic dermatitis	4
			6
General Expression of Discomfort/ Pain	Crying, facial grimacing, screaming	Allergies, sinus headache, dental, gastrointestinal seizures	2
			3
			6
			7
			8

TARGETED QUESTIONNAIRE TO IDENTIFY CHAPTERS OF INTEREST

Questions	Chapter
Disease/Syndrome	
Does the child have PKU, biotinidase deficiency, Smith-Lemli-Opitz syndrome, cerebral folate deficiency, pyridoxine-dependent epilepsy, Lesch-Nyhan syndrome, tuberous sclerosis, or PANS/PANDAS?	1
	4
	7
Is there evidence of craniofacial dysmorphism, brain damage, and/or head trauma?	3
Does the individual have limbic encephalitis or herpes simplex encephalitis?	3
Is there a history of seizures/epilepsy in the family?	3
If epilepsy, does the individual not respond to anti-convulsant medications?	3
Did SIB worsen after suffering from a viral syndrome?	6
Does the individual suffer from asthma, allergies (rhinitis, food allergy, etc.), and/or sinusitis?	6
	7
Does the individual suffer from celiac disease?	2
	6
	8
Epilepsy/Seizures	
Does the individual have seizures or appear to have seizures?	2
	3
	4
Gastrointestinal-Related Issues	
Does the individual also have gastrointestinal issues that may be painful? (For example, constipation, flatulence, bloating, GERD.)	2
	7
	8
Are stools normal? (For example, diarrhea, oily or greasy, grainy, blood, mucus.)	8
Does the individual have food allergy or intolerance?	6

Sensory-Related Issues	
Does the individual avoid strobe lights?	3
Is the individual a picky eater?	8
Does the individual appear to receive pleasure from the SIB?	9
Does the SIB appear to be associated with craving and seeking sensory input (stimulation) related to SIB?	9
	10
Is the individual insensitive to pain, such as not feeling the SIB?	9
Does the individual receive sensory stimulation from the SIB to reduce anxiety, such as to escape an uncomfortable sensory stimulation or panic?	4
	12
Stress/Anxiety	
Does the SIB often occur under anxiety and/or stress? (Examples: humming, antsy, repeats/perseverates on words/phrases, rapid breathing, sweating, trembling, pacing, more active, agitated, irritable.)	2
	4
	5
	6
	7
	9
	12
	13
Did the SIB start after sexual abuse, especially in the genital area?	7
Social/Behavioral	
Does the SIB function to obtain some form of attention, such as a social interaction or to receive comfort?	5
	10
	11
	12
Does the SIB function to obtain a tangible item or setting? (For example, food item, activity, toy.)	5
	10
	11
	12
	13
Could the SIB be interpreted as a form of communication to get his or her needs and wants met? (For example, "I want to leave" or "Leave me alone.")	10
	11
	12

Does the SIB serve the function of escape or avoidance of an aversive or anxiety-provoking task or situation?	4
	5
	10
	11
	12
	13
Additional Questions	
Does the individual appear to have a headache or migraine?	2
	3
	6
	7
	8
Does the individual have sleep problems, such as nocturnal awakenings? If so, are nocturnal awakenings associated with respiratory symptoms? (For example, nasal congestion, coughing, wheezing.)	2
	6
	7
	8
Is there excessive silliness, hyperactivity, or irritability?	8
Is the SIB associated with impulsivity?	3
	9
Are the SIB episodes not recalled later by the individual?	3
Did the SIB begin after the start of the menstrual cycle (if the individual is female)?	2
	5
	10
Are there episodes of loss of consciousness or unexplained falls? Does the individual look groggy at times?	3
Did the individual's autism symptoms appear after 1 year of age (late onset)?	3
Does the individual engage in self-restraint, such as wrapping shredded clothing or rope around his or her wrist?	4

PKU: phenylketonuria; PANS: pediatric acute neuropsychiatric syndrome; PANDAS: pediatric autoimmune neuropsychiatric disorder associated with streptococcal infections; SIB: self-injurious behavior; GERD: gastroesophageal reflux disease

THE STRUCTURED INTERVIEW FOR ASSESSMENT OF MEDICATION SIDE EFFECTS (SIAMSE)

Reproduced from Bleiweiss and Carr (2007, unpublished) with kind permission.

A. Demographics

1. Your Name: _____ Date: _____

2. Address: _____ Phone: _____

3. Relationship to Child (e.g., mother, father, guardian, etc.): _____

4. Child's Name: _____ Child's Age: ___ Child's Sex (circle one):   M   F

5. Child's Diagnosis: _____

6. Please list any chronic health problems that your child has (e.g., asthma, diabetes, seizures): _____

7. Is your child able to communicate with you through speech, sign language, PECs, or another Augmentative Communication Device? (Please describe.)

   _____

   _____

B. Medication History

1. Is your child presently on medication for problem behavior (i.e., for a period of at least two weeks)?   Circle one: Yes   No

2. Is your child currently experiencing adverse side effects while on medication for problem behavior?   Circle one: Yes   No

3. What type of problem behavior led to your child being put on medication? (Circle all that apply on the attached Problem Behavior Table.)

   Please describe: _____

   _____

   _____

4. For each medication (or combination of medications) that your child is currently on, and/or has been on in the last 12 months, please provide the following information (beginning with the most recent and working backwards):

   a. Name of medication: _____

   b. Date started: _____

   c. Dosage level: Initial: _____ Current: _____

   d. Type of problem behavior currently being treated by the medication:

   _____

   —

   How many times per day is the medication given? (For example, 3 times a day.)

   _____

   What time of day is the medication given? (For example, before meals.)

5. _____

   For each medication listed in Question 4, please answer the following questions:

   a. After the medication was started, did your doctor change the dosage level? Circle one: Yes   No

   b. Why did your doctor change the dosage level? Check ALL that apply:

     ☐ My child experienced acute negative side effects (physiological, motor, cognitive, affective)

     ☐ My child's problem behavior got worse (new/different problem behavior was exhibited)

     ☐ My child's problem behavior did not decrease

     ☐ My child's problem behavior did not decrease to a satisfactory level

     ☐ My child's problem behavior improved and he/she required less medication

     ☐ Other (please specify)

   c. Was the dosage level increased or decreased? _____

C. Nature of Side Effects

For each medication identified in question 5 of Part B (i.e., dosage change), please answer the following:

1. What are the current side effects of the medication(s) he/she is receiving? (Please circle all that apply on the attached Side Effects Table.)

For each side effect identified:

2. How do you know when your child is experiencing this side effect? (That is, what does he/she do/say/look like when the side effect is present?)

   _____

   _____

3. How frequently (number of days per week), on the average, is the side effect present? _____

4. When your child is experiencing the side effect, how long, on the average, does the side effect episode last? (How many minutes or how many hours?)

   _____

5. When your child is experiencing the side effect, how intense is it, on the average, using the following scale?

Mild		Moderate		Severe
1	2	3	4	5

6. For each side effect (e.g., fatigue) you identified, specify whether the overall level (i.e., frequency, duration, and intensity combined) of the symptom described (i.e., fatigue) is now slightly worse, somewhat worse, or much worse than what it was before your child went on medication. Alternatively, you may indicate that the current overall level of symptoms is the same as it was before the medication.

Slightly Worse		Somewhat Worse		Much Worse	Same
1	2	3	4	5	X

7. Have other people mentioned/commented on the presence of side effects?

   Circle one: Yes   No

   If so, who? Teacher/Friend/Neighbor/Other relative: _____

   Other person: _____

D. Impact on Context

1. Since your child has gone on medication, is he/she having more difficulty with any activities at home or in the community?

   Circle one: Yes   No

2. If you answered "Yes," then specify which activities. (Please circle all that apply on the attached Home and Community Activities/Routines Table.)

3. During the activities you specified, have you noticed the presence of any of the medication side effects you mentioned earlier?

Circle one: Yes   No

4. If you answered "Yes," then specify which side effect(s) was (were) present that made each activity more difficult: _____

5. If you answered "Yes" to Question 3, please specify whether the presence of the side effect (described in Question 4) has made successful completion of each activity slightly more difficult, somewhat more difficult, or much more difficult than was the case before your child went on medication. You may also circle No Impact if that was the case.

Slightly More Difficult		Somewhat More Difficult		Much More Difficult	No Impact
1	2	3	4	5	X

E. Impact on Problem Behavior

1. For each activity you identified in Part D, in which the activity became more difficult because of the presence of side effects, please specify whether your child sometimes shows problem behavior during the activity.

Circle one: Yes   No

Type of problem behavior(s) (please refer to the Problem Behavior Table):

_____

2. If you answered "Yes," then specify whether the level of problem behavior during the activity is slightly greater, somewhat greater, or much greater since your child has been on the medication, as compared to before he/she was placed on the medication. You can also circle No Change or Less if that was the case.

Slightly Greater		Somewhat Greater		Much Greater	No Change	Less
1	2	3	4	5	X	Y

3. If you answered "Greater" (ratings between 1 and 5), please describe the type of problem behavior, and indicate if this is an increase in an existing problem

behavior (i.e., behavior that the medication was intended to treat), or a new type of problem behavior.

a. Is this an increase in an EXISTING problem behavior?

Circle one: Yes   No

b. Is this a NEW type of problem behavior?

Circle one: Yes   No

F. Impact on Motivation/Consequences

1. When your child displays problem behavior while experiencing a side effect during an activity, describe how you or other members of your family respond to the behavior. What do you say? What do you do? (For example, do you change how you carry out the activity?) Do you discontinue the activity?

2. Do you now try to avoid the activity more so than was previously the case?

Circle one: Yes   No

PROBLEM BEHAVIOR TABLE

Aggression/Irritability:
Physically hurts others—hits, kicks, pinches, bites, head butts, punches, scratches, pulls hair, pokes eyes, spits
Verbally aggresses toward others—curses, insults, threatens, "talks back," verbally "nasty"
Destroys property—angrily breaks, rips, tears objects
Other (please specify)

Self-injury:
Hits head, bangs head on walls or other objects, bites hands, slaps or punches own face, pinches self, pulls out own hair, picks at skin/scab until it bleeds
Other (please specify)

Tantrum behavior:
Angry crying/screaming, stomping around/throwing self on floor/thrashing body around
Other (please specify)

Noncompliance:
Task refusal; pushes away work materials; runs away from adults/peers; falls to floor and refuses to move when requested; whining/complaining
Other (please specify)

Repetitive behavior:
Self-stimulatory behavior/repetitive motor movements (e.g., body rocking, hand flapping); stereotypy
Repetitive speech, obsessive speech
Compulsive/ritualistic behaviors, tics
Other (please specify)

Depressive features/ Mood disturbances:
Depressed mood/sadness/crying/weepy, withdrawn, moody, "no personality," overly sensitive
Mood changes/swings, excessive elation/manic episodes
Other (please specify)

Anxious/obsessive traits:
Excessive worry/anxiety/fearful; intrusive thoughts; obsessive thoughts
Other (please specify)

Hyperactivity/Attention difficulties:
Overactive/impulsive/fidgeting, difficulty concentrating, off-task behavior
Short attention span, easily distracted
Other (please specify)

Disruptive behavior:
Yelling, making weird noises, acting silly
Other (please specify)

Sleep disturbances:
Insomnia, difficulty falling/staying asleep, excessive sleep
Other (please specify)

SIDE EFFECTS TABLE

Physiological:

Sleep problems
- onset/trouble falling asleep
- night awakenings
- early awakenings
- too much sleep
- nightmares
- night terrors
- daytime sleepiness/drowsiness

Urinary problems
- nighttime bedwetting
- daytime bedwetting
- bowel accidents/encopresis
- increased urge to urinate
- decreased urge to urinate
- painful urination

Fatigue/lethargy

Gastrointestinal problems
- abdominal pain
- nausea
- vomiting/retching
- diarrhea
- constipation
- bloating

Eating problems
- weight gain (____lbs)
- weight loss (____lbs)
- appetite increase
- appetite decrease
- binging (driven eating)
- driven quality to drinking/ excessive thirst
- dry mouth

Vision problems
- blurred vision
- watery eyes
- red/itchy eyes

Sexual/reproductive side effects
- orgasmic/masturbatory problems
- amennorhea/irregular/ painful periods
- hypersexual behavior

Headache

Dizziness

Fainting

Seizure

Fever/flushed

Sweating

Itchy skin/rash/infection

Nasal congestion/runny nose

Breathing problems

Other (please specify)

Motor:

Clumsiness/awkward movements

Slurred speech

Stuttering

Fine motor impairments

Tardive dyskinesia/jerky movements

Tics/twitching

Rigidity in muscle tone

Drooling

Lack of coordination

Difficulty walking

Overactivity

Restlessness

Tremors/shakiness

Loss of muscle tone

Repetitive motor behavior (new behavior or increase in old behavior)

Other (please specify)

Cognitive:
Difficulty concentrating/
paying attention
Confusion/loss of
orientation/delirium
Difficulty with memory/memory loss
Latency to speak (speech hesitancy)
Spaciness/haziness
Hallucinations (visual/auditory)
Word finding problems
Less speech output
Other (please specify)

Affective:
Irritable/agitated/jittery/jumpy
Inappropriate affect/laughing/silly
Mood swings/emotional lability
Sadness/crying spells/feelings
easily hurt/seems depressed
Intrusive/obsessive thoughts/
compulsive behaviors
(e.g., finger picking)
Blunted/flat affect
Anxious/fearful/worried
Anhedonia/loss of interest
Other (please specify)

HOME AND COMMUNITY ACTIVITIES/ROUTINES

Home activities:
Waking up/getting out of bed
Brushing teeth
Showering/bathing
Grooming (comb hair, etc.)
Getting dressed
Eating breakfast
(preparing breakfast)
Talking with parents
Getting to bus stop/on bus
Practicing instrument/
karate/dance, etc.
Playing by oneself
(reading, TV, computer)
Eating/preparing lunch
Getting/eating snack
Doing homework
Chores (cleaning house, room, etc.)
Playing with siblings/friends/pets
Setting table/clearing table/
helping at dinner
Sitting down at table/eating dinner
Preparing for bed/going to sleep
Getting ready for community activity
Other (please specify)

Community activities:
Supermarket
Movies/museum/library
Mall/shopping
Parents' office/place of work
Local park
Car/train/bus/plane rides
Sports: team and individual
(e.g., soccer, bowling, mini-golf)
Relatives' houses/family gatherings
Friends/peers' houses (play dates)
Amusement park
Restaurants
Lessons (e.g., music,
dance, karate, etc.)
Doctors' offices
Religious services
Special entertainment (e.g., concerts,
professional sports events, theatre)
Vacations
Other (please specify)

COMPREHENSIVE LIST OF BEHAVIORAL INDICATORS OF ANXIETY

Physical/Physiological Symptoms Associated with Anxiety	Present	Absent
Rigidity or tenseness (visible muscle tension or stiffness)		
Hyperventilating, heavy breathing, rapid breathing, gasping		
Sweating or perspiration		
Flushed face or neck		
Trembling or shaking		
Lips clenched		
Lips quivering		
Behaviors Associated with Anxiety	**Present**	**Absent**
Withdrawal/avoidance		
Cowering		
Pacing		
Freezing		
Fidgeting		
Twitching or jerky/jumpy movements		
Frowning (turning down of mouth)		
Eyebrows raised in inverted V shape		
Tears		
Rapid clenching and unclenching of fists		
Avoiding eye contact		
Difficulty maintaining eye contact (e.g., eyes rapidly darting back and forth)		
Unusual movements (e.g., eye blinking, twitching, lip licking, head jerking)		

Unusual vocal sounds (e.g., coughing, throat clearing, sniffling, grunting)		
Picking or scratching (e.g., picks nose, skin, or other parts of body)		
Hand wringing		
Teeth grinding		
Compulsions (i.e., repeats certain acts, words, phrases, sentences, or movements over and over)		
Talking, singing, or vocalizing excessively (more than usual)		
Talking, singing, or vocalizing too loudly (more than usual) or for longer than usual		
Escalation (movements or vocalizations increase in volume, speed, or intensity)		
Stuttering or dysfluent speech, such as repetitions, interjections, pauses/blocks, or revisions		
Reassurance seeking		

SUBJECT INDEX

Page numbers in *italics* refer to figures and tables.

5-methyltetrahydrofolate (5-MTHF) 21

abdominal pain and discomfort 28, 30
abilify 121
Abnormal Involuntary Movement Scale (AIMS) 79
acetaminophen 111
adaptive skills, teaching 175–6
ADD (attention deficit disorder) 57
ADHD *see* attention deficit hyperactivity disorder
adrenalin 59
adversives, use of 15
Affex Facial Coding System for Negative Facial Expressions 208
aggressive behavior 39, 40–1
    caused by lead overload 116–17
    and epilepsy 45–7
    PANDAS-associated 119
AGRE (Autism Genetic Resource Exchange) 21
allergic diseases 91–108
    diagnostic approach 105–6
    neuropsychiatric conditions 94–8
        allergic rhinitis 96–7
        asthma 96
        atopic dermatitis 97–8
        celiac disease 98
        sinusitis 97
    neuropsychiatric disorders 98–100
    neuropsychiatric symptoms 92–4
        antigen sensitization 93
        effector cells 94

T-helper cell differentiation 93–4
SIB in individuals with limited expressive language 100–5
    case studies 102–4, *103, 104, 105*
allergic rhinitis (AR) 95, 96–7, 99, 102, 103, 105
    case studies 104, 114–15
allergies *see also* food allergy (FA)
allergy-elimination diets 131–2
amantadine 113
amoxicillin 120, 121
amygdala 42, 47, 144, 146
anti-inflammatory medications 30, 102, 121
antibiotics 63–4, 102, 119, 120, 121
anticonvulsants 31, 39, 44, 46–7, 51
antidepressants 57, 59, 60, 62, 65, 73, 76
antifungal treatments 117, 123
antihistamines 115
antipsychotic medications 56, 57, 58, 59, 62, 73, 74, 121
    see also individual medications
anxiety: assessment and intervention 198–230
    assessment 203–12
        behavioral component of anxiety 208–9
        cognitive/affective component of anxiety 205–8
        physiological component of anxiety 205
        step 1: describing the problem behavior 204–9
        step 2: measuring the behavior, antecedents, and consequences 209–12
    conceptualizing anxiety and SIB functionality 200–3

definitions of anxiety 199
intervention 212–25
    consequence strategies 222–5
    counterconditioning and generalized reinforcement 216–18
    differential reinforcement 223–4
    extinction 224–5
    functional communication training 219–20
    graduated exposure 216
    incorporating perseverative interests 218–19
    increasing predictability 212–15
    positive reinforcement 222–3
    prevention strategies 212–19
    priming 214
    providing advanced warning 214–15
    providing choices 215–16
    relaxation training 220–1
    replacement strategies 219–22
    Social Stories 213–14
    teaching coping skills 221–2
    visual schedule 213
    why is it often overlooked? 199–200
Anxiety, Depression, and Mood Scale (ADAMS) 206–7
anxiety disorders 101, 147
Anxiety Disorders Interview Schedule (ADIS) 205, 206, 207–8
anxiolytics 73, 121
applied behavior analysis (ABA) 152, 153
aripiprazole 73, 74, 113, 114, 124
arthritis 122
artificial food colors (AFCs) 133–4
ASD *see* autism spectrum disorder
asthma 92, 95, 96, 98, 99, 103
atopic dermatitis (AD) 97–8

attention deficit disorder (ADD) 57
attention deficit hyperactivity
    disorder (ADHD) 44, 45, 85,
    91, 95, 96–7, 97–8, 99, 134,
    147, 148
Autism Comorbidity Interview
    (ACI) 206
Autism Genetic Resource Exchange
    (AGRE) 21
Autism Research Institute, San
    Diego, California 15
autism spectrum disorder (ASD)
    definitions 27
    late development of 50
    see also high-functioning autism
Autism Spectrum Disorders—
    Comorbidity for Children
    (ASD-CC) 206
autoimmune diseases 122
    see also individual diseases
automatic nervous system (ANS)
    242
azithromycin 119, 121

Baby and Infant Screen for
    Children with aUtIsm Traits
    (BISCUIT) 43–4, 207
baclofen 113, 124
behavioral momentum 171
Behavioral Relaxation Scale (BRS)
    208
benzodiazepine 57, 59, 113, 124
biochemical abnormalities, targeted
    medical therapies 23–4
biome depletion 122
biotinidase deficiency 19–20
bipolar disorder 57, 58, 100, 102
BISCUIT (Baby and Infant Screen
    for Children with aUtIsm
    Traits) 43–4
biting 14, 15, 22, 40, 45, 47, 109,
    114, 139, 152, 153, 186, 187,
    195, 201, 202, 204, 223, 234
    case studies 58–9, 64, 78, 115,
    117, 121, 125, 175, 180,
    220, 231, 256–7, 260
blindness 15, 22, 40, 62, 231
borderline personality disorder 147
Brief Psychiatric Rating Scale 235

calcium 12, 13, 23–4, 114, 121,
    135
California, neonatal screening
    programs 20
cancer 49
carbamazepine 44, 73

carbohydrates, specific
    carbohydrate diet (SCD) 136
Carr, Ted 15, 109–10
casein 100
casein-free diet 129, 135
Caucasians 20, 102–3
cefuroxime 119, 120
celecoxib 113
celexa 113
celiac disease (CD) 98
cerebral folate deficiency (CFD) 21
cerebral palsy 29–30, 43–4
Challenging Behavior
    Questionnaire 49
challenging behaviors
    behavioral interventions for
        69–72
    four-term contingency model
        70–1, 71
    three categories of setting
        events 71–2
    and epilepsy 42–3
    prevalence 39
    use of term 38
Child and Adolescent Symptom
    Inventory (CASI) 206
chloral hydrate 260
chloresterol 20
chlorpormazine 56, 58, 62
chromatography 20
chronic rhinosinusitis (CRS) 97
ciprofloxacin 121
clindamycin 121
clonazepam 112, 113
clonidine 121
cogentin 263
cognitive behavior therapy (CBT)
    191, 212
cognitive picture rehearsal (CPR)
    248–9, 252–6, 255, 257, 258,
    259, 263, 270–1
communication skills, teaching
    173–4, 193, 194–5
constipation 113, 114, 118, 123,
    130, 132
Contextual Assessment Inventory
    (CAI) 166, 210
coping skills 81–2, 84, 174–5,
    221–2, 245
corgard 260
Cornelia de Lange syndrome 39
cortisol 101–2, 272
countdowns 170, 215
counterconditioning 216–17, 222
Crohn's disease 28, 136
Cues for Tension and Anxiety
    Survey Schedule (CTASS) 208
cysteine 115
cytokine 122

dairy-free diet 125
data collection 16–17
deep-breathing exercises 82, 84,
    175, 220, 249, 250–1
Demand–Control–Support model
    245–9, 246, 261–3
Denmark 99
dental pain 31–2
depakote 113, 263
depression 33, 42, 45, 47, 48, 57,
    58, 206
    and allergic diseases 95, 96,
        98, 102
    see also antidepressants
detailed behavior analysis 235–9
Detailed Behavior Analysis
    and Intervention
    Recommendations (DBAIR)
    235, 237, 239
Detailed Behavior Report (DBR)
    235, 236, 237, 258
Detailed Behavior Report Summary
    (DBRS) 235, 237, 238
Developmental Behavior Checklist
    (DBC) 207
developmental disabilities (DD)
    151, 161, 171, 173–4
    see also anxiety: assessment and
        intervention
DHCR7 gene 20
diabetes 122
Diagnostic and Statistical Manual of
    Mental Disorders
    DSM-I 56
    DSM-II 56
    DSM-III 56–7, 58
    DSM-IV 58
    DSM-IV-R 58
    DSM-5 27, 56, 65, 139–40, 146
Diagnostic Assessment for the
    Severely Handicapped (DASH)
    206
Diagnostic Checklists, E-2 15
diarrhea 28, 130, 132
diazepam 61, 73
diet, and PKU 19
dietary and nutrition intervention
    128–37
    advising parents 132–3
    allergy-elimination diets 131–2
    Feingold diet 133–4
    gluten- and casein-free diet plan
        135
    grain-free specific carbohydrate
        diets 136
    rationale for assessment and
        intervention 130–1
differential reinforcement 177–8,
    223–4

direct observation 209, 235–7, *236, 238, 239*
discriminative stimuli 70
DMSA (succimer therapy) 112, 116
DNA 21, 64
dopamine 121, 146
Down syndrome 29–30, 43–4

ear infections 31, 72
Early Steps76 43
ecological validity 158–9
ecosystem, human 122
ECT (electroconvulsive therapy) 65
eczema 91, 95, 99
EEGs (electroencephalograms) 42, 46, 47, 49
electroconvulsive therapy (ECT) 15, 65
encephalitis
    herpes simplex 49–50
    limbic 49
endorphin hypothesis 59–60, 60
epilepsy 41–7
    aggression and 45–7
    challenging behaviors in 43–4
    frontal lobe seizures 42–3, 47, 49
    medications 57
    medications and comorbidities 44–5
    neonatal 21
    pyridoxine-dependent 21
    self-injurious behavior and 45, 61
    temporal lobe seizures 42–3, 45, 46
    see also seizures
episodic dyscontrol 45, 48
everolimus 22
expressive language, limited 100–5
    case studies 102–4, *103, 104, 105*

face slapping 40, 72, 187, 188
    case studies 62, 118–19, 124, 188–9, 191
FBA *see* functional behavior assessment
Fear Survey for Children with and without Mental Retardation (FSCMR) 207
Fear Survey Schedule for Children—Revised (FSSC-R) 207
Feingold diet 133–4
fluoxetine 73, 111
folinic acid 21

food additives 125
food allergy (FA) 92, 95, 103
    see also dietary and nutrition intervention
fractional anisotropy (FA) 144
fragile X syndrome 147, 148, 206, 213
France 23
Functional Assessment Interview (FAI) 166, 209–10, 240
Functional Assessment Observation Form (FAOF) 167
functional behavior assessment (FBA) 16, 154–5, 163–8, 189, 192, 257
    case study 180–3, *181*
    conducting an FBA 163
    information gathering 164–6, *164*
        antecedents 164
        consequences 165–6
        setting events 164–5
    methods 166–8, *168*
        direct observation 167, *168*
        functions of behavior 168
        interviews and checklists 166–7
    methods of conducting 166–8, *168*
    see also anxiety: assessment and intervention
functional communication training (FCT) 82, 156, 174, 186–97, 219–20
    evidence base for 195
    introduction and case study 188–92
    SIB as communication 187–8
    steps for using 192–5

gabapentin 113
gamma globulin 119, 121
gas chromatography 20
Gastaut-Geschwind syndrome 42–3
gastroesophagitis 117
gastrointestinal (GI) disorders 28–9, 77, 100, 105, 117, 129–30, 136
Genesight 64
genital self-abrading 123
Geschwind, N. 57
Geschwind syndrome 42–3
glucocorticoid receptors 102
glutathione 115, 116, 118
gluten 100
gluten- and casein-free diet plan (GFCF) 135

gluten-free diet 125
grain beetles (*Tenebrio molitor*) 122–3
grain-free specific carbohydrate diet 136
Grandin, Temple 60
Greece 19
Groden Center, Providence, Rhode Island *see* stress-reduction
growth problems 29, 129, 130, 131, 132
guanfacine 111
gut organisms 100
gynecological complaints 29–30

hallucinations 43, 47, 49, 50
haloperidol 56, 57, 58
hay fever 95
HDCs (*Hymenolepis diminuta cysticercoids*) 122–3
head banging 15, 31, 58, 62–3, 103, 104, 112
    case studies 112–14, 115, 120, 138, 140–1, 142, 155, 161–2, 260–7
headaches 32–3, 45, 97
heart, concerns over the 24
heart rate 242–3
helminth 122
herpes simplex encephalitis 49–50
high-functioning autism 64, 102–3, 114, 206, 221, 232
Hispanic patients 20
homocysteine 118
hormonal dysfunction 29–30
hydrocodone 111
hygiene hypothesis 94
hypothalamic–pituitary–adrenal (HPA) axis dysfunction 101–2

ictal aggression 46
ID *see* intellectual disability
IED *see* intermittent explosive disorder
immuglobulin 122
immuglobulin E (IgE) *see* allergic diseases
immune disorders *see* allergic diseases
immunotherapy 49
India 101
inositol 113
instinctual monomania 48
intellectual disability (ID) 30, 39, 151, 206, 208, 211
interictal dysphoric disorders 42

intermittent explosive disorder
(IED) 45, 48, 57
Intervention Description Form
(IDF) 263, *264–8*
IQ 39, 43, 140, 142, 206, 207
Italian Scale for the Assessment of
Self-Injurious Behaviors 45

*Journal of Autism and Childhood
Schizophrenia* 56
*Journal of Autism and Developmental
Disabilities* 56

Kanner's syndrome 15
ketamine 65
ketoconazole 123
Kiddie Schedule for Affective
Disorders and Schizophrenia
(KSADS) 206
kidneys 23, 24
klonopin 263
Kluver-Bucy syndrome 42
kryptopyrrole 125

lansoprazole 117
lead overload 116–17
Lesch-Nyhan syndrome 21–2, 39
life expectancy 40
lifestyle changes 158, 161–3, 179,
183
Likert scale 79
limbic encephalitis 49
limbic system 43, 47, 144
lithium 113
lorazepam 73, 111, 112, 113, 117
low-sugar diet 114, 123
low-yeast diet 123
luvoxamine 112

magnesium 110, 115, 125
magnetic resonance imaging (MRI)
21, 113
Malaysian patients 22
marijuana 111
Matson Evaluation of Drug Side
Effects (MEDS) 79
medical and nutritional approaches
109–27
case studies 111–26
allergic rhinitis and face
pounding 114–15
constipation and hand
wringing in Rett
syndrome 118

face slapping and scratching
responsive to melatonin
and methyl-B12 118–19
gastroesophagitis with wrist
biting 117
head banging with multiple
complex factors 112–14
loss of communication system
resulting in severe self-
facial beating 124
monilial triggering of genital
self-abrading 123
nasal foreign bodies and face
fisting 111–12
PANDAS-associated
aggression 119
PANDAS/PANS with severe
head banging 120
PANS and self-injurious
behaviors 121–3
plumbism with aggression
toward self and others
116–17
pyrroluria with aversive
measures leading to self-
slashing 124–5
self-pinching and bruising
in a perfectionistic boy
struggling with math
challenges 126
sulfur pathway disruptions
and self-injury 115
medication, impact of side effects
68–90
behavioral interventions for
challenging behavior
69–72
four-term contingency model
70–1, *71*
three categories of setting
events 71–2
context-based approach to
assessment and intervention
80–6
case study: Ellie 83–4
implications 84–6
context-based assessment and
intervention 72–3
emerging research examining the
paradox 79–-80
medication side effects 75–9
assessment of 79
case study: Emma 78–9
potential paradox 77, *78*
pharmacological intervention
73–5

prevalence, importance and
treatment of severe problem
behavior 69
melatonin 118–19
memantine 113, 124
meningoencephalitis 49
menstrual problems 29–30, 72,
172, 178–9, 203
MET gene 29
methionine 118
methyl-B12 118–19
methylphenidate 73
migraine headaches 32–3, 45
Mischer, Karen 138, 140–1, 142
mitigation strategies 81, 83, 84,
118, 126, 135, 172, 178, 179,
218
Monitoring of Side Effects System
(MOSES) 79
montelukast 115
mood stabilizers 57, 73, 125
morphine 59
Motivation Assessment Scale (MAS)
166, 189, 192, 209–10, 240
MRI (magnetic resonance imaging)
21, 113
MTHFR gene 21
Multidimensional Anxiety Scale for
Children (MASC) 207

N-acetyl cysteine (NAC) 115
naltrexone 59, 60
nasal foreign bodies 111–12
National Health Interview Survey
(NHIS) 45
National Institute on Drug Abuse
143
National Institutes of Neurological
Disorders and Stroke
(NINDS) 30
National Survey of Children's
Health 97
neonatal epilepsy 21
neonatal screening 19, 20
neurobiological mechanisms 141–3
Neurology (journal) 30
neuropsychiatric model 55–67
affective disorders, OCD, and
TD 62–3
case studies 58–61, 62–3
DSM-5 65
DSM-III 56–7
panic disorder 57–62
PANS/PANDAS 63–4
pharmacogenomics 64
progress from 1943 to 1985 56
SIB and epilepsy 61

SIB options emerging in neuropsychiatry 64–5
neutrophil extacellular traps (NET) 94
NINDS (National Institutes of Neurological Disorders and Stroke) 30
nitrotyrosine 116
nutrition *see* dietary and nutrition intervention; medical and nutritional approaches
nystatin 123

obsessive-compulsive disorder (OCD) 58, 63, 91, 99, 104, 121–2, 123, 206, 207, 211, 221, 224
ocular self-mutation *see* blindness
omeprazole 117
opiates 59
opiods 60, 142
optimistic parenting 190–2, 195
orofacial pain 31–2
otitis media 31, 72
oxcarbamazepine 73
oxidative stress 115

pain perception 29, 32, 110, 142
PANDAS (pediatric acute neuropsychiatric syndrome associated with streptococcal infections) 63–4, 119, 120, 122
panic disorder 57–62
  case studies 58–61
PANS (pediatric autoimmune neuropsychiatric disorder) 63–4, 102, 120, 121–3, 122
paroxetine 73
PBS *see* positive behavior support
Pediatric Anxiety Rating Scale (PARS) 208
penicillin 121
perfectionism 126
person-centered planning (PCP) 162
pessimistic attributional styles 190–1
pharmacogenomics 64
pharmacological interventions 73–5
phenol- and salicylate-free diet 133–4
phenylketonuria (PKU) 19
pica 129
PKU (phenylketonuria) 19

plumbism 116–17
polypharmacy 74, 76
positive assertions 248, 263
positive behavior support (PBS) 151–85
  basic assumptions 152–4
  case study 180–3, *181*
  consequence-based strategies to reduce SIB 176–8
    differential reinforcement 177–8
    extinction 178
    instructional approaches 177
  designing an intervention plan 169–78
  developing prevention strategies 157, 169–72
    alternative sensory stimulation 172
    behavioral momentum and embedding 171
    minimizing the effects of setting events 172
    providing choices 170–1
    task modifications 171
    using preferred activities or interests 172
    using timers or countdowns 170
    using visual supports 169–70
  developing replacement behaviors and teaching skills 156, 173–6
    teaching adaptive skills 175–6
    teaching communication skills 173–4
    teaching coping skills 174–5
  functional behavior assessment 154–5
  functional behavior assessment (FBA) 163–8
    information gathering 164–6, *164*
    methods 166–8, *168*
  importance of targeting SIB 151–2
  important considerations when using prevention strategies 172–3
  key features 154–63
  putting the plan together 178–9
  long-term support and lifestyle changes 179
  treatment options for SIB 152
positive reinforcement 156, 157, 176, 179, 215, 217, 218, 222–3, 247, 253, 262
positron emission tomography 29

post-traumatic stress 124
postictal psychosis 47
Prader-Willi syndrome 148
prednisone 113
probiotics 123
program decay 16
program delay 16–17
propanolol 121
Psychology Today (magazine) 60
psychosis 42, 46, 47, 49, 56, 147
psychotropic medications
  types 73–5
  see also medication, impact of side effects; *individual medications*
pyridoxine-dependent epilepsy 21
pyrroluria 124–5

Questions About Behavioral Function (QABF) 166

relaxation techniques 82, 84, 174, 175, 220–1, 248–51, *250*, 257, 270–1
Repetitive Behavior Scale 235
restraints, physical 39–40, 46, 124, 166, 177, 189, 260–1, 269
Rett syndrome 118
Revised Children's Anxiety and Depression Scale (RCADS) 207
Revised Children's Manifest Anxiety Scale (RCMAS) 207
Rimland, Bernard 15, 23
risperdal 189, 263
risperidone 48, 73, 74, 77, 111, 112, 117, 121, 124, 189
Romania 144
rTMS therapy 65

S-adenosylmethione (SAMe) 22
Saccharomyces serevisiae 100
schizophrenia 31, 57, 99, 100, 102
  misdiagnosis 19, 49, 56
Screen for Anxiety and Related Emotional Disorders (SCARED) 205, 207
screening, neonatal 19, 20
seizures
  and CFD 21
  frontal lobe 42–3, 47, 49
  and panic disorder 60–1

seizures *cont*
    and pyridoxine-dependent
        epilepsy 21
    seizure disorders 30–1
    temporal lobe 42–3, 45, 46
    and tuberous sclerosis 22
self-control triad 262
self-injurious behavior (SIB)
    automatic assessment of 243–4
    as communication 187–8
    comorbidity 147
    definitions 14, 39, 56–7
    diagnosis 15, 56
    and epilepsy 45, 61
    forms 15, 27–8, 40, 45, 139–41
    in individuals with limited
        expressive language 100–5
    neurobiological mechanisms in
        141–3
    prevalence 14–15, 40, 69, 139,
        147
    treatment options 39, 69, 152
    see also individual behaviors
sensory hyperactivity 32–3, 47
sensory processing disorder (SPD)
    138–50
    description and prevalence of
        SIB 139–41
    hypothesis related to sensory
        craving 143–6
    neurobiological mechanisms in
        SIB 141–3
    prevalence, comorbidity, and SIB
        147–8
    subtypes 146
serax 260
serotonin 101, 121
setting events 68, 70, 71–2, 76–7,
    85, 154, 164–5, 172
Setting Events Checklist 167
sham rage 47
Shriver, Eunice 57
SIB *see* self-injurious behavior
Simons Simplex Collection 39
sinusitis 97, 103
skin conductance responses (SCRs)
    221, 243
sleep problems 20, 28, 33–4, 118,
    121
Smith-Lemli-Opitz syndrome
    (SLOS) 20
Smith-Magenis syndrome 39
Social Stories 170, 213–14, 221
specific carbohydrate diet (SCD)
    136
starch-free diet 114
State-Trait Anxiety Inventory for
    Children (STAIC) 207

statins 20
steroids 115, 121
stimulants 45, 73, 75–6, 93
stoicism 111, 115
streptococcal infections *see*
    PANDAS
stress-reduction 231–75
    case studies 256–69, *258, 259,*
        264–8
    coping with stress 245
    designing a cognitive picture
        rehearsal program 253–6,
        255
    discussion 270–2
        generalization 271
        relaxation and cognitive
            picture rehearsal 270–1
        self-control 271
    future trends 272–3
    intervention 244–69, 263,
        264–8
    multimodal assessment of SIB
        234–44
        direct observation 235–7, *236,*
            238, 239
        rating scales and interviews
            240
        Stress Survey Schedule
            240–2, *241*
        using technology 242–4
    strategies to reduce stress 245–
        52, *246*
        cognitive picture rehearsal
            252
        producing low demand
            246–7
        providing high support 247
        relaxation 249–51, *250*
        teaching high control 248–9
    stress perspective 232–4
Stress Survey Schedule (SSS) 211,
    235, 240, *241*, 242
Structured Interview for the
    Assessment of Medication
    Side Effects (SIAMSE) 79–80,
    81, 85
substance abuse 48
succimer therapy (DMSA) 112, 116
sugar, reducing 125
suicidality 39, 64, 65, 97, 101,
    101–2
sulfur pathway disruptions 115,
    118–19

Taiwan 101
Taiwan National Health Insurance
    Research Database 99

targeted medical therapies 18–26
    and a biochemical abnormality
        23–4
    biotinidase deficiency 19–20
    cerebral folate deficiency 21
    Lesch-Nyhan syndrome 21–2
    phenylketonuria 19
    pyridoxine-dependent epilepsy
        21
    Smith-Lemli-Opitz syndrome 20
    tuberous sclerosis 22
team-based collaboration 160–1
technology, using in assessment
    242–4
thioridazine 56, 57, 58, 61
thorazine 260
tick-borne infections 63–4
tics 58, 63, 76, 99, 103, 147
Time Timer™ 214–15
timers 81, 170, 214–15
Tourette disorder (TD) 58, 62–3,
    99
Toxoplasma gondii 100
trazodone 263
trileptal 113
TSC genes 22, 48
tuberous sclerosis 22, 48–9

uninhibited hypothalamic
    discharge 47
urine samples 23–4, 59
U.S. Food and Drug Administration
    (FDA) 22, 134

vigabatrin 22
viral infections 49–50, 63–4
    case study 102–3
visual schedules 72–3, 83–4,
    169–70, 213
visual supports 81, 169–70, 246–7
vitamin B 115, 125, 135
vitamin D 23, 24, 122

World Health Organization 245

zinc 110, 125
zoloft 121
zyprexa 112–13

AUTHOR INDEX

Aidenkamp, A.P. 44
Akdis, C.A. 93
Akdis, M. 93
Akhtar, S. 38
Al-Baradie, R.S. 21
Al-Khouri, I. 50
Albano, A.M. 205, 207, 212
Albert, D.J. 40
Albin, R.W. 69, 152
Albinali, F. 244
Alcantara, J.I. 139
Alessandri, M. 41
Allen, L. 248
Alley, C.S. 35
Aman, M.G. 74, 235
Amelink, M. 96
American Psychiatric Association
    27, 56, 56–7, 65, 69, 146
Anderson, S.R. 194
Andersson, G. 85
Andrulonis, P.A. 56
Aneja, A. 20
Antonacci, D.J. 199
Arangannal, P. 31
Arelin, K. 29
Ashburner, J. 139
Aspinwall, L. 245
Athens, E.S. 178
Atladottir, H.O. 98
Attwood, T. 199, 200
Austin, J.K. 44

Baer, D.M. 70, 194, 196
Baer, L. 63
Baghdadli, A. 14, 27, 40, 55, 139,
    147, 148
Bahadori, K. 105
Bahreinian, S. 96
Bahrick, L.E. 141, 144, 145
Bailey, J. 195
Bailey, J.S. 31, 195
Baker, J.P. 65
Balazs, J. 101

Balciunas, B.A. 31
Bambara, L.M. 81, 173, 174, 176,
    179
Bandura, A. 210
Baranek, G.T. 139, 146
Barkley, R.A. 45
Barlow, D.H. 199, 215, 248
Barnhill, L.J. 48
Baron, G. 249
Baron, M. 234, 248
Barrett, R.P. 56
Bartak, L. 140
Basile, E. 39
Bates, E. 187
Bean, S.C. 50
Beaulieu, A.A. 73
Behrens, T. 144
Beitman, B.D. 55
Bellini, S. 199
Ben-Sasson, A. 33
Benda, C.E. 19
Bennett, C.L. 21
Bennetto, L. 141
Berkson, G. 146
Bernstein, G.A. 85
Betancur, C. 18
Betz, A. 235
Bhise, V.V. 44
Bijou, S.W. 70
Bilbo, S.D. 122
Binkoff, J.A. 71, 187
Bird, F. 195
Birmaher, B. 205, 207
Blair, K.C. 81
Blakeley-Smith, A. 84, 101
Bleiweiss, J.D. 79, 80, 85
Blumer, D. 60
Boctor, F.N. 20
Bodfish, J.W. 27, 40, 139, 145, 148
Bögels, S.M. 199
Borregaard, N. 94
Borsatto, T. 20
Bos, C.S. 81
Bosch, J. 72, 77

Bourgeois, B.F. 44
Boyce, J.A. 92
Boyd, B.A. 139
Braquehais, M.D. 101
Breau, L.M. 139, 142, 143, 147
Britton, S.B. 47
Browder, D.M. 213
Brown, F.R., III 50
Bruininks, R.H. 69, 151
Brunwasser, S.M. 199
Bryson, S.E. 146
Buie, T. 28, 129, 136
Bundy, A. 210
Buono, S. 45
Burack, G.D. 44
Burd, L. 21
Burke, L.M. 29–30
Buske-Kirschbaum, A. 98, 102

Cale, S.I. 215
Camacho, F. 74
Camaioni, L. 187
Cameron, M.J. 70, 79
Campbell, D.B. 29
Campbell, J. 235
Campbell, M. 56, 60
Cannon, W.B. 47
Carcani-Rathwell, I. 140
Carlson, G.A. 75–6
Carlson, J.L. 73
Carr, E.G. 29, 34, 69, 70, 71, 72,
    73, 79, 80, 82, 84, 85, 100,
    101, 152, 156, 158, 159,
    160, 161, 163, 164, 165, 166,
    167, 172, 173, 174, 175, 178,
    178–9, 182, 186, 187, 195,
    201, 203, 209, 210, 212, 213,
    217, 219, 220, 223
Carrera-Bojorges, X.B. 95
Carter, A.S. 69
Casanova, M.F. 32, 65
Casey, F. 218
Casey, P.H. 129

Cautela, J.R. 82, 208, 220, 249, 252, 262
Center, D.B. 216
Centers for Disease Control and Prevention 45
Chambless, D.L. 195
Chan, J. 39
Chan, Y.M. 20
Chang, K. 63
Chang, T.W. 94
Charlop-Christy, M.H. 218
Charlop, M.H. 218
Chaudhary, M.W. 21
Chen, B.C. 22
Chen, M.H. 95, 97, 99
Chess, S. 56
Choate, M. 248
Chorpita, B.F. 207
Chou, P.H. 99
Christian, L. 82, 175, 220
Christie, L. 130
Chrostowska-Plak, D. 98
Chugani, H.T. 144
Clarke, S. 72, 172, 218
Clarke, W.N. 22
Coe, D.A. 206
Coffey, M.J. 47
Cohen, D. 75
Cohen, D.J. 57–8, 232
Cohen, I. 233, 240
Cohen, M.S. 62
Cole, J.O. 62
Coleman, M. 18, 20, 22, 23
Comer, J.S. 74
Conners, C.K. 85
Consensus Statement NIH 139
Cooper, J.O. 222
Cooper, S.A. 69
Cordeiro, L. 206
Cornell, C.U. 74
Cortesi, F. 33
Coulter, D.L. 49
Coury, D.L. 73, 74
Creedon, M.P. 143–4
Crimmins, D.B. 166, 189, 192, 195, 209, 240
Cuccaro, M. 41
Cuijpers, P. 85
Cummins, R.A. 207
Cunningham, A.B. 141

Daley, D. 91–2
Daly, T. 193
Dattilo, J. 215
Davies, L. 151
Davis, C. 82
Davis, D.H. 71

Davis, E. 199
Davis, M.L. 28, 72
Davis, N.O. 69
Davis, T.E. 175, 199, 216
de Lissovoy, V. 31
de Vries, P.J. 48
DeBlasio, N. 32
Deckert, S. 97
DeLeon, L. 74
Delgado-Escueta, A.V. 46
Delli, K. 31–2
DeLong, G.R. 50
D'Empaire, I. 64
Depasquale, G.M. 129
Derby, K.M. 174
Deriaz, N. 45
Dettmer, S. 81, 215
Devine, D.P. 139, 141, 144
Diaz-Granados, N. 65
Dirrigl, K.H. 39
Dolcetta, D. 22
Dominick, K. 139
Dornbush, K. 151
Doss, L.S. 71
Dougherty, L.M. 208
Dove, D. 60
Doyle, C.A. 73, 75
Drager, K. 82
Duerden, E.G. 142, 147
Duncan, J. 233
Duncan, J.S. 61
Dunlap, G. 69, 72, 81, 151, 152, 158, 160, 163
Dunn, D.W. 44
Dunn, W. 146, 147
Durand, V.M. 73, 82, 156, 163, 164, 166, 173, 174, 187, 188, 189, 190, 192, 193, 194, 195, 209, 210, 213, 219, 220, 240
Dyck, M. 139

Ebrecht, M. 98
Edelson, S.M. 139, 141, 186, 187
Eden, K.E. 49
Egelhoff, K. 139
Einfeld, S.L. 207, 210
Elias, E.R. 20
Elliott, D.E. 122
Eluvathingal, T.J. 144
Emerson, E. 28, 38, 39, 69
Engbers, H.M. 21
Ermer, J. 147
Esbensen, A.J. 74, 74–5, 206
Essex, M.J. 95

Fadini, C.C. 33, 34
Farley, A.H. 146
Favell, J.E. 223, 224
Favreau, H. 96
Fee, V.E. 69
Felce, D. 39
Ferri, R. 33
Findling, R.L. 55
Finucane, B. 39
Fish, D.R. 47
Fisher, W. 235
Flannery, K.B. 81, 212
Flom, R. 144
Foldvary-Schaefer, N. 43
Folkman, S. 233
Fombonne, E. 19
Fornazzari, L. 43
Foster, L.G. 146
Fowler, S.A. 196
Frankovich, J. 63
Freeman, R.D. 147
Friedlander, A.H. 32
Fuster, B. 42
Fyffe, C.E. 195

Gabriels, R.L. 140
Gada, E. 96
Gadow, K.D. 206
Gal, E. 139
Gallese, V. 145
Garand, J.D. 170, 213
Garcia-Larrea, L. 30
Gardner, W.I. 31, 167, 206
Garg, N. 95
Gargus, J.J. 32
Gastaut, H. 42, 45
Gaultieri, C.T. 57
Gedye, A. 49
Geraghty, M. 129
Gerard, M.E. 47
Gergely, G. 145
Geschwind, N. 42, 43
Ghazanfar, A.A. 145
Ghaziuddin, M. 50
Ghaziuddin, N. 50, 101–2
Giannotti, F. 33
Gibbs, E.L. 42
Gibbs, F.A. 42
Gilfillan, A.M. 94
Gillberg, C. 20, 22, 142, 146, 199
Gillberg, I.C. 50
Gilliam, F. 42
Gipson, T.T. 22
Girija, A.S. 21
Gitlesen, J.P. 39, 148
Glick, N. 22
Goadsby, P.J. 32

Goin-Kochel, R.P. 21
Goldberg, D.A. 46
Gomes, E. 141
Goodwin, F.K. 55, 57
Goodwin, M.S. 205, 242, 243, 244
Goodwin, R.D. 96
Gorham, D. 235
Gotham, K. 199
Grace, E.G. 31
Grandin, T. 60, 232
Gray, C.A. 170, 213
Gray, J. 207
Green, S.A. 33
Greer, M.K. 50
Griffin, J.C. 14
Griffin, M. 65
Grillon, C. 212
Groden, G. 234, 235, 248
Groden, J. 82, 200, 211, 220–1,
    234, 235, 240, 242, 243,
    248, 249, 250, 252, 254,
    270, 273
Guico-Pabia, C.J. 64
Gullone, E. 207
Gunsett, R.P. 31
Gut, D.M. 213
Guthrie, D. 146
Guy, W. 79

Hacohen, Y. 49
Hagerman, E. 143
Hagopian, L.P. 200, 207
Haley, J. 187
Hall-Flavin, D.K. 64
Hall, S. 148
Halle, J.W. 194
Hallerbäck, M. 199
Hamburger, S. 233
Hamoda, H.M. 44
Hanley, G. 235
Hardy, P.M. 62
Hartley, S.L. 207
Harvey, S.T. 195
Hastings, R.P. 39, 207
Hattier, M.A. 43–4
Hatton, D. 208
Hawk, B. 57
Hayes, S.A. 69
Hayes, S.C. 221
Haymes, L.K. 218
Healy, O. 28, 40, 147
Hediger, M.L. 129
Hedtke, K.A. 221
Heffner, K.L. 98, 102
Hellhammer, D.H. 98
Hellings, J.A. 75
Hembree, E.A. 208

Hepburn, S. 147
Heron, T.E. 222
Hess, J.A. 75, 76
Hessen, E. 44
Heward, W.L. 222
Hieneman, M. 163, 210
Hill, B.K. 69, 151
Hillbrand, M. 48
Hinton, S. 200
Hirstein, W. 144, 221
Hirtz, D. 30
Hobfoil, S. 245
Hoch, T.A. 27
Hoffmann, W. 233
Hogan, K.L. 147
Hogdon, L. 247
Holden, B. 39, 148
Hollander, E. 17, 39, 58, 63
Hooper, S. 208
Horner, A.A. 94
Horner, R.H. 69, 81, 163, 167, 170,
    178, 212, 235
Horrigan, J.P. 48
Horvath, K. 129
Howlin, P. 225
Humphreys, J.S. 33
Hyman, S.L. 141

Iarocci, G. 145
Intille, S.S. 205, 244
Irons, M. 20
Itkonen, T. 72
Iversen, P. 144, 221
Iwata, B.A. 70, 71, 168, 234
Izard, C.E. 208

Jackson, J.A. 94
Jackson, J.R. 98
Jacobson, E. 249
Jallon, P. 42
James, S.J. 116, 118–19
Jamison, K.R. 55, 57
Jang, J. 40, 41
Janney, R.E. 151
Jenike, M.A. 63
Jennett, H.K. 200, 207
Jerrell, J.M. 75, 76
Ji, N.Y. 55
Jia, F. 24
Jobst, B.C. 43
Johnson, K.P. 33
Jolliffe, T. 232
Jonik, R.H. 40
Joosten, A. 210
Julien, R.M. 73, 76, 77
Jyonouchi, H. 93, 95, 98, 101, 131

Kalachnik, J. 79
Kanne, S.M. 39
Kanner, A.M. 42
Kanner, L. 27, 56, 139, 199, 272
Kantor, J.R. 70
Kao, J. 207
Kaufman, J. 206
Kearney, A. 252, 262
Kelchner, K. 82
Kellner, R.B. 85
Kelly, K.L. 75–6
Kemp, D.C. 195
Kendall, P.C. 212, 216, 221
Kennedy, C.H. 72, 100, 203
Kern, J.K. 141, 146
Kern, L. 81, 173, 174, 176, 179
Kerr, M. 39
Kerr, M.P. 46
Khandaker, G.M. 99
Kiecolt-Glaser, J.K. 98, 102
King, N.J. 207
Kinsbourne, M. 144
Kirkland, C. 213
Klein, D.F. 59, 60
Klein, R.G. 85
Klerman, G.L. 55
Klingman, D. 46
Knoster, T. 173
Koegel, L.K. 69, 151, 214
Koegel, R.L. 69, 151, 152, 214
Kohlboeck, G. 96
Kopkow, C. 97
Koplewicz, H.S. 63
Koudelka, C.W. 97
Kratochwill, T.R. 207
Krauss, G.L. 46
Kriegel, M.F. 43
Kung, S. 64
Kurtz, P.F. 218
Kuschner, E.S. 141
Kushak, R. 136
Kwon, H.J. 99
Kwon, J.A. 97

Lacey, C. 71
Lam, K.S.L. 74, 235
Lancioni, G.E. 71
Landsdown, R. 232
Lane, A.E. 129, 139
Lang, R. 195
Langdon, N.A. 209
Langer, S.N. 71
Langthorne, P. 154
Lazarus, R. 233, 245, 250
Leader, G. 28, 40, 147
Lecavalier, L. 206
Lee, L. 69

Lee, Y.S. 96
Lehmkuhl, H.D. 216
Lequia, J. 81, 169
Lesevre, N. 42, 45
Leslie, D. 74
Lesniak-Karpiak, K. 208
Letitre, S.L. 96
Leuzzi, V. 21
Levi, L. 245, *246*, 273
Lewin, A.B. 199, 209
Lewis, M.H. 145
Lewkowicz, D.J. 144
Leyfer, O.T. 200, 206
Li, X. 64
Lieberman, M. 231
Linck, L.M. 20
Lindsay, W.R. 221
Lipman, R.S. 57
Lishman, W.A. 46
Liss, M. 146
Lord, C. 199
Lovaas, O.I. 39, 187
Lowe, K. 69
Lucyshyn, J.M. 69, 84, 152, 212
Lugnegård, T. 199
Luiselli, J.K. 70, 79
Luscre, D.M. 216

McAlonan, G. 144
McAtee, M. 79, 166, 210
McClintock, K. 148
McCord, B.E. 71
McCracken, J.T. 74, 75
McDonald, J. 145
MacDonald, R.F. 71
McDougle, C.J. 73, 75
Mace, A.B. 170
Mace, F.C. 170, 171
McElhanon, B. 117
McGee, G.G. 193
McGill, P. 70, 154
McGimsey, J. 223, 224
Machalicek, W. 81, 169
McIntyre, R.S. 75, 76
MacLean, W.E. 151, 207
McTiernan, A. 148
Magito McLaughlin, D. 182, 217
Mahan, S. 75, 76
Mamounas, L.A. 30
Manalai, P. 100
Mandelbaum, D.E. 44
Mandell, D.S. 74
Manford, M. 47
Mapstone, E. 193
March, J. 207, 221
Marcus, R.N. 74
Marques, F. 49

Marsh, L. 46
Martin, A. 75
Massaro, T. 129
Matson, J.L. 39, 40, 41, 43, 45, 56, 69, 74, 75, 76, 79, 139, 166, 206, 207
Matsuo, M. 41
Matthews, T. 46
Mazefsky, C.A. 207
Mazurek, M.O. 39
Mazzocco, M.M. 208
Merzenich, M. 144
Mesibov, G.B. 213
Metcalfe, D.D. 94
Meyer, K.A. 72, 100, 203
Meyer, L.H. 151
Miano, S. 33
Mielke, H.W. 116
Miller, L.J. 146
Mills, P.B. 21
Minichiello, W.E. 63
Minkel, J.D. 33
Minshawi, N.F. 17, 55, 60
Moffitt, C.E. 207
Mojtabi, R. 74
Montavont, A. 30
Moore, D.J. 33
Moore, T.R. 195
Moree, B.N. 175
Moretti, P. 21
Morreau, L.E. 69, 151
Morrier, M.J. 193
Morrin, G. 42, 45
Moskowitz, L.J. 101, 203, 205, 208, 211, 213, 215, 219, 220
Mula, M. 42
Mulle, K. 221
Mullins, J.L. 82, 175, 220
Mulvihill, J.J. 20
Muris, P. 199
Murphy, D. 38
Murphy, G.H. 28
Murphy, O. 28, 40, 147
Murphy, T.K. 63

Nanayakkara, J.P. 97
Napolioni, V. 24
Nascimento, P.P. 41
National Institute for Health and Clinical Excellence (NIHCE) 39
Nauseef, W.M. 94
Neal, D. 74, 76
Needleman, H.L. 116
Nelson, D.S. 30
Neufeld, R. 233
Newell, K.M. 139

Newsom, C.D. 71, 187
Niehaus, D.J.H. 58
Noel, L.P. 22
Nwokoro, N.A. 20
Nyhan, W.L. 22

Oberman, L.M. 65
Ochs, H.D. 93
Okur, H. 59
Olfson, M. 74
Oliver, C. 139, 148, 151
Ollendick, T.H. 199, 207
Ollerton, J. 122
O'Neal, J.H. 75
O'Neill, R.E. 166, 167, 209, 240
O'Reilly, M.F. 71, 72, 203
Ornitz, E.M. 144, 146
Oster-Granite, M.L. 17
Oswald, D.P. 142, 207
Oukka, M. 93
Overall, J. 235
Owen-DeSchryver, J.S. 34, 100, 203, 209
Owen, R. 74
Owens, J. 33
Ozdemir, C. 93
Ozonoff, S. 233

Palmieri, L. 24
Pan, A.Y. 94
Pandey, G.N. 102
Parker, W. 122
Passmore, A. 139
Paterson, R. 233
Patterson, A.M. 98
Peavy, R.D. 94
Pedersen, M.S. 99
Pedroso, F.S. 141
Pellock, J.M. 45
Perman, J. 129
Perrin, S. 199
Petscher, E.S. 195
Plato 187
Plotz, T. 244
Poppen, R. 208
Post, R.M. 57
Praharaj, S.K. 38
Prather, P.A. 48
Preskorn, S.H. 64
Preston, J.D. 75
Prevey, M.L. 44
Price, R.B. 65
Prior, M. 233
Pyles, D.A.M. 31

Quadros, E.V. 21

Rabe-Hasketh, S. 140
Raiten, D.J. 129
Rajesh, R. 21
Ramachandran, V.S. 144, 221
Ramaekers, V. 21
Ramirez, S.Z. 207
Ratey, J.J. 143
Reaven, J. 221
Reich, A. 98
Reichle, J. 71, 82
Research Units on Pediatric
    Psychopharmacology Autism
    Network (RUPP) 48, 73, 74,
    208
Reti, I.M. 65
Rey, C. 195
Reynolds, C.R. 207
Richards, C. 139, 208
Richards, S. 82
Richdale, A.L. 33
Richler, J. 145
Richman, D.M. 148
Richmond, B.O. 207
Rieske, R.D. 206
Riley, J.L., III 29
Rilling, J.K. 29
Rispoli, M.J. 81, 169
Rivet, T.T. 39
Roberts, D.W. 43
Robinson, T. 232
Rod, N.H. 98
Rodger, S. 139
Rodin, E.A. 45
Rogers, S.J. 147, 200
Rojahn, J. 14, 27
Rosenberg, R.E. 74
Rosenberger-Debiesse, J. 23
Rosenhall, U. 143
Rosenthal, D. 23
Rosenthal, Z.M. 147
Ross, J.L. 208
Rossi, P.G. 30
Roszell, P. 248
Rousseau, J.J. 187
Rubenstein, J. 144
Rudy, B.M. 199, 209
Ruef, M. 152
Rumsey, J. 233
Rusch, F. 215
Russell, A. 38
Russell, P.S. 101
Rutter, M. 56, 57, 140, 248
Ryan, A.K. 20

Saeed, S.A. 199
Safran, S.P. 213
Safren, S.A. 85

Sandman, C.A. 111, 141
Sanna, L. 95
Santosh, P.J. 45, 140
Sapolsky, R. 242
Sarkhel, S. 38
Sarlani, E. 31
Savard, G. 47
Scariano, M.M. 60, 232
Scharre, J.E. 143–4
Schell, R. 223, 224
Schmitt, J. 97
Schoen, S.A. 146
Schopler, E. 56, 57
Schreck, K.A. 33
Schreibman, L. 40, 141, 214
Schretien, D.J. 39
Schroeder, C.E. 145
Schroeder, S.R. 17, 27
Schubart, J.R. 74
Schulte, C. 79, 166, 210
Schwartz, I.S. 194
Scott, O. 49
Selassie, A.W. 45
Seligman, M. 191, 254
Selye, H. 233
Sequeira, J.M. 21
Severance, E.G. 100
Shahed, H. 31
Shakya, D.R. 45
Shapiro, E.S. 170
Sharp, W G. 129
Shea, S. 73, 74
Sheline, Y. 42
Shentoub, S.A. 147
Shih, J.J. 46
Shogren, K.A. 81, 215
Shorvon, S.D. 47
Shyu, C.S. 96
Siegel, M. 73
Silverberg, J.I. 95
Silverman, W.K. 205, 207
Simeon, D. 17
Simmons, J.Q. 39
Simon, E.W. 39
Simpson, E.L. 97
Sinclair, D. 102
Skinner, B.F. 70, 217
Slattery, M.J. 95
Smith, C.E. 70, 201
Smith, K.R. 43, 45
Smith, R.G. 70
Smith, S.J. 61
Snell, M.E. 195
So, N.K. 47
Sofronoff, K. 200
Soulairac, A. 147
Sovner, R. 31
Spencer, D. 74

Spielberger, C. 207
Spilioti, M. 19, 21
Spradlin, J. 194
Sprafkin, J. 206
Sprague, R.L. 56
Stahmer, A.C. 214
Staley, B.A. 22, 48–9
Steed, E.A. 195
Steen, P.L. 82
Stein, B.E. 141
Stein, D.J. 58
Steingard, R. 63
Sterling, L. 207
Stern, J.A. 207
Stevens, L.J. 134
Stevenson, S. 235
Stigler, K.A. 74
Stoff, D.M. 40
Stokes, T.F. 196
Stone, W.L. 147
Storch, E.A. 199, 208, 209
Stores, G. 72
Sturmey, P. 225
Sullivan, J.C. 32, 32–3, 146
Sullivan, K. 208
Sumer, M.M. 47
Swedo, S.E. 63, 116
Symons, F.J. 28, 72, 139, 147
Szepietowski, J.C. 98

Talaga, M.C. 75
Tan, B.K. 97
Task Force Promoting
    Dissemination of
    Psychological Procedures 195
Tassinari, C.A. 46, 47
Taubman, M.T. 187
Tavares, H. 48
Taylor, J.C. 71, 187
Taylor, S. 245
Tecchio, F. 144, 146
The Free Dictionary 253
Thoits, P. 248
Thompson, S.A. 61
Thompson, T. 17, 28, 72, 147
Thomson, R.J. 71
Tierney, E. 20
Todd, J.T. 141, 144, 145
Tomchek, S.D. 146
Tonge, B.J. 207
Tordjman, S. 110, 111
Torgerson, T.R. 93
Touchette, P.E. 71
Treinman, D.M. 41, 46, 47
Tsai, J.D. 97
Tse, K. 94
Tsiouris, J.A. 60

Tu, C.H. 29
Tuchman, R. 30, 41
Tucker, G.J. 42
Tudor, M.E. 33
Tureck, K. 74
Turnbull, A.P. 152
Turner, J. 233
Turner, M. 145
Turner, R. 248

Umbreit, J. 81
Ung, D. 207
Unnwongse, K. 43
U.S. Food and Drug Administration
    74

Valicenti-McDermott, M.D. 98
Van Bourgondien, M.E. 74
van Karnebeek, C.D. 19
van Steensel, F.J.A. 199
van Straten, A. 85
Vaughn, B.J. 72, 152, 170
Veldhuijzen, D.S. 29
Velicer, W.F. 205
Victorio, M. 32
Vishnu-Rekha, C. 31
Vitiello, B. 40
Volkmar, F.R. 30, 58, 146, 232
Vollmer, T.R. 166, 178
Volterra, V. 187
Vuilleumier, P. 42

Wachtel, L.E. 65
Wagner, M.B. 141
Wainwright-Sharp, J.A. 146
Walker, V.L. 195
Walsh, M.L. 40
Waters, J. 62
Watson, S. 69
Waxman, S.G. 42, 43
Wehmeyer, M.L. 82, 215
Wehner, E. 147
Wehner, T. 43
Wender, P.H. 60
Westman, M. 245
Whalen, C. 214
White, S.W. 199, 200, 207
Wiggs, L. 72
Wilde, L. 214
Wilder, D.A. 195
Wilhelm, S. 38
Wilkerson, M.L. 20
Willemsen-Swinkels, S.H. 60
Williams, K. 19
Williamson, P.D. 47
Winner, J. 64

Winter, H. 136
Wiznitzer, M. 48
Woerner, M. 59
Wolf, M.M. 158
Wolpe, J. 199
Wong, C. 195
Wortis, H. 47
Wu, J.Y. 22

Xeniditis, K. 38

Yaghmaie, P. 97
Yankovsky, A.E. 47
Yen, C.F. 101
Youngblade, L. 193
Yuce, M. 99

Zaffanello, M. 19
Zahran, S. 116
Zeidan-Chulia, F. 31, 32
Zimmer, M. 129
Zito, J.M. 74–5
Zitrin, C.M. 59
Ziviani, J. 139
Zuriff, G.E. 82